# DOCUMENTING DISPLACEMENT

McGill-Queen's Refugee and Forced Migration Studies
Series editors: Megan Bradley and James Milner

Forced migration is a local, national, regional, and global challenge with profound political and social implications. Understanding the causes and consequences of, and possible responses to, forced migration requires careful analysis from a range of disciplinary perspectives, as well as interdisciplinary dialogue.

The purpose of the McGill-Queen's Refugee and Forced Migration Studies series is to advance in-depth examination of diverse forms, dimensions, and experiences of displacement, including in the context of conflict and violence, repression and persecution, and disasters and environmental change. The series will explore responses to refugees, internal displacement, and other forms of forced migration to illuminate the dynamics surrounding forced migration in global, national, and local contexts, including Canada, the perspectives of displaced individuals and communities, and the connections to broader patterns of human mobility. Featuring research from fields including politics, international relations, law, anthropology, sociology, geography, and history, the series highlights new and critical areas of enquiry within the field, especially conversations across disciplines and from the perspective of researchers in the global South, where the majority of forced migration unfolds. The series benefits from an international advisory board made up of leading scholars in refugee and forced migration studies.

# DOCUMENTING DISPLACEMENT

*Questioning Methodological Boundaries in Forced Migration Research*

Edited by
**Katarzyna Grabska**
and
**Christina R. Clark-Kazak**

McGill-Queen's University Press

Montreal & Kingston • London • Chicago

ISBN 978-0-2280-0832-3 (cloth)
ISBN 978-0-2280-0833-0 (paper)
ISBN 978-0-2280-0949-8 (ePDF)
ISBN 978-0-2280-0950-4 (ePUB)

Legal deposit first quarter 2022
Bibliothèque nationale du Québec

Printed in Canada on acid-free paper that is 100% ancient forest free
(100% post-consumer recycled), processed chlorine free

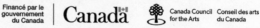

We acknowledge the support of the Canada Council for the Arts.

Nous remercions le Conseil des arts du Canada de son soutien.


Library and Archives Canada Cataloguing in Publication

Title: Documenting displacement : questioning methodological boundaries
in forced migration research / edited by Katarzyna Grabska and Christina R.
Clark-Kazak.
Names: Grabska, Katarzyna, 1973- editor. | Clark-Kazak, Christina R., 1975- editor.
Series: McGill-Queen's refugee and forced migration studies ; 8.
Description: Series statement: McGill-Queen's refugee and forced migration
studies ; 8 | Most of the chapters in this book were presented at the International
Association for the Study of Forced Migration (IASFM) at the University of
Macedonia, Thessaloniki, Greece, in July 2018. | Includes bibliographical refer-
ences and index.
Identifiers: Canadiana (print) 20210325461 | Canadiana (ebook) 20210325542 | ISBN
9780228008323 (cloth) | ISBN 9780228008330 (paper) | ISBN 9780228009498
(ePDF) | ISBN 9780228009504 (ePUB)
Subjects: LCSH: Forced migration—Research—Methodology. | LCSH: Refugees—
Research—Methodology. | LCSH: Research—Moral and ethical aspects.
Classification: LCC HV640 .D63 2022 | DDC 305.9/069140721—dc23

For Samir & Maxim – KG

For Anahita & Rustom – CCK

# Contents

# Figures and Tables

TABLES

# Acknowledgments

The process of making this book has been a beautiful collective journey, one that we started at the biannual meeting of the International Association for the Study of Forced Migration in Thessaloniki in July 2018. Inspired by the incredible methodological creativity and innovation and profound ethical honesty that we saw in several of the panels at the conference, we decided to embark on this journey. This book is the result of this collegial, collective, creative process, and this process would not have been possible without the support of so many people involved in it. First of all, a big thank you to all the contributors to this volume. You have all been incredibly responsive, patient, and ready to step up during the difficult times in which we happened to write this book. The pandemic and the restrictions on our lives as academics and as human beings have put the writing and research under serious strain. But this is also the reason why this volume is so important and why your contributions offer hope and new ways of thinking for doing ethically responsible and methodologically innovative and sound research with people in displacement situations. Your contributions have also offered a new, creative, and often fun way of seeing the field. You are making a difference with your work, and we thank you for it.

Second, we would like to thank McGill-Queen's University Press for accepting this project and recognising its value. We are grateful to our editor, Jacqueline Mason, for shepherding this book – and us – through the publication process. We acknowledge the support of the series editors, Megan Bradley and James Milner.

We also express gratitude to Cindy Horst for her early contributions to this project, which shaped our thinking at the beginning. We also would like to recognize Mansanga Tanga for helping us put the final touches on the manuscript and making sure that we delivered it on time. You have both been indispensable to this project.

We are extremely grateful to Marisa Cornejo, a Chilean born artist with her own history of displacement, for lending us use one of her thought-provoking, evocative art pieces for the cover of the book. Your work gives a deeper sense to the written words!

This book was inspired by many conversations and years of research that both of us have done for more than two decades. It is impossible to name all the people who influenced our thinking and our ways of doing research. You all know who you are – and we thank you for the advice, the guidance, and the belief that research in displacement situations requires going beyond standard ways of knowing. We are grateful to the research participants whose stories have been told and retold – by us and other researchers. We hope this manuscript honours your contributions and builds on our commitment to an ethics of care and solidarity.

And now it is time to open the book and start the journey through the maze of collective creative reflections of our authors. We hope you will enjoy reading this book as much as we enjoyed working on it – and will get inspired to move beyond what we know and how we know. Enjoy the reading!

# DOCUMENTING DISPLACEMENT

# Introduction:
## *Documenting Displacement beyond Methodological and Ethical Boundaries*

Christina R. Clark-Kazak and Katarzyna (Kasia) Grabska

## Why Focus on Methodology in Displacement Research?

This collection brings together researchers who have been working with innovative research methods to document displacement in order to reflect on the potentiality of different possible ways of knowing and less hierarchical and dominant approaches to research, through careful reflection on the ethical dilemmas involved in such research. The idea for this book grew out of a biannual meeting of the International Association for the Study of Forced Migration (IASFM) at the University of Macedonia, Thessaloniki, Greece, in July 2018. We both participated in the conference, and given our involvement in several methods-related panels there, and various presentations on the topic, we realized that an interdisciplinary collection would speak to the need to critically assess the ways in which knowledge is (co-)created in spaces of displacement and (re)produced, often through narratives.

Our interests emerged also from our respective involvements in debates related to methods and specifically to the ethics of doing research in the context of displacement and forced migration. During the conference, as we attended diverse panels that critiqued issues of methods, methodologies, and ethics in research on displacement, we realized there was a need to bring these innovative contributions to light. Most of the chapters in this book were presented at the conference in 2018. Some of the contributors were identified later through various networks and were invited to join as we felt that their methodological and ethical approaches had much to add to the debates around knowledge production in refugee and displacement studies.

We invited contributors who were using innovative and creative interdisciplinary methods to research individual and collective experiences of forced migration and exile. In what ways do these methods reveal different understandings of the temporal, spatial, and embodied aspects of displacement and forced migration? What challenges do they face in designing such research, and what types of insights can we develop as researchers? What are the limitations on using diverse methods? How are these diverse approaches proposed by our contributors a way of excavating both hidden agency and power hierarchies in displacement and forced migration?

The contributors to this book explore the ethics and methods of research in diverse forced migration contexts to share lessons learned and propose new ways of thinking about, and documenting, displacement. Research in migration contexts requires specific ethical and methodological approaches owing to the legal precarity, mobility, and criminalization that migrants face in politicized contexts. Each chapter delves into specific ethical and methodological challenges that researchers face in forced migration contexts, with particular attention to unequal power relations in the (co-)creation of knowledge, questions around representation and ownership, and the adaptation of methodological approaches to contexts of mobility. A defining feature of this book is its interdisciplinary, innovative use of collaborative arts-based methods, which have not before now been prominent in forced migration studies. The authors reflect critically on how engagements with methodologies that cross disciplinary boundaries has enriched their knowledge production about displacement. They also highlight how such methodological endeavours are able to bring into conversation other ways of knowing, including embodied and sensory experiences. While this book is not meant to serve as a textbook, we believe that the debates and examples presented here will be useful for graduate courses in methodology and research methods, as well as for researchers and practitioners undertaking research in diverse contexts. Another unique aspect of this book is that the contributors reflect honestly on both what has worked and what has not, thus providing useful points of discussion for future research. All of the contributors reflect on their positionalities within power asymmetries and politicized knowledge-making.

We have sought to "bring in" diverse contributions from colleagues working in a multitude of geographical locations, from a range of disciplinary perspectives and different positionalities. Collectively and individually, the chapters highlight both the opportunities and the challenges of meaningful research practice in refugee and displacement studies. They broaden and deepen ongoing debates about policy relevance, "north-south" divides, and "insider-outsider" dilemmas. While it is not meant to be exhaustive, this edited book offers unique insights into new ways of knowledge (co-)production and the multiple ways in which the lives and experiences of those in displacement and forced migration situations have been studied and how the results have been disseminated to date. All of the chapters in this volume share a strong commitment to ethical research and to providing spaces for knowledge co-creation with those whose experiences and voices are central to the research.

## Documenting Displacement: Methodological Opportunities and Challenges

This book explores innovative methodological and ethical strategies in diverse migration contexts. We deliberately chose "displacement" for our title to signal a broad conceptualization of migration contexts. Recognizing the politicized debates over "forced" versus "voluntary" migration (see, for example, Adelman and McGrath 2007; Hathaway 2007; Bakewell 2011; Long 2013; Erdal and Oeppen 2018; Crawley and Skleparis 2018) and mixed migration contexts (Van Hear et al. 2009; Long and Crisp 2010; Linde 2011; Crush et al. 2015), we prefer "displacement" as a descriptive term to refer to contexts in which people are dislocated from their original homes, communities, and networks. This book therefore includes research methodologies across different categories of migration (Zetter 1991, 2007; Black 2003; Bakewell 2008), including internally displaced persons, asylum seekers, refugees, and those with precarious status.

Each of the contributors to this book proposes innovative and empathetic ways of engaging in research in these diverse contexts. Our collective goal is to document the complexities of migration experiences through creative collaborative methods and epistemologies. We acknowledge our responsibility to not only bear witness to injustices in displacement contexts, but also to expose the ways in which research can exacerbate or attenuate these inequalities. In this way, the book aims to document research choices and the methodological and ethical dilemmas underpinning these decisions.

Research in displacement contexts poses specific methodological opportunities and challenges for several reasons. First, by definition, it takes place in situations of mobility. Research with mobile populations makes sampling (Bloch 1999, 2004) and longitudinal research (Jacobson and Landau 2003; Colson 2003; Ryan and D'Angelo 2018; Aziz, this volume; Oda and Hynie, this volume) difficult. Researchers may have less time to build rapport and can lose contact with participants, making continuous consent (Hugman et al. 2011; Gerver 2018; Godin and Donà, this volume) and the sharing of research results problematic or impossible (Lammers 2007; Mackenzie et al. 2007). The dynamic nature of mobility also affects researchers' access to sites of displacement (Wolf 2020) as people move and government policies respond to public opinion and changing realities on the ground (Aziz, this volume; Godin and Donà, this volume).

But it must also be pointed out that many displacement contexts are characterized by immobility and long periods of limbo as people find themselves "stuck" in refugee camps (Kaiser 2006; Hyndman and Giles 2011), behind closed borders (Van der Velde and van Naerssen 2011; Schewel 2020; Fitzgerald 2019; So anci this volume), in detention centres (Loyd and Mountz 2018; Tazzioli and Garelli 2018), or in protracted irregular situations (Brun 2015; Zetter and Long 2012; Grabska et al. 2019). This raises ethical questions about the voluntariness of consent by "captive audiences," who may believe that external researchers could provide a lifeline to escape immobility (Block et al. 2013).

Complicating all of this, researchers often enjoy different citizenship and immigration status than their participants (Goheen Glanville, this volume). Research projects are typically led by scholars in privileged positions who can come and go from research sites as they please, while the participants are much more constrained (Chatzipanagiotidou and Fiona Murphy, this volume; Aziz, this volume; Grabska, this volume). These power dynamics within the research process require more unpacking and honest reflexivity (Taha, this volume; Chatzipanagiotidou and Fiona Murphy, this volume; Grabska, this volume; Banki and Phillips, this volume). They also pose ethical questions in relation to confidentiality of information and how the research findings are used.

Finally, as noted earlier, displacement contexts are often highly politicized (Squire 2010). Migration policies are subject to contentious debates that are too often based on racism, xenophobia, and fear rather than evidence. Research material and documentation can help counter these problematic narratives but can also be manipulated or taken out of context to suit political agendas (Van Hear 2012; Andersson 2018; Baldwin-Edwards et al. 2019). Access to displacement sites is often controlled – physically and administratively – by governments, UN agencies, and NGOS (Aziz, this volume). Each of these actors will have a different agenda that can impact the type, quality, and quantity of data that researchers are allowed to collect and report on.

## Documenting Displacement within a Diverse Field of Study

Migration researchers have been grappling with these issues for many years (see, for example, Temple and Moran 2006; Voutira and Donà 2007; Bakewell 2007; Bose 2010; Berriane and de Haas 2012; Vargas-Silva 2012; McGrath and Young 2019). There has been a recent resurgence of interest in methodology and ethics, reflected in the number of related panels at IASFM conferences and in an expanding literature, partly cited here (for a more complete annotated bibliography, see Ghelani 2013, updated 2018). While this has generated important discussions both in person and in print, the field of (forced) migration studies still lacks both a codified methodology and a consensus on epistemological parameters. We are not suggesting here a rigid "how to" guide. Rather, we note that our field lacks methodological norms of the sort that are present in more established disciplines and even in other interdisciplinary fields of study. For example, conflict studies takes seriously the "do no harm" principle, while development studies has a strong normative orientation toward participatory approaches. The current methodological turn in migration studies is a welcome opportunity to collectively brainstorm norms and principles that we believe should provide a framework for research in our field. The present book is situated in this growing body of literature on methodology and ethics in forced migration. Our aim is to build on and amplify previous colleagues' work, but also to add new ideas and, in some cases, challenge dominant ways of knowing, doing, and being. All contributors offer critical and innovative ways of imagining and practising research ethically, grounding these ideas in relational ethics of care and solidarity.

One conversation to which this book contributes is the (co-)production of knowledge (Grabska et al. 2019; Godin and Donà, this volume; Grabska, this volume). To date, debate has focused primarily on inequalities between the "global north" and the "global south" (Bradley 2007; Hyndman 2010; Van Hear 2012; Landau 2012). To complement this discussion, this book delves more deeply into the micropolitics – or what Donà (2007) has called the microphysics – of knowledge production within contextualized research relationships (Chatzipanagiotidou and Murphy, this volume). Each contributor attends in a different way to their positionality within research processes.

This leads to another way in which this book builds on the existing literature: it seriously attends to power inequalities and ethical issues. Ethical concerns raised by scholars over the decades (for example, Mackenzie et al. 2007; Hugman et al. 2011a; Block et al. 2013; Krause 2017; FMR 2019) have recently led to the creation of guidelines (Clark-Kazak et al. 2017) and a code of ethics (IASFM 2018). However, these procedural ethics need to be complemented by serious attention to relational ethics. All of the authors in this book contribute to this discussion by highlighting the ethical tensions in their own work and reflecting honestly on the challenges of building sustainable, ethical relationships in research and praxis.

The interdisciplinary nature of our field is a source of great creativity but also serious challenges (Chimni 2009). On the one hand, the complexity of displacement necessitates collaboration across different disciplinary expertise. On the other, our field has tended to be dominated by only a few disciplines: law, anthropology, and political science. This book responds to this challenge by including underrepresented work in computer science (Frydenlund and Padilla, this volume), health (Oda and Hynie, this volume), communication studies (Goheen Glanville, this volume), social work, and music (Rodriguez and Cambròn, this volume).

As alluded to earlier, scholars have debated the opportunities and challenges of policy-relevant research in forced migration (Black 2001; Rodgers 2005; Bakewell 2008; Chimni 2011). Arguably, this is one of the greatest epistemological debates in our field, having been catalyzed by the widely cited "dual imperative" article by Jacobsen and Landau (2003). Based on the diverse contributions in this book, we would respectfully suggest that this is a false debate. People experiencing (im)mobilities are confronted on a daily basis by the consequences of policy decisions (Horst and Grabska 2015), which are often made by people who are the furthest from the issue and therefore have the least to lose (Harrell-Bond 1986). We contend that those of us who are serious about documenting displacement have no choice but to engage in the politics of knowledge production (cf. Taha, this volume). Indeed, contributions to this book illustrate that iterative reflexivity is necessary for us to understand our positionality within hierarchies of knowledge – both in high-level policy discussions and within the politics of everyday life in research contexts.

Finally, there is a rich literature on creative methodologies in displacement contexts. In particular, life stories (Powles 2002; Eastmond 2007; Sigona 2014; Cabot 2016; Chatty 2016) have been used effectively to humanize migration experiences. There is also a growing literature on participatory (Cooper 2005; Doná 2006; Ellis et al. 2007; Guerin and Guerin 2007; Moran, Mohamed, and Lovel 2011; Rodgers 2005) and arts-based or visual (Vecchio et al. 2017; O'Neill et al. 2019; Lenette 2019) methods. This book adds to this existing literature by expanding the scope of innovative methods – including computer modelling and simulation, graffiti analysis, film, multimedia packages, and soundscapes – to challenge colleagues to imagine new ways of researching with and for people in displacement contexts.

## A Roadmap to *Documenting Displacement*

This is a diverse book with contributions from a wide range of disciplinary perspectives and positionalities. In an attempt to provide some direction to the reader, we have grouped the chapters into three sections around some common themes. However, this grouping is somewhat limiting, for the innovative methodologies presented here defy categorization. Indeed, as alluded to in our subtitle, all of the contributors question disciplinary and methodological boundaries and many of the themes run across multiple chapters and sections. This methodological richness and creativity is what gives this book so much transformative potential. We hope that readers will engage with the full range of chapters and perspectives, even as we have tried to draw out common themes.

In section 1, the chapters speak directly to issues of ethics, power, and knowledge production. Anna Oda and Michaela Hynie, together with their peer researcher colleagues, consider the opportunities and challenges of community-based research (CBR) as an approach to co-production of knowledge. They reflect critically on how the involvement of community researchers is both important and beneficial to the process and outcomes of CBR studies; however, CBR comes with a number of complex ethical challenges. This chapter highlights some of the challenges that peer researchers, in particular, experienced while working on longitudinal mixed-method CBR that examines the integration and long-term health outcomes of Syrian refugees resettled in Canada. The authors reflect on these ethical challenges and provide some directions for future research and practice recommendations.

The second chapter in section 1, by Dina Taha, engages with decolonizing methodology and critical reflexivity – themes that run through most of the chapters in this book. She reflects on her interactions with Syrian refugee women in Egypt who married Egyptian men often as a coping strategy. Their stories did not simply challenge many Western hegemonic conceptions about intimacy, gender roles, and empowerment; they also challenged the author's research design (including interview questions) and her self-perception as an insider. She views critical reflexivity not only as a tool to sustain rigorous methodological and empirical practices but also as a means to decolonize narrative research. She discusses the limits of critical reflexivity by showing how it can further marginalize "Othered" stories by replicating colonial assumptions and reinforcing hegemonic discourses.

In the third chapter, Evropi Chatzipanagiotidou and Fiona Murphy critically analyze the ways in which researchers have engaged in the fetishization of the refugee "voice" through a methodological overemphasis on story-telling and narrative. They draw on ethnographic fieldwork with Syrian artists in Istanbul to demonstrate how engagement with art, both as a subject and as method of research, becomes a tool not only for transcending the confining and oppressive limits of structured speech but also for disrupting dominant and essentializing accounts of "refugeeness." As this chapter shows, much like others in the book (see Godin and Donà; Grabska;

Soğancı), a methodological focus on art is not a panacea for overcoming problems with "the voice" in documenting displacement and loss. As the authors argue, the process and ethics of art production have connections to ethnographic practice. They propose a project of "methodological dubiety" that does not and should not aim to resolve dilemmas around representation, experience, and aesthetics. They argue, instead, for a mode of highlighting further ethical, political, and methodological complexities in the ways that absence and loss is documented. This chapter, which shows the importance of going beyond the narrative and the representational, comes out of mutual and synchronic interaction in the field. The authors point to the importance of an ethical responsibility of refusal – the duty *not to* study particular silences (Weller 2017), losses, and invisibility/ies in the context of displacement.

Jason Hart's chapter focuses on specific ethical and methodological considerations in the context of research with children in displacement situations. He argues that the contemporary discourse of children's rights depicts them as social actors whose voices should be heard in all matters affecting them. As a result, there has been an insistence on involving children in research as subjects capable of offering meaningful commentary on their lives and communities. He reflects on the link between the imagining of children in settings of forced migration, on one hand, and the design of methodology and consideration of ethics, on the other. His chapter is particularly poignant in emphasizing ongoing self-reflection, careful attention to context, and enduring flexibility in research, given the different assumptions that researchers and institutions might hold about children's capacity in displacement.

The last chapter in this section, by Azza Aziz, reflects on challenges and opportunities as well as ethical dilemmas in her longitudinal research as a northern Sudanese female researcher engaging with southern Sudanese and then South Sudanese interlocutors (in light of the division of the country in 2011). Looking at how access to the field can be both constrained and facilitated by gender, class, and belonging to multiple places, she reveals complex ways of navigating the ever-changing political terrain of research.

In section 2, we group together chapters that speak to multisensory, creative, collaborative methodologies that aim to capture the emotions and embodiment of displacement. The chapters in this section also explicitly address questions of co-production of knowledge, ownership, and representation, echoing some of the ethical issues raised in the first section. They also emphasize the importance of embodied and sensory ways of knowing, which have been marginal in displacement studies to date.

In the first chapter of section 2, Andrea Rodriguez-Sànchez and Alfonso Cambròn present the creative method of sound postcards to capture embodied forms of displacement and to analyze changes in the social fabric in Colombia caused by prolonged armed conflict and displacement. The chapter describes the use of sound postcards as an ethnographic, participatory, embodied research method, one that was used with thirteen participants in the Music for Reconciliation Program of the Batuta National Foundation. The authors critically examine the limitations of art-based approaches and particularly the importance of sound for unravelling the emic perspectives of the changes in the types of bonds the subjects forge with the people and things in that environment.

Another arts-based collaborative method involves using graffiti. The next chapter is presented by Océane Uzureau, Marina Rota, Ine Lietaert, and Ilse Derluyn. Based on analysis of graffiti inscriptions collected within the framework of mixed-methods research on the transit experiences of unaccompanied refugee minors in Europe, the authors provide an alternative take on studying migrants' experiences in specific migratory settings in which their well-being can be strained (such as detention and transit camps for migrants and refugees). They carefully consider the methodological and ethical challenges encountered when studying this visual ethnography, particularly as these relate to access, informed consent, and interpretation. They show how graffiti is both a visual and a verbal form of expression that offers multiple ways of knowing.

Another arts-based collaborative method considered in this book is collaborative filmmaking. In her chapter, Katarzyna Grabska considers the experiences of filmmaking and dissemination of a documentary titled *Time to Look at Girls: Migrants in Bangladesh and Ethiopia* (2016). A collaboration among professional filmmakers, feminist researchers, and protagonists created points of tension and generated ethical reflections about the use of film, filming techniques, and visual methods as such. The protagonists were young women who had migrated as adolescents under dramatic circumstances. This chapter focuses on tensions in the co-creation of knowledge and the complex ways that different types of knowers need to let go in the process of the collaborative creation of knowledge. It argues that this type of collaboration provides insights into the struggle over the interpretative power of narratives and images – discussed in feminist writings, yet much less so in refugee and migrant studies.

Collaborative innovative visual methods used in research among refugees and the displaced is also considered by Marie Godin and Giorgia Donà. Their chapter offers a reflexive account of the use of participatory photography as a research and pedagogical methodology created with and by people on the move. It draws on the participatory photo-project *Displaces* (2015–16), which created a collaboration with displaced people in the space of transit of the "Calais jungle"; it also draws on ongoing work with a subgroup following the official conclusion of the project. The project belongs to a new visual (photographic) practice, situated within emerging spaces of political solidarity that challenge the politics of the border through the visual. The chapter addresses three issues in participatory visual research: ownership and copyright, sustained relationships, and the representations and voices of displaced people. Central to this approach was the ethics of care and respect; learners were given ownership of the cameras as well as copyright for the images they produced. The authors beautifully show how methodological and ethical approaches can move beyond standard guidelines and processes to adopt a broader array of political positions of care and solidarity.

Nihal Soğancı explores alternative methods for recollecting affective stories through engagement with everyday objects and images via collaging and a participatory art installation. During fieldwork conversations with displaced populations in North Cyprus, she realized that for most people, stories about homes and displacement were taboo; they were difficult to tell or would not go beyond certain common discourses. She used arts-based methods to access a different way of understanding displacement and memory. First, Soğancı organized three collage workshops during which she asked participants to use photographic materials that she had collected from her fieldwork (newspapers, magazine clippings, etc.) to create collages on what home means to them. Her second method involved a participatory art installation that was part of the Buffer Fringe Performing Arts Festival 2019 in Nicosia. *The Affective Garage: A Collective Junction* was a collective and creative journey to reimagine the buffer zone as an in-between space through everyday objects flashing beyond the webs of memory in which research participants engaged. Inspired by Walter Benjamin, Soğancı explores how bringing objects together on an unconventional plane in a random manner helped deconstruct and reconstruct understandings of the past, present, and future, particularly in the displacement context.

In section 3, we bring together chapters that question disciplinary boundaries and showcase mixed-methods approaches from disciplines that are underrepresented in refugee and forced migration studies. The chapters here highlight both the opportunities and the challenges of interdisciplinary research and inspire researchers to question their own methodological comfort zones.

Erika Frydenlund and Jose J. Padilla provide insight into an emerging method of modelling and simulation (M&S) that has been used in research on migration and displacement recently, from investigating the movement of people to safety and resource allocation. They discuss the types of data required and other potential uses of M&S in migration and displacement research by relying on a case study of Lesbos, Greece. The case study is explored through three modelling paradigms – system dynamics, discrete event simulation, and agent-based modelling – to illustrate how M&S can be useful depending on the research question and study objectives. The chapter concludes with a discussion of the limitations and ethical considerations of M&S for migration and displacement research. The authors argue that while simulation models may provide a means for communicating with decision- and policy-makers, the models could be used to undermine human rights.

Another set of innovative methods is discussed by Susan Banki and Nicole Phillips. They examine an adaptation of the "cultural probe" approach used in design studies, which, they argue, is particularly well-suited to conducting research on liminal and over-researched populations such as refugees. During their case study with a Bhutanese diaspora, they employed a multimedia package method (MMP) that allowed refugee respondents time to share their ideas through stories, video, objects, jokes, songs, and other non-traditional commentary. Given the oft-cited problem of hierarchical power imbalances between researchers and respondents in fieldwork, the authors show that this approach has the potential to develop a process that is, at its best, enjoyable and/or whimsical. Banki and Phillips reflect on the merits and drawbacks of MMP, focusing on, among other elements, design and preparation, the potential for participant involvement, and possibilities for large-scale research of this nature in the context of an approach that is exceptionally resource intensive.

Digital and arts-based methods of storytelling are addressed in the last two chapters in this section: by Shashini Gamage and Danesh Jayatilaka, and Erin Goheen Glanville. In their research project on urban displacement in Colombo, Sri Lanka, *The Unknown City: The (In)visibility of Urban Displacement*, Gamage and Jayatilaka integrated life-story narratives, memory mapping, and video documentation to produce what they call "mobility videos." This chapter examines how the intersection of these methods allowed the researchers to collaborate with participants, researchers, and video producers to digitize memories of displacement that primarily existed in cognitive modes. While these digitized memory-based narratives of displacement provide a tool for community engagement, for communicating research findings to macro-level development practitioners, and for understanding contexts that create social, political, and cultural conditions of displacement, they also require some critical reflexivity and raise particular ethical considerations, which the authors discuss.

Goheen Glanville examines the praxis of an educational media research project, *Worn Words*, in consultation with local refugee claimant support organizations in Vancouver, Canada. The project's methodology integrated the theory and practices associated with knowledge mobilization, digital narrative inquiry, and peace education and engaged communities in the research process. *Worn Words* moves between theory and practice to experiment with ethical media-making that can re-narrate the ordinary words of forced migration discourse, such as border, refugee, welcome, security, humanitarian, and trauma. The chapter focuses particularly on the value of nurturing informal relationships with migrant communities. As Goheen Glanville argues, informal relationality can accompany researchers and hold them accountable in ways that persist beyond the purview of the important formal processes of research ethics approval. She powerfully shows the importance of relationships that shape ethical community engagement but are not accounted for in established formal processes. Here again, we learn that small-scale, slow, and informal community engagement is a key site of knowledge for ongoing conversations about decolonizing forced migration research and for media-making about refugees.

## Conclusion: Amplifying and Deepening Methodological Conversations

Collectively and individually, these chapters contribute to the ongoing methodological, epistemological, and ethical discussions in the field of refugee and forced migration studies. We hope this book amplifies and enriches these conversations and provides food for thought for both seasoned and new researchers. A key point that emerges in all of these chapters is the need to attend to the specific, politicized contexts in which we work – for practical, methodological, and ethical reasons. A second recurring theme is creativity: innovation, adaptability, and resourcefulness in dynamic contexts of (im)mobility. Third, all authors in this book are deeply committed to continuously questioning the ethics of the methods and motives of research. There is an overarching call for attention to those whose lives we as researchers are studying, their own participation in the co-production in knowledge, and the representations of their experiences. Indeed, this book raises many questions, that, we believe, are not only the beginning of any good research project, but also a necessary element of reflexive, critical analysis throughout the research process.

REFERENCES

Adelman, H., and S. McGrath. 2007. "To Date or to Marry: That Is the Question." *Journal of Refugee Studies* 20: 376.

Andersson, R. 2018. "The Price of Impact: Reflections on Academic Outreach amid the 'Refugee Crisis.'" *Social Anthropology* 26, no. 2: 222–37.

Bakewell, O. 2007. "Editorial Introduction: Researching Refugees: Lessons from the Past, Current Challenges, and Future Directions." *Refugee Survey Quarterly* 26, no. 3: 6–14.

– 2008. "Research beyond the Categories: The Importance of Policy Irrelevant Research into Forced Migration." *Journal of Refugee Studies* 21, no. 4: 432–53.

– 2011. "Conceptualising Displacement and Migration: Processes, Conditions, and Categories." *The Migration-Displacement Nexus: Patterns, Processes, and Policies* 32: 14.

Baldwin-Edwards, M., B.K. Blitz, and H. Crawley. 2019. "The Politics of Evidence-Based Policy in Europe's 'Migration Crisis.'" *Journal of Ethic and Migration Studies* 45, no. 12: 2139–55.

Berriane, M., and H. de Haas, eds. 2012. *African Migration Research: Innovative Methods and Methodologies.* Trenton: Africa World Press.

Black, R. 2001. "Fifty Years of Refugee Studies: From Theory to Policy." *International Migration Review* 35, no. 1: 57–78.

– 2003. "Breaking the Convention: Researching the 'Illegal' Migration of Refugees to Europe." *Antipode* 35, no. 1: 34–54.

Bloch, A. 1999. "Carrying Out a Survey of Refugees: Some Methodological Considerations and Guidelines." *Journal of Refugee Studies* 12, no. 4: 367–83.

– 2004. "Survey Research with Refugees: A Methodological Perspective." *Policy Studies* 25, no. 2: 139–51.

Block, K., E. Riggs, and N. Haslam. 2013. "Ethics in Research with Refugees and Asylum Seekers: Processes, Power, and Politics." In *Values and Vulnerabilities: The Ethics of Research with Refugees and Asylum Seekers*, edited by K. Block, E. Riggs, and N. Haslam, 3–19. Toowong: Australian Academic Press.

Bose, P.K. 2010. "Refugee, Memory, and the State: A Review of Research in Refugee Studies." *Refugee Watch* 36: 1–30.

Bradley, M. 2007. "Refugee Research Agendas: The Influence of Donors and North–South Partnerships." *Refugee Survey Quarterly* 26, no. 3: 119–35.

Brun, C. 2015. "Active Waiting and Changing Hopes: Toward a Time Perspective on Protracted Displacement." *Social Analysis* 59, no. 1: 19–37.

Cabot, H. 2016. "'Refugee Voices': Tragedy, Ghosts, and the Anthropology of Not Knowing." *Journal of Contemporary Ethnography* 45, no. 6: 645–72.

Chatty, Dawn. 2016. "Refugee Voices: Exploring the Border Zones between States and State Bureaucracies." *Refuge: Canada's Journal on Refugees* 32, no. 1: 3–6.

Chimni, B.S. 2009. "The Birth of a 'Discipline': From Refugee to Forced Migration Studies." *Journal of Refugee studies* 22, no. 1: 11–29.

Colson, E. 2003. "Forced Migration and the Anthropological Response." *Journal of Refugee Studies* 16, no. 1: 1–18.

Cooper, E. 2005. "What Do We Know about Out-of-School Youths? How Participatory Action Research Can Work for Young Refugees in Camps." *Compare: A Journal of Comparative Education* 35, no. 4: 463–77.

Crawley, H., and D. Skleparis. 2018. "Refugees, Migrants, Neither, Both: Categorical Fetishism and the Politics of Bounding in Europe's 'Migration Crisis.'" *Journal of Ethnic and Migration Studies* 44, no. 1: 48–64.

Crush, J., A. Chikanda, and G. Tawodzera. 2015. "The Third Wave: Mixed Migration from Zimbabwe to South Africa." *Canadian Journal of African Studies/Revue canadienne des études africaines* 49, no. 2: 363–82.

Doná, G. 2006. "Children as Research Advisors: Contributions to a 'Methodology of Participation' in Researching Children in Difficult Circumstances." *International Journal of Migration, Health, and Social Care* 2, no. 2. https://doi:10.1108/17479894200600013.

– 2007. "The Microphysics of Participation in Refugee Research." *Journal of Refugee Studies* 20, no. 2: 210–29.

Eastmond, M. 2007. "Stories as Lived Experience: Narratives in Forced Migration Research." *Journal of Refugee Studies* 20, no. 2: 248–64. https://doi.org/10.1093/jrs/fem007.

Ellis, B.H., M. Kia-Keating, S.A. Yusuf, A. Lincoln, and A. Nur. 2007. "Ethical Research in Refugee Communities and the Use of Community Participatory Methods." *Transcultural Psychiatry* 44, no. 3: 459–81.

Erdal, M.B., and C. Oeppen. 2018. "Forced to Leave? The Discursive and Analytical Significance of Describing Migration as Forced and Voluntary." *Journal of Ethnic and Migration Studies* 44, no. 6: 981–98.

FitzGerald, D.S. 2019. *Refuge beyond Reach: How Rich Democracies Repel Asylum Seekers*. Oxford: Oxford University Press.

Gerver, M. 2018. "Refugee Repatriation and the Problem of Consent." *British Journal of Political Science* 48, no. 4: 855–75.

Ghelani, C.N. 2013. "Annotated Bibliography: Compiled for the Cluster on Methodology and the Knowledge Production in Forced Migration Contexts." Toronto: Centre for Refugee Studies, York University.

Grabska, K., M. De Regt, and N. Del Franco. 2019. *Adolescent Girls' Migration in the Global South: Transitions Into Adulthood*. Berlin and Heidelberg: Springer Verlag.

Guerin, P.B., and B. Guerin. 2007. "Research with Refugee Communities: Going Around in Circles with Methodology." PhD diss., APS Colleges.

Harrell-Bond, B.E. 1986. *Imposing Aid: Emergency Assistance to Refugees*. Oxford: Oxford University Press.

Hathaway, J.C. 2007. "Forced Migration Studies: Could We Agree Just to 'Date'?" *Journal of Refugee Studies* 20, no. 3: 349–69.

Horst, C., and K. Grabska. 2015. "Introduction: Flight and Exile – Uncertainty in the Context of Conflict-Induced Displacement." *Social Analysis* 59, no. 1: 1–18.

Hugman, R., L. Bartolomei, and E. Pittaway. 2011. "Human Agency and the Meaning of Informed Consent: Reflections on Research with Refugees." *Journal of Refugee Studies* 24, no. 4: 655–71.

Hyndman, J. 2010. "Introduction: The Feminist Politics of Refugee Migration." *Gender, Place & Culture* 17, no. 4: 453–9.

Hyndman, J., and W. Giles. 2011. "Waiting for What? The Feminization of Asylum in Protracted Situations." *Gender, Place, and Culture* 18, no. 3: 361–79.

Jacobsen, K., and L.B. Landau. 2003. "The Dual Imperative in Refugee Research: Some Methodological and Ethical Considerations in Social Science Research on Forced Migration." *Disasters* 27, no. 3: 185–206.

Kaiser, T. 2006. "Between a Camp and a Hard Place: Rights, Livelihood, and Experiences of the Local Settlement System for Long-Term Refugees in Uganda." *Journal of Modern African Studies* 44, no. 4: 597–621.

Krause, U. 2017. "Researching Forced Migration: Critical Reflections on Research Ethics during Fieldwork." *Refugee Studies Centre*. Working Paper series no. 123, 1–9.

Lammers, E. 2007. "Researching Refugees: Preoccupations with Power and Questions of giving." *Refugee Survey Quarterly* 26, no. 3: 72–81.

Lenette, C. 2019. "Arts-Based Methods in Refugee Research." Singapore: Springer.

Linde, T. 2011. "Mixed Migration – A Humanitarian Counterpoint." *Refugee Survey Quarterly* 30, no. 1: 89–99.

Long, K. 2013. "When Refugees Stopped Being Migrants: Movement, Labour, and Humanitarian Protection." *Migration Studies* 1, no. 1: 4–26.

Long, K., and J. Crisp. 2010. "Migration, Mobility, and Solutions: An Evolving Perspective." *Forced Migration Review* 35: 56.

Loyd, J.M., and A. Mountz. 2018. *Boats, Borders, and Bases: Race, the Cold War, and the Rise of Migration Detention in the United States*. Berkeley: University of California Press.

Mackenzie, C., C. McDowell, and E. Pittaway. 2007. "Beyond 'do no harm': The Challenge of Constructing Ethical Relationships in Refugee Research." *Journal of Refugee Studies* 20, no. 2: 299–319.

McGrath, S., and J.E.E. Young. 2019. *Mobilizing Global Knowledge: Refugee Research in an Age of Displacement*. Calgary: University of Calgary Press.

Moran, R., Z. Mohamed, and H. Lovel. 2011. "Breaking the Silence: Participatory Research Processes about Health with Somali Refugee People Seeking Asylum." In *Doing Research with Refugees: Issues and Guidelines*, edited by B. Temple and R. Moran, 55–74. Bristol: Policy Press.

O'Neill, M., U. Erel, E. Kaptani, and T. Reynolds. 2019. "Borders, Risk, and Be-
longing: Challenges for Arts-Based Research in Understanding the Lives of
Women Asylum Seekers and Migrants' at the Borders of Humanity.'" *Crossings:
Journal of Migration and Culture* 10, no. 1: 129–47.

Powles, J. 2002. "Refugee Voices: Home and Homelessness: The Life History of
Susanna Mwana uta, an Angolan Refugee." *Journal of Refugee Studies* 15, no. 1:
81–101.

Rodgers, G. 2004. "'Hanging Out' with Forced Migrants: Methodological and
Ethical Challenges." *Forced Migration Review* 21 (September): 48–9.

Ryan, L., and A. D'Angelo. 2018. "Changing Times: Migrants' Social Network
Analysis and the Challenges of Longitudinal Research." *Social Networks* 53:
148–58.

Schewel, K. 2020. "Understanding Immobility: Moving beyond the Mobility Bias
in Migration Studies." *International Migration Review* 54, no. 2: 328–55.

Sigona, N. 2014. "The Politics of Refugee Voices: Representations." In *The Oxford
Handbook of Refugee and Forced Migration Studies*, edited by E. Fiddian-Qasmiyeh,
G. Loeascher, and K. Long, 369–82. Oxford: Oxford University Press.

Squire, V. 2010. "The Contested Politics of Mobility: Politicizing Mobility, Mobilizing Politics." In *The Contested Politics of Mobility: Borderzones and Irregular-
ity*, edited by V. Squire, 1–26. New York and London: Routledge.

Tazzioli, M., and G. Garelli. 2018. "Containment beyond Detention: The Hotspot
System and Disrupted Migration Movements across Europe." *Environment and
Planning D: Society and Space.* https://doi.org/10.1177/0263775818759335.

Temple, B., and R. Moran, eds. 2006. *Doing Research with Refugees: Issues and
Guidelines*. Bristol: Policy Press.

Van der Velde, M., and T. van Naerssen. 2011. "People, Borders, Trajectories: An
Approach to Cross Border Mobility and Immobility in and to the European
Union." *Area* 43, no. 2: 218–24.

Van Hear, N. 2012. "Forcing the Issue: Migration Crises and the Uneasy Dialogue
between Refugee Research and Policy." *Journal of Refugee Studies* 25, no. 1: 2–24.

Van Hear, N., R. Brubaker, and T. Bessa. 2009. "Managing Mobility for Human
Development: The Growing Salience of Mixed Migration." Occasional paper,
UN Development Programme, New York.

Vargas-Silva, C., ed. 2012. *Handbook of Research Methods in Migration*. Cheltenham: Edward Elgar.

Vecchio, L., K.K. Dhillon, and Jasmine B. Ulmer. 2017. "Visual Methodologies for Research with Refugee Youth." *Intercultural Education* 28, no. 2: 131–42.

Voutira, E., and G. Doná. 2007. "Refugee Research Methodologies: Consolidation and Transformation of a Field." *Journal of Refugee Studies* 20, no. 2: 163–71.

Weller, R. 2017. "Salvaging Silence: Exile, Death, and the Anthropology of the Unknowable." *Anthropology of This Century* 19. http://aotcpress.com/articles/salvaging-silence.

Wolf, S. 2020. "Talking to Migrants: Invisibility, Vulnerability, and Protection." *Geopolitics* 26: 1–22.

Zetter, R. 1991. "Labelling Refugees: Forming and Transforming a Bureaucratic Identity." *Journal of Refugee Studies* 4, no. 1: 39–62.

– 2007. "More Labels, Fewer Refugees: Remaking the Refugee Label in an Era of Globalization." *Journal of Refugee Studies* 20, no. 2: 172–92.

Zetter, R., and K. Long. 2012. "Unlocking Protracted Displacement." *Forced Migration Review* 40: 34.

# SECTION ONE
## Ethics, Power, and Knowledge

Christina R. Clark-Kazak

In section 1 of this book, the contributors delve into the particular ethical dilemmas and power relations in knowledge production in contexts of displacement. The field of refugee or forced migration studies has long been dominated by researchers in the global north who lack direct experience of migration; thus, they have conducted research *on* rather than *with* displaced people. Our field is diversifying, but it is still undergirded by power asymmetries in knowledge production.

All of the authors of this book take seriously their positionality within these power structures. In this section, we have gathered together five chapters that illustrate some of the key questions and issues raised in the Code of Ethics adopted by the members of the International Association for the Study of Forced Migration (IASFM) in 2018. To be clear, this is a retroactive categorization by us as the editors and not an explicit attempt by the authors to endorse or "fit" within the code. In this section introduction, I use the key principles of the IASFM Code of Ethics (2018) to provide an analytic roadmap to the chapters that follow. In so doing, this section provides some examples of the ways in which relational ethics can be practically applied within real research projects.

The first principle in the IASFM code is *autonomy*:

We will respect and promote the right of people in situations of forced migration to make their own decisions about their lives, their participation in research projects, and the way they are represented in research findings. We acknowledge that too often forced migration researchers are positioned as "experts" on other people's lives and experiences, and too often speak for, or in the name of, people in forced migration. (IASFM 2018)

In the first chapter of this book, Oda and colleagues highlight the ethical and methodological dilemmas that peer researchers face when conducting longitudinal, community-based research in their own communities. They problematize the classic "insider/outsider" dichotomy by demonstrating how ethical research relationships are complicated by issues of representation and power: "They are seen to be insiders by the research team, but this position is challenged by the roles peer researchers take in research and the relationships peer researchers have within the community under study" (31). Similarly, the chapters by Taha and Aziz in this section speak to nuanced understandings of how researchers can be both insiders and outsiders. As forced migration research becomes more diversified, we need to take seriously these issues of representation and autonomy.

Both Taha and Aziz suggest that storytelling and narratives are methods that can foreground autonomy. Taha deliberately sought out "epistemological and practical ways of decolonizing knowledge," while Aziz used storytelling to "attenuate my own privileged structural positioning" and "establish a dialogue with my diverse interlocutors" (127). However, Chatzipanagiotidou and Murphy caution against assuming that any one method is inherently emancipatory. They argue that art-based methodology is "an ethically complex endeavour, which may sometimes reproduce rather than challenge hierarchies in the production of solidarity and empathy" (82). They challenge researchers to think carefully about not only the methods but also the topics of our research, including by practising refusal and the "the responsibility (not) to document loss." Ultimately, autonomy in practice requires foregrounding the dignity of the people with whom we are working and honouring their decisions and experiences.

The second principle in the IASFM Code of ethics is *equity*:

We acknowledge intersecting, unequal power relations, which are exacerbated in forced migration contexts, and will take steps to mitigate their effect on research relationships and results. We are mindful that power relations can never be fully resolved, but commit ourselves to actively challenging repressive social structures." (IASFM 2018)

In the chapters in this section, authors show how they engaged in practice with critical reflexivity. Taha provides specific examples of how she reflected on her position and her positionality, especially in relation to complicated insider/outsider relationships (noted above) and her commitment to decolonizing knowledge. Chatzipanagiotidou and Murphy (98) advocate for "methodological dubiety, an approach that moves beyond relying on specific methods to constantly reflecting on their application."

While community-based, participatory, and co-creation approaches are sometimes lauded as methodologies that address power inequalities, Oda and colleagues "(30) caution against this assumption: "The inherent power imbalance between the position of the academic researchers and peer researchers may be harder to acknowledge in community-based research and may lead to further marginalization and exploitation of researchers from marginalized communities." Moreover, Oda and colleagues as well as Aziz demonstrate how longitudinal research creates relationships beyond the research, with correspondingly complicated and intertwined power dynamics.

Hart, Oda and colleagues, Aziz, and Chatzipanagiotidou and Murphy, in very different research contexts, also highlight the importance of socio-economic class within intersecting power relations. This important positionality is often overlooked in forced migration studies dominated by binaries of migrant/settler, North/South.

Attention to intersecting power relations is linked to issues of *diversity*, the third principle in the IASFM code of ethics, which states:

We recognize the diversity of experiences of forced migration and culturally-specific research ethics. We will include a multitude of perspectives and proactively seek out those who are marginalized or excluded from decision-making and research processes.

Hart's chapter focuses on age as one such diversity issue – indeed, one that is often overlooked in forced migration studies: "Failure to attend to the perspectives of children in situations of displacement creates a limit to our understanding of forced migration: as unacceptable in both ethical and intellectual terms as ignoring the experience of say, adult women, or the elderly" (104). Aziz and Taha show how both the age and the gender identity of researchers and respondents affects the research process. This is nothing new, nor is it unique to migration studies, but awareness of it helps counteract homogenizing and essentializing research about "the refugee experience."

As the contributors to this section demonstrate, diversity also applies to methods, epistemology, and ethics. Taha advocates for "embracing other ways of knowing" as "a decolonizing approach that will require expanding one's sociological imagination to include other theoretical explanations and methodological tools that could help us understand Othered experiences" (59). Chatzipanagiotidou and Murphy (84) call on researchers to be aware of a "methodological fixation on collecting accounts of displacement, suffering, and loss," which can result in "the fetishization of the 'refugee voice' and forms of epistemic violence" (Cabot 2016).

The fourth principle in the IASFM code is *competence*:

We will use methodological approaches that are adapted to the cultural contexts in which we work, as well as the specific opportunities and challenges of forced migration. We will ensure adequate training for all involved in research projects, including students, research assistants, interpreters and gatekeepers. (IASFM 2018)

Hart's chapter highlights some child-specific and child-centred methodologies and ethical considerations that should be part of competent approaches to research with children in contexts of displacement. Oda and colleagues discuss the challenges of compassion fatigue among peer researchers, suggesting that competence extends beyond standard methodological training to care ethics, including self-care. Aziz speaks to the importance of personal responsibility and ethical competence, sometimes in addition to – or in opposition to – formal ethics protocols. Indeed, many kinds of research scenarios are not covered by procedural ethics. In fact, all of the chapters in this book provide some insights into dilemmas and lessons learned when messy research relationships arise.

Here, particularly Chatzipanagiotidou and Murphy's discussion of empathy can expand and enrich the IASFM principle of competence.

IASFM's final principle in the code of ethics – partnership – starts with a bold statement: "Forced migration scholarship often disproportionately benefits those who are least affected by displacement" (IASFM 2018). All of the contributors to this book reiterate this statement in different ways (cf. Banki and Phillips; Grabska). The IASFM code (2018) provides some ways in which researchers can implement partnership:

> To mitigate this problem and to promote maximum benefit from participation in research, we will include relevant partners throughout the research process, including, formulating the research question, design, data collection, analysis and dissemination. Research project budgets will include funding for all partners to reflect the time, talent and contributions to the research. Researchers may also consider actively contributing their time and labour to projects, activities, events or actions which unrelated to the research, but are undertaken by partners or the communities where research is being conducted.

The chapters in this section complement the IASFM code by offering insights into practical, methodological, and ethical challenges of partnership and how the authors and their colleagues addressed them. Oda and colleagues are refreshingly honest about the challenges – and opportunities – of community-based research built on partnerships, but within power asymmetries. Hart highlights the complexities of undertaking funded research, as well as that done in partnership with UN agencies, governments, and NGOs. He rightly highlights the dependence of forced migration researchers on this funding and collaboration and the ethical and methodological implications. Hart also underscores the importance of interacting with children as research partners. Similarly, Chatzipanagiotidou and Murphy (95) advocate for "a common, collaborative decision-making process with one's interlocuters." They also attend to collegial partnerships within research teams, which lead to "better access and the opportunity to forge a more collaborative interaction with artists who are themselves working in groups or collectives, and therefore value partnership and exchange" (86).

In conclusion, the chapters in this section provide particular insights into the importance of critical questioning in research relationships in displacement contexts. As Hart states at the end of his chapter, uneasiness is a good indication that researchers are aware of key ethical and methodological challenges and the importance of our research relationships, as well as the issues we are working with. "Methodological dubiety" (Chatzipanagiotidou and Murphy) and critical reflexivity are important themes running through this section and throughout the book.

# 1

## Ethical Challenges of Conducting Longitudinal Community-Based Research with Refugees: *Reflections from Peer Researchers*

Anna Oda, Adnan Al Mhamied, Riham Al-Saadi, Neil Arya, Mona Awwad, Oula Hajjar, Jill Hanley, Michaela Hynie, Nicole Ives, Rabih Jamil, Mahi Khalaf, Rim Khyar, Ben C.H. Kuo, May Massijeh, Rana Mohammad, and Kathy Sherrell

Research with resettled refugee populations is necessary to develop an understanding of their settlement and integration experiences and challenges, and thus for successful refugee settlement program planning and implementation. However, research with refugee populations also comes with many methodological and ethical challenges (Hugman et al. 2011, 1274). These challenges overlap with the ones encountered when recruiting and retaining ethnic minority populations in research, grounded in sociopolitical, historical, and cultural factors that can result in a lack of trust and negative attitudes toward scientific inquiry and the institutions and individuals engaged in research (Block et al. 2013, 78–81; Yancey et al. 2006, 15–17). People with refugee backgrounds face unique risks and concerns. These include a reluctance to revisit pre-migration experiences, political or ethnic conflicts within the community, and perceived or actual risks to migration status arising from certain lines of questioning (Clark-Kazak 2017, 12–13). For the recently arrived Syrian refugees settling in Canada, all of these concerns apply – for example, having lived precariously in refugee camps, leaving behind loved ones in dangerous situations, and finding themselves sharing their new communities with Syrians from another side of the conflict. To anticipate and address some of the challenges in research with refugees, a number of studies have adopted a community-based research approach (Ellis et al. 2007, 477), and it was decided from the inception that this would be the best approach for our project.

Community-based research (CBR) refers to a family of systematic inquiry approaches that share a commitment to community involvement and leadership in research design, implementation, results interpretation, and dissemination (Israel et al. 1998, 177). When members of the community are involved in the research, they are often called peer researchers (Greene 2013, 142). Many advantages of CBR have been reported in the literature – for example, it ensures culturally appropriate and relevant research questions at the outset, as well as appropriate data collection tools; it facilitates more informative analysis plans and interpretations of findings; it mitigates power imbalances between researchers and the community being researched; and it increases community trust (Minkler 2005, 4–7). Depicting vulnerable communities such as refugees as voiceless and lacking agency is harmful and can further marginalize the community; clearly, then, it is important to ensure that their voices are accurately represented throughout the research process (Wilson et al. 2018, 191–2). In this project, the hiring of peer researchers (including Syrian refugees, second-generation Syrian Canadians, and (im)migrants from Palestine and Lebanon) and close consultation with Syrian community and religious organizations as well as refugee resettlement agencies provided the base for our CBR approach. Our assumption was that CBR would allow for more relevant and sensitive research processes, and more accurate interpretations of the results, and would lead to stronger community interest in the findings. In our view, CBR methods support more ethical research from the perspective of the participants and communities, as well as better research overall.

However, while CBR has many benefits in terms of the quality and relevance of the research process and findings, complex ethical challenges can arise (Wilson et al. 2018, 192–7). Although peer researchers are often employed to help identify and address these challenges, their position and involvement throughout the research process can actually heighten these concerns. The inherent power imbalance between the academic researchers and the peer researchers may be harder to acknowledge in community-based research and may lead to further marginalization and exploitation of researchers from marginalized communities (Wilson et al. 2018, 192–3; Marlowe et al. 2015, 394). We juggled these challenges within our own project, with peer researchers who held various (and sometimes simultaneous) positions as community leaders, graduate students under the supervision of academic team members, or employees of settlement agencies.

Moreover, peer researchers are placed in a fraught position on the insider/outsider continuum. They are perceived as insiders by the research team, but this position is challenged by the roles they play in research and by the relationships they have within the community being studied. Insider status is about more than ethnicity, nationality, or shared experiences; it is a dynamic position when one takes into account demographic and contextual factors, both past and present (Ryan 2015, vol. 16; Leung 2015, vol. 16). For example, working on refugee research projects with peer researchers who have the same country of nationality as the research participants can be complicated by socio-political factors such as the ethnic, religious, or political affiliations of peer researchers vis-à-vis those of participants (Jacobsen and Landau 2003, 193). In our project, for example, dynamics of class and political sympathies played out between peer researchers and community participants, and those dynamics had to be carefully managed. Moving between insider/outsider spaces is a fluid process strongly affected by the context of each research interaction (Jacobsen and Landau 2003, 192–3). Literature exists that addresses the challenges of being an insider/outsider in the research process from the perspective of ethnography or other forms of qualitative studies (Ryan 2015, vol. 16; Leung 2015, vol. 16); less has been written about the challenges that may arise for insiders who are peer researchers in CBR. Indeed, more generally, analyses of the roles of peer researchers have tended to focus on the benefits or challenges they bring to the work or on protecting their well-being (Jacobsen and Landau 2003, 192–3). This chapter contributes to the academic reflection on these issues by focusing, instead, on the ethical issues that may arise when conducting CBR with peer researchers.

This chapter begins with a short description of the longitudinal community-based research study with Syrian refugees, including the background, methods, and process of involving peer researchers. The rest of the chapter focuses on the ethical challenges peer researchers faced during data collection (positionality, professional role conflict, compassion fatigue and burnout, and distress and secondary trauma), and how these challenges were addressed over the course of the study.

## Background and Process

Canada welcomed more than 47,735 Syrian refugees between November 2015 and July 2017 (IRCC 2017). In 2016, a team of Canadian researchers and practitioners in the field of refugee resettlement, including medical doctors, nurses, and social workers, received funding from the Canadian Institute of Health Research (CIHR) to conduct the Refugee Integration and Long-Term Health Outcomes in Canada study (SYRIA.lth). This four-year national mixed-method CBR project documented how various resettlement programs (Government Assistance, Private Sponsorship, or Blended-Visa Office) helped Syrian refugees settle in Canada and supported their long-term integration, and, ultimately, their physical and mental health. The project was a collaboration between settlement agencies, community organizations, and academics in three provinces (British Columbia, Ontario, and Quebec) across six research sites: Okanagan Valley and Vancouver, BC; Toronto, Kitchener, and Windsor, ON; and Montreal, QC. Arabic-speaking research assistants (including those who were Syrian refugees themselves, recent Syrian immigrants, second-generation Syrian Canadians, or (im)migrants from Palestine and Lebanon) were invited to participate as peer researchers in all aspects of the study. Peer researchers participated in selecting and refining the research questions; they were also involved in participant recruitment, translation, data collection, data analysis, and interpretation and dissemination of findings.

In 2017, peer researchers were able to identify potential participants across Canada; in all, 2,000 Syrian refugees were recruited to participate in this study. Ultimately, 1,957 were interviewed face-to-face in Arabic, using a structured survey, once every year for three years (2017, 2018, and 2019, with a fourth wave planned for 2020). Interviewers entered the participants' responses on project iPads. The interviews were conducted where most convenient to the participants, be it in the home, in a local public space (e.g., a coffee shop or park), or at the office of a partner organization. Survey topics included pre-migration socio-economic background, demographic information, migration pathways (both sponsorship routes and length and location of asylum), service use in the first and third years, social networks and social supports, gender roles, discrimination and belonging, employment, housing, and health (including mental health). In addition, focus groups were conducted at each site in year two with the goal of understanding participants' experiences of social networks and how they helped Syrian refugees resettle and find jobs. These focus groups were organized and conducted in Arabic by peer researchers and held in the offices of partner organizations.

Over the course of the study, the research team (including both academic and peer researchers) held multiple discussions related to the ethical challenges that peer researchers faced while working with participants on data collection; a number of measures were put in place each year to address these issues. At the end of Year Three, in 2019, the peer researchers decided to document their experience and reflect on it as insiders/outsiders. Our team collectively agreed that such issues were critical enough in themselves that they should be shared with larger audiences, especially those planning to engage in CBR projects with refugee communities. Similar to the efforts of Marlowe and colleagues (2015, 383–98) and Mistry and colleagues (2015, 27–35), this chapter offers peer researchers' personal reflections, addressing the challenges raised in the first three years of this study, in the hope that they will inform future practice and advance refugee research in general and community-based research in particular.

## Methods

The reflections described here are based on three exercises conducted over the course of the first three years of the study. After the first year of data collection, peer researchers were invited to write a short reflective piece about their experiences, as part of a debriefing procedure (described below). After the second year of data collection, peer researchers were invited to participate in an arts-based reflective process; each peer researcher was asked to draw a metaphor representing their Year Two experiences and then to describe in words what the metaphor represented. This chapter is being written following Year Three data collection and a series of conversations around ethical challenges as another step in our process of reflecting on and processing the challenges of engaging in this kind of research, including the strategies we use to address those challenges and what we could do differently. Thus, writing this chapter has been a community-based process as well.

The reflections in this chapter come from ten Arabic-speaking peer researchers: one from BC, five from Ontario, and four from Quebec (eight females and two males). All of them have worked on the research study since its inception. Not all peer researchers participated in the process of writing this chapter, but all were invited to do so, and the academic researchers were also invited to share their reflections and feedback. Four of the peer researcher authors are Syrian refugees themselves, while the other six are first- or second-generation immigrants from the Middle East who have been involved in the Syrian Refugee Resettlement Initiative since 2015. Six peer researchers have worked as settlement workers with Syrian refugee resettlement programs in Canada (these are not mutually exclusive categories). We met virtually on several occasions over two months, shared our contributions from the previous reflection exercises, and discussed our current reflections from the three years of data collection. Meetings were organized and led by the first author, who is the project coordinator and also a member of the data collection team, and is an immigrant to Canada from Syria. Notes were taken and incorporated into an ongoing, developing document, which was shared with the group for comments and reflections, which helped organize the next discussion. In discussing experiences and documents from previous reflections, the group identified and discussed a number of common themes and issues, which were again summarized and shared. Through this cycle of discussion and review, we eventually agreed that the experiences and reflections could be summarized under four themes: positionality, professional role conflict, compassion fatigue and burnout, and distress and secondary trauma. What follows is a summary of the main themes that emerged from our reflections.

## Reflections and Ethical Challenges

I see the role of peer researchers like a link and a bridge. This bridge's role is to link the institution to the participants, help bridge the gap in existing research, and reach out correctly to communities that might be distant otherwise. However, as a link, the peer researcher is required to ensure the delivery of information, different forms of information that the participants or the institution want to convey to one another.

Figure 1.1 Research assistant 1.

This role is not always easy to accomplish. (Research assistant [RA] 1, see figure 1.1)

*Positionality and the Insider/Outsider Position*

The term "community" typically refers to a group of people who share a certain characteristic. However, community boundaries are often contested (MacQueen et al. 2001, 1930–3). When we look more closely at groups that share salient characteristics, such as nationality, religion, or migratory path, we often find considerable heterogeneity. Members of the same ethnic community can have different demographic and socio-economic characteristics, as well as different religions, histories, and political views. Thus, the process of identifying communities and self-identifying as a "member" of a certain community can be very complex. The complexity and intersectionality of particular historic, social, economic, religious, and political positions of the peer researchers and the research participants created complex insider/outsider relationships. For example, the study sample included Armenians,

Arabs, and Kurds, Muslims and Christians, and people with very different political positions in relation to the conflict in Syria. Peer researchers represented a mix of religions and ethnicities, different migration trajectories into Canada, different ages and professions, and different political orientations. Moreover, most of the peer researchers had a university education, which set them apart from a substantial proportion of the research participants (see Hynie et al. 2019 for sample demographic information). Thus, there could be considerable social distance between peer researchers and those they were interviewing, despite their shared language and/or nationality. Deepening trust between peer researchers and participants as they got to know one another through the interview process and over the years of the study resulted in further complications in negotiating boundaries with participants (discussed below). Peer researchers felt an increased pressure of responsibility towards participants and also to disclose aspects of their personal identity, and this could be complicated, given that assumed similarities (e.g., around political orientation or religion) were not necessarily validated.

Tensions between researchers and participants arises from the inherent power imbalance at individual and structural socio-economic levels (Jachyra et al. 2015, 249). Building rapport is viewed as an ethical approach to mitigating the power imbalance between researchers and participants (251–4). Research also suggests that rapport contributes to the richness and accuracy of collected data (Collie et al. 2010, 147). Honesty and self-disclosure are essential to interpersonal communication, and these are recommended in qualitative research methodologies as means to build rapport with participants (Jachyra et al. 2015, 251–4). Being welcomed into participants' homes as a trusted community member almost always entailed answering their questions about oneself *before* starting the actual research survey. This was particularly noticeable during home visits; at times it felt uncomfortable and was perceived as a social burden by peer researchers.

> As Syrian peer researchers, we were consistently asked personal questions about where we are from in Syria, when we moved to Canada, our age, and if we were married or looking to get married! (RA 9)

> In the process of data collection and in order to be the researcher, you need to allow yourself to be questioned, surveyed, and observed. You

start asking your participant but hold on, you become the participant, the participant is now asking you "When did you arrive to Canada?" You answer "In 2016." Other questions follow: "How old are you?" "How often do you feel tired?" "How did you get to Canada?" "Do you have driver's licence?" "How often do you exercise?" "How did you get this job?" "Are you fasting?" "Do you smoke Shisha?" "How did you feel yesterday?" "Why aren't you married?" (RA 1)

Peer researchers sometimes felt uncomfortable with this questioning and sometimes felt they should refrain from full and honest self-disclosure or even misrepresent themselves – especially when participants started talking about sensitive topics such as Syrian politics – in order to avoid any potential conflict. So it was sometimes difficult to establish genuine relationships and be fully open, which challenged research ethics as they related to self-disclosure and rapport-building. Moreover, for those peer researchers who felt strongly about opinions the respondents shared with them, it was distressing to have to bite their tongue:

I knew that when I enter participants' houses, they would consider I am on the neutral side and that they won't try to open with me any political conversations. However, I had to listen many times to some political opinions that the participants shared with me and I personally totally disagree with, but I had just to listen and nod my head and try to pass to the next questions. That didn't feel easy all the time. (RA 6)

I had at certain point to do interviews with participants who questioned my political views or even expressed political opinions against their fellow Syrians. I had to ensure that I am distancing myself from the Syrian conflicts as if I am doing a research by expatriation [Beaud and Weber 2003, 47]. In many cases, I had to answer questions about my ethnic background or my original place of birth in Syria (RA 7)

One common challenge when working with those with a refugee background is that living under an authoritarian regime likely affects one's willingness to take part in investigative exercises and disclose personal information. Respondents' concerns about how information will be used and

what purpose it will serve are very important to address, given the reper-
cussions such disclosure could have for their situation; leaving Syria does
not necessarily mean that they have freed themselves from the culture of
fear. Trust-building was challenged by the conflict that Syrian refugees had
experienced and by their fears of being exploited in Canada. Consistent
with other research, peer researchers in this project were in the position of
representing another authority, in this case the research project, and having
to assure participants of confidentiality. This placed a great deal of responsibility on peer researchers for gaining the participants' trust and ensuring
their well-being (Marlowe et al. 2015, 392). Recruiting potential participants
and conducting the first-year interviews was one of the early challenges
peer researchers reported.

> When we told them about the consent forms' signature, they often
> would tell us stories about them being tricked by someone to sign
> something here in Canada. (RA 1)

> Being myself a Syrian refugee, I fully understand the reaction and the
> reluctance of some participants against taking part in such a detailed
> socio-economic survey. Four years now after being resettled in Canada
> I am still concerned with the confidentiality of the information I
> shared as part of my refugee application. (RA 7)

> I struggled to get accurate answers from my participants, especially
> males. They told me many times: "We do not want any problems with
> the government." One participant asked me, "Are you sure no one will
> read these answers?" Every time I have to assure them that their con-
> fidentiality is our priority, but it is hard for people who came from the
> culture of fear. (RA 5)

Building trust remained a challenge until Year Three of the study. Since
this research study was longitudinal, many participants felt more comfortable participating during follow-up surveys in Years Two and Three, especially if it was conducted with the same research assistant; they developed
trusting relationships over time. However, this growing trust and relation-

ship likely deepened some of the social distress that is reported below, and in subsequent sections.

> Conducting the interviews for three years in a row with some families made the participants feel more comfortable with the questions and the research process. They felt more comfortable to ask more questions about existing resources and express their opinion about their current life and well-being. (RA 6)

The researcher role is privileged, and this often made peer researchers feel like community outsiders, because of their more powerful position but also because they had been trained in how to establish professional boundaries during the research study, which meant distancing themselves from the community. These professional boundaries and the assumed political neutrality of peer researchers in a community that has been undergoing a conflict for the past decade sometimes made peer researchers feel forced to alienate themselves from the community, put aside their identity and personal, social, and political stance, and refrain from self-disclosure during interviews. The contradiction between the need for self-disclosure and professional boundary-setting caused an internal struggle in peer researchers' identity as it related to their insider/outsider role. This had an impact on peer researchers' mental health and well-being. Many struggled with the notion of neutrality and professional boundaries:

> I often meet participants in public places such as the mall or grocery store. For confidentiality reasons, I know that it is better not to talk too much to them, but it was challenging to do so tactfully, especially because the study is longitudinal. (RA 8)

> As peer researchers, we share the status of trauma survivors, we are from within the community, but we had to distance ourselves, at least during the interview time, from our identity as refugees and put forward our role as field researchers ... All these intrapersonal challenges had to be mitigated by re-emphasizing the research objectives and framework. In short, fieldwork was an ongoing back-and-forth between my position

as research assistant (outsider) and identity as peer refugee (insider). While the former was essential to prove neutrality and confidentiality, the latter was key in strengthening the trust relation and showing our understanding of the context they are experiencing. (RA 7)

Insider/outsider roles not only impact relationship dynamics with participants and the mental well-being of peer researchers (as the previous reflections indicate) but also have hidden implications in terms of data validity and trustworthiness, potential biases, miscommunication, and misrepresentation. When peer researchers and participants come from different socio-economic and political structures within a vulnerable community, peer researchers' position may shift from insider to outsider as they may not have the knowledge and experience participants have. Thus, there is a risk of preconceived assumptions that can compromise the quality of the collected data. Peer researchers' insider knowledge can lead to disagreements or doubts about the accuracy of responses shared by participants, doubts that may or may not be warranted, further challenging the establishment of trust and leaving peer researchers feeling uncomfortable.

Another challenge is the trust from my side. Some refugees tend to tell stories that, as a Syrian, I know they are fake or at least far away from reality. But as a researcher I am not there to examine the reality of these stories, so I have to ignore the stories despite the psychological impact on me. (RA 5)

Reflexivity and examination of how tension arising from different socio-economic conditions, attitudes, beliefs, values, and assumptions influences data collection processes, as well as the well-being of researchers and participants, is therefore critical throughout the research process (Finlay 2002, 535; Block et al. 2013, 84–5). But delineating their position in relation to the research study and the research participants in order to locate and acknowledge bias may be particularly challenging for peer researchers (Sánchez 2010, 2258).

*Professional Role Conflicts*

The second intrapersonal challenge peer researchers faced was related to conflict between their different professional roles. Almost half the peer researchers also worked in the settlement sector in various professional capacities, including as settlement workers, translators, social workers, and psychologists. This specific positionality, in terms of different simultaneous professional roles, created unique ethical challenges. Completely distancing oneself from the primary service provider role is difficult during research with vulnerable populations who could benefit from services. Newly resettled refugees often need and ask for support during their initial resettlement, support that some of the peer researchers had been trained to provide. Efforts were made to ensure that those peer researchers who worked in the settlement sector refrained from recruiting and interviewing clients at the settlement agencies they worked with. This strategy helped avoid possible coercion, conflict of interest, or confusion around the study's purpose. However, as news travels quickly in small communities, some participants knew about peer researchers' settlement roles and requested settlement support. To address this challenge, peer researchers were instructed to establish professional boundaries, explain their role as peer researchers, and spend adequate time obtaining informed consent and explaining the study's purpose (Yassour-Borochowitz 2004, 183).

One of the challenges that I faced is that of professional roles conflict, due to multiple roles and relationships with the participants. I worked at a settlement agency, where potential research participants receive regular services and support. While familiarity was positively related to participants' trust and willingness to participate in this project and being interviewed, this "dual relationship" led to some unique challenges as well. First, in some cases, Syrian participants were hesitant to share negative experiences or challenges about the agency for which I work [even if they were not my direct client]. Secondly, the other challenge in managing the dual roles is that, in some instances, participants during the interviews were seeking further settlement-related support, which clearly contravened the purpose of the research interview. In this case, I had to reaffirm my role specifically for the project data collection and also provided the participants with a resource handout. I encouraged these participants to access their assigned social service or settlement workers and get the support they need. (RA 4)

Participants were expecting my help as they were talking about problems during the survey. Others even asked if I could help by giving information about (good family doctor, a good house for rent or how could they find a job). One woman even asked me if I can be her friend because she is so lonely here. After I had this problem, I started stating my role and its boundaries from the very beginning and telling people what am I expected to do and not to do and, actually, this was helpful. (RA 3)

When we went through the question about family members abroad, it always got research participants talking about finding opportunities for sponsorship for them. Since I work at a settlement agency, participants always requested support to sponsor their family members abroad. As a peer researcher, when faced with this request, I would always go back to explaining the purpose of the study and how this has nothing to do with my work as a settlement worker. I would recommend they see a settlement agency for support with this matter. (RA 9)

Some of the young adults interviewed would ask me about college applications and acceptance. I try to answer their questions with the knowledge that I have and within reason. Keeping the relationship to strictly research was also tough for me. (RA 7)

This was not an intervention study. Moreover, many peer researchers were not qualified to provide settlement support, and there were ethical concerns linked to participants joining or continuing the research in order to obtain services. Nonetheless, some participants had high expectations of help from peer researchers, the effect of which was compounded by the peer researchers' desire to provide help. In advance of conducting the study, each research site had developed resource handouts with contact information for different settlement agencies that participants could access for support in their communities. Despite such efforts to address the challenge of dual roles, some situations proved more complex. For example, peer researchers were sometimes asked to help with simple tasks such as interpreting letters from schools or government. Although the main underlying argument behind avoiding such practice was to avoid turning this longitudinal study into intervention research and avoid coercion because participants might feel the need to participate in order to receive services, peer researchers working in service provision fields such as social work and nursing argued that researchers have the ethical obligation of not only doing no harm but also of doing good, and that performing small courtesies is part of the ethical obligation (Bloor 2010, 17–20). To decline to offer simple help and instead refer participants to settlement agencies was painful, and even felt unethical at times.

> I've faced various challenges being a research assistant interviewing the same target group and community that I interacted with in another capacity as a settlement worker serving specifically the Syrian community. The first logistical challenge was trying to avoid interviewing my own clients, which was easy to solve by participant distribution lists; however, I still faced some issues while interviewing participants who were recruited through my clients because they already knew I was a settlement worker and would ask me questions hoping to get the kind of support that I cannot offer as a researcher. Creating this wall between my two capacities was extremely difficult because when I clarify my role as a researcher, to them, that's basically refusing to offer help. It was sometimes very difficult to provide participants with a list of organizations they can seek for help, while I can give my own card or number, because the two offers are perceived in a totally different way, from my experience. Providing them with a list of community organizations sometimes seems useless to them, as I realize in their eyes while I am handing them the sheet. I suppose they don't feel it's going to be easy to contact or search for those organizations due to the language barrier and if they did contact them, it's going to be difficult to find the person who can actually help them. (RA 2)

## Compassion Fatigue and Burnout

Strongly linked to the issue of professional role conflicts, peer researchers identified compassion fatigue and burnout as another consequence of working on data collection. The stress resulting from wanting to help those who are suffering and in need, beyond one's abilities, can result in compassion fatigue (Hesse 2002, 295–6). When compassion fatigue is not addressed and managed in time, it can lead to further complications and even to professional burnout (Adams et al. 2008, 246–7). Burnout was also a big concern given the demanding nature, length of time, and location of these interviews. Data collection occurred during the spring and summer of every year, and peer researchers had around four months in total to conduct interviews at each site. Interviews occurred mostly at participants' homes, and since the majority lived far from city centres, travel time was another factor that added stress to intense data collection work. Also, interviews were relatively long, with more than 200 questions, so the total interview (including the pre- and post-interview chats that were so important) could take between one and two hours per participant, and a session could take up to eight hours when several participants lived in one household and each was interviewed.

> As days of work passed, I discovered that my limit of interviews for one day is five; each one would be around an hour to two hours. It is within that limit that I can give the participant my best, while considering my emotional and physical state as well as the travel time, which varied between two hours to three hours each time. (RA 1)

Peer researchers were encouraged to do home visits in pairs. Logistically, this strategy made each home visit shorter, and families felt less overwhelmed, as having researchers at their house for an extended time could be burdensome. It was also important for ensuring the safety and well-being of our peer researchers. The strategy also facilitated informal support opportunities, in that peer researchers had a companion with whom to share emotional support.

> I was teamed up with another peer researcher through the work duration to facilitate the work, have a travel companion and assure our safety all the time. (RA 1)

Compassion fatigue and burnout was exacerbated by the limited ability that peer researchers had to provide support to participants.

The highest level of compassion fatigue was triggered by the issues that, even as a settlement worker, I have no solutions, such as the language barrier, especially for elders who cannot learn a language easily. One participant described his feelings about this issue as "being deaf"; he said this is how he feels in Canada with a very painful tone, as if he actually lost his voice and sense of hearing. Another common problem without any solution is family reunification, which to some people is the only solution to their sorrows. (RA 2)

Perhaps one of the most valuable things peer researchers and participants identified was the opportunity to share and listen. On the one hand, it was sometimes difficult and draining being present and actively listening to participants and their stories. On the other, it felt very rewarding to both peer researchers and participants. Many participants, especially those who experienced isolation, shared their feelings of gratitude for having someone to listen to their stories.

For me, to create this trust and this comfortable ambiance during the interviews took a lot of my energy, sometimes. You want to give them as much care as you can and listen to every detail and show them how they are valuable beyond this research and that they are not just a number and a code (even though you want to emphasize the fact that their name is not mentioned anywhere and that for confidentiality and research purposes they will be just a code assigned to them). (RA 6)

Working as a researcher with people – I consider myself to belong to them – was enjoyable. Through this work I was not only able to enter their places, they opened their hearts to me. Many times I left, elderly women hugging me. During Ramadan, people (especially Christians) gave me candies, some of them offered to me to break my fast with them. Even though it was painful to listen to stories from elderly people, it was a pleasant moment for me to close my iPad and listen to women who are struggling from isolation and they want someone to listen. A lady told me once "You are the first one to knock on our door in a week. (RA 5)

## Distress and Secondary Trauma

The thing about working in social research is being able to see deeper
layers in people that are often not reflected by their outer facial impres-
sions. While listening to participants' stories and feelings, a lot of the
smiles turned out to be misleading. Even with the questions they prefer
not to answer, a spark in their eyes after hearing the question always
uncovers their spontaneous reaction to the topic of the question, and
whether they feel good about it or not, whether they remembered a
happy or a sad story. The misleading image is not only associated to
sadness being hidden by smiles, but is also a factor of personality, as
interviewing participants, to me, was like finding their most human
nature, showing how each and every person is beautiful from within.
(RA 2, see figure 1.2)

Many Syrian refugees had faced hardships and traumatic life events during their migration journey, which some shared with peer researchers. The
nature of these face-to-face interviews created opportunities for additional
disclosures, and almost all participants (90 per cent) chose to share additional information that was not part of the survey. It is important to acknowledge that all peer researchers experienced emotionally distressing
situations while collecting data:

When participants recalled their difficult migration stories and the
losses they experienced, I found myself involved and cried as she was
crying. I let her finish her story and then I asked for a break for both
of us before we could continue the survey. This situation was very difficult. (RA 3)

I was touched by each story I came to hear and learn from my participants. The experiences of escape, exposure to losing a friend or a loved
one due to a bullet or a bomb made me tearful. (RA 4)

I think what I found to be most challenging part to me throughout the
process was listening to the stories. Most of the time, participants were

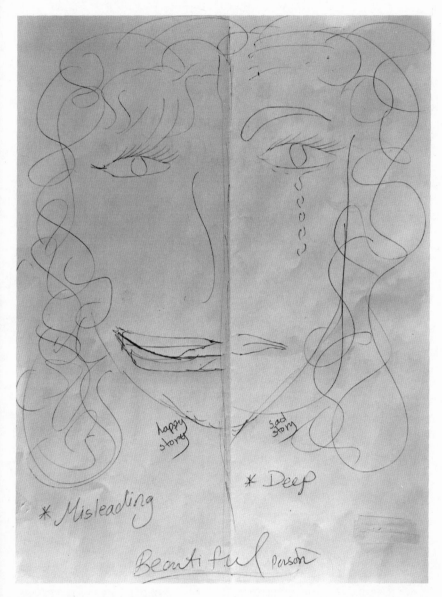

Figure 1.2 Research assistant 2.

willing to share their personal stories with us, some of which are re-
markably painful. I would listen to these stories and try to absorb their
frustration and sorrow. I remember in one interview, I ended up crying
with my participant and feeling down about their story the entire week.
It is in those moments I think that it gets complicated to separate your
researcher self from your human and Syrian self. (RA 1)

Sometimes it was very difficult for me to see that my questions provoked negative emotions related to the trauma. Sometimes I felt a lot
of guilt and their stories confronted me with the injustice of the world.
I often asked myself at night, before going to bed, if the participants
felt better. (RA 8)

Secondary trauma, also known as vicarious trauma, can occur as a result
of working with trauma survivors (Hesse 2002, 295–6; Adams et al. 2008,
246–7). Research indicates that working with trauma survivors and listening to their stories can have profound emotional and psychological effects
on service providers' well-being (Hesse 2002, 296); this can also be true of
those collecting information about these experiences for research purposes,
who are, by virtue of their role, even less able to provide comfort or assistance. Those who work with trauma survivors and listen to traumatic stories can become traumatized themselves and experience symptoms similar
to post-traumatic stress disorder (PTSD) after such encounters (Hesse
2002, 296–7); symptoms can include feelings of initial shock, grief, pain,
and psychological distress that can lead to unhealthy behavioural outcomes
such as avoidance (Hesse 2002, 296–7). Due to its serious negative consequences, secondary stress syndrome is now being viewed as an occupa-
tional hazard when working with trauma survivors (Bride 2007, 64). The
likelihood of secondary trauma increases when practitioners have experienced traumatic life events themselves (Adams et al. 2008, 246–7). Since
more than half of peer researchers had similar experiences of migration,
refuge, and hardship to those experienced by participants, the risk for retraumatization was even higher.

I felt sad when I saw during the first year how people are hopeful and are
eager to find jobs, while I am aware as an immigrant myself of all the

barriers that immigrants face in the job market. You can predict barriers that they could be facing but that they can't see at the moment because they are still in their honeymoon phase in regard to the Canadian government and all the welcoming they have received so far. (RA 6)

In one interview, a refugee father shared his concerns about the increasing anxiety and feeling of loneliness. "Don't leave me until next year, let's have a coffee from time to time," this is how he ended the interview. As a refugee and a father myself, I was unable to distance myself from this issue. I share the same concerns. That evening was very difficult. (RA 7)

Give the importance of this issue, several measures and strategies have been implemented in order to prevent or manage situations of emotional distress and create formal and informal support opportunities. These measures include encouraging peer researchers to do home visits in pairs for time, safety, and support purposes; an annual online workshop prior to data collection led by a principal investigator with expertise working with immigration officers around secondary trauma, compassion fatigue, and self-care; weekly local team debrief meetings during data collection; regular one-on-one check-ins with local research coordinators; and private WhatsApp group chats. Regular team meetings and ongoing communication were particularly valuable as a means for informal support:

By having the team's support and our weekly meetings, it allowed me to share my feelings and thoughts, which helped me to deal with the uneasy task of listening to the participants' emotional stories. (RA 1)

It is important to note that the research team is multidisciplinary, with mental health counsellors accessible at every research site. Each site thus had at least one resource person that peer researchers or local coordinators could turn to for professional help; regular check-ins between local coordinators and the resource person in each site ensured that any concerns could be addressed immediately.

## Discussion and Conclusions

This chapter has presented reflections from peer researchers working on the Syrian Refugee Integration and Long-term Health Outcomes in Canada study, a community-based national longitudinal mixed-methods research project. Given the study's complexity and multidimensionality, many challenges have emerged, and it has been a continuous learning journey to address these challenges. Despite the recent popularity of research with refugee populations in general, and community-based research in particular, research in the area of ethics related to engaging peer researchers in such complex projects is scarce.

Peer researchers occupy a delicate and variable insider/outsider position (Jacobsen and Landau 2003, 192–3). They move back and forth between insider/outsider positions between interviews and even within interviews as they negotiate their relationships with their participants. This positionality creates further strain when peer researchers come from and do research with vulnerable populations such as trauma survivors and refugees. Conducting research with refugees, especially those who come from countries divided by civil war, can pose a challenge to building trust and rapport and place peer researchers at risk for retraumatization (Clark-Kazak 2017, 12–13; Grabska et al. 2019).

The longitudinal aspect of research creates additional ethical challenges around how peer researchers can maintain and nurture relationships they have created with participants over time, and build rapport while setting professional boundaries. Peer researchers routinely walk a fine line between insider and outsider as they maintain ongoing consent, preserve professional boundaries, and at the same time negotiate the kinds of support they are able to offer participants. Studies of qualitative longitudinal research have highlighted the challenges researchers face with regard to attending to the relational aspects of research practice (Mauther and Parry 2013, 58). Although peer researchers were candid with participants about their role as researchers, those participants often disregarded the verbal descriptions of that role, relying instead on culturally grounded reciprocity norms. For peer researchers who worked in settlement services and/or who knew of settlement services from a client perspective, it was difficult to determine "how much and what kind of support may be legitimately provided and received as part of an ongoing, reciprocal relationship" (Neale 2013, 10). This created more stress than it would have for researchers with no relationship to or affiliation with the participant population. Part of the ongoing reflexive process for peer researchers will be paying attention to the ways in which their relationships with participants have changed over the four-year arc of the project.

If researchers are to conduct ethically sound research, there is a tremendous need for the scientific community to further explore and address peer researchers' involvement in research with vulnerable communities. The ethical obligation of minimizing the risk of harm not only to participants, but also to peer researchers, has become a serious issue that demands attention. Peer researchers in this study identified four main ethical issues: positionality, professional role conflict, compassion fatigue and burnout, and distress and secondary trauma. Multiple strategies were implemented to support peer researchers, including strategies to address the stress related to their research participation. These strategies highlight the collective importance of self-care, defined as practices for addressing one's own emotional, psychological, spiritual, and physical well-being (Monk 2011). Regular individual and weekly team meetings were scheduled for research staff at each site, led by research coordinators and supervised closely by project investigators. These meetings served as a safe space where peer researchers were encouraged to share stories and reflect on issues that had arisen before, during, and after interviews. Also, discussion groups were created on WhatsApp for additional informal support so that peer researchers could connect with one another following difficult interviews. This collective engagement provided opportunities for peer researchers to "counteract feelings of isolation and stress ... [and] process challenging emotions and work toward maintaining personal–professional balances" (Ives et al. 2020). All research sites have mental health practitioners on their team, including psychologists, physicians, nurses, and social workers, with whom peer researchers can schedule one-on-one meetings to discuss emotionally distressing situations.

As noted at the start of this chapter, since the beginning of the study, peer researchers have been encouraged to reflect on their experiences, incorporating individual and group exercises at the end of each wave of data collection. The value of reflective practice has been well-established in the nursing, social work, and other community service professions and goes beyond individual self-assessment and professional development (Johns 1995, 23–9). Engagement in reflective practice can be a therapeutic process that helps individuals make sense of their environment, perceptions, feelings, and actions. Recognizing the collective impact of participation, peer researchers moved from self-care to group care. They transitioned into a reflexive practice space, propelled by the need to critically reflect on how identity and power relations shaped their interactions with participants and with one another. In the first three years of data collection, peer researchers journalled about their experiences, integrated arts-based reflections, and engaged in a series of conversations around ethical challenges in the research study's process of reflecting on and processing the challenges of engaging in this type of research. As they step into the final year of the project, strategies for supporting one another on this journey will also evolve, contributing to the knowledge base of ethically grounded research and highlighting the ethical imperative for strategies to support peer researchers both individually and collectively.

REFERENCES

Adams, R.E., C.R. Figley, and J.A. Boscarino. 2008. "The Compassion Fatigue Scale: Its Use with Social Workers Following Urban Disaster." *Research on Social Work Practice* 18, no. 3: 238–50. http://dx.doi.org/10.1177/1049731507310190.

Beaud, S., and F. Weber. 2003. *Guide de L'Enquête De Terrain*. Paris: La Découverte.

Block, K., D. Warr, L. Gibbs, and E. Riggs. 2013. "Addressing Ethical and Methodological Challenges in Research with Refugee-Background Young People: Reflections from the Field." *Journal of Refugee Studies* 26, no. 1: 69–87. https://doi.org/10.1093/jrs/fes002.

Bloor, M. 2010. "The Researcher's Obligation to Bring About Good." *Qualitative Social Work* 9, no. 1: 17–20. http://doi.org/10.1177/1473325009355616.

Bride, B.E. 2007. "Prevalence of Secondary Traumatic Stress among Social Workers." *Social Work* 52, no. 1: 63–70. http://dx.doi.org/10.1093/sw/52.1.63.

Clark-Kazak, C. 2017. "Ethical Considerations: Research With People in Situations of Forced Migration." *Refuge: Canada's Journal on Refugees* 33, no. 2: 11–17. https://refuge.journals.yorku.ca/index.php/refuge/article/view/40467.

Collie, P., J. Liu, A. Podsiadlowski, and S. Kindon. 2010. "You Can't Clap with One Hand: Learnings to Promote Culturally Grounded Participatory Action

Research with Migrant and Former Refugee Communities." *International Journal of Intercultural Relations* 34, no. 2: 141–9. http://doi.org/10.1016/j.ijintrel.2009.11.008.

Ellis, H.B., M. Kia-Keating, S. AdenYusuf, A. Lincoln, and A. Nur. 2007. "Ethical Research in Refugee Communities and the Use of Community Participatory Methods." *Transcultural Psychiatry* 44, no. 3: 459–81.

Finlay, L. 2002. "'Outing' the Researcher: The Provenance, Process, and Practice of Reflexivity." *Qualitative Health Research* 12, no. 4: 531–45. https://doi.org/10.1177/104973202129120052.

Grabska, K., M. de Regt, and N. Del Franco. 2019. *Adolescent Girls' Migration in The Global South – Transitions into Adulthood*. New York: Palgrave Macmillan.

Greene, S. 2013. "Peer Research Assistantships and the Ethics of Reciprocity in Community-Based Research." *Journal of Empirical Research on Human Research Ethics* 8, no. 2: 141–52. http://doi.org/10.1525/jer.2013.8.2.141.

Hesse, A.R. 2002. "Secondary Trauma: How Working with Trauma Survivors Affects Therapists." *Clinical Social Work Journal* 30, no. 3: 293–309.

Hugman, R., E. Pittaway, and L. Bartolomei. 2011. "When 'Do No Harm' Is Not Enough: The Ethics of Research with Refugees and Other Vulnerable Groups." *British Journal of Social Work* 41, no. 7: 1271–87.

Hynie, M., S. McGrath, J. Bridekirk, A. Oda, N. Ives, J. Hyndman, N. Arya, Y.B. Shakya, J. Hanley, and K. McKenzie. 2019. "What Role Does Type of Sponsorship Play in Early Integration Outcomes? Syrian Refugees Resettled in Six Canadian Cities." *Refuge: Canada's Journal on Refugees* 35, no. 2: 36–52. https://doi.org/10.7202/1064818ar.

IRCC. 2017. "Syrian Refugees – Monthly IRCC Updates." IRCC open-source data. http://open.canada.ca/data/en/dataset/01c85d28-2a81-4295-9c06-4af792a7c209.

Israel, B.A., A.J. Schulz, E.A. Parker, and A.B. Becker. 1998. "Review of Community-Based Research: Assessing Partnership Approaches to Improve Public Health." *Annual Review of Public Health* 19: 173–202. https://doi.org/10.1146/annurev.publhealth.19.1.173.

Ives, N., M. Denov, and T. Sussman. 2020. *Introduction to Social Work in Canada: Histories, Contexts, and Practices*. 2nd ed. Toronto: Oxford University Press.

Jachyra, P., M. Atkinson, and Y. Washiya. 2015. "'Who are you, and what are you doing here': Methodological Considerations in Ethnographic Health and Physical Education Research." *Ethnography and Education* 10, no. 2: 242–61. http://doi.org10.1080/17457823.2015.1018290.

Jacobsen, K., and L.B. Landau. 2003. "The Dual Imperative in Refugee Research: Some Methodological and Ethical Considerations in Social Science Research on Forced Migration." *Disasters* 27, no. 3: 185–206. http://doi.org/10.1111/1467-7717.00228.

Johns, C. 1995. "The Value of Reflective Practice for Nursing." *Journal of Clinical Nursing* 4, no. 1: 23–30.

Leung, M.W.H. 2015. "'Talk to her, she is also Chinese': A Reflection on the Spatial-Temporal Reach of Co-Ethnicity in Migration Research." *Forum: Qualitative Social Research* 16, no. 2. http://dx.doi.org/10.17169/fqs-16.2.2332.

MacQueen, K.M., E. McLellan, D.S. Metzger, S. Kegeles, R.P. Strauss, R. Scotti, L. Blanchard, and R.T. Trotter. 2001. "What Is Community? An Evidence-Based Definition for Participatory Public Health." *American Journal of Public Health* 91, no. 12: 1929–38. https://doi.org/10.2105/AJPH.91.12.1929.

Manderson, L., E. Bennett, and S. Andajani-Sutjahjo. 2006. "The Social Dynamics of the Interview: Age, Class, and Gender." *Qualitative Health Research* 16, no. 10: 1317–34. https://doi.org/10.1177/1049732306294512.

Marlowe, J.M., L. Lou, M. Osman, and Z. Zeba Alam. 2015. "Conducting Post-Disaster Research with Refugee Background Peer Researchers and Their Communities." *Qualitative Social Work* 14, no. 3: 383–98. http://doi.org/10.1177/14733 25014547252.

Mauthner, N.S, and O. Parry. 2013. "Open Access Digital Data Sharing: Principles, Policies, and Practices." *Social Epistemology* 27, no. 1: 47–67.

Minkler, M. 2005. "Community-Based Research Partnerships: Challenges and Opportunities." *Journal of Urban Health* 82, no. 2: 3–12. http://doi.org/10.1093/jurban/jti034.

Mistry, J., A. Berardi, E. Bignante, and C. Tschirhart. 2015. "Between a Rock and a Hard Place: Ethical Dilemmas of Local Community Facilitators Doing Participatory Research Projects." *Geoforum* 61: 27–35. https://doi.org/10.1016/j.geo forum.2015.02.010.

Monk, L. 2011. "Self-Care for Social Workers: A Precious Commodity, an Ethical Imperative." *Perspectives: Newsletter of the BC Association of Social Workers* 33, no. 1: 4–7.

Neale, B. 2013. "Adding Time into the Mix: Stakeholder Ethics in Qualitative Longitudinal Research." *Methodological Innovations Online* 8, no. 2: 6–20.

Ryan, L. 2015. "'Inside' and 'Outside' of What or Where? Researching Migration through Multi-Positionalities." *Forum: Qualitative Social Research* 16, no. 2. http://dx.doi.org/10.17169/fqs-16.2.2333.

Sánchez, L. 2010. "Positionality." In *Encyclopedia of Geography*, edited by Barney Warf, 2258. Thousand Oaks: SAGE.

Wilson, E., A. Kenny, and V. Dickson-Swift. 2018. "Ethical Challenges in Community-Based Participatory Research: A Scoping Review." *Qualitative Health Research* 28, no. 2: 189–99. https://doi.org/10.1177/1049732317690721.

Yancey, A.K., A.N. Ortega, and S. Kumanyika. 2006. "Effective Recruitment and Retention of Minority Research Participants." *Annual Review of Public Health* 27, no. 1: 1–28. http://doi.org/10.1146/annurev.publhealth.27.021405.102113.

Yassour-Borochowitz, D. 2004. "Reflections on the Researcher-Participant Relationship and the Ethics of Dialogue." *Ethics and Behavior* 14, no. 2: 175–86. http://doi.org/10.1207/s15327019eb1402_5.

# 2

## Critical Reflexivity and Decolonizing Narrative:
### *Reflections from the Field*

Dina Taha

Gheith's study of Gulag memories (2007) challenged the (Western) assumption that narrative should be at the centre of the experience. Instead, she explored silence and other creative non-narrative means for remembering and surviving. Further research has sought to challenge how Eurocentric analysis fails to capture non-Western experiences, especially those of depression, trauma, and coping (Shoeb et al. 2007; Tilbury 2007). This chapter builds on the body of work that seeks to decolonize methodology by focusing on critical reflexivity not only as a tool to sustain rigorous methodological and empirical practices but also as means to decolonize narrative and narrative analysis. In particular, I aim to extend the notion of critical reflexivity to unravel how research can further marginalize the "Othered" stories of forced migrants by replicating colonial assumptions and reinforcing hegemonic discourses. I reflect on examples from interactions with my respondents during my fieldwork in 2017, when I interviewed Syrian refugee women in Egypt who had married Egyptian men, often as a coping strategy. Their stories did more than challenge many Western hegemonic conceptions about intimacy, gender roles, and empowerment; they also challenged my research design (including my research questions and interview questions) as well as my self-perception as an insider to the culture, highlighting both my vulnerability and my bias as a researcher. Questions that served as constant checkpoints during fieldwork and throughout the analysis included these: Is my research grounded in binaries? Are my interview questions promoting polarized (either/or) and stereotypical perceptions of the Other? And above all, is my research contributing to social justice and attempting to offer a platform for the marginalized or Othered participants from which they can speak?

There is an increasing focus within the social sciences on personal accounts, stories, or narratives as the basis for analysis. This chapter emphasizes the contribution of a decolonizing approach to refugee research. In particular, I focus on strategies for decolonizing when engaging with narrative analysis. Case studies such as Sugiman (2008), Hatoss (2012), and Kimura (2008) offer striking examples of researchers using their participants' accounts as a tool for understanding how a story can help explain human experiences beyond what is explicitly mentioned. More accurately, narrative analysis helps us analyze accounts beyond the true/false binary, viewing them instead "as the moment of – and space for – subject-formation, where subversive agency can also emerge" (Kimura 2008, 18). This can be attained by highlighting the relationship between the past and the present as well as the (transforming) conception of identities and agency (Sugiman 2008). We can also approach this by reflecting on how participants project themselves, especially vis-à-vis the researcher, and what possible impact this would have on the narrative's outcome (Hatoss 2012, 51).

Discourse analysis also informs narrative analysis, in that the researcher traces how some discourses are more privileged than others through power relations or the ideological implications of a discourse (Bischoping and Gazso 2016, 160–2). For instance, Sigona (2014) suggested that the international humanitarian discourse about refugees impacts how we choose to listen to the "voice" of refugees. In his review, he tracks instances of refugee agency that challenged the discourse of the agentless refugees and demonstrated how "Western humanitarian organizations frequently resort to a vocabulary of trauma and vulnerability to describe the condition of refugees and others" (372). Thus, this chapter sets out to demonstrate how a decolonizing approach could inform both narrative and discourse analysis to reveal underprivileged and under-recognized experiences and expressions of refugees' subjectivities, agencies, and trajectories. The aim is to illustrate how different cultural references and power relations shape these non-Western narratives and discourses. Sigona's reference to Western discourses raises questions about decolonizing methodology and various past attempts to challenge assumptions – initially colonial and Western-centric – about both qualitative methods and refugee research.

This chapter applies the concept of critical reflexivity as a guide to data collection, analysis, and, more importantly, research design. I start by revisiting the meaning of decolonizing methodology and how literature has addressed it specifically as it concerns empowering the marginalized. I then provide a brief background about my own fieldwork and how I sought to apply decolonizing principles not just at the analysis stage but throughout the process, by "immersing the research in a decolonizing mindset." Next, I pave the way for discussing critical reflexivity by reflecting on my own position and positionality in relation to the participants and how these might have impacted the narrative "co-creation." Finally, I reflect on encounters with some respondents during which critical reflexivity was used not just for the sake of methodological rigour but also as a means to decolonize research. As I discuss below, it is possible that my religious, linguistic, and ethnic proximity enabled access and rapport on some fronts. However, such access was paradoxically a reason for suspicion or fear of judgment, hindering such rapport in some occasions.

## Decolonizing Methodology, Reciprocity, and Empowerment

Scholars like Homi Bhabha (1991) introduce postcolonial critiques as means to acknowledge the inequality of ontological and epistemological explanations and cultural representations fostered by the Western political and social "authority" of what is referred to as the modern world order. Such authority has created "ideological discourses of modernity that attempt to give a hegemonic 'normality'" when trying to understand non-Western cultures (245). Thus, I understand postcolonialism as a theory that took root within other theoretical frameworks, especially Marxism and post-structuralism, but that resists any attempts at grand or "holistic forms of social explanation" (248). In particular, I use the term *decolonizing* to explore "alternative model[s] of social organization, which challenge modernist conceptions of the state" (Ayyash 2018, 23) and reject Western hegemonic and Orientalist modes of knowledge production (Herr 2014).

We cannot start our discussion without Linda Tuhiwai Smith's distinguished work, *Decolonizing Methodologies* (1999), in which she draws researchers' attention to the fact that the term *research* is of Western coinage and may strike many indigenous cultures as a "dirty word" – they are sick of it and have suffered from previous fieldwork (1). She shares throughout her book many strategies for decolonizing research, with examples. At the core of these ideas, we find two overarching principles for pursuing a decolonizing approach to qualitative research in the future.

The first such principle is *reciprocity*, which in decolonizing research is regarded as defining the relationship between the researcher and the researched. Reciprocity as a notion has been addressed differently by different scholars (see, for instance, Lincoln 1995; Carlson 2016; Maiter et al., 2008; Grabska 2014; Harrell-Bond and Voutira 1992; Voutira and Donà 2007). Here a decolonizing understanding extends beyond deep trust and mutuality (Lincoln 1995; Creswell and Poth 2016) to include accountability to the researched group through seeking guidance and feedback from them. The objective is to pursue a more egalitarian research experience, one that ensures that our interpretations are not made in isolation from the research participants. By egalitarianism, I am not referring to a romantic form of interview in which rapport and trust are emphasized in order to draw out true or intimate "confessions" from the participants (Roulston et al. 2003). On the contrary, egalitarianism here links back to the idea of viewing the participants as experts and constantly striving to minimize positions of inequality between the researcher and the researched (see Roulston et al. 2003; Smith 1999; Grabska et al. 2019). Thus, in a decolonizing approach, the principle of reciprocity should be complemented by a second principle: *embracing other ways of knowing*.

Much of the forced migration literature attempts to problematize the political representation of refugees as well as hegemonic assumptions about the "refugee voice" (see, for instance, Sigona 2014; Anthias 2002; Malkki 1995). Thus, by *embracing other ways of knowing*, I am referring not only to respecting or recognizing the Other's underprivileged discourse but also to a decolonizing approach that will require expanding one's sociological imagination to include other theoretical explanations and methodological tools that could help us understand Othered experiences. This approach extends beyond "reporting back" to the participants to include "borrowing their ways of knowing" in defining the research problem, conceptualizing the theoretical and methodological notions we are using, designing the project, and analyzing the findings. For instance, both Shoeb and colleagues (2007) and Tilbury (2007) challenged the Western (conventional) psychiatric diagnoses of sadness/depression, trauma, coping, and survival, accusing those who made them of failing to understand some non-Western populations. As mentioned earlier, Gheith's study of Gulag memories (2007) also challenged the idea that narrative should be at the centre of the experience, especially for the purpose of healing, emphasizing that such connotation is a Western conception. Instead, she explored silence and other creative non-narrative means for remembering and surviving.

At the core of this chapter, I reflect on my encounters with some of the respondents during which I exercised critical reflexivity not just as a form of rigour and to narrow the gap between "experiences" and "interpretations" (i.e., the crisis of representation) but also as a way to decolonize methodologies. But let us start with a brief background to the fieldwork and the case study to set the course regarding the dynamic between the researcher and the participants.

## Methodology: Immersing the Research in a Decolonizing Mindset

The interviews were conducted in Egypt from April to July 2017. I interviewed Syrian refugee women who had escaped the conflict in Syria and married Egyptian men after 2011 once they settled in Egypt. The data were collected in the greater Cairo area and Alexandria, the two areas with the highest concentration of Syrians. I relied on personal connections, snowballing, and social media, as well as perseverance, to get in touch with key informants for my sample. Some ethnographical observations were incorporated into this project to complement the picture. As someone with cultural fluency with regard to this case study, I also relied on some anecdotes and known facts from my upbringing in Egypt and in the Middle East; as we will see in Diab's story, this was a factor that emphasized my "vulnerability" as a researcher.

Since a primary objective of this decolonizing attempt is to listen to the accounts of the participants as "experts" on and not "witnesses" to their contexts, a qualitative approach was selected. That approach tends to give a face to the "data." Additionally, and again informed by a decolonizing approach, this chapter uses longer direct quotes by my respondents. This serves a few purposes. First, it allows more space for their voices and stories. Second, it addresses the issue of the crisis of representation or the gap between the research and the interpretation on one side and the actual lived experiences on the other by minimizing filtered and biased interpretations between the reader and the respondents. Third, it emphasizes the respondents' epistemic privilege and portrays them as capable of telling their own stories and articulating their own experiences with minimal interference. A parallel objective to these long direct quotations is to minimize viewing my respondents as mere numbers or simply the "Other," by emphasizing the flow of the conversation between myself and my respondents. Through these longer quotations and interactions, I show how our intersubjectivities intertwined to produce this particular narrative. My approach stems from the belief that the data are not "out there" waiting to be collected and analyzed; rather, they are a co-construction between the researcher and the researched (See Halai 2007; Grabska et al. 2019). What lies beyond the words and beyond the texts – laughter, tears, and sarcastic intimations – is integral to my analysis. These things breathe new meaning into their words and narratives. From a decolonizing perspective, these extended quotes and conversations, and the emotions and body language attached to them, do not just correspond to rigour. More importantly, they serve as strategies to humanize the respondents and add faces to their narrative.

In translating the interviews for this study, I acknowledge that translation "cannot fully capture a culture because cultures are not autonomous, discrete, or homogenous. Translation is, thus, always partial and incomplete" (Abdelbaki 2021, 8). There are many approaches to converting the original language to the translation (see, for instance, Van Nes et al. 2010; Halai 2007). In this research, I opted for one that captured the cultural and contextual aspects of the conversation and, more importantly, the voices of the women respondents. Allowing the respondent a voice is a central concept in decolonizing literature, and to that end, I used two strategies when translating excerpts from the interviews. First, and importantly, in my analysis preceding or following excerpts or quotes, I did not interpret or explain the text so much as make "the context of the source visible" (Abdelbaki 2021,

12). In many instances, I spent time giving context and backgrounds that had produced a certain proclamation or term by one of the respondents or to deconstruct the meanings of some of the packed terms or statements. A second strategy was to "mediate between two contexts through bilingual and bicultural texts" (Abdelbaki 2021, 14). I opted to use the transliteration of some of the packed terms such as *sutra*, *ghorba*, and *sanad*. Some of my respondents talked, for instance, about the notion of *ghorba*, which literally means estrangement but is rhetorically used to express meanings and experiences of exile and uprooting. Thus, translating such notions as *exile* would have undermined accompanying experiences such as alienation, desolation, dreariness, forlornness, and loneliness. Translation inevitably sheds some meaning; the extended direct quotes in this research should be viewed as an effort on my part to listen to Othered stories in more depth and with less distortion.

Finally, in examining these stories, I utilized strategies to uncover the narrators' position and their agentic choices vis-à-vis other individuals in their stories, the events they considered to be transitional or fateful in their lives, and how they made sense of them and connected them to their own cultural references. I relied on discourse analysis strategies to highlight how power and hegemonic discourses shape accounts and perceptions and thereby rank some ways of knowing more valid than others. Thus, when considering the immersive nature of decolonizing methodology, I focus on strategies for decolonizing during the analysis stage *per se*. In particular, I focus on exercising critical reflexivity, for which the first step is to reflect on the researcher's position and positionality in relation to the participants and how these might impact the data "co-creation."

*Position, Positionality, and Legitimacy*

The insider/outsider consideration is essential to this chapter in order to reflect not just on notions such as authority and positionality but also to respond to other issues such as legitimacy. Legitimacy refers to who has the right to study and validate the experiences of a particular group and how our position as researchers always reflects some complex dialectical relationship between the native and the Other. As a diasporic researcher, I grappled a lot with this. Narayan (1993) offered some helpful insights as she argued against a native/non-native dichotomy. She suggested that, for a researcher who might be perceived as a native, "fieldwork might be considered a deepening of the familiar rather than a discovery of the other" (672). This recognition of my hybrid position – of being simultaneously an insider and outsider – helped me identify subtle cultural discourses. This will become apparent, for example, in Diab's story.

I am an Egyptian Muslim woman born and raised in the Arab world, so my linguistic and cultural fluency offered me ease of access to my respondents. In the same vein, that I was of a similar religious, ethnic, and linguistic background as most of the participants may have facilitated some encounters and allowed me to build rapport more quickly than someone with a different background. Paradoxically, however, the latter was sometimes a reason for participants to be suspicious of me or fear my judgment, as they likely expected me to be aware of shared cultural and religious traditions and restrictions that they might not have been able to uphold. As well, the fact that I have a family and children may have offered common ground for building rapport and cultivating a safe space, for the participants felt that I could relate to their concerns and responsibilities.

At the same time, there were other factors that had implications for my perceived native/insider position. For instance, though I was a migrant, I had never been a refugee and had never faced the same trauma or sense of uprootedness. I tried to leverage my immigration to Canada from Egypt to understand my respondents' experiences better, but there will always remain unique elements that signify refugeeness that I will never have "lived." During the interviews, I encountered certain common aspects to all forms of migration (such as loss of social capital) that I was able to relate to. That said, I always reminded myself that there were other elements that could only be understood by those who had been exposed to the refugee experience. For that, I relied on a lot of probing, asking questions that might seem to have obvious answers. As we will see in Nour's story, such questions can be eye-openers even to those who are familiar with the culture.

Two other factors affecting my native/insider position are my socioeconomic status and being from the academic ivory tower. The fact that I live and receive education in Canada may create a gap between myself and the participants. Such gaps can be sensed – on both sides – whether in terms of rapport-building or in terms of understanding conveyed meanings. Thus, the respondents could, for instance, understand the meanings behind the interview questions in ways quite different than what I intended (see Hollway and Jefferson 2012, 26). A central question that I am still grappling with is this: As an immigrant from a visible minority, and as a female researcher who is returning home equipped with "Western" education, can I represent subaltern voices? And do I have the authority to communicate my participants' voices and their interpretations of their experiences? And can I do so with less distortion than other researchers with different backgrounds? I have sought to respond to these questions by constantly reflecting on my own position and my engagement with my respondents, as will be evident in some of the examples I give.

In discussing the insider/outsider (native/Other) dilemma, my objective is not to offer a conclusive answer but rather to draw attention to the subtlety and complexity of the issue of representation. When designing or conducting our fieldwork, and especially when exercising reflexivity, "whether native or other, we are all 'another's' in the field because there will always be facets of ourselves that connect us with the people we study and other facets that emphasize our difference" (Chawla 2006, 2).

## Critical Reflexivity: Examples from the Field

In the previous sections, I have discussed how data (and narratives) are almost always a co-construct between the researcher and the researched. Unlike romanticized forms of interviews, for example, where the researcher and researched emphasize rapport and trust in order to engage in a revealing "egalitarian sharing" process (Bishoping and Gazso 2016, 47; Lincoln 1995; Roulston et al. 2003), the data co-construction process is dictated by power dynamics and hegemonic discourses. What can be said? Which discourses are more privileged? Which texts come across as more "plausible," and why? These are questions that should guide researchers' ongoing reflexivity during the fieldwork, throughout the research project, and particularly during the writing and interpretation phases. Here I want to propose reflexivity – that is, asking "how one's self and one's methods are implicated in the knowledge one produces" (Bischoping and Gazso 2016, 43) – as a tool/strategy that should be central to rigorous methodological and empirical practices and as a means for decolonizing research.

In the three examples that follow, I apply reflexivity to trace how factors such as my position and positionality (including my demographic characteristics and my ideological biases) have intertwined with those of my respondents to produce a particular narrative that is not necessarily objective. Instead, it is a product of negotiations between myself and my respondents regarding power balance and taking control of the conversation. In the process, reflexivity has led me to:

a) reflect on the initially hidden "outsider" aspect of my positionality (i.e., how I replicated hegemonic and stereotypical perceptions of non-Western experience – reflecting on Nour's story);
b) reflect on my vulnerability as a researcher who is a product of the same cultural and social milieu as my respondents (the insider element) (i.e., how I was affected by cultural/patriarchal discourses in a way that shifted the power balance in the conversation and made me lose control of the interview – reflecting on Diab's story); and
c) reflect on how I used reflections on both the above incidents to strive for a fine line that would turn the conversation into a negotiation that would recognize the alternating power imbalance between the researcher and the respondent (i.e., arrive at a somehow healthy balance where I intentionally let go of being in charge).

### Nour's Story: Reflexivity and Ideological Bias

Nour[1] was twenty-five years old when her husband was killed in Damascus a year and a half before our interview. She and her daughter were forced to catch up with her family in Egypt a few months later, after ill-treatment in her in-laws' household. Just a few months after their arrival, a family friend introduced them to an Egyptian man who was married with children but was searching for a Syrian widow with whom he could engage in *sutra* (protection or sheltering). *Zawaj al-sutra* (protection or shelter marriage) is a familiar notion even if not practised widely in Egypt. In such cases, the man is motivated to marry a widow, especially that of another man who died in war, with the intention of providing her and her children with a livelihood and emotional support. This practice is arguably recurrent throughout Islamic history, and many have suggested that Islamic tradition encourages it

(*Quraan* and *sunnah*). He and Nour had a religious marriage[2] three weeks
after they first met. She noticed a change in her new husband's treatment of
her after the first month of their marriage; he became more aloof, and they
separated just four months into the relationship. Despite her negative experience, Nour was actually pleased with her ex-husband's interest in applying
*sutra* to a widow and her orphaned children. As a researcher who is a product
of Western institutions, I was astonished that she would be happy that someone was marrying her almost out of charity. She clarified that she appreci-
ated his honesty and noble intentions; she was certain that love, an essential
factor, was a gradual process that would come later:

R: *So he told you he is married and he wants to marry again in secret?*
N: Yes.
R: *And what was your impression?*
N: That his wife will eventually know by time. Nothing can be hidden.
R: *Didn't you think, why would I be a second wife, I want to be a first wife?*
N: No.
R: *Why?*
N: Because I have unique circumstances, I am not a normal girl.
R: *Do not you think that this is lowering one's standards?*
N: Dear, it's not us. It's the world around us that forces us (to think and
act this way). Even if you are convinced, the society around you won't
be convinced.
R: *You are right.*
N: Excuse me, I'm sure your study showed you, but most of our society
is not like that. Even if you convince yourself.
R: *Do you mean that you might be convinced with one thing, but the society obliges you to another?*
N: Exactly. So why would I bother/pressure myself? If I wanted to
marry a single man, no one would want my daughter ...
R: *Oh, so you mean you do not care if you are a first or a second wife as
long as your daughter is with you?*
N: Yes, dear. Excuse me, but for women like us, we do not think about
ourselves, we think about our children. When you buy anything for the
house, do you think of yourself or your son? ... In my country, I had
my rights, and I was able to manage. Here I am in a strange country.

Why would I work and degrade myself, meet this and meet that, the good and the bad? No, I apply *sutra* to myself and my daughter and find a human being who is honest and straightforward and offers me a decent life. I'm not saying that I want a car and a big house. Middle ground. A decent life …

When I reflected on my encounter with Nour and my astonishment at her rationale, I could trace elements of a hegemonic understanding of intimate relations as it relates to the nuclear family, individual perceptions, commercialized romantic expressions, and monopolized affections. After reminding myself again and again during the interview and throughout the analysis that Nour was the expert on her own situation, the interview took a more conversational trajectory, one that allowed for a deeper narrative that portrayed her as a narrator who demonstrated a clear and coherent rationale for this marriage. For her, other solutions such as working as a hairdresser – which was her job before she married her first husband – would keep her away from her daughter and expose her to a relatively foreign culture, thus leaving her more vulnerable to exploitation and "degradation," as she described it. For her, then, marriage was the safe or decent, if not the obvious, option in her situation, especially given that her child was her priority.

Here, I go back the principles of reciprocity and embracing Other(ed) ways of knowing in order to utilize critical reflexivity that extends beyond "reporting back" to the participants to include adopting their world views and ways of knowing in understanding and defining the research problem, conceptualizing the theoretical and methodological notions we are using, designing the project, conducting fieldwork, and analyzing and writing down the findings. By reflecting on my own shortcomings as a product of a Western-centric environment and by actively seeking to rebalance the power relations between my respondent and me through reframing the questions to be directed to an "expert," not a mere witness or a victim, I was able to push the boundaries of my project toward rethinking central notions such as liberal versus moral agency, victimhood versus vulnerability, and malleable and non-Western embodiments of marriage. Decolonizing reflexivity thus extends beyond one's position and positionality to include how one's approach is replicating or reinforcing colonial assumptions.

*Diab's Story: Reflexivity and the Researcher's Vulnerability*

Diab was in his early twenties at the time of our interview. He was the only Syrian husband (to an Egyptian wife) that I interviewed. He shared with me his unusual point of view, which reinforced the impression about the Syrian husbands that they are stricter than their Egyptian counterparts. He explained to me the positive qualities he saws in his Egyptian bride-to-be, all of which revolved around obedience and her recognition of their hierarchy in the marriage:

> D: Allah has granted me a woman … I mean … Milk, is it black?
> R: *Excuse me?*
> D: Milk … is it black? Yes, it is.
> R: *Oh, you mean she listens to you on every matter?*
> D: Allah has granted me someone like this. If I tell her that milk is black, she will agree. But of course, that was after she understood that when I tell her it's black, that I am not wrong. That I am correct. That I am not trying to harm her. That I am not trying to control her. She understands that he is a prince above, and I am below, he is a man, and I am …

Diab was not trying to boast, or provoke me. Throughout the interview, he was very cooperative and interested in my research. The above quote is consistent with his opinions throughout our interview. He even made a couple of friendly comments implying that my *hijab* was not put in the proper way because a few hairs were showing. For him, this was his way of looking after women (sisters) and protecting them. This hierarchy preserved the decency and the harmony in the marital household and in society in general. Diab's interview has left a strong but subtle effect on me as a researcher who is also a Middle Eastern woman. He was very outspoken and charismatic. He was persuasive and echoed hegemonic masculinist ideas and rhetoric that are very common in the Middle East. In revisiting the audio recording of this interview, I was surprised to note my response to this iteration of hegemonic masculinity and to hear the ease with which I, at the time, accepted his patriarchal conviction about gender roles. I had reverted to a form of femininity that was commensurate with the brand of masculinity that he embodied. I share this not to highlight my own latent inclinations or "feminist deficiencies," but rather to note that power permeates research differently. Here, the gendered dynamics trumped the epistemic disparity between Diab and I, inadvertently and unexpectedly shifting the power balance in that encounter.

Reflecting on the intentional and unintentional manipulation exercised by respondents such as Diab might have been damaging to this interview. That said, I found it enlightening to exercise critical reflexivity on my positionality vis-à-vis Diab: as an insider from the same culture, I found myself complicit in replicating gender roles, which I would seek to challenge in later interviews. For example, as one would expect, it was not just men who accepted the world view that Diab shared with me; women had internalized rather similar ideas. In particular, some of my women respondents agreed with Diab regarding the importance of this hierarchy in the marital relationship, for it guaranteed the satisfaction of both the husband and the wife. Applying critical reflexivity after my encounter with Diab has served as a reminder (or given me more experience and self-awareness) to learn how to nudge and tease the conversation about hegemonic discourses such as gender roles using similar cultural and religious references in order to craft more meaningful interviews that allow the respondents to reflect better on their realities. This also highlights the subtle advantage that researchers with cultural "liminality" as both insiders and outsiders have over other researchers. While beyond the scope of this chapter, I posit that further research to identify the salient role that "liminal researchers" could play in decolonizing research with non-Western participants is necessary (see, for instance, Enosh and Ben Ari 2016).

## Ghalya's Story: Negotiations and Balance of Power

Ghalya, a respondent in her mid-forties, chose to stay in an abusive relationship because, as she explained, "a shadow of a man is better than a shadow of a wall." She was contemplating going back to the war zone rather than bearing the harassment in Egypt. Her god-sent solution was marriage; however, she kept rejecting all proposals that do not include her son and his best interests.

R: *Did you get a lot of proposals?*
G: Oh, too, too, too many! I think a woman who lived nearby was a matchmaker [girls' realtor was her expression]. She would get them married and get paid a commission. She brought me so many suitors, and I would tell her, "No, I want to raise my boy." Seriously it wasn't an option even among Syrians. ... I would tell them, "I don't want to get married. I hated all men." One of the suitors proposed, and he asked me to give him a chance and that he will change my point of view about men. I gave him a chance, but he made me hate them even more. He simply told me why you don't send your boy to a boarding school?" ... I sacrificed my whole life for my son, and I was able to bear his father for him, and I explained that to him [the suitor], and now he wants me to prevent him from me and throw him in a boarding school in the *ghorba*?

Similarly, other respondents, such as Nour (whom I spoke about earlier) and her sister Marwa, understood *sutra* as primarily about protection for their children. That is to say, many of my respondents chose marriage because they viewed it as their motherly duty. Nazira, a middle-aged divorced woman, only considered marriage after *ghorba*[3] and displacement because in Syria she would have had a support system and motherhood status. For her, "wifehood," or marriage, was a way to compensate for her lost motherhood status. Thus, one can identify a central theme in many of my respondents' narratives (Ghalya, Nazira, and Nour, among others): all of their narratives turned constantly back to the idea of Motherhood. They found empowerment *in* and *through* motherhood. Besides giving these women a sense of purpose and a motivation to survive and adapt, it often also gave them social status. Once we have decolonized the perception of traditional gender roles and avenues toward empowerment, we can see how motherhood status can be perceived by the woman herself as well as the members of her community as more important than socio-economic or educational accomplishments (Bawa 2016); it can offer a woman an elevated status in her community, one that offers respect and a strong social network.

Here, I want to focus on how the notion of empowerment has various cultural interpretations when analyzed outside liberal humanitarian understandings. I contend that some refugee women can find empowerment in cultural practices, such as *sutra* marriage and traditional gender roles (including motherhood). As I demonstrated earlier, many studies have explored conjugal relationships that challenge the idea of the nuclear family as the natural and only form of family, and of love and attraction as the main reasons for marriage (see Al-Sharmani 2010; Kim 2014; Szczepanikova 2005; Säävälä 2010). Other studies have revealed that a primary motivation for women to enter the public sphere, mainly in the form of paid work, has been "the survival and well-being of their families rather than their own individual development or progress" (Franz 2003, 102). This is reinforced in my respondents' narratives, which expressed that their children's interests outweighed any other priorities.

In the examples of Nour and Diab, I was reflecting on my struggle to balance the power with my respondents and regain some control over the conversation. In this final example, of Ghalya, I reflected on how I had to let go of this control in a way that would allow the women to reshape their perceptions of the case study and of the research question. Here, I am referring to utilizing critical reflexivity in a search for an appropriate balance between gaining control of the conversation and letting go of this control for the sake of decolonizing the narrative and narrowing the crisis of representation. When I was designing the project, a central question I was planning on investigating was this: Had my respondents' forced migration and displacement experiences (re)shaped their perception of the meaning, purpose, and form of marriage? I was fixated on the idea of their identity as "wives," and my questions mostly investigated how they reflected on themselves as "wives." But as I started engaging with my respondents, I started noticing that they were pushing for a different identity when reflecting on themselves: motherhood.

## Discussion: Critical Reflexivity and Decolonizing Research

Throughout the planning phase, as a self-declared postcolonial researcher, I was consumed with the idea of the crisis of representation: the gap between the author's (often colonized) text and the lived experiences of the population being researched. In addition to having an empirical interest in the stories behind "Syrian refugee brides," I was also interested in theoretical and methodological questions such as, how do hegemonic ideas affect academic research? *Which* narratives and ideas, and *whose* narratives and ideas, are more privileged? How do the researcher's social location, ideological motivations, and theoretical convictions determine how the message will be received? How do factors such as academic privilege implicate knowledge production? How do the different cultural, social, and intellectual references between the researcher and the researched contribute to losses of meaning?

Like any researcher in a Western academic institution, I had to start with a clear research question about how the fieldwork would "fit" within previous literature and dominant theories. My initial/official interest was in exploring how Syrian women interpret their decision to marry Egyptian men. How did they use marriage as a survival tool? And how did elements such as agency, exploitation, and patriarchy affect this decision? But as I familiarized myself with the field, my concern about academically privileged and countering hegemonic ideas about non-Western contexts started to dominate my approach. I was slowly letting go of my initial questions and cautiously letting my respondents' narratives lead the way, and this would enable me to explore more exciting avenues and dimensions of their stories. While exploring how these women have used the concept of marriage creatively and flexibly to promote their own interests, I have developed another question: have their forced migration experiences (re)shaped their perceptions of marriage – it meaning, purpose, and nature? That is, how do their stories challenge what is hegemonically viewed as morally correct? Who gets to define notions such as human rights, human dignity, empowerment, and victimhood? What really constitutes an agentive act, and what constitutes an act of exploitation?

Critical researchers often use reflexivity as a tool for ensuring that the message conveyed about what the participants "tell us" about their interpretations of their own experiences and subjectivities is as close as possible to their actual interpretations of these experiences. This encourages researchers to reflect on how their own positions and positionalities have impacted their interpretations and findings. Many researchers have addressed issues that require them to apply reflexivity at different stages of their research projects. For instance, Halai (2007) reflected on her concerns regarding the accuracy of transcribing and translating bilingual interviews from Urdu to English. Since the issue has not been addressed enough in literature, she had to come up with her own customized (but consistent) guiding rules to make sure her participants' stories were conveyed correctly. Clarke (2003) has reflected on some of the strategies she has employed to "overcome ambivalence" from her respondents and pursue higher authenticity in their accounts. Building rapport, managing alternating positions between insider and outsider wisely, and paying heed to the locations in which interviews are conducted are some of her strategies for ensuring rigour and proper representation of her respondents' experiences. Another example is Anim-Addo and Gunaratnam (2013), who reflected on the limits of oral history and tried to unravel the relationship between facts and fiction in their respondents' accounts in a systematic way. Thus, while exercising reflexivity in my own fieldwork, I started posing the question of how researchers can use reflexivity to decolonize research. That question soon evolved into this one: How can we decolonize reflexivity?

The examples I used in this chapter demonstrate how critical reflexivity revealed instances of my ideological bias even though I initially identified as an insider to the culture. Yet it also revealed my vulnerability as a researcher who is a product of the same culture as the respondents. This affected the gendered powered dynamics with my male respondents, which affected in turn the trajectory of the interviews. Critical reflexivity accentuates the non-uniform balance of power between researcher and participant in a way that questions the meaning of objective data, researcher neutrality, and the participant's role in research design.

Furthermore, decolonizing methodology helps push the boundaries and function of critical reflexivity by problematizing concepts such as "participation" and "empowerment" and how the former still works within the conventional academic agenda to reinforce hegemonic and homogenous conceptions of the research participants and their experiences. In this chapter, I have explored whether critical reflexivity can foster "some" position for Othered ways of knowing by helping us design a decolonizing methodology. I have argued that reflexivity would thereby extend beyond identifying one's position and positionality to include how one's overall methodological approach is replicating or reinforcing colonial assumptions. Questions central to a decolonizing approach include these: Is my research grounded in binaries? Is my research promoting a polarized (either/or) and stereotyped perception of the Other (as opposed to the self)? And above all, is my research contributing to social justice and attempting to offer a platform for the (indigenous or subaltern) participants from which they can speak?

## Conclusion

My reflections on my fieldwork and particularly on my encounters with respondents like Diab, Nour, and Ghalya identified potentially helpful strategies that are dynamic and open for expansion and refinement. First, coupling narrative analysis with discourse analysis helped me reflect on questions such as these: Whose narratives and perceptions are more privileged, whether in Western hegemonic cultures or local patriarchal cultures? How do the researcher's social location, ideological motivations, and theoretical convictions determine how the message is going to be received? How do factors such as academic privilege implicate knowledge production? How do the different cultural, social, and intellectual references between the researcher and the researched contribute to losses of meaning?

Second, it took some commitment to stay true to the notion that I should practise critical reflexivity consistently throughout the different stages of my research. While the analysis stage might seem like an obvious space to apply a decolonizing framework, it was as important to ensure it was present during other stages such as when designing the research (which ideologies and assumptions are informing it?) and identifying the research questions as well as the interview questions (do they reflect biases or hegemonic assumptions?). The principles of reciprocity and embracing other ways of knowing were crucial in designing (and redesigning) an empirical project that perceived the participants as experts, not just witnesses or mere bearers of evidence. There is literature that discusses how Eurocentric analysis fails to capture non-Western experiences, especially those of depression, trauma, and coping. My reflections in this chapter have traced how listening to my respondents as experts moved my research away from its initial assumptions. That is, instead of focusing on my respondents' identities as wives, as refugees, and as survivors, I allowed them to push their own narratives of what they constituted as morally justified in their role as mothers.

Third, logistically during data collection, I tried to be reflexive about adopting ways that would minimize power inequality between researcher and participant. This included designing and explaining the consent form as well as subtle gestures such as giving honorariums (if any) in advance and emphasizing the participants' right to end the conversation whenever they chose. Similarly, reflexivity should inform other, often underemphasized stages, such as transcription and translation, which can result in meanings being lost. One strategy I utilized involved relying on direct and extended quotes from my respondents that indicated not just their opinions but also the dynamics between them and myself as a researcher. Also, I made sure to emphasize gestures and body language – pauses, laughs, sarcasm, and so on – that emphasized multiple aspects of identity and personality, beyond that of refugee.

Finally, applying critical reflexivity to the researcher's position and that person's location on the insider/outsider continuum can be a serious challenge. This mostly goes back to the non-uniform power relations and constant negotiations between researcher and participant, which depend on the context, the topic, and even the demographic and ideological backgrounds of both sides. This was evident when, for instance, with Nour, I found myself replicating a colonized understanding of the nuclear family. At the same time, my assumption that, as a researcher, I always have more power than the respondent was challenged by my encounter with Diab, which triggered my vulnerability as a researcher who is also a product of the Middle Eastern culture and its own (sub)hegemonic discourses. It is important, then, to treat the interview process as a negotiation while remaining aware of the process of co-constructing the narrative. This highlights the advantages of intentionally giving up control of the interview. I slowly let go of my initial questions and allowed my respondents' narratives to lead the way. This allowed me to explore more interesting avenues and dimensions of their stories.

This highlights the unique position of those I refer to as *diasporic or liminal researchers* – those who acquire the traits and position of being both an insider and an outsider researcher – and the role they could play in decolonizing empirical research with non-Western participants. Such people, with their distinctive cultural liminality, face different challenges and acquire different strengths than other researchers. They consequently require different kinds of support and academic discussion, especially when it comes to reflecting on their position and positionality. While beyond the scope of this project, further discussion is needed to explore the uniqueness and the contribution of this group at the methodological and theoretical levels when it comes to decolonizing research.

On a final note, the reflections in this chapter are also intended to make the case for small-scale qualitative research. Rodgers (2004) argues that such smaller studies, which allow for more intimate interaction with the respondents, are "relevant, important and ethically desirable" 49). Building on Rodgers's argument through a decolonizing lens, a call for larger-scale projects that emphasize validity, reliability, replication, and representation underscores certain assumptions: (a) that the researchers (who are largely located in or are from the global north) already know what the relevant questions and gaps are; (b) that objectivity is not ideologically biased; and (c) that "generalizability" is the only desirable outcome from research with forced migrants, which dismisses the importance of recognizing the diversity and intersectionality, never mind the cultural differences and subjectivities, of refugee populations. The objective of the case study I reflect on in this chapter was to showcase how certain marginalized groups, especially those from the global south, carry different non-hegemonic interpretations of what humanitarian notions such as agency and empowerment mean to them and how they translate in their own realities. A decolonizing research design highlights the importance of recognizing the discrepancies between the "norm" and the "hegemonic" and the challenges to both. Small-scale qualitative research designs have their own shortcomings and should be designed so that they contribute to deconstructing and humanizing the refugee experience with its many trajectories. This offers the potential for more effective decolonized responses.

NOTES

1 All names used in this chapter are pseudonyms.
2 So, she would be his lawful wife religiously, but socially she still stays with her parents until they prepare for the wedding and the new place. This facilitates his visitation and them getting to know each other. Having sex would be lawful, but it is socially frowned upon. If they separate, she is considered divorced, but there is usually no documentation to prove the marriage and divorce.

3   The Arabic word *ghorba*, sometimes used to mean emigration, literally
    means estrangement; or it is a noun for the status of being an outsider. In
    Arab culture, the term is associated with other meanings such as alienation,
    desolation; dreariness; estrangement; forlornness; loneliness. While these do
    not capture the full meaning, the closest terms that are used in refugee liter-
    ature to refer to the experience of *ghorba* is uprooting or exile. Said (2000),
    for instance, explained exile as "the unhealable rift forced between a human
    being and a native place, between the self and its true home: its essential
    sadness can never be surmounted" (174). Malkki (1995) pointed out the
    commonalities between the refugee experience and the exile experience,
    which is again centred around isolation, loss, and disruption.

REFERENCES

Abdelbaki, R. 2021. "Translating the Postcolony: On Gender, Language, and
    Culture." TOPIA: *Canadian Journal of Cultural Studies* 42, no. 9: 117–31.
Al-Sharmani, M. 2010. "Transnational Family Networks in the Somali Diaspora
    in Egypt: Women's Roles and Differentiated Experiences." *Gender, Place, and
    Culture* 17, no. 4: 499–518.
Anim-Addo, J., and Y. Gunaratnam. 2013. "Secrets and Lies: Narrative Methods
    at the Limits of Research."Research." *Journal of Writing in Creative Practice* 5,
    no. 3: 383–96.
Anthias, F. 2002. "'Where do I belong?': Narrating Collective Identity and
    Translocational Positionality." *Ethnicities* 2, no. 4: 491–514.
Ayyash, M.M. 2018. "An Assemblage of Decoloniality? Palestinian Fellahin Resis-
    tance and the Space-Place Relation." *Studies in Social Justice* 12, no. 1: 21–37.
Bawa, Sylvia. 2016. "Paradoxes of (Dis)empowerment in the Postcolony: Women,
    Culture, and Social Capital in Ghana." *Third World Quarterly* 37, no. 1: 119–35.
Bhabha, H.K. 2012. *The Location of Culture.Culture.* New York and London:
    Routledge.
Bischoping, K., and A. Gazso. 2015. *Analyzing Talk in the Social Sciences: Narra-
    tive, Conversation, and Discourse Strategies.* Thousand Oaks: SAGE.
Chawla, D. 2006. "Subjectivity and the 'Native' Ethnographer: Researcher Eligibil-
    ity in an Ethnographic Study of Urban Indian Women in Hindu Arranged
    Marriages." *International Journal of Qualitative Methods* 5, no. 4: 13–29.
Clarke, L.H. 2003. "Overcoming Ambivalence: The Challenges of Exploring
    Socially Charged Issues." *Qualitative Health Research* 13, no. 5: 718–35.

Creswell, J.W., and C.N. Poth. 2016. *Qualitative Inquiry and Research Design: Choosing among Five Approaches*. Thousand Oaks: SAGE.

Denzin, N.K., and Y.S. Lincoln. 2008. *Collecting and Interpreting Qualitative Materials*. Vol. 3. Thousand Oaks: SAGE.

Duneier, M., and O. Carter. 1999. *Sidewalk*. New York: Farrar, Strauss and Giroux.

Enosh, G., and A. Ben-Ari. 2016. "Reflexivity: The Creation of Liminal Spaces – Researchers, Participants, and Research Encounters." *Qualitative Health Research* 26, no. 4: 578–84.

Gheith, J.M. 2007. "'I never talked': Enforced Silence, Non-Narrative Memory, and the Gulag." *Mortality* 12, no. 2: 159–75.

Grabska, K. 2014. *Gender, Home, and Identity: Nuer Repatriation to Southern Sudan*. Woodbridge: James Currey.

Grabska, K., M. De Regt, and N. Del Franco. 2019. *Adolescent Girls' Migration in the Global South: Transitions into Adulthood*. Berlin and Heidelberg: Springer Verlag.

Hajdukowski-Ahmed, M., N. Khanlou, and H. Moussa, eds. 2008. *Not Born a Refugee Woman: Contesting Identities, Rethinking Practices*. Vol. 24. New York: Berghahn Books.

Halai, N. 2007. "Making Use of Bilingual Interview Data: Some Experiences from the Field." *Qualitative Report* 12, no. 3: 344.

Harrell-Bond, B.E., and E. Voutira. 1992. "Anthropology and the Study of Refugees." *Anthropology Today* 8, no. 4: 6–10.

Hatoss, A. 2012. "'Where are you from?': Identity Construction and Experiences of 'Othering' in the Narratives of Sudanese Refugee-Background Australians." *Discourse and Society* 23, no. 1: 47–68.

Herr, R.S. 2014. "Reclaiming Third World Feminism: Or Why Transnational Feminism Needs Third World Feminism." *Meridians: Feminism, Race, Transnationalism* 12, no. 1: 1–30.

Hollway, W., and T. Jefferson. 2012. *Doing Qualitative Research Differently: A Psychosocial Approach*. Thousand Oaks: SAGE.

Kim, K. 2014. "'I Am Well-Cooked Food': Survival Strategies of North Korean Female Border-Crossers And Possibilities For Empowerment." *Inter-Asia Cultural Studies* 15, no. 4: 553–71.

Kimura, M. 2008. "Narrative as a Site Subject Construction: The Comfort Women debate." *Feminist Theory* 9, no. 1: 5–24.

Lincoln, Y.S. 1995. "Emerging Criteria for Quality in Qualitative and Interpretive Research." *Qualitative Inquiry* 1, no. 3: 275–89.

Maiter, S., L. Simich, N. Jacobson, and J. Wise. 2008. "Reciprocity: An Ethic for Community-Based Participatory Action Research." *Action Research* 6, no. 3: 305–25.

Malkki, L. 1995. *Purity and Exile: Violence, Memory, and National Cosmology among Hutu Refugees in Tanzania.* Chicago: University of Chicago Press.

Narayan, K. 1993. "How Native Is a 'Native' Anthropologist?" *American Anthropologist* 95, no. 3: 671–86.

Robben, A. 1995. "Seduction and Persuasion: The Politics of Truth and Emotions among Victims and Perpetrators of Violence." In *Fieldwork under Fire: Contemporary Studies of Violence and Survival*, edited by Carolyn Nordstrom and Antonius C.G.M. Robben. Berkeley: University of California Press.

Rodgers, G. 2004. "'Hanging Out' with Forced Migrants: Methodological and Ethical Challenges." *Forced Migration Review* 21 (September): 48–9.

Roulston, K., K. DeMarrais, and J.B. Lewis. 2003. "Learning to Interview in the Social Sciences." *Qualitative Inquiry* 9, no. 4: 643–68.

Säävälä, M. 2010. "Forced Migrants, Active Mothers, or Desired Wives: Migratory Motivation and Self-Representation in Kosovo Albanian and Russian Women's Biographies." *Journal of Ethnic and Migration Studies*, 36 no. 7: 1139–55.

Said, E. 2000. *Reflections on Exile and Other Essays.* Cambridge, MA: Harvard University Press.

Shoeb, M., H.M. Weinstein, and J. Halpern. 2007. "Living in Religious Time and Space: Iraqi Refugees in Dearborn, Michigan." *Journal of Refugee Studies* 20, no. 3: 441–60.

Sigona, N. 2014. "The Politics of Refugee Voices: Representations." In *The Oxford Handbook of Refugee and Forced Migration Studies*, edited by E. Fiddiah Qasmiyeh, G. Loescher, K. Long, and N. Sigona, 369–82. Oxford: Oxford University Press.

Smith, L.T. 2013. *Decolonizing Methodologies: Research and Indigenous Peoples.* London: Zed Books.

Sugiman, P. 2008. "'*Days You Remember*': Japanese Canadian Women and the Violence of Internment." In *Not Born a Refugee Woman: Contesting Identities, Rethinking Practices*, edited by M. Hajdukowski-Ahmed, N. Khanlou, and H. Moussa, 113–34. New York: Berghahn Books.

Szczepanikova, A. 2005. "Gender Relations in a Refugee Camp: A Case of Chechens Seeking Asylum in the Czech Republic." *Journal of Refugee Studies* 18, no. 3: 281–9.

Tilbury, F. 2007. "'I feel I am a bird without wings': Discourses of Sadness and Loss among East Africans in Western Australia." *Identities: Global Studies in Culture and Power* 14, no. 4: 433–58.

Van Nes, F., T. Abma, H. Jonsson, and D. Deeg. 2010. "Language Differences in Qualitative Research: Is Meaning Lost in Translation?." *European Journal of Ageing* 7, no. 4: 313–16.

Voutira, E., and G. Doná. "2007. "Refugee Research Methodologies: Consolidation and Transformation of a Field." *Journal of Refugee Studies* 20, no. 2: 163–71.

# 3

## Exhibiting Displacement:
## *Refugee Art, Methodological Dubiety, and the*
## *Responsibility (Not) to Document Loss*

Evropi Chatzipanagiotidou and Fiona Murphy

On 2 September 2015, a young Syrian boy was found dead on a beach near Bodrum in Turkey. His lifeless body was photographed by Turkish journalist Nilüfer Demir and quickly made international headlines. The young boy, Aylan Kurdi, a name now familiar to millions around the globe, died trying to cross into Europe with his family. This photograph wounded in a way that many other images of refugee suffering, death, and loss had not and, subsequently, elicited public responses in transnational affective terrains (Prøitz 2018). The photo of Aylan Kurdi became iconic, underscoring the lack of solidarity, responsibility, and action that has come to define Europe as a place where refuge has become a dangerously contingent concept.

More than a year and a half later, Chinese artist Ai Weiwei re-enacted the photograph of Aylan Kurdi, this time on a stony beach on the Greek island of Lesbos, where the artist has a temporary studio (*India Today Magazine* 2016). Persecuted by the Chinese state and self-exiled in Europe, Ai Weiwei aimed at drawing on his own experiences of loss and displacement to evoke empathy for the plight of refugees. The photo was circulated with alacrity but also condemnation and outrage, by audiences, activists, and the press (see for instance Dhillon 2016; Ratnam 2016), who raised concerns about the state and purpose of modern art. Ai Weiwei had been attempting to evoke silences, absences, and erasures, yet he was accused of appropriating suffering and essentializing the experiences of those he had intended to represent (Atkinson 2018).

Similar critiques of Ai Weiwei's portrait have grown around the work of other artists documenting displacement and loss. Artists like Marco Tiberio, Henk Wildschut, Jeroen van der Most, and Magnus Wennman, to name only a few, have been subjected to intense public debates about who has the right to represent whom, and how. These artistic engagements, therefore, open up a space for us to think about political activism and art as ethically complex endeavours that may sometimes reproduce rather than challenge hierarchies in the production of solidarity and empathy. Similar ethical shifts and imbalances arise in ethnographic practice, even though ethnographic fieldwork is often conducted in more cautious and self-reflexive ways. We argue in this chapter that, as ethnographers, we often find ourselves navigating comparable ethically dubious landscapes in our research, documentation, and representation of displacement. Not least in the ways we use art as both a subject and a method of research to speak about loss and refugeehood.

Reflecting on ongoing ethnographic fieldwork with Syrian artists in Istanbul, Turkey, we discuss the complexities of how methodological attention to art provides insights into how refugees choose (or not) to articulate experiences of displacement and loss. These emerge as forms of "counter-memorial aesthetics" (Tello 2016) that transcend the confining and oppressive limits of structured speech and disrupt dominant and essentializing accounts of "refugeeness." This is a crucial move away from a persistent anthropological fetishization of the refugee "voice" that endures through a methodological overemphasis on storytelling and linear narratives.

Further to this, we trace the tensions and power imbalances that are embedded in the production of "refugee art" as an essentialized and commercialized category. We posit that a methodological focus on art is, as such, not a panacea in the scholarly project of documenting displacement and loss and overcoming problems with "the voice." We return to the ethical and political dilemmas raised by the example of Ai Weiwei, thereby highlighting art's relevance for ethnographic practice. As a way forward, we propose a project of "methodological dubiety" in the context of displacement that does not and should not aim to resolve dilemmas around representation, experience, and aesthetics. Instead, we argue for a mode of highlighting further ethical, political, and methodological complexities in the ways in which absence and loss are documented and empathy is mobilized or evoked.

Methodological dubiety also involves the enactment of ethnographic refusal, the dialogic and collaborative determination between researchers and research participants to craft representations in ways that speak openly to the need to maintain certain kinds of gaps, erasures, and absences. This methodology involves a keen preparedness as well as an acceptance that there may also be an ethical responsibility *not to* articulate particular kinds of admittances and indeed, silences (Weller 2017), losses, and invisibility/ies.

## Art at Work

The material discussed in this chapter is based on ethnographic fieldwork conducted in Istanbul in 2018–19. Our broader project was designed to examine refugeehood, loss, and the politics of labour in Turkey;[1] a focus on art had not been included in our original research plans. While art is a long-established way of engaging refugees in articulating experiences of displacement and loss, it has been examined less as a form of work and more predominantly as a therapeutic and expressive tool. For instance, "agency empowerment" projects (Arda 2019), which mobilize art to empower refugees, have grown in the past few decades, especially since the start of the recent "refugee crisis." These projects are usually supported by national and international NGO, academic, and policy endeavours around the world to involve refugee artists and non-artist refugees in diverse forms of creative practice. Some of the best-known examples have been in encampment contexts, including the Za'atari project in a Jordan refugee camp and the UNHCR-funded "Artists for Refugees" in Kenya. Underpinning these kinds of projects is the idea that art offers refugees an alternative way to articulate experience and acquire a "voice" (Chatzipanagiotidou and Murphy 2020), beyond oral structured accounts and testimonies, which can be restrictive and silencing when conducted in official environments or for the purposes of rights-claiming and recognition (Hastrup 2003; Ross 2003; Wilson 2003; Das 2003, 2007). Art, therefore, constitutes a potentially therapeutic tool for articulating and overcoming trauma (see O'Neill 2008; Kalmanowitz 2016) without traumatizing refugees by forcing them to "speak."

In spite of theoretical and methodological efforts to address the dominance of the oral narrative in accounting for and representing experience, there seems to be an enduring anthropological emphasis on the documentation of "voices" and stories (see for instance, McGranahan 2012; Jackson 2013; Maggio 2014). In relation to refugees, however, this methodological fixation on collecting accounts of displacement, suffering, and loss has raised concerns about whether anthropologists are engaging in the fetishization of the "refugee voice" and forms of epistemic violence (Cabot 2016). Ethnographers have historically attempted to move away from privileging oral linear narrative as the main site of subjectivity production (Good 2012) by shifting attention to the unspoken and "unspeakable" (Weller 2017). Art – indeed, creative expression more broadly – has emerged as a significant tool for articulating experience in alternative ways and transcending the confining and oppressive limits of structured speech (Abu-Lughod 1986; Hogan and Pink 2010; Tello 2016).

However, as we have argued elsewhere (Chatzipanagiotidou and Murphy 2020), the use of art in refugee engagement does not offer a cure-all to problems around "the voice." Instead, and especially through the (re)production of "refugee art" as an aesthetic and commercial category, we run the risk of moving from the fetishization of the "refugee voice" to the aestheticization of displacement and loss. The market, policy, and academic demand for refugee art, therefore, further essentializes the category of the refugee and alienates artists who do not fit within or resist this categorization. While it offers the opportunity to break established silences around the refugee experience in the public sphere, art, in this form, also generates other silences and processes of silencing.

All these power hierarchies, struggles, and contestations became apparent to us when we shifted attention to "art as work" for refugees living in Istanbul. Through ethnographic fieldwork, which we describe in detail below, it became apparent that for some Syrians, art was not only an expressive and creative tool but also a way of making a living, and, more crucially, a potential "passport" for further mobility, at least for those who hoped to achieve some international recognition and audiences. In a broader neoliberal context, however, artistic work comes with experiences of income instability, insecurity, and anxiety that precarity engenders (Hesmondhalgh and Baker 2011; McRobbie 2016). These conditions are often internalized and normalized through processes of "self-precarization" (Lorey 2011), through which artists "seem able to tolerate their living and working conditions with infinite patience because of the belief in their own freedoms and autonomies, and because of fantasies of self-realization" (Lorey 2011, 87). When it comes to refugee artists, however, such precarity is further aggravated by limited access to citizenship and labour rights, as is very much the case in Turkey (Erdoğan and Uyan Semerci 2018). While artistic practice may appear as a self-imposed "choice" in other cases, for some Syrians in Istanbul it becomes one of the very few work avenues available. To deal with economic anxiety, some artists respond to calls by NGOs, academics, policymakers, or galleries for artistic projects that focus on the "Syrian perspective." Thus, the spheres of "refugee art" and "art as labour" are not separate; rather, they overlap, especially when "refugee art initiatives" offer opportunities for employment and income generation. Some artists participate in this genre of artistic creation, which expects a focus on articulations of displacement, war, and loss; some do so reluctantly, others through processes of self-essentializing and commodification. A number of refugee artists, however, abstain from such initiatives, which they deem to be both creatively limiting and economically exploitative.

This chapter draws on a series of semi-structured interviews with artists who fled the 2011 civil war in Syria, have since settled in Istanbul, and work in private studios or in partnerships.[2] Originally, we did not limit ourselves to any specific category of artistic practice in our research. However, through snowballing, we tended to encounter mainly visual artists and musicians, and for the purposes of this chapter we focus mainly on the former group. Most artists are in their thirties or forties and have received university qualifications, including art degrees. There is a strong gender dynamic to this: male artists dominate the scene in Istanbul. So, while we interviewed both male and female artists, the majority of our research participants are male.

By contrast, the research team was all women. It included the two authors, who were also the project's main principal investigators, and two researchers, one Arabic-speaker and one Turkish-speaker. Both authors are anthropologists, based in Northern Ireland and with ongoing research interests in the themes of migration, displacement, memory, and loss across a number of ethnographic contexts. The two researchers were political science and international relations postgraduate students at Istanbul Bilgi University, our collaborating institution, and were recruited and supervised by our research partners at the Center for Migration Research. We conducted interviews with a core group of nine artists, and engaged in a number of informal conversations with a larger number of artists in studios and social gatherings as well as online through follow-up communications. Most interviews were conducted in English, as the artists were fluent speakers, except for one interview, which was conducted in Arabic, with synchronous translation for the other researchers, who were also present. A number of exchanges and interviews took the traditional form of one-to-one, involving one researcher and one research participant, but a large portion of our fieldwork involved "team ethnography," a collaborative endeavour that involved the two authors or even, at times, the entire research team conducting fieldwork together (Erickson and Stull 1998; Clerke and Hopwood 2014). This was mainly due to the way in which the original project and research trips had been designed, which veered from the traditional practice of the "lone ranger" ethnographer (Scales, Bailey, and Lloyd 2011, 22). This methodological approach raises further opportunities and challenges that are beyond the scope of this chapter to discuss. However, one point to note here is that working as a team afforded us better access as well as the opportunity to forge a more collaborative interaction with artists, who were themselves working in groups or collectives and therefore valued partnership and exchange. It also enriched the process of data collection and analysis, given the multiplicity of our experiences, backgrounds, and disciplinary theoretical approaches, and thereby allowed us to parse and frame key insights in dialogue with diverse fieldsite readings and interpretations. Co-writing or writing in consultation with one another and our research participants also accrued enormous benefit to this project.

Our fieldsite, however, was highly complex. Turkey, laudably, has been the greatest recipient of displaced Syrians, yet Syrians there find themselves hemmed in by a broad range of temporary protections as well as by escalating anti-Syrian sentiment (Erdoğan and Uyan Semerci 2018). Since 2014, when the Law on Foreigners and International Protection (LFIP) was passed, displaced Syrians have been assigned the status of "temporary protection." LFIP, conceived as a step toward harmonizing Turkish law with EU legislation, outlines provisions for foreigners in need of international protection (including "temporary protection") when they have been forced out of their country and cannot return (Içduygu and im ek 2016, 61). However, LFIP also makes it clear that temporary protection is not the same as a residency permit, nor does it offer any specific time frame for possibly acquiring permanent status (Rygiel, Baban, and Ilcan 2016, 9). Syrian refugees, then – especially those residing in urban centres as opposed to camps – face significant challenges in accessing education, employment, and economic support (Erdoğan and Uyan Semerci 2018).

Because of their temporary legal status and precarious living conditions, "some Syrians are anticipating resettlement in a third country or repatriation once the war comes to an end, and others are travelling or hoping to travel to Europe in an effort to receive a more secure life, one that leads to permanent residency or full citizenship" (Erdoğan and Uyan Semerci 2018, 2). Many of our research participants lived elsewhere before settling in Istanbul. Others view their residency in the city as merely temporary. By the time of writing, some had already departed for the United States or Britain.

Our research practice was conducted through multiple sites that reflected multiple ways of being an artist, a Syrian artist, and a refugee artist in Istanbul. This included examining the intersections these artists occupy in their everyday practice/s. As already noted, our fieldsite exchanges were complemented by follow-up virtual interviews and interactions. We also conducted interviews with a number of NGOs and civil society advocates, who work with or commission artistic works by refugees. To break the dominance of oral accounts, we also engaged in participant observation in art spaces and at refugee-led projects.

In the next section, we follow one of these refugee-led projects to trace the ways in which art emerges as mode of survival, place-making, and solidarity, and at the same time as a critical space from which the representation politics of refugeeness, trauma, and loss are interrogated and confronted.

## Arthere

Arthere is a well-known project established by displaced Syrian artists. It brings together communities of – mainly visual – artists of different nationalities, and connects to other refugee initiatives. It is located on a small street off a very busy part of Kadıköy in Istanbul. Kadıköy, a historic neighbourhood on the Asian side of the city, has become a popular commercial and recreational centre; it is also home to a number of alternative spaces, including co-operatives, social enterprises, and art collectives. Arthere occupies a two-storey building. The front room hosts works by various artists and also serves as a working and social area with a small café attached. The building also houses a studio, a darkroom, an open space for musical performances and cinema screenings, and a small patio, where Nabil,[3] one of the founders of Arthere, cuts wood to manufacture frames for his photographs.

Arthere provides refugee artists with a creative environment for developing their artistic practices that have been disrupted by war and displacement, as well as a workspace for those with limited access to a professional studio. The artists do not receive salaries but can sell their art in the gallery. Arthere operates through external funding and offers an "artists in exile" residency program. Nabil started the project in 2014, a year after he left Syria, with funding from local and international NGOs. He explains why he did:

Artists can actually find work here, they can have exhibitions, they can practise. Artists have lost all their support and networks, and this is what we try to do here, to build these connections. You are an artist, but you need to work in a factory or a restaurant [to make a living]. So, we try to give them some time through giving residency. This program started in 2017 with 10 artists.

Reflecting our own misconstructions and methodological bias, we had expected to find a place overwhelmingly dominated by projects referring directly to the war in Syria, displacement, and loss. Instead, we found that the visual art exhibited around the gallery was extremely diverse, covering a wide range of topics, genres, and techniques. Even so, we insisted on asking Nabil and other artists how the war and refugeehood had affected their artistic practice. Nabil's answer gave a twist to what was otherwise implied by our loaded question:

We have more freedom here to create. This is not an NGO, not a company, not an organization, not a business, not a café, not a gallery. It's, in a way, our reaction to what is happening in Syria. People were afraid [to produce art in Syria] and took the opportunity to leave. But now we say let's do it from outside [Syria] …

The idea was for Syrian artists to meet and work together and learn. To also work with Turkish and international artists. Art spaces had to have the approval of the regime and intelligence in Syria, so it was impossible to do the sort of art you wanted in Syria because there was very little funding and support.

Art is always a threat. It used to look like we had [art] things but it was always elite and small. Video makers had to show their films illegally. You spend your life trying to find your way through. And that's how they kill you, how they kill creativity, going from one government organization to another trying to get permission.

Arthere, then, offers artists greater freedom to engage in creative practices that had been restricted, suppressed, or ignored in Syria. From this entanglement of political and artistic freedom has flowed a socio-political critique of the Syrian regime, conflict, and displacement, expressed not through direct references but rather through an aspiration to expand and internationalize creativity in ways that were not possible in Syria. Arthere's artists, as "frustrated cosmopolitans" (Tsioulakis 2011), seek to diversify through experimentation and collaboration with Turkish and other international artists. These collaborations allow artists to engage in "cosmopolitan imaginaries" (Tsioulakis 2011, 176), and become modes of sociality, solidarity, and place-making, especially given that a number of artists spend long hours almost every day sharing this space. Arthere gives artists a place to work, but also a network and a physical presence and visibility in the bustling city of Istanbul.

So it is understandable that the artists there express uneasiness about queries that steer them toward the categories of the "displaced artist" and "refugee art." Jamal, one of our research participants, commented that "in Syria, I used to be an artist, but now I have to be a *Syrian artist*." Such categorizations and discursive constructions pressure artists to produce "art on demand" in response to particular thematic expectations or to value their existing work in accordance with an assumed scale of authenticity implicit in "refugee art." Some artists *do* produce art that speaks to these themes. A number of the exhibitors in Arthere have reflected on how experiences of violence, conflict, and loss have directly impacted their work, and some of the displayed art vividly conveys this. However, they reject the abstracting and essentializing effects of categorical thinking, which devalues their art as lacking universalistic aspirations. This "Othering" underscores the ways in which a number of others' arts are constructed against the Western canon. In this cultural predicament (Clifford 1988), indigenous, ethnic, tribal, and any "other" art is seen as valuable only in the context of the category that Western art has assigned it. As Clifford (1988) writes, the cultures associated with these categories have been objectified and commodified as timeless and ahistorical exhibits to be consumed by a Western "gaze." In this way, "refugee art" not only becomes part of global aesthetic hierarchies of value but also defines and further essentializes the category of the "refugee" as a timeless "Other" (Malkki 1996).

There are also ethical dilemmas that emerge in this process as well as issues of responsibility and accountability. Nabil, for instance, explained that he has another job outside photography that allows him to make a living and therefore be selective in terms of his art. Others, though, who do produce or engage in projects of "refugee art" are often excoriated by other artists and other Syrians for "taking advantage of the revolution" and capitalizing on the traumatic communal histories of uprootedness and loss. "But you can't victimize the victims," continues Nabil, pointing out that in the current context of precarity, limited access to employment, and scarce state support, "refugee art" projects are one of the very few available options for Syrian artists. Not least because involvement in these projects, through which some artists can achieve international recognition and networks, is perceived as a positive resource for further mobility outside Turkey. In such cases, being a successful "refugee artist" enables one to become a "successful" refugee. Some artists, therefore, choose to essentialize themselves in order to develop a livelihood and possibly secure relocation for themselves and their families in Europe or North America. But such hopes for further mobility are not often fulfilled, and the resulting dependency on unpredictable humanitarian or commercial work locks artists into cycles of "protracted uncertainty" (Horst and Grabska 2015, 2) and precarity.

There are, however, others who fully abstain or withdraw from the broader market for "refugee art" in order to protect their own personal and communal histories of trauma and suffering. Conforming to art forms that require the recollection and aestheticization of war, pain, and displacement is simply a step too far for these artists, who choose either to engage in art through spaces like Arthere, or (sometimes) to fully withdraw from artistic practice as it becomes non-viable. Paradoxically, "refugee art," in its mission to give "voice" to and empower the displaced, can have the opposite effects of silencing, pushing them out of creative practice and thereby increasing their precarity.

## Art, the Politics of Empathy, and Methodological Dubiety

Thus far, we have drawn on two examples that highlight the ethical and political issues that arise at the intersection between art and refugee representation, one involving a non-refugee celebrity artist, the other involving displaced artists themselves. These examples provide a lens through which to examine our particular ethnographic practice and methodological approach. Indeed, the problematics and challenges contained therein have had a direct impact on how we do research on displacement.

Ai Weiwei has long been an activist committed to promoting the rights of the displaced. When Denmark toughened its policies to discourage refugees and asylum-seekers, he cancelled his scheduled exhibition there in protest. His re-creation of the Aylan Kurdi photo was in fact an attempt on his part to remind his international audience that a year after the boy's death, people were still dying trying to find safe haven in Europe. He was trying to raise awareness, solidarity, and support. In speaking about his chosen method, however, he argued that his own experiences paralleled that of the dead Syrian boy: "For me to be in the same position [as Kurdi] is to suggest our condition can be so far from human concerns in today's politics" (cited in Ratnam 2016, 1). This unfiltered comment outraged his critics and provoked a backlash against his intentions. His art was deemed thoughtless and dangerous, and his equation of his own experiences with that of a dead child was viewed as helping devalue human suffering and loss. If he had intended to activate feelings of empathy among international audiences, his artistic effort had probably resulted in the opposite.

The notion of empathy has featured heavily in debates about how to mobilize support for the displaced in an era of rising nationalism and xenophobia. As much as it is seen as central for some, there are others who view empathy as a weak response to what is a human rights issue. Some recent popular arguments informed by public psychology, for instance, have come out *against* empathy (Bloom 2016; Greene 2015). The premise here, based on universalistic conclusions about morality, is that empathy is an irrational emotion applied through personal biases and therefore often reproduces inequality and injustice. Rational decision-making instead is and should be encouraged as the main way of being moral in modern society.

This debate on the politics of empathy and solidarity has long roiled ethnographic research and writing. Anthropologists have for decades problematized the idea of empathy and have often shied away from it in analytical and methodological approaches, to the point that the editors of a special issue on the topic felt motivated to ask: "Whatever happened to empathy?" (Holan and Throop 2008). Unlike social psychologists, however, anthropologists have warned that empathy is an elusive concept, mainly because it is defined, applied, and observed so differently depending on the socio-cultural environment (Holan and Throop 2008). In addition, popular understandings of empathy assume fixed perceptions of inter-subjectivity, intentionality, and experience. As Desjarlais (1994, 2018) has argued, such approaches become challenged not only across cultures but also in sensorial contexts of illness, pain, and suffering.

If we as anthropologists are hesitant to evoke empathy as both a method and a result of the ethnographic worlds we present, the question that remains is *how* we are supposed to "understand" our research participants' experiences and *what* we are supposed to understand them *for*. In the study of displacement, this is a crucial epistemological, ethical, and political question. As Joel Robbins (2013) has noted, contemporary anthropology has replaced its non-Western "Other" with the "suffering subject," and "refugees" have acquired a central place in recent years in this process of subject-making (Ramsay 2019, 6). A fundamental anthropological concern, therefore, remains preoccupied with privileging experiences and stories of suffering and loss. As anthropologists, we have criticized our own epistemological insistence on "the voice" and oral narrative (see Hastrup 2003; Ross 2003; Wilson 2003; Das 2003, 2007), yet we have been less reflexive about how we engage in alternative methodologies, including art. Especially given that we still apply particular frameworks that position displacement at the centre of the ethnographic encounter when we deploy such methodologies.

As demonstrated, however, focusing on "refugee art" is not a panacea for overcoming problems with "the voice," as the politics of artistic articulation and production in this case (re)produce hierarchies and inequalities in the process of representing. Such processes, coupled with the ethics of art production, also have implications for ethnographic practice. Like art, and metaphorically close to Ai Weiwei's endeavour, participant observation involves "mimicking": we learn through participating in and enacting our research participants' practices. But mimicking, as Taussig (1993) argues, produces simultaneously interactions of both empathy and alienation. Through participant observation we can often contribute to the essentializing and objectification of trauma and suffering. As anthropologists, therefore, we often deal with complex ethical spaces. The question that remains here is how to navigate such spaces and how to produce accounts of displacement and loss without either fetishizing voices or aesthetizing loss.

In addition to how we engage and interact in the field, we also have to question what we do with the products of our research. Why do we keep collecting stories of loss and suffering, and what do we do *with/to* our participants' "voices," artworks, objects? If it is not to evoke the empathetic reaction of our reading audiences but rather to offer an understanding of other worlds, what gets compromised, and silenced, here? Are we not yet again abstracting from broader histories and politics? And does any sort of change happen? In this case, why do we need more stories of trauma and suffering? What is the point of them?

These are not easy questions to answer, and by all means, we are not suggesting that we should stop documenting displacement and suffering altogether. But instead of taking up this task as central to the anthropological undertaking, we should first critically reflect on the broader structural conditions that deem such documenting necessary, desirable, valuable, or even fundable. An anthropology of displacement and loss does not, and should not, aim to resolve dilemmas around representation, experience, and aesthetics; rather, it should follow what we call here a "methodological dubiety" that highlights further ethical, political, and methodological complexities in documenting absence. In line with what Ingold (2014) calls "correspondence," ethnography in this context should go beyond the narrative and the representational and arise from mutual and synchronic interaction in the field so that it is not just inter-subjective but multi-subjective, including

landscapes, objects, ideas, and artistic encounters. This is a space of continuous interrogation and disruption, as opposed to a straightforward context
of ethical conduct and empathetic production.

This interrogation is not solely the product of methodological and ethical
self-reflexivity and the researcher's questioning of her own positionality. It
is the result of the ethnographic encounter and can come directly from the
research participants themselves. Such commentary can emerge both in narratives and in critical dialogue, as well as in what is unspoken about – in silences, whispers, gaps, and absences (Navaro-Yashin 2012). It often emanates
from bodily, affective, and material exchanges (Kidron 2009; Navaro-Yashin
2009; Dragojlovic 2015), all of which may tell a different story than the verbal
accounts that both researchers and research participants (re)produce. In her
study of post-division North Cyprus, Navaro-Yashin (2009) remarks that
although Turkish Cypriots may appear to deploy dominant state narratives
in their accounts of the war, their interactions with ruined houses and objects left behind by Greek Cypriots reveal alternative responses of *maraz*, a
particular melancholia that operates as a critique of the status quo.

However, such interactions have the potential to disrupt not only the participants' oral accounts but also the ethnographic process and the methodological approach, besides pushing for a reorientation of the ethnographic
encounter and the knowledge production that stems from it. In our case,
while our research participants were willing to engage with our specifically
framed questions around loss and displacement and how such experiences
redefined their creative lives, the artworks exhibited in Arthere visually in-
tervened, interrupted, and interrogated. It challenged our preconceived categories and redefined what refugee art entailed in this context through
alternative displays of humanist and cosmopolitan aspirations. This diversity
of artworks adds an interpretive element of complexity to the creative lives
and experiences of refugeehood. It was this particular empirical encounter
between the research participants, their art, the space, and us as researchers
that challenged categorical thinking and opened up opportunities for a
paradigm shift.

## Ethnographic Refusal and the Responsibility (Not) to Document Loss

The notion of empathy we work with here is subject to a degree of termi-
nological and epistemological anxiety; nonetheless, it is a necessary frame
through which we have been motivated to act, document, and represent displacement. Our research and our interlocuters inhabit contexts of political
contention, so our quest for a blend of methodological dubiety and ethnographic refusal arises from a place of grave ethical responsibility for our interlocuters. This position on refusal follows the work of Zahara (2016), which
argues for a form of "ethnographic refusal" that goes beyond Ortner's (1995)
notion of simply protecting participants unilaterally. It calls instead for a
common, collaborative decision-making process with one's interlocuters.
This project reorients academic analyses away from "harmful pain-based
narratives" (Zahara 2016, 1) in a way that emphasizes research participants'
agency with respect to their own self-representations (Zahara 2016). There
is a strategic decision here on what to include or exclude, thus making omission a political and ethical act. In carving out this perspective through the
particularities of our ethnographic endeavour, we also evince the ethical
complexities engendered through this positionality.

As academic scholars, we work in a context of what Neves and colleagues
(2018, 242) have noted is ever increasing "institutional surveillance" in the
shape of neoliberal institutional regulatory ethics. They argue that "hypothetical, speculative procedural ethical concerns are no match for the phenomenology of real-world situations packed with existential dilemmas"
(242), and it is here that our position of methodological dubiety and ethnographic refusal confronts the neoliberal framing of ethics in the corporate
university. In our decision to omit – to occlude in conjunction with our research interlocuters – we are methodological and ethical shapeshifters, practising an ethnography that resists, protects, and advocates far beyond the
remit of institutional ethics would have us do. This is the kind of ethics necessary for any work with individuals seeking refuge. This position is dis-
tinctly decolonizing (Tuhiwai Smith 1990; see also Taha, this volume) in a
research area troubled by a surfeit of narratives of suffering and pain put
to work in ways that decentre refugee experience in often harmful ways. To

evolve methodological dubiety and refusal in this regard, we need to recentre relationality, subjectivity, and agency in a manner that cultivates care and collaboration in the form of what Hammersley and Traianou (2014) call the "new ethics." Such an ethical positionality pays attention to participatory action and collaborative engagements with research participants, activism and advocacy, care and justice, and omission as a political act. It is this "new ethics" that institutional regulation is attempting to curtail in order to protect itself while suffocating the modes and methods of the social sciences more broadly.

As we work with Syrians in Turkey, many of whom are highly precarious in relation to the state, our refusal comes out of an awareness that in telling their stories they run many different but also intersecting risks with respect to their status in Turkey and their relationship to Syria. This is especially the case for those with families remaining there. As the interviews in this chapter demonstrate, a number of the artists we engaged with were very open about the degree to which their creativity had been monitored and even curtailed in Syria, in comparison to their new-found freedoms in Turkey. Others were more veiled in their criticism, citing concerns for their families and themselves. For some, our discussion centred solely on art, and they shielded from us their stories of escaping Syria; for others, the focus was on journeying and the reclamation of their art through that journeying. These tensions also played out in the open analysis of "refugee funding" and "refugee art." What "methodological dubiety" entails here is the preparedness not to unravel – and crucially, not to follow up – on particular stories, especially in contexts where research participants actively resisted telling or exhibiting their stories in public. Empathy here is not just about evoking positive intersubjective identification; it may also involve forced intimacy. To develop empathy or understanding, we intrude into knowledge that our research participants may not want us to have or share that presents sharp ethical challenges. Through our co-writing, collaborations, and team ethnography, we have adopted an approach of ethical caution in our reckoning with the politics of our research participants' strategic omissions, absences, and silences. The carving out of a collaborative analytical position was conducted with and through the knowledge that these types of omissions and silences were not only necessary but often imposed by our interlocutors.

In paying attention to the weave of conflict, refugee, and artistic lives in our interviewing, we listened to the refusal in their narratives – sometimes overt, sometimes existing as silence and absence (Chatzipanagiotidou and Murphy 2020), but always markedly distinguishing of different registers of speakability. It is this very plurality of register, which runs counter to how neoliberal regulatory ethics understands practices of informed consent, that allows ethnographic refusal to maintain its model of illusionary control and efficiency with respect to research practice.

In our practice of ethnographic refusal, informed consent figures as a longitudinal and collaborative configuring and reconfiguring of the constellation of refugee experience vis-à-vis artistic experience rather than as a signature releasing a particular narrative into the world of academia. This informed consent necessitates an ongoing dialogue with and concern for the lives of one's research interlocuters that extends far beyond how the corporate university and the associated institutional regulatory ethics conceive of notions of consent in research. Here in this space of ethnographic refusal, what is troubling for institutional ethics is the attentiveness to relationships, sociality in the life of a research project, advocacy, and even friendship (Murphy 2019). Inherent in this is a kind of empathetic openness (Hollan and Throop 2008, 9) that functions as a kind of disruption of the demands of the behemoth institutional and regulatory form of ethics. Our approach then of refusal and dubiety allows us a space in which absences, silences, and losses are in constant negotiation with their putative framings and representations, thus allowing researcher and interlocuter to navigate much more open spaces of worlding in the documentation of artistic and refuge-seeking lives.

## Conclusion

As discussed at the start of this chapter, Ai Weiwei's artistic re-enactment of Aylan Kurdi's photo was motivated by his intention to mobilize support. Instead, it provoked criticism for insensitivity and ethical myopia. We have argued that as ethnographers, despite the best of intentions, we may often also find ourselves in the position of reproducing categorical thinking in the study of displacement and loss that essentializes and silences. Replacing one method with another, however, is not a solution as we navigate this ethically challenging landscape. Ethnographers have attempted to move away from the problematic and restrictive dominance of oral narrative in documenting displacement, by deploying art as a methodological tool for accessing refugee experiences. However, as we have shown, art does not always offer an ethical solution to problems with the "voice," especially when it narrows down on suffering and loss as the central loci of experience. Here, ethnographers contribute to the static understanding of "refugee art" in similar ways to those of policy-makers, NGOs, and art dealers. Our stumbling upon art-as-work offered the opportunity to interrogate what "refugee art" constitutes, but also the ethnographic encounter itself. It revealed gaps, silences, and inequalities that remain unaccounted for in a number of "refugee art" projects, as well as spaces of alternative artistic articulations. Exhibiting displacement, as the chapter title suggests, both in its literal and metaphorical sense, allows us to deploy visual art production as an example of the interplay of the tensions and dynamics of representation.

The result has been the development of a methodological dubiety, an approach that moves beyond relying on specific methods toward constantly reflecting on their application, contributing thereby to the ongoing anthropological commitment to reflexivity. The issue of intention is critical in this endeavour. As we have discussed, having the best of intentions in the ethnographic endeavour is not good enough. Instead, we have to monitor how these intentions are framed by broader structural and discursive domains of power, including demands by our own institutions to produce "impactful" research and engage with "real life" issues. These we may find often contrast with what is at stake for our research participants.

We also need to question the role of empathy as an intended ethnographic tool and research outcome. Its application in the ethnographic encounter, especially if it is done unilaterally, can lead to further alienation and the reproduction of power dynamics between researcher and researched. Especially when it also involves breaking silences that participants prefer to maintain. If our intention is also to write ethnography in order to evoke empathy from our audiences, we have to realize that this often relies on reproducing essentialized categories of displacement, loss, and refugeehood.

Instead of relying on established methods and categories, however, we align here with Pandian's (2019) call for a "transformative anthropology," an anthropology of possibilities. As he advocates, "wherever we go and whomever we seek out in curiosity or solidarity, the stories we bring back are only worth telling when they complicate the humanity of those we share them with" (5). This becomes a testing task in our times, during which claims to a universal common humanity are being mobilized to contest the rise of racist, xenophobic, and anti-migrant politics. Our effort to present displaced lives and experiences in their complexity may be challenged by broader political stakes to support and protect. Such precautions may be attenuated if they do not fully engage the disruptions and interventions that our research participants seek. As such then, a commitment to collaboration with our research participants, one that opens space for interrogating categories, methods, and canons, emerges as the only viable way for an anthropology of displacement and loss to continue as the "effort to unsettle and remake what would seem to be given in human being" (5).

NOTES

1   The project is titled "Counting Our Losses: Social Entrepreneurship, Refugees, and Urban Transformation in Turkey" and is funded by the British Academy under the program "Tackling the UK's International Challenges 2017."

2   Although Syrians started fleeing to Turkey in 2011, the numbers peaked after 2013.

3   All research participants have been anonymized, and the names used here are pseudonyms suggested by the authors.

REFERENCES

Abu-Lughod, L. 1986. *Veiled Sentiments: Honor and Poetry in a Bedouin Society.* Berkeley: University of California Press.

Arda, B. 2019. "Contemporary Art on the Current Refugee Crisis: The Problematic of Aesthetics versus Ethics." *British Journal of Middle Eastern Studies* 46, no. 2: 310–27. http://doi.org/10.1080/13530194.2019.1569307.

Atkinson, A. 2018. "The I in the Past." *History Australia* 15, no. 3: 578–90.

Bloom, P. 2017. *Against Empathy: The Case for Rational Compassion.* London: Random House.

Cabot, H. 2016. "'Refugee Voices': Tragedy, Ghosts, and the Anthropology of Not Knowing." *Journal of Contemporary Ethnography* 45, no. 6: 645–72.

Chatzipanagiotidou, E., and F. Murphy. 2020. "'Devious Silence': Refugee Art, Memory Activism, and the Unspeakability of Loss among Syrians in Turkey." *History and Anthropology.* https://doi.org/10.1080/02757206.2020.1830383.

Clerke, T., and N. Hopwood. 2014. *Doing Ethnography in Teams.* London: Springer Briefs in Education. http://doi.org/10.1007/978-3-319-05618-0_1.

Clifford, J. 1988. *The Predicament of Culture.* Cambridge, MA: Harvard University Press.

Das, V. 2003. "Trauma and Testimony: Implications for Political Community." *Anthropological Theory* 3: 293–307.

– 2007. *Life and Words: Violence and the Descent into the Ordinary.* Berkeley: University of California Press.

Desjarlais, R. 1994. "Struggling Along: The Possibilities for Experience among the Homeless Mentally Ill." *American Anthropologist* 96, no. 4: 886–901.

– 2018. *The Blind Man: A Phantasmography.* New York: Fordham University Press.

Dhillon, N. 2016. "Ai Weiwei's Photo Reenacting a Child Refugee's Death Should Not Exist." *Hyperallergic.* https://hyperallergic.com/272881/ai-weiweis-photo-reenacting-a-child-refugees-death-should-not-exist.

Dragojlovic, A. 2015. "Affective Geographies: Intergenerational Hauntings, Bodily Affectivity, and Multiracial Subjectivities." *Subjectivity* 8, no. 4: 315–34.

Erdoğan, E., and P. Uyan Semerci. 2018. "Fanusta Diyaloglar: Türkiye'de Kutuplaşmanın Boyutları" [Dialogues in the Bell Jar: Dimensions of Polarization in Turkey]. Istanbul: Istanbul Bilgi University.

Erickson, K.C., and D.D. Stull. 1998. *Doing Team Ethnography: Warnings and Advice.* Qualitative Research Methods Series. Vol. 42. Thousand Oaks: SAGE.

Good, B.J. 2012. "Phenomenology, Psychoanalysis, and Subjectivity in Java." *Ethos* 40, no. 1: 24–36.

Greene, J. 2013. *Moral Tribes: Emotion, Reason, and the Gap between Us and Them.* New York: Penguin Books.

Hammersley, M., and A. Traianou. 2014. "Foucault and Research Ethics: On the Autonomy of the Researcher." *Qualitative Inquiry* 20: 227–38.

Hastrup, K. 2003. "Violence, Suffering, and Human Rights: Anthropological Reflections." *Anthropological Theory* 3, no. 3: 309–23.

Hesmondhalgh, D., and S. Baker. 2011. *Creative Labour: Media Work in Three Cultural Industries.* London and New York: Routledge.

Hogan, S., and S. Pink. 2010. "Routes to Interiorities: Art Therapy and Knowing in Anthropology." *Visual Anthropology* 23, no. 2: 158–74. http://doi.org/10.1080/08949460903475625.

Hollan, D., and C.J. Throop. 2008. "Whatever Happened to Empathy? Introduction." *Ethos* 36: 385–401. http://doi.org/10.1111/j.1548-1352.2008.00023.x.

Horst, C., and K. Grabska. 2015. "Introduction: Flight and Exile – Uncertainty in the Context of Conflict-Induced Displacement." *Social Analysis* 59, no. 11: 1–18.

İçduygu, A., and D. Şimşek. 2016. "Syrian Refugees in Turkey: Towards Integration Policies." *Turkish Policy Quarterly* 15, no. 3: 59–69. http://turkishpolicy.com/files/articlepdf/syrian-refugees-in-turkey-towards-integration-policies_en_2781.pdf.

*India Today Magazine*. 2016. "Artist Ai Weiwei Poses as Aylan Kurdi for India Today Magazine." 1 February. https://www.indiatoday.in/india/story/artist-ai-weiwei-poses-as-aylan-kurdi-for-india-today-magazine-306593-2016-02-01.

Ingold, T. 2014. "That's Enough about Ethnography!" *Hau: Journal of Ethnographic Theory* 4, no. 1: 383–95.

Jackson, M. 2013. *The Politics of Storytelling: Variations on a Theme by Hannah Arendt*. Vol. 4. Copenhagen: Museum Tusculanum Press.

Kalmanowitz, D. 2016. "Inhabited Studio: Art Therapy and Mindfulness, Resilience, Adversity and Refugees." *International Journal of Art Therapy* 21, no. 2: 75–84.

Kidron, C.A. 2009. "Toward an Ethnography of Silence: The Lived Presence of the Past in the Everyday Life of Holocaust Trauma Survivors and Their Descendants in Israel." *Current Anthropology* 50, no. 1: 5–27.

Lorey, I. 2011. "Virtuosos of Freedom: On the Implosion of Political Virtuosity and Productive Labour." In *Critique of Creativity: Precarity, Subjectivity, and Resistance in the "Creative Industries,"* edited by Gerald Raunig, Gene Ray, and Ulf Wuggenig, 79–91. London: Mayfly.

Maggio, R. 2014. "The Anthropology of Storytelling and the Storytelling of Anthropology." *Journal of Comparative Research in Anthropology and Sociology* 5, no. 2: 89–106.

Malkki, L.H. 1996. "Speechless Emissaries: Refugees, Humanitarianism, and Dehistoricization." *Cultural Anthropology* 11, no. 3: 377–404.

McGranahan, C. 2012 "Anthropology as Theoretical Storytelling." In *Writing Anthropology: Essays on Craft and Commitment*, edited by C. McGranahan. Durham: Duke University Press.

McRobbie, A. 2016. *Be Creative: Making a Living in the New Culture Industries*. Cambridge: Polity Press.

Murphy, F. 2019. "Friend or Foe?: A Reflection on the Ethno-Politics of Friendship and Ethnographic Writing in Anthropological Practice." *Ethnofoor* 31, no. 1: 11–28.

Navaro Yashin, Y. 2009. "Affective Spaces, Melancholic Objects: Ruination and the Production of Anthropological Knowledge." *Journal of the Royal Anthropological Institute* 15, no. 1: 1–18.

– 2012. *The Make-Believe Space: Affective Geography in a Postwar Polity*. Durham: Duke University Press.

Neves, T., C. Holligan, and R. Deuchar. 2018. "Reflections Concerning Ethnographic Ethical Decisions and Neo-Liberal Monitoring." *Etnográfica* 22, no. 2: 241–58.

O'Neill, M. 2008. "Transnational Refugees: The Transformative Role of Art?" *Forum Qualitative Sozialforschung/Forum: Qualitative Social Research* 9, no. 2: 54–65.

Ortner, S.B. 1995. "Resistance and the Problem of Ethnographic Refusal." *Comparative Studies in Society and History* 37, no. 1: 173–93.

Pandian, A. 2019. *A Possible Anthropology: Methods for Uneasy Times*. Durham: Duke University Press.

Prøitz, L. 2018. "Visual Social Media and Affectivity: The Impact of the Image of Alan Kurdi and Young People's Response to the Refugee Crisis in Oslo and Sheffield." *Information, Communication, and Society* 21, no. 4: 548–63. http://doi.org/10.1080/1369118X.2017.1290129.

Ramsay, G. 2020. "Time and the Other in Crisis: How Anthropology Makes Its Displaced Object." *Anthropological Theory* 20, no. 4: 385–413. https://doi.org/10.1177/1463499619840464.

Ratnam, N. 2016. "Ai Weiwei's Aylan Kurdi Image Is Crude, Thoughtless, and Egotistical." *The Spectator*. https://blogs.spectator.co.uk/2016/02/ai-weiweis-aylan-kurdi-image-is-crude-thoughtless-and-egotistical.

Robbins, J. 2013. "Beyond the Suffering Subject: Toward an Anthropology of the Good." *Journal of the Royal Anthropological Institute* 19, no. 3: 447–62.

Ross, F. 2003. "On Having Voice and Being Heard: Some After-Effects of Testifying before the South African Truth and Reconciliation Commission." *Anthropological Theory* 3, no. 3: 325–41.

Rygiel, K., F. Baban, and S. Ilcan. 2016. "The Syrian Refugee Crisis: The EU-Turkey 'Deal' and Temporary Protection." *Global Social Policy* 16, no. 3: 315–20.

Scales, K., S. Bailey, and J. Lloyd. 2011. "Separately and Together: Reflections on Conducting a Collaborative Team Ethnography in Dementia Care." *Enquire* 6: 24–49.

Taussig, M. 1993. *Mimesis and Alterity: A Particular History of the Senses*. London: Routledge.

Tello, V. 2016. *Counter-Memorial Aesthetics: Refugee Histories and the Politics of Contemporary Art*. Radical Aesthetics Radical Art series, Bloomsbury Philosophy. London: Bloomsbury.

Tsioulakis, I. 2011. "Jazz in Athens: Frustrated Cosmopolitans in a Music Subculture." *Ethnomusicology Forum* 20, no. 2: 175–99.

Tuhiwai Smith, L. 1990. *Decolonizing Methodologies: Research and Indigenous Peoples*. London: Zed Books.

Weller, R. 2017. "Salvaging Silence: Exile, Death, and the Anthropology of the Unknowable." *Anthropology of This Century* 19. http://aotcpress.com/articles/salvaging-silence.

Wilson, R.A. 2003. "Anthropological Studies of National Reconciliation Processes." *Anthropological Theory* 3, no. 3: 367–87.

Zahara, A. 2016. "Ethnographic Refusal: A How-To Guide. *Discard Studies*. https://discardstudies.com/2016/08/08/ethnographic-refusal-a-how-to-guide.

# 4

## Ethical and Methodological Issues When Conducting Research with Children in Situations of Forced Migration

Jason Hart

According to recent figures, more than half of the roughly seventy million people living in a situation of forced migration around the globe are under the age of eighteen (UNHCR 2019, 3). This includes children who have been internally displaced as well as those who have fled across national borders in search of sanctuary. It also includes the thousands born each year in the world's many displacement camps, often to parents who grew up in the same location.

Failure to attend to the perspectives of children in situations of displacement weakens our understanding of forced migration. In both ethical and intellectual terms, this is as unacceptable as ignoring the experience of say, adult women, or the elderly. At the same time, the fields of childhood studies and children's rights must pay attention to the perspectives of young forced migrants in order to move beyond normative assumptions about the role of the state – assumptions reinforced by research with child citizens, who are rarely identified as such (Boyden and Hart 2007).

Recognizing the value of investigating children's experiences of forced migration leads to consideration of the approach to such inquiry, in terms of both methodology and ethics. In this chapter, my aim is not to provide a comprehensive guide to the issues surrounding research with children in situations of forced migration. That would require a far lengthier discussion than is possible here. Rather, I intend to offer prompts for reflection when considering how best to conduct research with children in such situations. These are organized around the themes of positionality, specificity, and power.

## Positionality

Across the social sciences the vision of the researcher as a neutral observer has been questioned to varying degrees. Those who see research, instead, as an intersubjective process highlight the need to attend to one's own assumptions, values, and experiences as a researcher with regard to their impact on the questions we ask and the manner in which we conduct ourselves. Moreover, our approach and the responses of others to us in the course of research will be mediated by factors such as gender, age/generation, class, ethnicity, and (dis)ability. Going further, many would argue that it is vital to attend to the distribution of power and the impact of consequent inequality on the relationship between researcher and researched. This is an epistemological as well as an ethical issue. Within the "new sociology of childhood," considerable attention has been paid to differences in status and social power between adult researchers and children. Reflecting on one's positionality as a researcher entails considering the impact of the complex interplay between personal characteristics; the nature of one's power – not least to frame exchange and to represent – within the research encounter; and the effects of disciplinary orientation.

Exploration of children's experiences of forced migration has involved researchers from a range of disciplinary backgrounds: from law and human rights to social work, from anthropology to psychology, and from politics and international relations to education studies. Each of these disciplines conceptualizes children in settings of displacement in a particular manner, attributing certain properties (such as agency, vulnerability, or resilience) or foregrounding certain experiences (such as victimization, exploitation, or empowerment). For some, displacement is the central focus, and thus their object of study may be labelled as "forced migrant children." This is common among disciplines oriented toward immediate solutions or remedies, such as social work, law and human rights, and psychology. By contrast, anthropologists and sociologists, in particular, tend to locate their study of the impact of displacement within the daily lives of children, attending to the mediating effects of social, cultural, and political forces. Reference to "forced migrant children" may be rejected by scholars in these fields since it implies that displacement defines the experience, if not the identity, of children. Instead, a term such as "children in situations of forced migration" leaves open questions about the manner in which displacement shapes children's lives.

Disciplinary differences typically, but not necessarily, also have methodological implications. Inquiry focused on specific issues to be addressed through intervention – such as psycho-emotional distress, rights violations, and educational access – is likely to approach field-based research in a narrowly focused manner such as through the application of a questionnaire or through the employment of some means of diagnostic evaluation. By contrast, inquiry that begins with the children themselves, seeking to understand the issues and experiences that are most meaningful for them, is likely to be more open-ended, using a range of interactive methods in an iterative manner. The point here is not to suggest that certain disciplines are better suited to the study of children and displacement but rather to encourage reflection among researchers about the ways that their own disciplinary training may have led them to conceptualize and approach inquiry. This chapter focuses particularly on the qualitative and more open-ended approach typically pursued by researchers trained in anthropology, sociology, and allied disciplines. Inevitably this approach comes with its own limitations, such as in terms of time needed and relatively small sample size compared to the approaches typically favoured by mental health and social work researchers, for example.

Discipline isn't everything, however. In addition, it is important to consider how our approach as researchers is informed by personal background, experience, and outlook. For example, class position may shape in a significant manner the way in which each of us considers the situation of unaccompanied asylum-seeking children. Those brought up in middle-class homes in the global north, where risk to the young is managed carefully by constraining their lives to spaces overseen by trusted adults, may make assumptions about the extent of distress experienced by children away from a customary home and familiar care relationships. Whether and how such experiences impact the young may prove more difficult to unpack, and researchers must be aware of and willing to challenge their own assumptions. Again, there is no background that renders some researchers, as individuals, inevitably better suited than others to investigating children's lives in settings of forced migration. What matters is the willingness to consider one's own outlook and to be open to alternative perspectives.

Finally, one's positionality as a researcher should also be considered in relation to the source of funding and the expectations of the most immediate consumers of one's work. Financial support for academic research is increasingly instrumental in its aims. For example, the *Global Challenges Research Fund* (GCRF), which was introduced by the UK government in 2015 and has become a key framework for public spending on research, directs inquiry toward "innovative solutions to intractable development issues,"[1] including forced migration. The stated strategy behind this initiative conceptualizes the challenges that research should address in localized terms, overlooking the significance of connections between, for example, UK government policy, including support for the arms industry or for certain rights-abusing regimes, and displacement in locations around the globe. The increasingly explicit effort to encourage a focus on solutions of a typically technical nature risks obscuring the political reasons that lie behind the "intractable development issues" noted by the GCRF. How might the principle of independence from government agendas, which is core to the field of "modern humanitarianism" – at least in rhetorical terms – apply to researchers focused on issues of broad humanitarian interest (Hart 2021)?

The shift in balance away from funding research projects of intellectual interest toward inquiry that promises to deliver "innovative solutions" to predetermined "challenges" has implications for the methodology that may be pursued. For example, securing funds for open-ended research involving children to define the issues of greatest interest or concern becomes harder when funders require a clear statement of outcomes and impact before funds are allocated and research begins. A participatory approach to research with children in situations of forced migration has become popular among scholars from sociological and anthropological backgrounds especially (e.g., Evans 2012; de Wildt and Murk 2014). However, it is necessary to anticipate the limits on the extent and depth of such participation in light of the expectations of funders.

Research commissioned by United Nations or non-governmental humanitarian organizations working with children is often particularly narrow in its scope, focused on providing data around a specific issue of direct relevance to the development of practice. It is also commonly framed by particular definitions of and world views about childhood. In constant need of funding for their own survival and reliant on the willingness of host governments to allow their operations, UN agencies and NGOS are often especially sensitive about research that strays beyond a prescribed remit. This is particularly likely when findings draw attention to powerful actors such as governments and private corporations that are both sources of support *and* are implicated in harm to the young. Researchers may, therefore, find themselves in an ethical dilemma when their work contradicts the agenda of their employer, particularly if those findings have been meaningfully informed by the input of children and their communities. How to resolve such a dilemma, should it occur, is a question that might be considered in advance of accepting a contract, taking into account both ethical and professional implications.

## Specificity

Within the academy and among practitioners there is now plentiful material to help inform choices about research methodology. There are also guides and procedures intended to ensure that research is carried out with sufficient anticipation of basic ethical issues such as confidentiality, informed consent, and anonymity. However, fieldwork with children in settings of displacement entails attention to additional, specific concerns.

A body of work exists that attends to the ethical and methodological aspects of research with people who are displaced (e.g., Clark-Kazak 2017; Ghorashi 2008; Temple and Moran 2006). Many of the issues raised in this work are relevant to research with children in situations of forced migration. For example, Clark-Kazak draws our attention to the fact that people going through the asylum system are required to give repeated accounts of painful experiences; this creates a burden of which researchers need to be mindful. This concern applies not only to adults: unaccompanied asylum-seeking children and those who have been trafficked are also routinely subjected to this demand, with all the potential it creates for psycho-emotional harm (2017, 11).

At the same time, there are particular considerations that should be given to the young in situations of forced migration, beyond those pertaining to adults. For example, the manner in which the ethical obligation to obtain informed consent is realized entails negotiation of specific issues in the case of children. It is standard practice, commonly reinforced by ethical review boards, that a responsible adult should always give consent for someone under the age of eighteen to participate in research. However, violent conflict and the forced migration to which it gives rise often result in a child fending for themselves or even taking on a primary caregiver role. In such cases it is debatable whether the opportunity for a child to describe experiences and articulate needs should be subject to the gatekeeping of an adult who may have scant knowledge of that individual and the situation at hand (Hopkins 2008, 40).

In recent years, debate about the ethical and methodological dimensions of research with children has burgeoned (e.g., Alderson and Morrow 2011; Farrell 2005). Authors have commonly taken children's rights as a framework for thinking about research ethics. This framework is founded upon the conviction that there is an obligation to attend to the perspectives of children in research, rather than rely on the commentary of adults about the concerns of the young. According to Beazley and colleagues (2009, 370), a rights-based approach to research with children entails "children being participants in research; using methods that make it easy for them to express their opinions, views and experiences; being protected from harm that might result from taking part in research conducted by researchers who use quality, scientific methods and analysis."

All of these points – about the importance of a participatory approach, about the appropriateness of methods, about protection from harm, and about rigorous methodology and analysis – are relevant to research with children in situations of forced migration. However, each may have particular implications in such research. The most urgent of these concerns is the duty to ensure that the heightened risks typically encountered by the young in displacement settings do not translate into harm to them as a result of involvement in research. For example, when undertaking inquiry with children living "under the radar" in a country of refuge, the need to ensure anonymity may be especially important. Research activities that draw attention to children in such a situation may result in them and their families being deported, detained, or relocated to displacement camps. The timing and location of research activities become issues of pressing security, and thus ethical, importance.

On the other hand, the invisibility of children may, in some settings, result in them failing to access the support and protection they need. Thus, the apparently "safe option" of not engaging with children in situations of particular vulnerability out of the wish to preserve their low profile raises ethical issues of its own. Standard ethical checklists and procedures generally fail to capture the particular ambiguities and sensitivities of situations such as this. Instead, the most ethical approach must be identified through careful judgment based on a detailed understanding of the specific context.

Literature focused on research with children in situations of forced migration is still fairly limited. There is, however, some discussion of child-focused research in relation to humanitarian emergency, usually with particular emphasis on settings of armed conflict (e.g., Berman et al. 2016; Boyden 2004; Hart 2012). This has relevance in many ways to inquiry around displacement. For example, exposure to armed conflict may have impacts – psychological and practical – upon the lives of children that remain with them long after they have fled. Such continuity notwithstanding, settings of forced migration are, by definition, often distant from the violence that gave rise to displacement. New dangers may exist as well as new opportunities. Displacement may entail not only loss of a familiar environment but also the dispersal of household and community and thereby raise significant challenges in achieving safety and integration somewhere entirely new. It may also provide the chance to access education of a kind or standard previously unavailable; or offer the possibility of renegotiating intra-household or community hierarchies built on gender, age, birth order, and so on. Participatory research in which children explore both possibilities and difficulties can serve as a learning experience for all, by increasing awareness of resources available to them (Hart et al. 2007, 43). Handled well, such discussions can also serve to build networks of mutual support –something that may have particular benefit in settings of forced migration, where families and communities are dispersed and familiar sources of care and assistance are unavailable.

Settings of forced migration are, of course, extremely diverse. Although media reports often feed the assumption that people displaced by conflict primarily end up in camps, the reality is more complex. There are, indeed, a large and growing number of displacement camps around the world, many of which have existed for decades, such as those of the Palestinians in the Levant region, of the Sahrawi people in the camps of southern Algeria, and the numerous camps in Uganda, Kenya, Tanzania and other countries in East Africa housing refugees from various neighbouring countries. However, it remains the case that the majority of forced migrants, including children, take refuge in urban settings, typically in countries adjoining their own, often without full civil status and sometimes illegally. Whether people displaced by conflict end up in a camp or in an urban area may be due, in part at least, to socio-economic class and social capital. The better off and those with professional skills may have greater choice over where they reside and may be able to avoid residence in camps, which often constitute the least desirable option.

The situations of forced migration in which children find themselves also include being trafficked; seeking asylum in a status-granting country; and resettlement with leave to remain. There are situations where children are travelling across national borders, often over long distances, toward a country of intended asylum. Finally, we may consider return to the country if not the actual home of customary residence as a situation of forced migration. Although commonly depicted as the ideal solution to forced migration, numerous ethnographic studies show that "return" may entail not an end to displacement but a new stage in an enduring experience of loss and alienation (e.g., Grabska 2014; Hammond 2014; Stefansson 2006). This is particularly likely for children who are "returning" to a place in which they have never lived or from which they left at a very early age.

Careful inquiry that minimizes assumptions and that seeks, instead, to understand vulnerability and risk in each specific context is needed. Furthermore, our thinking about the ethical and methodological issues of research with children should take the multiplicity of settings into account, instead of assuming that "displacement" gives rise to a ubiquitous set of issues or that children's diverse experiences are reducible to those of a generic "refugee child." To underscore the importance of specificity, we can identify potential ethical and methodological considerations that are particularly likely in one or another of the situations noted. Again, the aim is to be illustrative rather than provide a comprehensive guide. To that end, I take three different situations of forced migration.

### Children Resettled with Leave to Remain and Full Access to Services

In the resettlement setting researchers must develop a methodological approach that is sufficiently flexible and multi-faceted to enable capture of the inevitably complex ways that the experience of displacement impacts the everyday lives of children. At the same time, there are potential sensitivities to be negotiated due to inter-generational differences in outlook. It is vital to build trust so that a space may be created in which children feel able to articulate their experience and aspirations. Even so, intra-familial conflict may be provoked if the research depicts these children as fully committed to and enjoying their new environment while their parents struggle to integrate or are ambivalent in their attitude toward life in the country of resettlement. In such a situation there may be pressure on the young to express a desire to "return" as an act of loyalty to the adults in their family. Moreover, the researcher needs to take into account that in some families any discussion of violence and displacement in the country of origin may be taboo (Miller et al. 2008). Opening up this topic with children may thus require immense caution. When it comes to sharing findings, the researcher may face the dilemma of how to remain true to the broad experience of children with all its potential contradictions without provoking tensions or conflict between generations.

### Children Seeking Asylum Alone

Recognition of the complexities, even burden, of children's relationships with adult caregivers in settings of resettlement encourages one to avoid assuming that being "accompanied" is necessarily easier in all respects than the situation of children seeking asylum alone. Yet this has long been the conviction among practitioners when it comes to "unaccompanied asylum-seeking children" (UASC). The presence of adult caregivers may well have a considerable impact upon children's personal safety and access to support and basic services, but it is not inevitable that they will function effectively to "mediate or buffer the effects of difficult experiences" (Goodman 2004, 1177). Indeed, in situations of forced migration children may take on the role of translators (culturally as well as linguistically) and provide significant support to parents (Hinton 2000). There may be particular obstacles to overcome in locating unaccompanied children and gaining access to them in order to engage them in research (Hopkins 2008). However, research with this group of young forced migrants also illustrates the need to adopt a highly nuanced approach when working with notions currently central to research with children in difficult circumstances. These notions include agency, resilience, vulnerability, victimhood, and trauma. Assumptions that unaccompanied children are particularly vulnerable may obscure the ways in which they exercise ingenuity and are effective in pursuing their path to a more secure life. Indeed, those who have succeeded in travelling to a country of asylum alone will commonly have displayed immense capacity to manage an array of psychological-emotional, practical, and safety-related difficulties. Research should acknowledge this and avoid presenting the young in simplistic terms as purely passive victims. At the same time, the ways in which children may be rendered vulnerable by their past experiences as well as by the system in which they find themselves should also be kept keenly in mind. As Hopkins illustrates in his reflections on research with unaccompanied asylum-seeking children in Scotland, current ideas around ethical research, such as the importance of involving children in dissemination activities (Jones 2005), may need rethinking in light of concern about the potential for distress as a result of insensitive or invasive questioning (Hopkins 2008).

## Children Living in Countries of First Asylum

A cursory glance at the figures compiled by UNHCR reveal that the overwhelming majority of people displaced across national borders reside in neighbouring countries. Many of the nations currently hosting the largest numbers – including Jordan, Lebanon, Bangladesh, and Pakistan – typically do not grant the right to work to most displacees. Thus, even families that arrive with some financial resources are vulnerable to extreme poverty over time. When adults are forbidden to work or earn very little in informal and precarious employment, the pressure on the young to engage in economic activity may be considerable. In many socio-cultural settings the distribution of work is likely to be highly gendered. While boys in gender-segregated and socially conservative societies take on work outside the home, girls are confined to the domestic realm, acting as carers for younger children, thus enabling parents to seek some form of work outside, often with very long hours. The invisibility, relative to that of adults, that enables (male) children to pursue work illegally also makes it hard to engage them in research. Yet even they may be more visible than their sisters, who are obliged to remain at home. From the perspectives of humanitarian protection and research ethics it is vital that the experiences of displaced children in a situation of such marginalization be brought into view. For that to happen, a multi-sited approach that takes the researcher beyond the normative spaces of children's lives such as school, community-based activities, and adult-run households is vital. However, connecting with young people absent from such spaces is likely to require detailed understanding of the context, considerable trust-building, and great flexibility and sensitivity. Findings must be handled with awareness that revealing their economic activities could result in stigmatization or, worse, criminalization and the possible punishment of them or their families.

## Power

Numerous social science scholars have noted the importance of attending to power relations in research with children (e.g., Mayall 2000). As Morrow and Richards (1996, 98) wrote a quarter century ago, "ultimately, the biggest ethical challenge for researchers working with children ... is the disparities in power and status between adults and children."

In the context of research with children in settings of forced migration, attending to the distribution of power is a crucial ethical responsibility. Such distribution of power is likely to occur along lines of (relative) age, gender, "race," class, and so on. Although disparities in the power of individuals are never entirely fixed, there may be significant structural limitations to efforts to resist or renegotiate the dominance of others. Settings of forced migration may open up opportunities for the renegotiation of conventional hierarchies built upon (relative) age and gender. Displacement may weaken the basis of power – socio-cultural, economic, and political – within the household or community. Yet at the same time, there may also be the risk of a conservative backlash when, for example, parents seek to exert greater control over the young out of concerns for safety or cultural continuity (Grabska 2014). When it comes to research ethics and methodology, we might think about power in three distinct domains: (1) the power of the researcher, (2) relations among children, and (3) larger political-economic forces that shapes children's lives in settings of displacement.

## The Power of the Researcher

Article 12 of the UN Convention on the Rights of the Child states that children have a right to be involved in decisions that affect them. This has been taken as encouragement to engage the young as active partners in research – a move that has been heralded as allowing children's voices to be heard and their concerns to be identified and addressed. However, the reality is that in most societies young people enjoy less social power than adults. This basic fact has important implications for the possibility, manner, and focus of inquiry with children.

Inevitably, the power imbalance between adults and children will extend to the relationship between the researcher and young people in any given setting. In situations of forced migration, the power of the researcher may be particularly enhanced by their social status as highly educated, well-resourced, and mobile in comparison to the populations that are impoverished or otherwise marginalized as a result of forced migration. As a consequence, adults acting as gatekeepers may feel embarrassed or unable to decline requests for access to children in their care, while children themselves lack the confidence to withhold consent. Creating an atmosphere in which children and gatekeepers feel able to terminate inquiry is an important responsibility of the researcher. Certainly, there should be clarity that participation or refusal to participate will have no impact on the support offered by agencies responsible for aid and protection. This task may be more complex when researchers are clearly associated with known humanitarian and governmental actors – perhaps they are travelling in agency vehicles or are seen associating with agency personnel in a familiar manner.

For this reason, researchers need to think clearly in advance about the potential benefits and problems of any institutional association.

Researchers enjoy relative power in relation to the communities in which they conduct inquiry; yet they themselves encounter constraints and lack of cooperation on the part of local authorities – both governments and humanitarian organizations. In many locations, obstacles have arisen as a result of frustration generated by decades of research experienced as extractive – authorities have gained little of practical value, and neither have the displaced child populations they assist and manage. In many countries hosting large numbers of refugees, particularly in camps, systems of permission and monitoring have evolved that limit access to displaced children, their families, and their communities. A sense of entitlement to conduct research wherever and with whomever a researcher chooses – a sense nurtured in many elite academic and humanitarian organizations in the global north – is thus being increasingly challenged. Ideally, such constraints will provoke reflection on the purpose and benefit of planned programs of inquiry with the young.

Present-day guides to ethical social research commonly highlight the need to check findings with children involved in inquiry and to build agreement about key findings and the mode of dissemination (Berman et al. 2016; Gibbs et al. 2013; Laws and Mann 2004). This is seen as an important element of a participatory approach that seeks to involve the young as full partners and thereby reduce the power imbalance between children and researchers. However, the process entailed may take considerable time, with weeks or months in between periods of primary research, finalization of findings, and dissemination. Meanwhile, children directly involved may have moved on to a new location or even a new country. There is no direct remedy for this. However, the involvement of a "contact group" of children, including those from the same community who were not involved in the original research, may go some way toward ensuring that the perspectives of young people are embraced throughout and inform the content and form of outcomes.

## Power Relations among Children

While the imbalances of power that commonly exist between adults and children are widely understood, there is less appreciation of the fact that such differences are also inevitably present among children themselves.

Factors of age, gender, birth order, educational attainment, caste/class, ethnicity, and (dis)ability, as well as individual personality and physical stature, all play a role in the disparities between children. Vitally needed is an approach to research that attends to the consequences for children of the intersection of say, gender and ethnicity. In the context of forced migration, it is important to also include within such an approach a focus on legal status. This has implications that are both methodological and ethical.

Research conducted with a participant group formed on the basis of geographical proximity or involvement in the same institutions, such as a school, may engage children with different legal statuses. A group formed at random might include children with full citizenship, others who have leave to remain, and some awaiting the outcome of an asylum application. Such differences in legal status may translate into differences in social status, with significant implications for intra-group dynamics. In a piece reflecting on the use of focus group discussions with children, Michell (1999) observes that "focus groups can facilitate the exploration of mutual experiences and identities, but this is not necessarily the case. I urge researchers always at least to consider the voices which may be silenced in the particular group research settings they employ" (36).

Children who have experienced forced migration may feel bullied into silence by citizen peers due to their lesser/marginal legal status in combination, potentially, with factors of "race"/ethnicity, gender, disability, and so on. Ethically and methodologically, it may be necessary to create an alternative forum or, as Michell did, conduct one-to-one interviews with children otherwise silenced. However, the risk that such separation may lead to stigmatization and further marginalization also needs to be considered carefully. In any case, to the extent that non-citizen children seek to blend into a new society, do they wish to be identified by researchers as "forced migrants" and thus as different?

### Political Economy

Since its emergence in the latter decades of the twentieth century, the field of childhood studies, led principally by sociologists and anthropologists, has paid scant attention to the question of political economy (Hart and Boyden 2018). Although consistent efforts have been made to situate young people's experiences in social and cultural context, a tradition of inquiry into the manner in which political-economic forces shape the lives of children and the contours of childhood is yet to be established. The importance of making such a connection is particularly clear in the case of children in situations of forced migration. Normative assumptions about the role of the state in protecting and providing services to children are starkly revealed when young people are forced to flee from the physical or structural violence of the state or when that state is unable to prevent harm from other quarters.

Researchers commonly seek, through their work, to contribute to improving the lives of children in situations of forced migration. However, as long as the physical, psycho-emotional, and socio-economic difficulties experienced by these young people are individualized or localized, larger root causes of such suffering are kept largely out of the picture. Ethnographic inquiry, along with research that pursues a mental health or social work approach, commonly runs the risk of obscuring the causes of suffering through a narrow focus on children and their communities in isolation from the forces that provoke and sustain displacement, in turn producing harm, poverty, and marginalization. How, for example, might we situate the conditions of children's lives in relation to the failure of Western nations to uphold their stated commitment, through the 2018 *Global Compact on Refugees*, to share the "burden" of hosting displaced populations? Huge numbers of children are warehoused with their families in countries of first asylum that lack the resources to ensure their basic rights. Meanwhile, wealthy countries close their borders to all but a tiny number. What are the forces that keep children in such dire circumstances? Who profits from this situation, and who has the power, if not the political will, to change it? Situating research in such a manner that brings together the local, the national, and the global is a methodological challenge. But I would argue that it is also a fundamentally ethical one as well.

## Conclusion

In this chapter I have chosen not to centre discussion on the core themes of ethical research such as confidentiality, anonymity, and informed consent, which are ubiquitous within pre-fieldwork approval processes in academia. Instead, my focus has been largely upon the dynamics of displacement and the specific ethical and methodological issues that may arise when undertaking inquiry with and about children in situations of forced migration. While this discussion may be helpful to those completing ethics forms, my aim has been to encourage reflexivity throughout the life of a research project – from design to dissemination. No one can anticipate and provide a detailed guide to all of the dilemmas that might potentially emerge through the life of a project. However, we can each continue to develop our sensitivity to the issues and problems that may arise, while building our capacity to respond in a timely and appropriate manner. Sometimes it may feel that the difficulties of working with children in situations of forced migration are insurmountable and that the possibility of doing harm is too great. Such feelings, I would suggest, are healthy when they cause us to ask ourselves whether we are conducting our inquiry in a manner that safeguards the children on whom we seek to focus, along with their families and communities.

NOTE

1　UK Department of Business, Energy and Industrial Strategy, UK *Strategy for the Global Challenges Research Fund (GCRF)*, 2017, 2. https://www.ukri.org/files/legacy/research/gcrf-strategy-june-2017.

REFERENCES

Alderson, P., and G. Morrow. 2011. *The Ethics of Research with Children and Young People*. London: SAGE.

Beazley, H., S. Bessell, J. Ennew, and R. Waterson. 2009. "The Right to Be Properly Researched: Research with Children in a Messy, Real World." *Children's Geographies* 7, no. 4: 365–78.

Berman, G., J. Hart, D. O'Mathúna, E. Mattellone, A. Potts, C. O'Kane, J. Shusterman, and T. Tanner. 2016. *What We Know about Ethical Research Involving Children in Humanitarian Settings: An Overview of Principles, the Literature, and Case Studies*. Florence: UNICEF Innocenti Centre. https://www.oecd-ilibrary.org/docserver/ce5b9789-en.pdf.

Boyden, J. 2004. "Anthropology under Fire: Ethics, Researchers, and Children in War." In *Children and Youth on the Front Line*, edited by J. Boyden, and J. de Berry, 237–58. Oxford: Berghahn Books.

Boyden, J., and J. Hart. 2007. "The Statelessness of the World's Children." *Children and Society* 21, no. 4: 237–48.

Clark-Kazak, C. 2017. "Ethical Considerations: Research with People in Situations of Forced Migration." *Refuge* 33, no. 2: 11–17.

de Ruijter de Wildt, L., and J. Murk. 2014. "The Right to Be Heard and Participation of Unaccompanied Children: A Tool to Support the Collection of Children's Views on Protection and Reception Services." Stockholm: Save the Children. http://www.connectproject.eu/PDF/CONNECT-NLD_Tool1.pdf.

Evans, R. 2012. "Towards a Creative Synthesis of Participant Observation and Participatory Research: Reflections on Doing Research *with* and *on* Young Bhutanese Refugees in Nepal." *Childhood* 20, no. 2: 169–184.

Farrell, A., ed. 2005. *Ethical Research with Children*. Maidenhead: Open University Press.

Ghorashi, H. 2008. "Giving Silence a Chance: The Importance of Life Stories for Research on Refugees." *Journal of Refugee Studies* 21, no. 1: 117–32.

Gibbs, L., C. Mutch, P. O'Connor, and C. MacDougall. 2013. "Research with, by, for and about Children: Lessons from Disaster Contexts." *Global Studies of Childhood* 3, no. 2: 129–41.

Goodman, J. 2004. "Coping with Trauma and Hardship among Unaccompanied Refugee Youths from Sudan." *Qualitative Health Research* 14, no. 9: 1177–96.

Grabska, K. 2014. *Gender, Identity, and Home: Nuer Repatriation to Southern Sudan*. Oxford: James Currey.

Hammond, L. 2014. "'Voluntary' Repatriation and Reintegration." In *Oxford Handbook of Refugee and Forced Migration Studies*, edited by E. Fiddian-Qasmiyeh, G. Loescher, K. Long, and N. Sigona, 499–511. Oxford: Oxford University Press.

Hart, J. 2012. "The Ethics of Research with Children in Situations of Political Violence." In *Cross-Cultural Child Research: Ethical Challenges*, edited by H. Fossheim. Oslo: Norwegian National Committee for Research Ethics in the Social Sciences and Humanities (NESH).

– 2021. "Humanitarianism in Principle and Practice" In *Handbook on the Governance and Politics of Migration*, edited by E. Carmel, K. Lenner, and R. Paul, 98-109 Cheltenham: Edward Elgar.

Hart, J., and J. Boyden 2018. "Childhood (Re)materialized: Bringing Political-Economy into the Field." In *Reimagining Childhood Studies*, edited by S. Spyrou, R. Rosen, and D. Cook. 75-90 London: Bloomsbury Academic.

Hart, J., A. Galappatti, J. Boyden, and M. Armstrong. 2007. "Participatory Tools for Evaluating Psychosocial Work with Children in Areas of Armed Conflict: A Pilot in Eastern Sri Lanka." *Intervention: International Journal of Mental Health, Psychosocial Work, and Counselling in Areas of Armed Conflict* 5, no. 1: 41–60.

Hinton, R. 2000. "Seen but Not Heard: Refugee Children and Models for Intervention." In *Abandoned Children*, edited by C. Panter-Brick and M. Smith, 199–212. Cambridge: Cambridge University Press.

Hopkins, P. 2008. "Ethical Issues in Research with Unaccompanied Asylum-Seeking Children." *Children's Geographies* 6, no. 1: 37–48.

Jones, A. 2005. "Involving Children and Young People as Researchers." In *Doing Research with Children and Young People*, edited by S. Fraser, V. Lewis, S. Ding, M. Kellett, and C. Robinson. London: SAGE.

Laws, S., and G. Mann. 2004. *So You Want to Involve Children in Research? A Toolkit Supporting Children's Meaningful and Ethical Participation in Research Relating to Violence against Children*. Sweden: Save the Children.

Mayall, B. 2000. "Conversations with Children: Working with Generational Issues." In *Research with Children: Perspectives and Practices*, edited by P. Christensen and A. James, 120–35 Abingdon: Falmer Press.

Michell, L. 1999. "Combining Focus Groups and Interviews: Telling How It Is; Telling How It Feels." In *Developing Focus Group Research: Politics, Theory, and Practice*, edited by R.S. Barbour and J. Kitzinger. London: SAGE.

Miller, K., H. Kushner, J. McCall, Z. Martell, and M. Kulkarni. 2008. "Growing Up in Exile: Psychosocial Challenges Facing Refugee Youth in the United States." In *Years of Conflict: Adolescence, Political Violence and Displacement*, edited by J. Hart, 58–86. Oxford: Berghaan Books.

Morrow, V., and M. Richards. 1996. "The Ethics of Social Research with Children: An Overview." *Children and Society* 10: 90–105.

Stefansson, A. 2006. "Homes in the Making: Property Restitution, Refugee Return, and Senses of Belonging in a Post-War Bosnian Town." *International Migration* 44, no. 3: 115–37.

Temple, B., and R. Moran, eds. 2006. *Doing Research with Refugees: Issues and Guidelines*. Bristol: The Policy Press

UNHCR. 2019. *Global Trends: Forced Displacement in 2018*. Geneva. https://www.unhcr.org/uk/statistics/unhcrstats/5d08d7ee7/unhcr-global-trends-2018.html.

# 5

## Modalities of Knowing in Difficult Circumstances: *Methodological and Ethical Parameters of Engagement with Southern/South Sudanese Residing in the Capital of Sudan*

Azza Ahmed Abdel Aziz

This chapter contends with some methodological challenges related to conducting longitudinal research with Southern/South Sudanese interlocutors
about the quest for health and well-being.[1] Within this initial endeavour
during doctoral research, I explored experiences of internal displacement
and identity formation among Southern Sudanese people who had relocated
to Khartoum, the capital of Sudan. This venture elucidated how therapeutic
events and therapeutic sites were integral to the process of knowledge production. It demonstrated that the structural relationships among space, illness, and identity within Khartoum were continually being challenged and
reworked through new forms of therapeutic practice through which people
remade the city, overcame the difficulties of displacement, and moved toward remediation. This often involved adopting new beliefs, about the nature of healing that replaced or called into question pre-existing beliefs and
practices. In this context people used therapy and narrative creativity to craft
new ways of being, belief, and self-understanding in their quest for health
in the context of displacement.

The project involved an ethnographic analysis of formal and informal
therapeutic spaces, through close relationships with patients and healers
who were willing to share their experiences and practices, as well as within
residential neighbourhoods that are marginalized and therefore allow healing practices that are not sanctioned in the city centre (which represents the
locus of power and social practices perceived as superior, as will be elabo-
rated further down).

Internally displaced persons (IDPS) in Sudan confront different forms of marginalization in circumstances that are difficult and that present in two significant ways. First, they relate to the status of Southern Sudanese in Khartoum as displaced people considered superfluous both by the state and the by wider society (Abdel Aziz 2018; Denis 2005). Thus, Southerners have to navigate a city that imposes different levels of alterity on them and that is predominantly reluctant to recognize their heterogeneous socio-cultural identifications. Second, they evoke a binary between a historically dominant hegemonic northern culture and a southern one.

Northern culture permeates Khartoum – which is imbued with the dominant and hegemonic cultural signifiers of northern/central riverine (Nile Valley) Sudan – even while, paradoxically, that city provides the locus of refuge and protection for Southerners. Ideally, this capital city should have offered the same opportunities for socio-economic advancement and cultural expression to all Sudanese citizens on an equal basis, but it failed to do so. As a consequence, it was ravaged by the differences between the diverse population groups that inhabited it. Under such circumstances, populations that did not share or adhere to the dominant frameworks, be they cultural (ethnicity, religion, cultural practices, and so on) or structural (class privilege), associated with Northern Sudan found themselves having to negotiate those frameworks, which meant either embracing or rejecting them according to specific circumstances and situations that arose in their everyday lives in the city.

In 2011, Sudan divided into two separate countries: Sudan and South Sudan. These contextual elements impinge directly on the aims of this chapter. Therefore, this piece equally addresses some of the key challenges related to research methods that I, a Northern Sudanese researcher who is a woman,[2] have faced conducting longitudinal research with Southern/South Sudanese interlocutors. Thus, this chapter equally addresses methodological forays with South Sudanese while they continue to reside in Khartoum and to maintain a special relationship to the rump country of which they were no longer citizens.

## The Parameters of Inquiry and Ethical Theorizations

Sudan is a highly contested country, and many of its challenges manifest themselves in various forms of violence that have informed its construction as a state. These disturbances are largely tied to historical processes that were tied to the Islamo-Arabization (Hassan 1967; Spaulding 1985) of the country's north and central regions, which eventually exerted cultural and economic hegemony. This resulted in unequal development (Young 2018), which fed a "war of visions" (Deng 1995) regarding how Sudan should be defined and which cultural signifiers should govern its formation as a nation that includes all members of its diverse populations in an equitable fashion given that it had been assembled from diverse cultural, linguistic, and social structures. These cleavages manifested themselves clearly through the two civil wars between the north – the locus of Sudan's central government – and the south (Khalid 2003). This eventually led to the splitting of Sudan.

During the initial phase of field work highlighted here (2003–11), the 1.8 to 2 million Southerners living in Khartoum as IDPs (Pérouse de Montclos 2001, 7) were subjected to control by the state in its attempts to implement its Islamic ethos (civilizational project/*mashru al hadari*) (Simone 1994). Despite their presence in Khartoum in such large numbers, Southern IDPs were subjected to "structural invisibility" (Turner 1967, 98, 99). As an undifferentiated mass, their socio-cultural allegiances did not have a place within the valued structuring order of Khartoum society.

For the most part, long-time residents of Khartoum did not question the fact that its dominant culture (Abu Sin and Davies 1991; Wani 2006) was simply one among various possibilities. Thus its socio-cultural signifiers remained largely unarticulated to others arriving from outside. Furthermore, IDPs' frames of reference were not attended to by the hosting society, and no active dialogue developed between different life-worlds.

Long before the government and the Sudan People's Liberation Movement (SPLM) signed the Comprehensive Peace Agreement in January 2005, many long-established informants in Khartoum stated that "these people [IDPs] are destined to leave once the war is over" (interview, December 2004). Based on numerous field testimonies in this vein, these new arrivals in Khartoum were clearly viewed as temporary guests. Thus, alternative cultural manifestations remained spatially and temporally bound.

I was interested in exploring the agency of different interlocutors. Diverse groups engaged in efforts to manage the uncertainty that informed their lives, through productive force or by acting on a plethora of signifiers existing within the social landscape. Specific forms of social action and social experiences were thus enacted (Dewey 1984). Notwithstanding, I was invested in simultaneously maintaining the significance of their choices without circumventing important structural constraints that made their everyday lives difficult, and thus I was equally guided by my observations of their constrained agency. In this respect, I was mindful of conveying their efforts to tame the vicissitudes of life in displacement without overly romanticizing their agency or trivializing the weight of the challenges they faced as they exercised it. This implied striking a balance between presenting the travails they faced and conveying (in writing) their resourcefulness in contending with them. Any other approach would have ultimately absolved the state of its persecution of individuals and groups (El Bushra and Hijazi 1995; Fouad 1991; Motasim 2008) who for religious and cultural reasons did not fit the mould of its Islamizing project – a project that was being imposed on large swathes of Khartoum society and tangibly making the lives of those not invested in that project more difficult.

Both Northern and Southern Sudanese are diverse in terms of ethnicity, class, generation, gender, and religion. So it was essential not to confound the authoritarian apparatus of the state and its capillary power structures (Foucault 1979), along with the privileges it attained and distributed to its partisans and opportunistic individuals, with a different form of power available to a plethora of Northern Sudanese, who, despite variations in privilege and access to power, benefited from cultural hegemony either through the "contingency" or "destiny" (depending on one's epistemological perspective) of birth. Potentially, such populations were more amenable to the Islamic ethos imposed by the state.

Conversely, a southern Muslim minority had to negotiate the terms of its Islamic identity by less straightforward means and by conceding sociocultural signifiers perceived as contradictory to Islam. These signifiers included rituals associated with possession and those involving communication with otherworldly ancestors as an intrinsic part of the constitution of the lifeworlds of Southerners in Khartoum.

To avoid the facile binary of Northern Muslim versus Southern Christian and (more rarely) adherents of indigenous traditional spiritual beliefs, when accessing the socio-cultural worlds of diverse Southern groups I opted for a methodology based on in-depth interviews, participant observation, and multi-sited research. This facilitated the triangulation of data, thus providing salient themes, which were discussed with the interlocutors before findings were drafted. My diverse methodological orientation kept sight of the fact that I was offering only partial and "situated knowledges" (Haraway 1988), which were mediated through the occupation of specific spaces and which elucidated the workings of time in tracing some of the pathways of possibly vast social processes and experiences. Given that this knowledge was perspectival, I had to contend with the ethical contemporary duty – incumbent on anthropologists – to take heed of how social actors interpret their own actions and world views in order to overcome the problematic history of the discipline (Asad 1973; Clarke 2010). I took into serious consideration that the production of knowledge is always tied to positionality and the limits of neutrality. Therefore, this chapter underscores and traces how access and ethics are informed by gender, class, and belongings to multiple places (structural positions that convey signs based on social interpretations/conventions rather than individual realities and choices).

Indeed, I was sensitive to my position as a middle-class, educated northern Sudanese.[3] While my gender as a woman was an element that I had to negotiate in the field, I was for the most part privileged by social power. My task was complicated by the fact that the "kinds of violences in the social reality of [participants'] everyday life" (Kleinman 2000, 228) affecting the people I was dealing with were largely emanating from the cultural landscape to which I belonged. I therefore opted to centre my inquiry on an ethnographic analysis of social violence characterized by Kleinman (2000, 227) as one that "implicates the social dynamics of everyday practices as the appropriate site to understand how larger orders of social-force come together with micro-contexts." In this respect I elected to adopt theoretical and methodological tools that would facilitate an intersectional reading of the social realities of the different people with whom I spoke.

To attenuate my own privileged structural positioning, I invested in storytelling as a means to relate some of the experiences I was witnessing and also, equally, to establish a dialogue with my diverse interlocutors. "Story telling is never simply a matter of creating either personal or social mean-ings, but an aspect of 'the subjective inbetween' in which a multiplicity of private and public interests are problematically in play" (Jackson 2006, 11, citing Arendt 1958, 182–4). I was convinced of Jackson's position that "to re-constitute events in a story is no longer to live those events in passivity, but to actively rework them, both in dialogue with others and within one's own imagination" (15) and that this would facilitate "an interplay of intersubjec-tive ... processes" that were essential building blocks to the ethical orienta-tion I adapted in conducting this research.

I was aware of the theoretical portent of asymmetrical power relations and took care to apply methods targeted at enacting a professionally guided ethical position that would do no harm.[4] However, my attempt was fraught with other ethical considerations regarding my legitimacy to mediate these processes. In particular, I was concerned about "stealing the pain of others" (Razack 2007) and usurping their narratives and muting their voices.

Aware that I was working within a socio-cultural landscape informed by inequality, I looked for ways to set aside my fears of speaking on behalf of my interlocutors. Habermas writes that "the life worlds and voices of marginalized classes ... tend to be privatized by being denied public recog-nition" (cited in Jackson 2006, 12). So I chose to position myself as an inter-locutor and as an individual committed to hearing and listening. Because of my ethical trepidations about appropriating the narratives of my infor-mants, I chose to engage with the idiom of the researcher as interpreter rather than author, in this way allowing a place to be created where culture could be negotiated and reframed (Tribe and Thompson 2009, 5, 6).

From this vantage point I underscore two important methodological is-sues: first, the function of the interlocutor in being in the right place at the right time to hear these stories while also exploring why certain things are said to certain people; and second, the position of the interlocutor – in this instance the anthropologist – and their importance in creating a *transitional space* (my emphasis) through narratives that might otherwise not exist. It is indeed worth interrogating whether the people I spoke to would share these stories with one another. I tried to ensure that my questions and out-sider position would generate alternative narratives that had not been widely heard. I equally felt that this space could perform a bridging function be-tween different cultural understandings, both dominant and subordinate, in the form of narrative constructions.

## Identifying the Spaces of Research

IDPS were predominantly the subject of other people's classifications, and their experiences were generally muted. So I tried to reverse this trend by conducting multi-sited research. This was my attempt to attenuate bias as well as the risk that any discourse about displacement would shadow the experiences, voices, and views of the subjects of this study and their re-sponses to the situation.

My research took me through a range of "official" and "non-official" spaces and healing contexts. The official spaces I worked in were the Khar-toum Teaching Hospital in central Khartoum and the Médecins sans fron-tières Clinic; the non-official spaces included various healers' and patients' homes in the Mayo district in South Khartoum, in IDP camps (Mandela in Mayo and Dar-el-Salam in Omdurman), and in various residential areas hosting marginalized populations.

The largest IDP camps were on the western edge of Omdurman (part of greater Khartoum alongside its sister cities Bahri and Khartoum; see figure 5.1 below).[5] However, I conducted most of my fieldwork in Khartoum since the tensions contained in its relative prosperity and development in relation to the other principal sectors of the city, Omdurman and Khartoum North and in the discrepancy between them affected IDPS most starkly in Khar-toum.[6] The bulk of my research was done in Mayo – comprised of Mayo city and the displacement camp Mandela/Mayo Farms – since it was located in Khartoum province. That area hosted a diversity of Southern groups. My choice was justified by several other factors besides:

a) Médecins sans frontières (MSF) France ran a therapeutic feeding centre within the IDP camp in that district. Thus this location allowed me access to two sites: the local community and traditional healers within this setting, and the aforementioned clinic. In addition, during the time of fieldwork the area was continuously being integrated into

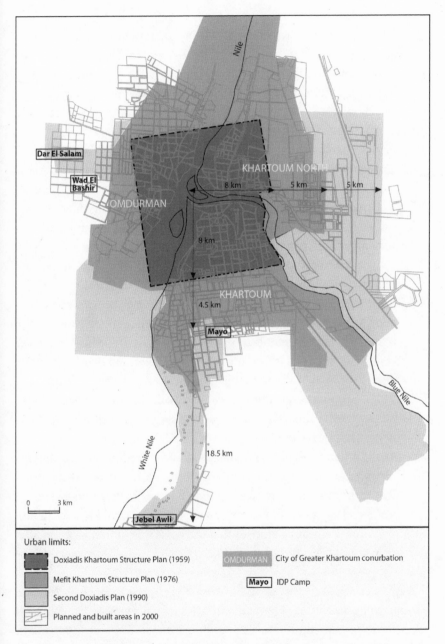

Dar El Salam

Wad El
Bashir

OMDURMAN

KHARTOUM NORTH

8 km    5 km    5 km

Nile

8 km

KHARTOUM

4.5 km

Mayo

Blue Nile

White Nile

18.5 km

0    3 km

Jebel Awli

Urban limits:

Doxiadis Khartoum Structure Plan (1959)

Mefit Khartoum Structure Plan (1976)

Second Doxiadis Plan (1990)

Planned and built areas in 2000

OMDURMAN    City of Greater Khartoum conurbation

Mayo    IDP Camp

Figure 5.1: The expansion of Greater Khartoum: the location of Mayo
in relation to the three other official IDP camps. *Source*: Abdel Aziz 2013.

the urbanisation process and a large hospital, Bashair, was constructed. If anything, the construction of this site of biomedical care in an area largely inhabited by IDPs reinforced the pertinence of choosing Mayo as the principal site of research, since it could not be argued that they resorted to alternatives to biomedicine on the basis of its unavailability. This draws attention to the need to question the significance of medical pluralism in relation to displacement.

b) I had difficulties early on in developing more than superficial contacts with Southerners. But I had made the acquaintance of an Equatorian Southern Sudanese who lived in Mayo and who was willing to introduce me to the community, and this also influenced my choice of this site. He introduced me to a key local healer who was a woman, who in turn introduced me to other healers, both women and men. The density of information gained from this location allowed me to situate the information gained in other peripheral areas of the city.

c) The area's residents hailed mainly from Southern and Western Sudan (the loci of marginalized ethnic groups). As a location, it was singular in that it was not as remote from the centre as the other areas inhabited by IDPs; it was also sufficiently close to the centre to be readily influenced by it. So it was ideal for the purposes of my study. Mayo reflected the dynamics of a society in flux – the contradictions, negotiations, and representations of marginal healing systems as well as more dominant ones – since these elements existed in Mayo side by side.

d) Since Mayo was eighteen kilometres south of the city centre and populated mostly by IDPs, it readily exposed the diversity of healing practices in Khartoum. The combination of marginalized people and a peripheral location allowed for a greater spectrum and higher visibility of alternative healing systems that the government had prohibited at the heart of the city.

Mayo was removed enough to be "forgotten" by the authorities yet close enough to be accessible. This accessibility enabled me to grasp the sheer range of clientele within this setting. For instance, I crossed paths with Northern Sudanese women who would typically have had nothing to do with the area owing to its notorious reputation for profluent vice – specifically, crime and alcohol (also illicitly provided to people outside the area) use as determined by codes of morality imposed by the state and the wider society of Khartoum. These women were seeking particular healing systems that were no longer tolerated in the centre. I also opted for this location because other groups of the displaced made their way there from other locations around the city (see figure 5.1).

My first concerns were linked to access to IDPs. This difficulty was part of the general atmosphere of Khartoum: war and displacement were sensitive topics in the city, and this made it difficult to pose direct questions about them to Southern IDPs. So I began with what I term "casual auditory" participation: listening and noting conversations and comments that I heard in my interactions outside the field (asking friends and acquaintances and paying attention to everyday interactions), simulating enough disinterest that I did not interfere with either topic if it arose in conversation. This approach enabled me to convey the general mood of daily life Khartoum and served as the backdrop to the narratives and case studies I later selected.

Accessibility issues influenced the order of the different sites I visited as I moved from auditory participation to participant observation. I started my active fieldwork by addressing myself to hospitals and NGOs around Khartoum while simultaneously seeking ways to reach IDPs at the community level. My decision to deal with the public hospital at this initial stage was justified by my endeavours to locate southern IDPs within the wider social context of Khartoum. This would facilitate a comparison between their health concerns and those of other residents of the city.

It was relatively easy for me to access Khartoum's teaching hospital because I knew doctors practising there. However, this ease of access raised some ethical discomfort related to the fact that the public hospital dealt with the health needs of those who were most vulnerable. This placed me in a position of control that misaligned with my actual role as a research student.

The patients I interviewed in the wards often assumed I was a doctor. Despite my efforts to convince them I was not, this belief persisted, the result being a "forced" compliance to my inquiries that I was uneasy with; it also led to over-codified factual responses to questions (yes/no, lists of medicines, elaborations on logistical difficulties). In addition, I felt that patients were responding according to what they perceived would meet with my approval.

All of this made it more difficult to gather personal life histories, which was an element that depended on the individual temperaments of the patients. Another limiting factor was the possible number of southern patients present at any given time.

This last point did not prove to be unduly problematic, for I found a good distribution of southern patients at hospital sites. Even so, the information elicited at this site had to be supplemented by the community sites, for three reasons. First, hospital settings brought to the surface the discrepancy between official medical discourse and its practice in Khartoum and the social realities of disease, but without fully elaborating the latter. Thus I would have to explore those realities outside these spaces. Second, I was concerned that the idiosyncrasies of individual narratives in the hospital context would lead me to make generalizations and assertions that would then delineate the concerns of a collective through the prism of individual narratives.

At the hospital, I traced the profiles of Southern IDPs and their health-seeking patterns as well as their areas of residence around the capital. I did this by consulting patient files after gaining permission from both patients and their doctors, conducting interviews in the wards, and attending clinics. My concern with patients' consent was motivated by contemporary/global disciplinary ethical requirements, since there were no strict and precise ethical directives in this space. Given that the information gathered at this site did not sufficiently reflect the lives of IDPs, I proceeded to explore their presence in Khartoum at the community level.

## Engagements at the Community Level

This second phase of fieldwork was significantly more challenging, since it was to highlight the ever-present atmosphere of surveillance that shrouded Khartoum. Complications were driven primarily by the profile of the population I envisaged spending time with. My first obstacle arose early during my first forays into the district of Fitihabe (Abu Seid) Omdurman. When I visited the local council to gain information about that community, I found myself being closely questioned by two young men. They appeared on the scene just as the young official I had initially met was providing me with data. It quickly became apparent that they were security agents and that I needed to convince them that my research was centred on health issues and had no element of political activism.

In the end, they assured me there would be no problem and that their questions were merely a precaution for my own protection. Clearly, though, this was a covert warning – I should be careful in the area since not all the people I encountered were civil.[7] This incident was the first of many that demonstrated that conducting sensitive research in Khartoum – within the heavily inspected areas on the fringes of the city – was always accompanied with the need to negotiate and manoeuvre carefully with the authorities.

Throughout my time in Mayo and other peripheral areas of Khartoum, my access was limited to daylight hours. I was obliged to leave before night-fall because the level of alcohol consumption in those areas rises at night. Also, most people had no electricity supply, which throws their neighbour-hoods into pitch-blackness after sunset. Fear, as well as the likelihood that security patrols would not comprehend the presence of a northerner – and a woman at that – in this area at night, led me to restrict my presence to day-light hours. On one occasion I was refused entry to Mayo by a security agent recruited from the area because it was after sunset; I was told to come back the next morning. This was sufficient testimony to how far removed the dis-placed are from the social fabric of Khartoum.

### Gaining Trust and Access

As noted earlier, I found that in public hospitals under the state's mandate, patients were somewhat distant and yet would try to figure out the "right" responses expected of them. Also, the doctors and nurses left me to my own devices, which meant that I could do little more than observe them at their work. They were willing to respond to any questions I posed, and they al-lowed me access to patient charts and files, but they showed little interest in engaging with my project.

Most of the hospital patients hailed from socio-economically disadvan-taged groups. They perceived the power asymmetry between themselves and health providers – viewing me as one of the latter – and so they did not ex-pect to be consulted.[8] Interestingly, while patients did not interfere with tech-nical aspects of the therapeutic sessions, at times they exerted some control over them by giving curt responses and not being expansive in conveying information about their "sickness" (socially recognized) experience.

All of this stood in sharp contrast to my dealings with patients and healers in community spaces. Patients here were more voluble about their illnesses (subjective experience), explaining why they consulted particular therapeutic pathways, and healers expanded on both epistemological and practical aspects of their practice. These spaces implicated me more directly and allowed us all to come together more intimately to discuss the meanings behind diverse forms of illness – what being unwell meant and how this governed and informed health-seeking behaviour.

### Gauging the Collaborative Process of Gaining Access

With this contrast in mind, in this section I expand on how I overcame challenges to gain access to community informants. As I became more embedded in Mayo, my level of access evolved. I recount how this occurred to show how I produced this work in conjunction with my informants. As it turned out, the approach I developed was more efficient than simply gathering statistics and conducting interviews (of which I did 148). The ethnographic material and analysis in my work was the fruit of a collaborative process of producing knowledge, one in which my informants were at the centre. Without their engagement, interpretations, and readiness to dialogue with me I would not have gained the wealth of information I did, and they were consulted about the material included in the text.

Even so, this collaborative process needs to be problematized: the ebbs and flows of relationships with diverse actors in the field are intrinsic to that process. The grievances of many Southern IDPs revolved around entrenched notions of their alterity. Culturally and socially, they were perceived as radically different from northern Sudanese, with the result that they were obliged to fight for their own Southern Sudanese values (in all their diversity) in the face of the onslaught by the dominant socio-cultural signifiers that prevailed in Khartoum. They felt pressure – from the state, the host community, religious institutions, medical institutions, and international organizations and NGOs – to embrace a multitude of hegemonic discourses that they had not authored, though they lived under them.

So this process of eliciting the perspectives of Southern IDPs was characterized by moments of tension: when informants showed reluctance to
talk to me as a northerner, when they expressed their anger at their poverty
and the dearth of programs to alleviate it, when they railed against being
unacknowledged and unheard, and when their core socio-cultural identities remained submerged. But at the same time, all of this eventually allowed me to attract the testimony of diverse Southern IDPs – to frame this
status of displacement in Khartoum in ways that related to their concerns
and dilemmas.

My access to the community was informed by multiple factors that
emerged through multiple spaces and social variables, such as my ethnicity,
education, gender, and even personal affinity and trust (categories set and
interpreted by my informants characterizing how they perceived me). Over
the course of their multiple interactions with me, I had to negotiate my informants' biases and interests.

Those biases and interests extended beyond my individuated self to reflect how informants framed me "sociologically" at different stages. I needed
to remain aware that while the elements with which Southern IDPs framed
me were important, I personally was not at the centre of my informants'
concerns. Indeed, my approach provided an opportunity for me to examine
how my categorization(s) reflected wider social variables influencing the
interactions and reflecting the engagement of IDPs with their lives in Khartoum under specific circumstances of war displacement. As such, they epit-
omized a diversity of Southern voices and vantage points.

This affirmed that it was just as important to address these social variables (that implicated me) from the perspectives of my informants: their
ethnicities, educational levels, professions, genders, and personalities were
equally expressive of their willingness to interact with me, besides being
pivotal to encounters that sometimes ran smoothly and other times proved
more challenging, but that always danced to the drum of what life in Khartoum allowed or prohibited. This positioning allowed a reading of what
gender, education, and understandings of interpersonal relationships came
to signify to Southern IDPs.

It was I who had approached Southern IDPs in Khartoum, not the other
way around, and this positioned them to exhibit their own centrality in the

city – that is, to exercise moments of agency through self-definition. At times this was achieved by a refusal to engage with elements associated with systems and societal forces of domination except on the terms they set. At other times, they reflected a choice to assimilate in Khartoum, by framing the city through their own narratives and actions so that their lives there gained value.

## Gendered Encounters

While I have presented the intersectional parameters of my ethnic and class privileges, in this chapter I expand more fully on the variable of gender. Many of the positive interactions I enjoyed in Mayo were based on my gender, which helped present me as "safe," that is, not hostile or threatening. I quickly learned – when I visited households within the community – that news of northerners being present in Mayo always spread rapidly. I found that they had been awaiting my arrival since word had spread that a Northern Sudanese "girl" was conducting research. My gatekeepers informed me that pillars of the community in Mayo (healers, clinic staff, elders, those who presided over the local courts in Mandela, and members of the community at large) had already questioned them about my identity and my reasons for being in the area.

I quickly became aware that my gender afforded me a distinct advantage, since it reduced the risk of rejection posed by my belonging to a Northern Sudanese ethnic group. I was informed that presence of a Northern Sudanese man would have been met with more open confrontation. A Northern Sudanese man in Mayo was always potentially suspected of "illicit behaviour" (Northern value system) in their zone (i.e., he was there to buy and consume alcohol). Clearly, the people of Mayo were aware that their culture was more accepting of drink,[9] and they situated this recognition within their awareness of another value system that deemed drinking alcohol morally reprehensible. This engendered the hostility among my interlocutors arising from the fact that their culture is perceived as being opportunistically used by Northerners who are too weak to stand against their own domineering culture, and do not acknowledge that this supposedly "inferior" culture offers them a breathing space from a dominating culture.

In addition to that, and more contentiously, northern men in Mayo could frequently be suspected of being part of the security apparatus that arbitrarily roamed the district. From time to time, security agents would arbitrarily confiscate the utensils that Southern Sudanese women used to brew alcohol, an essential activity that provided them with a living and enabled them to support an extended network of displaced kin – no small thing in the difficult economic climate of Khartoum.

My gender allowed me to avoid being subjected to the ever-present risk of the brutality of state security agents. Indeed, I was characterized as benign, and often framed as a girl, not even a woman (see Grabska 2014). In Arabic this gendered designation as *bint* (in southern vernacular, *binaya*) implied that I was in reality harmless and to be protected and indulged. This brings to mind Butler's notion of performativity, which stipulates – through allusion to Austin's formulation of performatives as linguistic declarations that perform actions calling objects or situations into being (Austin 1962) – that through the exercise of performatives, gendered categories are created. In this way, performative speech acts "bring into being that which they name" (Butler 1996, 112).

In the field, I embraced this definition even though it did not correspond to my understanding of my gender role. I was well aware that by not resisting it I was facilitating my presence in Mayo in public spaces where there was a dominant masculine presence, such as markets. This framework also served me well in my dealings with southern Sudanese men in Mayo's public domains (Customary Law Courts that mediated and resolved local disputes, international organizations, churches, community organizations). This label that was imposed on me was not a heavy one to bear since it represented an aspect of my social identity within specific spaces in Mayo: I did not have to condition my persona to it everywhere and with all the individuals I encountered. Unlike Southern IDPs who carried their designation through a large swathe of social contexts (being defined as such by others or by the difficult nature of their lives), once I left the field every evening, I could shed the word assigned to me.

I also noted the community's widespread patrilineal understanding of the role of women. This allowed me insight into what was expected from women in the community and how this directly addressed the importance of their staying healthy. Good health defined their positions within the community and clarified understandings in the community about the importance of reproductive capacity, the relationships between women and their children, and more general notions of well-being.

I found that their need to make sense of their own lives made most of the women I visited (more than 100 households) respond to me as an ally. My questions and home visits were perceived as an opportunity to share their life narratives. They felt that as a fellow woman, I would empathize with the enormous pressure men put on them (threat of divorce or abandonment, and so on). They also expressed that it was a relief to be able to narrate their difficult lives and that doing so was easier with a woman. Some expressed their hope and trust that I would do justice to their problems.

## Interrogating and Revisiting Ethics

The issue of ethics arose mainly with regard to how I would frame the information gained from the field. My concerns about the ethical dimensions of research manifested themselves differently at the hospital and community sites. This issue had two significant dimensions. The first had to do with the information I gathered in hospital settings and how I would present myself to my informants, the patients. The second was related to the marked difference these concerns held in the community setting, where there was no undue concern for confidentiality or ethical considerations.

In the Khartoum hospital I did not have to explain my position to the patients – it was enough to tell them that I was conducting research. The researcher role was in itself sufficient to draw responses, but the quality of those responses was greatly at the discretion of the individual patients. I opted to pursue my inquiries by declaring my role as a researcher, which served to highlight what was to become a crucial theoretical question related to understandings of power. I had been told by several individuals at the hospital (a psychologist and some nurses) that if I posed as a doctor I would get better and quicker responses from the patients. Although I chose not to do so, this suggestion by hospital staff clarified the dimensions of power that medicine and doctors had in practice and the social distance between them and the patients at the public hospitals.

This impinged on ethical concerns. I was under no obligation from the hospital to obtain patients' permission before consulting their files, and I had gained access to patient files through permission from the consulting doctors, who directed the nursing staff to allow me access. When I was in the hospital I chose to apply the code of ethics, namely the "ethics of consent" required by UK-based institutions (hospitals, universities etc.). This was a conscious decision on my part, since the codes that existed on paper (i.e., the rules of the Sudanese Medical Council) are often not applied rigorously in Sudan.

Given the gulf between doctors and patients that I witnessed, I had to overcome my discomfort when attending rounds. These were conducted in English, and most of the patients looked on with no comprehension of what was being discussed. A Sudanese woman doctor practising in the UK later told me that she only became cognizant of the power she had wielded while practising in Khartoum when she compared it to her experience in the UK, where she had to explain and discuss everything with her patients.

Research ethics were of no concern to my interlocutors in Mayo. They were neither aware of the importance of ethical frameworks nor concerned about confidentiality or what I was planning to do with the information they provided (mostly, they expressed a desire to appear in my "book," as they called it). All of the information that I elicited was offered based on the amount of time I spent in the area and the levels of trust that I managed to build with different people.

### Personal Responsibility versus Ethical Protocols

I was extremely uneasy about how simple it would have been for me to gain information in the hospital setting by adopting an identity that was not mine (i.e., a biomedical doctor). I was equally disturbed that hospital staff saw no problem with this. Later, in the community once I gained access, I could have used the information I obtained as I saw fit.

These excesses of power, without adequate ethical oversight, left me deeply perturbed. This discomfort would propel me toward another line of interrogation spurred by introspection about my understanding of ethics. I came to realize that the ethics I knew were part of a cultural and academic tradition outside Sudan. This was corroborated by the observations of the aforementioned woman doctor I had encountered at the Khartoum teaching hospital.

I realized that I had a tremendous amount of leeway and limited accountability and therefore a disproportionate amount of power to portray IDPS in any manner I liked. I was completely unimpeded and could use the information IDPS gave me in ways that, however interesting intellectually, might perhaps not serve the best interests of my informants in Khartoum.

I had two important concerns. First, I was preoccupied with maintaining a project of engaged anthropology – directed toward mediating the voices of a diverse group of southern IDPS – that would convey their dilemmas as well as their agency in difficult circumstances characterized by ill health, poverty, and social marginalization. Second, I wanted to produce a text that was to the best of my ability in synchrony with the concerns of my informants and that would transmit information in a manner that would prove safe for them.

These objectives made it necessary for me to exercise my power to mobilize my decision to adhere to ethical frameworks that did not necessarily resonate with my informants. For example, I chose to anonymize the identities of my Southern interlocutors despite their willingness to have their names used. I was well aware that security was tight and ruthless in Khartoum and that censorship and political suppression were endemic.

I made one important exception to this: one informant insisted that I use their real name (which I could do without pinpointing their identity, though they would be able recognize themselves in the text) as acknowledgment of their resilience and achievements in difficult circumstances.[10]

One might question why this concern with anonymity and the ethical impetus to continue to protect the social subjects – who willingly relinquished their time and trust – remains relevant and persistent, given that many IDPS have returned to the south or are planning to do so. I witnessed Southerners leaving only to return to Khartoum after finding settlement in the south too difficult. Also, I noted on subsequent visits to the camp – over the *longue durée* – that upon leaving, many families had maintained a member of the family in Khartoum to ensure that they would not lose their dwellings and the land, on which they had been built, to other people arriving in Khartoum (notably, having fled conflict in Darfur and the Nuba mountains).

The privilege of hindsight comes into play with regard to how crucial anonymity can be, given the outbreak of civil unrest in South Sudan on 15 December 2013, which resulted in yet another mass movement. The links between Sudan (Khartoum) and South Sudan had not been entirely severed – the two countries remain somewhat interdependent owing to shared economic interests related to oil pipelines and border disputes (Copnall 2014). This has taken on added salience, with some South Sudanese fleeing the violence by returning north. As South Sudanese, they have been citizens of another country since 2011, so they no longer enjoy protection under the law as Sudanese citizens. So they may once again become vulnerable to the whims of security agents in Khartoum (this time with diminished legal rights). In this circumstance, anonymity becomes all the more timely, as well as pressing.

## Conclusion

This chapter has underscored methodological and ethical concerns – the latter inspired by professional and disciplinary vantage points rather than philosophical ones – from a time when Sudan had not yet split into two countries. It has aimed to interrogate how these concerns both withstand and are vexed by the workings of the field, and explored their imbrications.

Furthermore, it has raised ethical concerns coloured by the break-up of Sudan into two countries. That momentous event would have ramifications for how South Sudanese expressed their experiences on the landscape of Khartoum.

My research with South Sudanese since separation bears testimony to different concerns. In the past, Southern Sudanese expressed their issues within the framework of being marginalized citizens, and hence their confrontations and demands had a different tone than those that followed South Sudan's independence. Ironically, after 2011 they enjoyed the freedom to discuss South Sudanese politics more freely within designated spaces in the heart of Khartoum. It is noteworthy that South Sudanese women could now walk freely in the centre of Khartoum without being harassed about their sartorial choices or head coverings. Ironically, as non-citizens, both men and women wielded more space within the Islamic landscape of Khartoum and were visible under the images they wished to present in the heart of the city; this was instead of being tucked away at its peripheries, which is where I had predominantly engaged with them when Sudan had been one country.

But all of this was tempered by the fact that they still inhabited these peripheries. My interviews with South Sudanese in limbo (i.e., no longer citizens yet not refugees) – given the status of *wafidin* (arrivals) and brothers and sisters (Abdel Aziz 2018, 206), which did not confer any rights – conveyed changed tones that require engagements on the basis of new methods and ethical concerns.

NOTES

1  I refer to populations hailing from the south as either Southern or South Sudanese according to ethnographic temporality. When Sudan was a single entity they were Southern; after country split in July 2011 they become South Sudanese.

2  This chapter uses the terms *women/woman* and *men/man* consistently, instead of the more habitual adjectives *female/male* used in classical English writing. While this choice might appear controversial, it is justified academically by the fact that the former terms relate to gendered socially allocated identities, whereas the latter refer to biological attributions.

3  While position may be structural, it is worth mentioning – at this juncture – that it is also arbitrarily manipulated as subject to the gaze of shifting fields and diverse actors within them. In Sudan, studies observe the vantage points of other Northern Sudanese middle-class researchers (Abusharaf 2009; Elsanhouri 2017; Fadlalla 2019). Musa (2018) a Darfuri researcher who is a woman, states her social background and professional experience to authoritatively expound the role of powerful women (*hakkamat*) in that region. For the divergent positions of Caucasian researchers who are women, see Boddy (1989); Hale (1996); Grabska (2014); Kenyon (2012); and Willemse (2001). Significantly, while the American historian and "woman of colour" Brown (2017) evokes this aspect of her identity in acknowledgment of how her mentor teaches her its significance, she does not engage it in the face of the Sudanese women whose lives she documents.

4  For examples of guiding frameworks, see the American Anthropological

Association Code of Ethics, https://www.theasa.org/ethics, and
https://www.soas.ac.uk/research/ethics. Such documents convey an "archaeology of knowledge" production that is historically contingent. While they
bind professional manoeuvrings, one should be aware of their limits in
addressing social complexities. See Fassin (2010) and Tickten (2010).

5   According to Denis (2005, 93) six years after the first settlements in 1993 the
population was 73,000, and by 2002 it had risen to 200,000 (an increase
of 12 per cent per year).

6   After independence, "Khartoum" become the favoured residential location
for Sudanese educated elites, who tended to claim its totality as their own
in the face of more recent migrants. This preference led to construction of
areas such as Khartoum 2, Amarat; and in the 1980s, Riyadh linked to the
bourgeoisie of Khartoum, although it remained important to maintain
memories of an extended family abode in Omdurman as a symbol of being
a legitimate city dweller.

7   I have no inkling whether they were referring to a menace posed to me
by the local population or to other security agents, who were constantly
lurking and were perhaps less inclined to be indulgent with researchers.
Subsequently, I discovered that during unfamiliar initial encounters the
southern local population could be hostile to questions posed by Northerners, but it was not violent.

8   This speaks to the corpus elaborating the hegemony of biomedicine in
different world settings (Foucault 1973; Gordon 1988). Under scrutiny, this
monolithic edifice has been deconstructed, with the diversity within it explored (Hahn and Gaines 1985). It also appears as one therapeutic system
among others (Good and Good 1993; Kleinman 1995) Notwithstanding,
this theoretical orientation does not apply to the context of contemporary
Sudan, where biomedicine stands at the pinnacle of diverse healing modalities and bestows power and prestige that they cannot match.

9   Different varieties of alcohol are brewed in the area: *merissa* (sorghum beer),
*keni muru* (sesame), a*byad damir* (ginger), *teylibun* (millet), *lachi* (made
by *acholi* only), *duma* (honey). The most popular in terms of consumption
are *merissa* and *aragi* (date wine, preferred by northern men) and form
a good client base.

10  See Abusharaf (2009, 6) for a similar request by a southern Sudanese

internally displaced woman informant in a Khartoum shantytown as testimony to the suffering she had endured through violence and as an expression of her grievances.

REFERENCES

Abdel Aziz, A.A. 2013. "Confronting Marginality and Otherness: Knowledge Production and the Recasting of Identity through Therapeutic and Embodied Encounters among Internally Displaced People from Southern Sudan." PhD diss., University of London.

– 2018. "Customary Courts: Between Accommodating and Countering the Hegemony of the Laws of the State: The Case of Mayo." In *Anthropology of Law in Muslim Sudan: Land, Courts, and the Plurality of Practices*, vol. 7, edited by B. Casciarri and M.A. Babiker, 203–35. Leiden: Brill.

Abusharaf, R.M. 2009. *Transforming Displaced Women in Sudan: Politics and the Body in a Squatter Settlement*. Chicago: University of Chicago Press.

Abu Sin, M.E., and H.R.J. Davies, eds. 1991. *The Future of Sudan's Capital Region: A Study in Development and Change*. Khartoum: Khartoum University Press.

Arendt, H. 1958. *The Human Condition*. Chicago: University of Chicago Press.

Asad, T., ed. (1973) 1996. *Anthropology and the Colonial Encounter*. London: Rowman and Littlefield.

Austin, J. 1962. *How to Do Things with Words*. Oxford: Clarendon.

Boddy, J. 1989. *Wombs and Alien Spirits: Women, Men, and the Zar Cult in Northern Sudan*, Madison: University of Wisconsin Press.

Brown, M.G. 2017. *Khartoum at Night: Fashion and Body Politics in Imperial Sudan*. Stanford: Stanford University Press.

Butler, J. 1996. "Gender as Performance." In *A Critical Sense: Interviews with Intellectuals*, edited by P. Osborne. London: Routledge.

Clarke, K.M. 2010. "Toward a Critically Engaged Ethnographic Practice." *Current Anthropology* 51, supp. 2: 301–12.

Copnall, J. 2014. *A Poisonous Thorn in Our Hearts: Sudan and South Sudan's Bitter and Incomplete Divorce*. London: C. Hurst.

Deng, F. 1995. *War of Visions: Conflict of Identities in Sudan*. Washington, DC: Brookings Institution.

Denis, E. 2005. "Khartoum: ville refuge et métropole rentière." In *Cahier du Grémamo, La ville arabe en mouvement* no. 18: 87–124.

Dewey, J. 1984. "The Quest for Certainty." In *John Dewey: The Later Works, 1925–1953*, vol. 4, *1929*, edited by A. Boydston. Carbondale: University of Southern Illinois Press.

El Bushra, E.S., and N.B. Hijazi. 1995. "Two Million Squatters in Khartoum Urban Complex: The Dilemma of Sudan's National Capital." *Geojournal* 35, no. 4: 505–14.

Elsanhouri, T. 2017. "Backstage with 'Fuzzy Wuzzy': Reflections on the Representational Influences on Filming *Our Beloved Sudan* (2011)." In *African Film Cultures: In the Context of Socio-Political Factors*, edited by W. Mano, B. Knorpp, and A. Agina, 162–85. Cambridge: Cambridge Scholars Publishing.

Fadlalla, A.H. 2019. *Branding Humanity: Competing Narratives of Rights, Violence, and Global Citizenship*. Stanford: Stanford University Press.

Fassin, D. 2010. "Humanitarianism as a Politics of Life." In *A Reader in Medical Anthropology*, edited by B.J. Good, M.M.J. Fischer, S.S. Willen, and M.J. Delvecchio Good, 452–66. Hoboken: Wiley Blackwell.

Fouad, I.N. 1991. "The Southern Sudanese Migration to Khartoum and the Resultant Conflicts." *Geojournal* 25, no. 1: 13–18.

Foucault, M. 1973. *The Birth of the Clinic: An Archeology of Medical Perception*. New York: Vintage Books.

– (1975) 1979. *Discipline and Punish: the Birth of the Prisons*. Translated by Alan Sheridan. Harmondsworth: Penguin Books. Originally published in French by Gallimard, as *Surveiller et Punir: la naissance de la prison*.

Good, B., and M.J. Delvecchio Good. 1993. "'Learning Medicine': The Constructing of Medical Knowledge at Harvard Medical School." In *Knowledge, Power, and Practice: The Anthropology of Medicine and Everyday Life*, edited by S. Lindenbaum and M. Lock. Berkeley: University of California Press.

Gordon, D. 1988. "Tenacious Assumptions in Western Medicine." In *Biomedicine Examined*, edited by M. Lock and D.R. Gordon, 19–56. Dordrecht: Kluwer Academic.

Grabska, K. 2014. *Gender, Home, and Identity: Nuer Repatriation to Southern Sudan*. Woodbridge: James Currey.

Hahn, R., and A. Gaines, eds. 1985. *Physicians of Western Medicine*. Dordrecht: D. Reidel.

Hale, S. 1996. *Gender Politics in Sudan: Islamism, Socialism, and the State*. Boulder: Westview Press.

Haraway, D. 1988. "Situated Knowledges: The Science Question in Feminism and the Privilege of Partial Perspective." *Feminist Studies* 14, no. 3: 575–99.

Hassan, Y.F. 1967. *The Arabs and the Sudan.* Edinburgh: Edinburgh University Press.

Jackson, M. 2006. *The Politics of Storytelling: Violence, Transgression, and Intersubjectivity.* Copenhagen: Museum Tusculanum Press.

Kenyon, S.M. 2012. *Spirits and Slaves in Central Sudan: The Red Wind of Sennar.* Hampshire: Palgrave Macmillan.

Khalid, M. 2003. *War and Peace in Sudan: A Tale of Two Countries.* London: Kegan Paul.

Kleinman, A. 1995. *Writing at the Margin: Discourse between Anthropology and Medicine.* Berkeley: University of California Press.

– 2000. "The Violences of Everyday Life: The Multiple Forms and Dynamics of Social Violence." In *Violence and Subjectivity,* edited by V. Das, A. Kleinman, M. Ramphele, and P. Reynolds. Berkeley: University of California Press.

Motasim, H. 2008. "Deeply Divided Societies: Charting Strategies of Resistance." *Respect: Sudanese Journal for Human Rights Culture and Issues of Cultural Diversity* 8 (August): 1–25.

Musa, S.M.E. 2018. *Hawks and Doves in Sudan's Armed Conflict: Al Hakkamat Baggara Women of Darfur.* Woodbridge: James Currey.

Pérouse de Montclos, M.-A. 2001. "Migrations forcées et urbanisation: Le cas de Khartoum." *Les dossiers du CEPED* no. 63 (September), Paris.

Razack, S.H. 2007. "Stealing the Pain of Others: Reflections on Canadian Humanitarian Responses." *Review of Education, Pedagogy, and Cultural Studies* 29, no. 4: 375–94.

Simone, T.A.M. 1994. *In Whose Image? Political Islam and Urban Practices in Sudan.* Chicago: University of Chicago Press.

Spaulding, J. 1985. *The Heroic Age in Sinnar.* East Lansing: African Studies Centre, Michigan State University.

Tickten, M. 2010. "Where Ethics and Politics Meet: The Violence of Humanitarianism in France." In *A Reader in Medical Anthropology,* edited by B.J. Good, M.M.J. Fischer, S.S. Willen, and M.J. Delvecchio Good, 245–62. Hoboken: Wiley Blackwell.

Tribe, R., and K. Thompson. 2009. "Opportunity for Development or Necessary Nuisance? The Case for Viewing Working with Interpreters as a Bonus in

Therapeutic Work." *International Journal of Migration Health and Social Care* 5, no. 2: 4–12.

Turner, V. 1967. "Symbols in Ndembu Ritual." In *The Forest of Symbols: Aspects of Ndembu Ritual.* Ithaca: Cornell University Press.

Wani, N.H. 2006. "Reading Khartoum." *Politique Africaine* 100: 302–14.

Willemse, K. 2001. *One Foot in Heaven: Narratives on Gender and Islam in Darfur, West Sudan.* Leiden: Colofon.

Young, A. 2018. *Transforming Sudan: Decolonization, Economic Development, and State Formation.* Cambridge: Cambridge University Press.

# SECTION TWO
## Reimagining Displacement Research through Creative Collaborative Methodologies

Christina R. Clark-Kazak

In this section we have grouped together chapters that demonstrate how documenting displacement can be reimagined through creative methodologies but also through thoughtful, meaningful collaboration. The contributors to this section present innovative ways to engage with multisensory displacement experiences through sound, touch, and images. They also challenge themselves and researchers to critically reflect on ownership and representation, with careful attention to relational ethics. Their engagements with relationships and positionalities in the research process and their questioning of hierarchical power relations offer an empathetic, in-depth discussion of the situated co-production of knowledge. The result is a powerful collection of chapters that individually and collectively have transformative potential for refugee and forced migration studies, but also for academia more generally.

## Amplifying Multisensory Experiences of Displacement

The authors in this section think beyond a predominant reliance on the written word to engage in innovative methodologies that reflect the multisensory experiences of displacement and, hence, embodied ways of knowing. Rodríguez-Sánchez and Alonso-Cambrón enrich methodological possibilities by detailing their use of sound postcards and the emotions and memories evoked by music and sounds. Soğancı explains the tactile experience of collaging and the emotional value of discarded objects for people who have been displaced across generations. Similarly, Uzureau and colleagues explore the physicality of graffiti as a counterpoint to transient migration. Through film, Grabska engages participants, researchers, filmmakers, and viewers with sounds and images. As she argues, film is an accessible medium that can be both powerful and dangerous. Godin and Donà similarly explore the use of participatory photography to disrupt stereotypical imaginings of migrants and refugees as either victims or dangers.

It would not be an overstatement to claim that the chapters in this section have the potential to transform our field. Engaging creatively across sensory experiences and acknowledging the importance of other ways of knowing allows for a more holistic understanding of embodied (im)mobility. As Soğancı (250) argues, "Displacement of any form implies a disruption of our understanding of time and space." Researchers will be inspired by the innovative ways in which the contributors engage with sound, touch, and sight to evoke deep memories and meanings, as well as by the sensorial and embodied knowledges that emerge about displacement. The chapters describe and reflect in detail on these nuanced sensorial and embodied ways of knowing.

## Opportunities and Challenges in Collaboration and (Co-)Creation

The chapters in this section also engage meaningfully with epistemological and methodological questions of collaboration and co-creation. Through the collage-making workshops and the participatory art installation *the Garage*, Soğancı (254) deliberately sought out collaborative processes where "participants would become part of the creative thinking process." Grabska highlights the opportunities and challenges of co-creating films as a "less hierarchical process of knowledge production" (205) involving women with direct experience of migration, researchers, and documentary filmmakers. Godin and Donà (231) explain how *Displaces* was conceived of first and foremost as a "civic engagement project" for which photographers were invited as "authors of their own work." This "allowed migrants and refugees to move away from a 'performed refugeeness' (Georgiou 2019, 663) and express themselves, at least temporarily, as visual artists" (Godin and Donà, 239). Rodríguez-Sánchez and Alonso-Cambrón explain that the sound postcards were intended as "an active process of creating meaning that would more than likely have transformative potential" (169) – both for those who created the sound postcards and for those who heard them in the sound gallery.

While all authors in this section took seriously their responsibility to create safe spaces for collaboration, the research presented here was not without ethical challenges. For example, Uzureau and colleagues grappled with how to obtain consent to use graffiti left in "semi-public places" and with minors who had no legal caregivers. Grabska highlights the different agendas of filmmakers, researchers, and those whose stories are being told in terms of how narratives are portrayed. Similarly, Godin and Donà "acknowledge the messiness that operates in collaborative endeavours when contacts are lost, priorities differ, deadlines diverge, unequal power dynamics have not disappeared, and intersectional identify markers of race, age, gender, and class play a role in collaborations" (240).

## Representation and Ownership in Creative Methodologies

The "messiness" and power asymmetries were manifest as authors navigated issues of representation and ownership. Grabska's title – "In Whose Voice? And for Whom?" – sums up the central questions that authors in this section continuously asked themselves and their collaborators. Soğancı "reminded participants that they are the actors of the study and the exploration was not on them, not about them but it was together with them" (252). Godin and Donà (234) highlight the "politics of representation" that all researchers must navigate, especially when engaging in visual, audio, and material methods.

While informed consent is a standard procedural ethics requirement, not enough attention has been paid to issues of ownership and copyright – generally in academia and specifically in refugee and forced migration studies. Godin and Donà squarely addressed these by "giving learners ownership of the cameras and giving them the copyright to the images they produced." Extending copyright to the photographers also meant that consent to use photographs had to be obtained on an ongoing basis. In contrast, because Uzureau and colleagues were accessing graffiti that is often deliberately anonymous, it was challenging to acknowledge artistic ownership, and they often needed permission from third parties – such as government officials or NGOS – to access controlled spaces in which the graffiti was made, and to take photographs. Similarly, Grabska and colleagues negotiated anonymity and ownership so that the young women in the films could use them to advocate in their own communities.

## Embodying Solidarity

While navigating the opportunities and challenges of co-creation, all contributors to this section directly or indirectly emphasized what Grabska articulates as a "feminist methodological commitment to care and solidarity in research" (205). The affective qualities of sensory experiences lend themselves to an empathetic politics and ethics of care. Godin and Donà draw on Bassel's (2017) notion of "political listening": "to hear multiple voices of knowledge and allow people on the move to challenge knowledge hierarchies, as well as hierarchies of credibility" (234). This section has transformative potential for displacement research – not only because of the innovative sensory-based methods, but also because of this epistemological commitment to co-creation.

# 6

## Sound and Memory:
### Collaborative Reflection on Using Sound Postcards in Rebuilding Social Fabric with Victims of Forced Displacement in Colombia

Andrea Rodríguez-Sánchez and Miguel Alonso-Cambrón

> From a mountainside, camping with their household goods, Ersilia's refugees look at the labyrinth of taut strings and poles that rise in the plain. That is the city of Ersilia still, and they are nothing. (Calvino 1972)

Like the inhabitants of this invisible city, people who have been forcibly displaced from their homes and spaces of familiarity look to their past, to memories about their places of origin, with feelings of nostalgia, loss, and attachment to something they view as no longer existing, to a reality they can no longer see or touch but whose echoes still resonate within. This chapter presents and discusses a research project, its methodology and theoretical basis. But it also reflects on an object of study (which more than an object is a subject, or subjects, in a plural sense) that has existed throughout the history of our species to the point of being the origin of many traditions and rituals around hospitality, familiarity, and, in the end, sociability: forced migratory movements.

In this chapter, we discuss the development and an adaptation of a research technique known as the *sound postcard*. It was created within the research group Ciutat Sonora, in which Miguel Alonso-Cambrón, co-author of this article, participated. Ciutat Sonora (Sound City) was a Barcelona-based action research collective that existed from 2005 to 2010 and that was part of the Catalan Institute of Anthropology's (ICA) working group network. Founded by Noel García, Sandra Anitua, Claire Guiu, Íñigo Sánchez,

Anna Juan, and Miguel Alonso-Cambrón, its research focus has contributed to the creation of the field of socio-acoustics, a discipline primarily derived from cultural anthropology and social psychology, and influenced by geography and ethnomusicology, whose objective is to cover the spectrum of variables and constants related to sound production and perception. During the time it was active, the group carried out a research project called "Acústiques del litoral de Barcelona. Una aproximació etnogràfica a l'espai sonor urbà" [Barcelona Littoral Acoustics: An Ethnographic Approach to Urban Sound Space], which generated the theoretical framework on which the research presented in this chapter is based.

The sound postcards were used as an exploratory methodology to determine the relevance of deepening the ethnographic description of certain spaces in the city of Barcelona, Spain. Six years after this technique was first developed, during the review of methodological approaches for the doctoral research "A Study of Collective Musical Programs as Spaces for Rebuilding the Social Fabric of Victims of the Armed Conflict in Colombia," the second co-author, Andrea Rodríguez-Sánchez, discovered Alonso-Cambrón's publications related to this methodology (Alonso-Cambrón 2003, 2005, 2011, 2013). This led to a series of conversations between us that provided important inputs for the methodological direction of Andrea's doctoral research. These conversations made it possible not only to understand and adapt the method to the doctoral study but also to reach an agreement regarding the analysis criteria for the results derived from the sound postcards. This chapter presents the entire process: from the conception and design of the technique, to its adaptation during the fieldwork, which led to a purpose different from the intended one.

Our objective here is to present and evaluate the sound postcard methodological technique. The chapter is based on a double narrative line, in that it describes both the birth and the evolution of the technique itself, as well as the research during which it was inserted *a posteriori*. We begin by describing the initial contexts of both the technique and the research in which it was conceived. Then we detail the process and results of its adaptation to the research with displaced populations in Colombia. We end with a series of reflections on ethical aspects of working with displaced populations and on the effectiveness of this particular methodology.

## The Sound Postcard

The sound postcard technique emerged during the first decade of the twenty-first century in the context of the establishment of the paradigm of sound anthropology or socio-acoustics. Although the social sciences had previously shown interest in research around listening (Augoyard and Torgue 2005; Erlmann 2004; Feld 1990; Sterne 1990), as had other disciplines related to cultural creation (Cage 1961; Oliveros 2005; Schafer 1997; Truax 2001), it was not until the beginning of the twenty-first century that a disciplinary branch was specifically created in this regard.

Its origin must be attributed to the hybridization of proposals for an anthropology of the body and an anthropology of the senses (Classen 1993; Howes 2008; Le Breton 1997) with investigations that have emerged since the 1970s around the concept of *soundscape*, both from the French school (Augoyard and Torgue 2005; Schaeffer 1966) and from the Canadian school (Schafer 1977; Truax 2001). Its starting point is the idea that *sound* as a process includes a whole series of physical, physiological, spatial, and architectural constants and variables that can be observed, described, and analyzed, as well as – and herein lies the innovation – social, cultural, and psychosocial ones. Thus, the notion of *sound* varies, from its objectual understanding to a procedural one, in which sound phenomena only occur when certain conditions arise. Thus, a sound phenomenon cannot occur without a source emission – a series of means (environmental and physiological) through which sound waves are propagated – and a final receiver, which would include the systems of interpretation based on the social imaginaries of the territory or of the social group within which said phenomena occur (Alonso-Cambrón 2011).

Thus, sound phenomena provide a large amount of information about all of the variables related to the sound process and can be classified according to the hierarchy among the elements that interact in the process. According, then, sound phenomena provide a large amount of information about all of the variables related to the sound process and can be classified not only according to the hierarchy among the elements that interact in the process but also regarding the acoustemological taxonomies of each cultural group (Feld 1990). The primary interest and attention of both sound anthropology and sound ethnography is *sociophonic* phenomena (Alonso-Cambrón 2011). That is, they are rooted in those socially based sound phenomena in which the human being has a hegemonic role, while also taking into account other phenomena (biophonic, geophonic, etc.) that could not occur without the presence of the mechanisms of acoustic communication (Truax 2001) even if the human factor (regarding both the presence and the agency of the medium) had a subaltern role.

The aim of sound anthropology or socio-acoustics is to describe and reflect on two fundamental features of all human societies: the production of sound forms by social groups – that is, the *sociophonic* phenomenology of a social group (Alonso-Cambrón 2011) – and their listening patterns and hierarchies – that is, their *acoustemological* patterns (Feld 1990). For this purpose, a series of qualitative and quantitative methodologies for the observation, treatment, and analysis of data have been developed that give shape to what is known as sound ethnography, as well as a series of hermeneutical lines that make it possible to reflect on and give name to the knowledge thereby generated.

The sound postcard technique was developed by Claire Guiu[1] within the collective Ciutat Sonora in the context of the research project "Barcelona Littoral Acoustics: An Approach to Urban Sound Space" (Anítua et al. 2010) in order to explore the social imaginaries around sociophonic phenomenology. The technique was first used to establish contacts with potential informants during the exploration phase of the fieldwork. Survey participants were sought, after which they were asked a simple question related to the their own spatial context. The question was as follows: "If you had to send a postcard to someone you know but who has never been here [in the space in question], what (visual) images would you select?" The number of responses to the question varied depending on the needs of the particular moment, but the recommended number ranged from one to three. Then the same question was asked, this time requesting sound phenomena instead of visual images. Initially, the technique was tested only with the question related to sound phenomena, but great difficulty was encountered when the interviewees were asked to reflect on their contexts in sonic terms. That is why the Ciutat Sonora research team introduced the visual question – it made it easier for informants to then think of their environments in terms of sound (Anítua et al. 2010).

This methodology was used as an exploratory technique in the aforementioned research, in order to detect spaces and phenomena related to identity and territorialization, both objects of study. Later it was used in other investigations by the same research group as well as in the research projects of individual members (Sánchez Fuarros 2015; Alonso-Cambrón 2011, 2013, 2016), always for exploratory purposes. However, until Rodríguez-Sánchez incorporated it into her research, it only appeared in the context of research related to sound anthropology.

## Violence and Displacement in the Colombian Context

Andrea Rodríguez, the co-author of this chapter, transferred the technique of sound postcards to a different field of research: peacebuilding. In this study, she sought to understand the changes in the social fabric of people who had been forcibly displaced in Colombia.

Colombia has more forcibly displaced persons within its borders than almost any other country. They include 8 million survivors of that country's six-decade violent struggle for land tenancy (CMH 2013; Zuluaga-Nieto 2009). The nation's rich lands are highly sought after for their expression of multiple economic, political, and social interests (Agudelo 2009; Palacios 2012). Zuluaga-Nieto (2009) writes that many of Colombia's conflicts revolve around the struggle for land tenancy.

The land is desired for its subsurface minerals and fuel resources (Massé and Camargo 2012); for agricultural purposes, including cattle-ranching (Reyes 2014); for the production of illicit crops and highly lucrative substances such as cocaine (Mantilla 2012); for trafficking various illegal materials along strategic corridors (Pérez 2003); and for megaprojects with high rates of economic return for some financial sectors (Villa e Insuasty 2016). Hence Mondragón's classic statement: "It is not that there are displaced people because there is war, but rather there is war so that there might be displaced people" (Valderrama and Mondragón 1998, 58). From this perspective, displacement in Colombia is a low-cost historical strategy for clearing the land of its people.

In Colombia, two main laws have been enacted to protect displaced populations. The first one, in 1997 (Law 387), established the status of displaced persons and steps to address that status, based on a government policy to

158    ANDREA RODRÍGUEZ-SÁNCHEZ AND MIGUEL ALONSO-CAMBRÓN

help them reclaim rights that had been taken from them. The second one (Law 1448, aka the Victims' Law), was enacted in 2011 at a time when peace agreements were being negotiated. This law confirmed many of the points of the previous one and set out the concept of "integral reparation": rights would be restored by returning lands and territories, including to ethnic populations such as indigenous peoples and Afro-descendants, as well as through accompanying productivity strategies, urban and rural development policies, the rebuilding of the social fabric, emotional recovery, and the guarantee of non-repetition (Camacho and Jiménez 2013).

Under this law, the Music for Reconciliation (MpR) program of the Batuta National Foundation (FNB) was established in 2012. This program's participants were young survivors (children, adolescents, and young people) of the armed conflict in Colombia. A very similar program had existed since 1991, but the Victims' Law led to the inclusion of psychosocial treatment alongside the music classes. Andrea's doctoral research project (2014–19), titled "We Have Been Taught to Be in Company," examined how a music program such as MpR could help rebuild the social fabric for victims of the armed conflict. For this purpose, social fabric was taken as the central concept. As Rodríguez and colleagues (2019) describe it, the social fabric amounts to a network or mesh, a network of threads, interconnected pieces that are made up of human relationships, and the resulting interactions generate links in the context of everyday life. The constituent elements of social fabric include networks, tangible resources, intangible resources, experiences, and social bonds. These elements served as initial categories for analyzing the information gathered during the fieldwork.

The study took a qualitative approach, going deeper into the research question through narrative techniques. Life stories (Goodson and Gill 2011) were created by way of sound postcards (Alonso-Cambrón 2005). The research had two stages, starting with an initial, documentary phase that corresponded to the literature review (state of the field) and to the construction of a theoretical framework, from which an article and a book chapter emerged (Rodríguez and Cabedo 2017; Rodríguez et al. 2019). This was followed by the fieldwork stage, during which the methodological considerations were set out and *in situ* research was undertaken by Andrea in four Colombian cities: Tierralta, Bogotá, Cali, and Florencia. Andrea lived for one month in each of the chosen cities, and this enabled her to experience first-hand the daily life of the music centre and to develop an appreciation of the socio-political reality of each site, while she carried out the fieldwork itself.

The participants were selected based on the following criteria: they were victims of the armed conflict; they had participated in the MpR program for a year or more; they were older than ten; they had time to participate in the research; and they agreed[2] to allow the information derived from the interviews to be used for academic purposes. Parents gave consent on behalf of those participants who were under eighteen. Later, Rodriguez analyzed and interpreted the data, taking into account the categories of *social fabric* that had emerged: networks, tangible resources, intangible resources, experiences, and social bonds. A total of fifty-seven people were interviewed: students, relatives of students, and members of staff. But the sound postcard methodology was implemented only with the students and their relatives, mainly their mothers.

## Methodological Adaptation

The sound postcard has undergone a transformation based on exchanges between the authors of this chapter. The following timeline shows how it originated and was later developed and adapted.

Based on the above, the *sound postcard* technique underwent some adaptations for the aforementioned research project "We Have Been Taught to Be in Company" so that it would better suit a different population and objective (see below). The research was implemented with children and displaced families, with the goal of better understanding the changes the war had inflicted on the social fabric of the interviewees, as well as how participation in the musical/psychosocial program had contributed (or not) to their recovery. *Sound postcards* was chosen as a method because they might allow us to identify data from more sensory approaches.

As noted earlier, and as Alonso-Cambrón (2010, 31) has shown, sound has the capacity to "untie memories and feelings associated with people's history." It contrasts with the dynamic of life histories – the other technique chosen for the research – since, as Goodson and Gill (2011) suggest, narrators often organize their material in a way that is acceptable to those hearing it. Thus, the sound postcards were a way of balancing the possible lack of spontaneity of the life histories. Sound postcards are capable of describing the

Figure 6.1 Timeline describing the life and modifications of the sound postcard technique and the collaboration between the authors.

sound phenomena present in a given space-time. These descriptions contain useful information for understanding the social dynamics of that time. For the case analyzed, the technique managed to reveal the changes in the socio-acoustic dynamics before and after the interviewees' forced displacement.

The sound postcards were carried out as part of the life histories. Each person would relate their experiences from before the forced displacement, and from afterwards, as well as those of their participation at the centre. At certain points, they were invited to create a sound postcard based on this question: "If you could send a postcard, but with sounds from where you are at the moment, what sounds would you send?"

Three individual interviews were conducted with the two participating mothers and children in each city. These were then transcribed verbatim, resulting in a total of forty-eight transcripts, twelve for each city. Each participant was invited to create two or three sound postcards. It was not easy for people to talk about sounds. Some sound postcards lacked sufficient details for us to make further use of them. In the end, we selected seventy sound postcards. We opted to use the sound postcards to elicit relevant memories and to allow for the creation of the subject's "life sound stories" to the present day. In this way, the transformations in the lives of the interviewees would be revealed by way of changes in their sonic environments.

The sound postcards indeed enabled us to gather information concerning the research objectives related the social fabric of the interviewees before the acts of violence, after the acts of violence, and currently. The categories proposed by sound anthropology and set out in the theoretical section were used to analyze the postcards.

Through the sound phenomena they described, the sound postcards enabled us to understand the subjects' different networks, uses of space-time, and gathering spaces at each of the times discussed. We were thus able to observe that the *domestic symphony* before the acts of violence associated with the countryside evinced the bonds between the subjects and their environment, be it nature, their networks, or the activities that filled their time. Likewise, they revealed a kind of sound territorialization marked by a symbiosis between the sounds of human activities and those of nature. Sergio, a seventeen-year-old member of Batuta, told us that "the sounds that I would choose, would be something that I've never heard anywhere else, except in the countryside. You hear a calm silence, but it's also the sound of the birds and the insects, which is something that, I would say for me, I would like to hear again and feel at home in again, because that would be my home" (second interview, 26 July 2016, Florencia).

Figure 6.2  Link to the re-creation of the sound postcard.

The contrast with the sound environment after the acts of violence in the city leads to questions about all the changes that victims of violence have had to deal with, which are not merely geographic; they are also related to a ways of life and how people monopolize time and spaces. The loss of their relationship with nature – that is, the lack not only of its presence but also of all their affective and subjective (resources) bonds with it – signals a life change. It is clear that the sound territories the interviewees now found themselves in were alien to them. Esperanza, the fifty-two-year-old mother of Sergio, a member of Batuta, remembered, "well, the sounds of the village, the music, squabbling, gossiping, because you go from one place to another and suddenly people are nosy, trying to see what they hear or heard someone say. People gossiping, but not the birds, because you can hardly hear any birds" (second interview, 28 July 2016, Florencia).

Figure 6.3  Link to the re-creation of the sound postcard.

Faced with these losses, the families found that the musical space could help them appropriate new places where the victims could learn and make music together. Alejandra, a ten-year-old member of Batuta, told us that "there are the sounds from when people are talking, laughing, you can also hear instruments, when the teacher is talking, the guitar, that's what you hear. My favourite song is a song called 'La niña cumbia.' No, I didn't used to like music, I didn't like to dance, so Batuta has released an emotion inside me, a talent, something I wasn't even aware of" (second interview, 20 May 2016, Cali).

Figure 6.4 Link to the re-creation of the sound postcard.

These are some examples of the sound postcards and of the findings identified by way of the sounds described in each of them. The analyses were based on the information brought forth by the narrators when they created their postcards regarding present networks (human, nature), what those people did, what the narrator was saying about the situation or place they were describing, what emotions were explicitly aroused; this also encompassed changes in the tone of voice or gestures. The sound postcards made it possible to go into the changes in density of the social fabric so that we could interpret and understand the meanings of the elements thereof that were present in the postcards: networks, tangible resources, intangible resources, experiences, and social bonds.

Thus we were able to analyze qualitatively the density of the social fabric – that is, the quality of relationships and of the exchanges that took place within them. Clearly, sound postcards seem able to describe the sound phenomena present in a given space and time. That is why the descriptions contain useful information for understanding the social dynamic of the time.

The method succeeded in revealing changes in the socio-acoustic dynamic before and after the forced displacement of the interviewees.

## Ethical Considerations in Sound-Based Research

Regarding ethical questions arising from the methodology, we identified two important concerns: we were drawing information from children, and the participants were victims of armed conflict. In this respect, we took on board guidelines on research with children (Greig et al. 2007), as well as literature related to undertaking research with victims of armed conflict (Riaño-Alcalá and Baines 2011; Bello 2014), especially with children (Euwema et al. 2008; Hart 2014). As Hart (this volume) suggests, researchers should create spaces where children and young people can feel safe when expressing their wishes. Likewise, researchers should avoid traditional classifications that overlook the specific experiences that individuals can draw from similar situations.

The main ethical implications in our study concerned (1) the emotional stability of the participants selected for interview (preferably, they had received treatment to ameliorate the impact of violence); (2) guaranteeing confidentiality with regard to both the research sample and the dissemination of results, as well as proper management of data; and (3) seeking the participants' emotional tranquility, owing to the possible consequences arising from recalling traumatic events from the past.

The research participants were identified in collaboration with the Batuta Foundation, which had information on the emotional health of each participant. Likewise, the expertise of workers in the psychosocial field (social workers and psychologists at the music centres) was available, to help select the most suitable profiles. None of the research participants were undergoing psychiatric or psychological treatment. The trust that Batuta's backing had instilled in the participants was of great value. Without this bridge, it would have been very difficult to gain access to them, given that the violence they had experienced in the past and present meant they felt very afraid to talk about their lives.

Also, the decision was taken not to delve into traumatic events during the interviews, in particular vis-à-vis the sound postcards. No references were created to violent acts, in order to protect the dignity of the victims and their mental health.

## Sound Gallery

We also assembled a sound gallery as a means to disseminate the findings. However, we displayed only twelve of the seventy postcards so that the exercise would be more manageable. We selected for the gallery the richest descriptive testimonies with regard to the interviewees' sound environments, from before as well as after displacement.

The equipment included wireless headphones containing each of the postcards, along with supporting images with text in both English and Spanish. Although our intention was to take the gallery to the communities where the information had been collected, the money for this purpose has not yet become available. However, the link to the website where the sound postcards are found has been shared with all participants in the study.[3]

The gallery has been used to disseminate the research, as an auxiliary tool at presentations or in other spaces where the results of the study have been communicated. On some occasions, it has been the basis for explaining the results. In these cases, the presentation has analyzed the sounds that can be heard in the postcards.

## Participants' Reflections

Recalling the reactions to how the sound postcard technique was outlined, we can say that it struck participants as a strange request. The question about sounds took them by surprise, perhaps because they were unaccustomed to paying attention to the sounds around them, so it was unusual to talk about them. When one of the families participating in the MpR program was asked to relate moments from their lives by way of sounds, the son found that identifying them was a simple task, while the mother said it was difficult. She confessed that the idea of talking about sounds had never occurred to her, that it seemed remote. She went on to explain that in her life she only had time for work, implying that she could not find spaces to go beyond everyday obligations: "For me, too, it was difficult [to make the postcards] because as I'm used to having a photo taken and that's it, I thought that they couldn't be done [laughs]. Because technology still catches me out, I didn't think it was possible, but now I've heard it all, how beautiful it was, I liked it … But at work all the time, you forget about so many beautiful things" (7 May 2016).

On the other hand, when we recall what making the sound postcards stirred in people, nostalgia figures strongly: people remembered their places of origin, their lives prior to being displaced. It was also an opportunity for them to demonstrate their strong resilience vis-à-vis events that had driven them from their homes. Remembering sounds somehow enabled a re-evaluation, and allowed people to generate positive feelings about their lives, especially how they had recovered from difficult moments. The mother of a participant in the music program recounted that "I also liked [the postcards] about the birdies, because when you listen to those sounds of the music, it takes you back to where you called home. The little birds, the waterfalls remind me of my childhood. Listening to that, I remembered when I was a child and felt nostalgic, you want to go back to how things were before" (7 May 2016).

The sound postcards were a pleasant way to talk to people who had experienced very complex circumstances. Indeed, instead of increasing people's trepidation about being interviewed, they increased interest in participating in the research. One student affirmed that the sound postcards encouraged him to take part in the research. When the sound gallery was being configured, some photographs were taken of the interviewees. The same young person saw this moment as one of the most meaningful, for it allowed him to feel part of something, acknowledged and integrated: "I thought that it was an interview, not with sound photos or anything like that, I didn't think it was anything as cool as that … The day we took the photos, I enjoyed that day. It was one of the few times I have felt integrated into something" (Diomedes, seventeen years old, 6 May 2016).

Trust between the researcher and the narrators was important here. Overall, the sound postcards allowed calm and generous conversations to take place, reducing the anxiety that displaced people might have felt when looking back on armed conflict. Similarly, our requests that they remember events on the basis of sounds seemed to allow them a place where they did not feel vulnerable. Clearly, then, there is value in exploring innovative methodologies that seek alternative channels for knowledge creation and that at the same time allow the participants to engage in a "creative" process.

## Final Thoughts and Conclusions

In this chapter, we have presented the sound postcard technique, exploring its origins, its theoretical-methodological bases, and how it has evolved since being applied in different research contexts. We have also examined a research project where it has been used, related to people's displacement within Columbia as a result of violent conflict there. We conclude by reflecting on the changes the methodological tool of the sound postcard has undergone, on its effectiveness, and on its suitability for research in similar contexts. We then make some final observations.

Communication between the authors of this chapter was vital. Miguel Alonso-Cambrón was the first to encounter this tool. Long-distance conversations enabled the genesis of sound postcards – and their original objectives – to be understood. This allowed us to identify their potential to capture sound environments and territorialization processes. They struck us as a useful tool for tracking changes in interviewees' social fabric in terms of its sound content.

This chapter also highlights the importance of collaborative work to develop knowledge around emerging areas such as socio-acoustics and sound ethnography, explained here using sound postcards. Replicating the work undertaken in Barcelona, and adapting it for use in Colombia, involved a series of conversations to scrutinize the various conceptual constructs that had shaped the sound postcard tool. This "collegiate" approach, developed over a number of years, was of great value, for it enabled a new version of sound postcards to come into being.

The choice of sound postcards as a research tool in the field of forced displacement was motivated by the responsibility we felt toward the study's participants, those who would receive the results, and the academic community. We needed to create methodologies that would respect the participants' dignity, to avoid revictimizing those who had suffered violence. This can happen if the logic of objectification is reproduced in order to suit other people, leaving the victims in a state of passivity, without voice or agency (Martínez 2012). To place individuals at the centre of affairs is to empower them to participate in the artistic act, to assume the role of protagonist in the research.

Regarding the intended audience, this technique allowed us to convey the results clearly and eloquently. The sound gallery served as a point of departure that enabled us to penetrate both the interviewees' sensoriality and that of the gallery's visitors/listeners. This was a non-conventional way to bind the listeners to the interviewees. For the academic community, the sound postcards produced rigorous results, given that they generate both qualitative and quantitative outcomes, thereby engendering a richness that strengthens analysis and the findings derived from the sounds.

Likewise, the resort to artistic materials allowed the research to benefit from some of the positive qualities of art. First, those materials enabled expression. This was important because it allowed new narratives about experiences to be created, with an emphasis on resymbolizing and re-evaluating the past. According to Walsh (2006), resymbolizing is partly a process of rereading and rewriting our experiences. It is possible that sound, as an expressive material, favours this process insofar as it creates new epistemologies of experience. As Saks (1996) notes, the arts "offer the reader access to content that would otherwise be inaccessible ... Some things can only be known through touch, through insinuation, through involvement, through one's mood."²² Thus, the choice of methodology can open up spaces to review past experience and build new narratives. Many survivors embrace a narrative that they then repeat; therefore, openness to other lenses through which to view their experiences may be a defining element in their personal development. The sound descriptions embedded in the postcards provided interviewees with alternative narratives.

At the same time, methodologies that offered the possibility of using artistic materials enabled the interviewees not only to go deeper into their own accounts but also to explore their own creativity. Many of the participants admitted to feeling surprised at the possibility of creating artistic pieces such as illustrated sound postcards. They viewed it as worthwhile and as outside their everyday circumstances. Many of them had never had access to spaces where they could interact with artistic materials; this methodology enabled them to experience that. It was valuable for them to feel themselves to be active protagonists. Over the course of the research, they were not simply sources of information; the project offered them a place where they could strengthen their own voices, and this, as noted, proved restorative for them.

As Knowles and Cole (2008) emphasize, using art in research is not simply for the sake of art; it is also linked explicitly to the moral purposes of responsibility. The goal is to involve the interviewee in an active process of creating meaning that has transformative potential. And, we might add, transformative not only for those who undertake it as interviewees, but also for those who hear the result – in this research, that was in the sound gallery. In this way, the sound postcards enabled a re-evaluation of the facts and the well-being of the interviewees.

Regarding the objectives of the research, the tool showed itself to be uniquely capable of evoking sound in order to bring to light changes in the social fabric. At the same time, it proved beneficial for spontaneous accounts – that is, those that were less likely to be organized by the narrator. This was due to the unexpected nature of the invitation to offer a version of places or situations by describing sound phenomena. What emerged was what was expected: the sounds present at different points in their lives, and their relationships to them. As it turned out, the initial theoretical basis for the postcards, developed in Barcelona, was successfully applied to the project in Colombia. The only thing that varied was how the results were used and interpreted, and that was a function of the objectives of each project. Clearly, this methodology can be adapted successfully.

Even so, it is important to recognize the limits of the tool. The sound postcard should be understood as an appetizer, or an initial approach, to a topic. We must avail ourselves of other tools if we are to go into greater depth.

NOTES

1 A researcher from Ciutat Sonora trained in geography and currently a professor at the University of Nantes (https://www.univ-nantes.fr/version francaise/claire-guiu-533315.kjsp).
2 https://musicsocialfabric.wixsite.com/sound-postcards.
3 Author's translation.

REFERENCES

Agudelo, G. 2009. "La economía frente al conflicto armado interno colombiano, 1990–2006." In *Perfil de coyuntura económica* 8: 141–74. Medellín: Universidad de Antioquía.

Alonso-Cambrón, M. 2003. "El entorno sonoro. Un ensayo sobre el estudio del sonido medioambiental." In *Revista Resonancias*. Madrid.

– 2005. "Sonido y sociabilidad: consistencia bioacústica en espacios públicos" In VVAA: *Espacios sonoros, tecnopolítica y vida cotidiana. Aproximaciones a una antropología sonora*. Barcelona: Orquesta del Caos, Institut Català d'Antropología, Generalitat de Catalunya.

– 2011. *Sociofonía identidad y conflicto. La vida sonora de la Part Alta de Tarragona*. PhD diss., Barcelona: Generalitat de Catalunya.

– 2013. *Ambulans Londinensis. Notas dispersas a la toma de registros sonoros del Londres pre-olímpico*. Valencia-Gijón: La Escucha Atenta Ediciones.

– 2016. "O son da cidade vella. Diagnose socioacústica dos cascos vellos de cidades galegas. Achegamento inicial a Betanzos e A Coruña." In *Fol de Veleno. Anuario de Antropoloxía e Historia de Galiza* 6. Pontevedra: Sociedade Antropolóxica Galega.

Anitua, S., M. Alonso-Cambrón, N. García López, C. Guiu, A. Juan Cantavella, and I. Sánchez Fuarros. 2010. "Acústiques del litoral de Barcelona. Una aproximació etnogràfica a l'espai sonor urbà." Barcelona. https://www.academia.edu/ 1539340/Acu_stiques_del_litoral_de_Barcelona._Una_aproximacio_etnogra_ fica_a_lespai_sonor_urbà_Barcelona_Littoral_Acoustics._An_ethnographic_ approach_to_urban_sound_space_.

Augoyard, J.F., and H. Torgue, eds. 2005. *Sonic Experience: A Guide to Everyday Sounds*. Montreal and Kingston: McGill-Queen's University Press.

Bello, M. 2014. "Daños, devastación y resistencia." In *Desde el jardín de Freud: revista de psicoanálisis* 14: 203–11. Bogotá: Universidad Nacional de Colombia.

Cage, J. 1961. *Silence: Lectures and Writings*. Middletown: Wesleyan University Press. Published in Spanish by Ediciones Árdora (Madrid, 2002) as *Silencio*.

Calvino, I. (1972) 2019. *Las ciudades invisibles*. Madrid: Siruela.

Camacho Torres, G.C., and A.J. Jiménez Ramírez. 2013. *Alcance real de la ley de víctimas frente al desplazamiento forzado*. MA thesis, Universidad Católica, Colombia.

Classen, C. 1993. *Worlds of Sense: Exploring the Senses in History and Across Cultures*. London and New York: Routledge.

Erlmann, V. 2004. *Hearing Cultures: Essays on Sound, Listening, and Modernity*. Oxford and New York: Routledge.

Euwema, M., D. De Graaff, and A. De Jager. 2008. "Research with Children in War-Affected Areas." In *Research with Children: Perspectives and Practices*, edited by P. Christensen and A. James. New York and London: Routledge.

Feld, S. 1990. *Sound and Sentiment: Birds, Weeping, Poetics, and Song in Kaluli Expression.* Philadelphia: University of Pennsylvania Press.

GMH (Grupo de Memoria Histórica). 2013. *¡Basta Yá! Colombia: Memorias de guerra y dignidad.* Bogotá: Imprenta Nacional.

Goodson, I., and S. Gill. 2011. *Narrative Pedagogy: Life History and Learning.* New York: Peter Lang.

Greig, A., J. Taylor, and T. Mackay. 2007. *Doing Research with Children: A Practical Guide.* London: SAGE.

Hart, J. 2008. "'Can these dry bones live?': An Anthropological Approach to the History of the Senses." *Journal of American History* 95, no. 2: 442–51.

– 2014. "Children and Forced Migration." In *The Oxford Handbook of Refugee and Forced Migration Studies,* edited by E. Fiddiah Qasmiyeh, G. Loescher, K. Long, and N. Sigona, 383–94. Oxford: Oxford University Press.

Knowles, J.G., and A.L. Cole. 2008. *Handbook of the Arts in Qualitative Research: Perspectives, Methodologies, Examples, and Issues.* New York: SAGE.

Le Breton, D. 1997. *Du Silence.* Paris: Editions Métailié.

Mantilla Valbuena, S. 2012. "Economía y conflicto armado en Colombia: los efectos de la globalización en la transformación de la guerra." In *Latinoamérica. Revista de estudios Latinoamericanos* no. 55: 35–73. México: Centro de Investigaciones sobre América Latina y el Caribe de la Universidad Autónoma de México.

Martínez, F. 2012. El investigador social como otro. Conflicto, límites y reconocimientos. In *Itinerario Educativo: revista de la Facultad de Educación* 26, no. 59: 79–96. Bogotá: Editorial Bonaventuriana.

Massé, F., and J. Camargo. 2012. "Actores armados ilegales y sector extractivo en Colombia." In *V Informe.* Colombia: CITpax.

Oliveros, P. 2005. *Deep Listening: A Composer's Sound Practice.* iUniverse, 2005.

Pérez, M. 2003. "La conformación territorial en Colombia: entre el conflicto, el desarrollo y el destierro." In *Cuadernos de desarrollo rural* 51. Bogotá: Editorial Pontificia Universidad Javeriana.

Reyes, P.G. 2014. "Tierra, palma africana y conflicto armado en el Bajo Atrato chocoano, Colombia. Una lectura desde el cambio en los órdenes de extracción." In *Estudios Socio-Jurídicos* 16, no. 1: 207–42. Bogotá: Universidad del Rosario.

Riaño-Alcalá, P., and E. Baines. 2011. "The Archive in the Witness: Documentation in Settings of Chronic Insecurity." *International Journal of Transitional Justice* 5, no. 3: 412–33.

Rodríguez-Sánchez, A., and A. Cabedo-Mas. 2017. "Espacios musicales colectivos durante y después del conflicto armado como lugares de preservación del tejido social." *Revista Co-herencia* 14, no. 26: 257–91. Colombia: Universidad EAFIT.

Rodríguez-Sánchez, A., A. Cabedo-Mas, M. Pinto, and G. Zapata. 2019. "Artistic Spaces for Rebuilding Social Fabric: The Colombian Case." In *Handbook of Research on Promoting Peace through Practice, Academia, and the Arts*, edited by M. Walid Lutfy, and C. Toffolo, 251–77. Pennsylvania: IGI Global.

Saks, A.L. 1996. "Should Novels Count as Dissertations in Education?" In *Research in the Teaching of English* 30, no. 4: 403–27. Chicago: National Council of Teachers of English.

Sánchez Fuarros, I. 2015. "Mapping Out the Sounds of Urban Transformation: The Renewal of Lisbon's Mouraria Quarter." In *Toward an Anthropology of Ambient Sound*, edited by C. Guillebaud. New York: Routledge.

Schaeffer, P. 1966. *Tratado de los objetos musicales*. Madrid: Alianza Editorial.

Sterne, J. 2003. *The Audible Past: Cultural Origins of Sound Reproduction*. Durham: Duke University Press.

Truax, B. (1984) 2001. *Acoustic Communication*. Norwood: Ablex Publishing.

Valderrama, M., and H. Mondragón. 1998. *Desarrollo y equidad con campesinos*. Bogotá: TM Editores.

Villa Gómez, J.D., and A. Insuasty Rodríguez. 2016. "Significados en torno a la indemnización y la restitución en víctimas del conflicto armado en el municipio de San Carlos." In *Revista El Agora USB* 16, no. 1L, 165–91. Cali: Editoral Bonaventuriana.

Walsh, Ş. 2006. "An Irigarayan Framework and Resymbolization in an Arts-Informed Research Process." *Qualitative Inquiry* 12, no. 5: 976–93.

Zuluaga-Nieto, J. 2009. "Orígenes, naturaleza y dinámica del conflicto armado." In *Las otras caras del poder. Territorios, conflicto y gestión en municipios colombianos*, edited by F. Velásquez, 45–95. Bogotá: Fundación Foro Nacional por Colombia, Deutsche Geselleschaft für Technische Zusammenarbeit (GTZ) GmbH.

# 7

## Transient Lives and Lasting Messages:
## *Graffiti Analysis as a Methodological Tool to Capture Migrants' Experiences While on the Move*

Océane Uzureau, Marina Rota, Ine Lietaert, and Ilse Derluyn

Refugees and migrants fleeing from poverty, war, and discrimination are often compelled to rely on irregular migration and smuggling networks to facilitate their journey due to tightened migration policies and lack of legal pathways for migration and asylum (Derluyn et al. 2010; Mavris 2002; Van Impe 2000). Thus, transit migration is known to be fragmented, unpredictable (Collyer 2007), and highly traumatic (BenEzer 2002; Pineteh 2017). Irregular migrants must therefore develop strategies of invisibility and anonymity to conceal their final destination and avoid interception by border officers (Bridgen and Mainwarning 2016; Derluyn 2010; Nardone and Correa-Velez 2015). Until recently, transit experiences during the journey were not perceived as a significant part of the migratory process and for that reason were overlooked by scholarly investigation (BenEzer and Zetter 2015). Research called for more empirical evidence on transit migrants' everyday experiences and trajectories (Hess 2012) by means of multisited ethnography (Marcus 1995) and trajectory ethnography (Grabska 2014; Schapendonk 2012; Schwarz 2018), suitable for longitudinal research with migrants on the move.

In this chapter we focus our analysis on irregular migrants' experiences of immobility and transit after arrival and identification in Greece and Italy. However, capturing experiences of people on their way constitutes a significant challenge due to the hidden nature of their journey, but also because of transit migrants' shifting decisions to leave or to remain in one country (Papadopoulo-Kourkoula 2008). Therefore, this chapter introduces graffiti research as a relevant visual method for analyzing inscriptions left by migrants engaged in different forms of transit migration and shows how such research offers insights into their feelings and experiences (Derluyn et al. 2014; Tsoni and Franck 2019). We first describe the nature and functions performed by graffiti inscriptions. Here, we address the broad context and characteristics of transit migration, with a particular focus on the central role of migrants' and refugees' camps, emphasizing the visibility of transit migration in Greece, Italy, and France through hotspots, self-organized camps, detention centres, and shelters for unaccompanied minors. After that, we highlight the functions of graffiti in relation to migration studies and transit migration. In the final section, based on our own empirical data on migrant children's trajectories in Europe, we reflect on the opportunities and methodological challenges encountered when applying graffiti research in migrant transit settings.

## Graffiti Research in Social Sciences

Graffiti inscriptions are anciently known evidence of human presence in a given setting (David and Wilson 2002), so research has paid particular attention to its definition, characteristics, and functions. Graffiti is defined by Willett as an "inscription, word, figure, painting or other defacement that is written, marked, etched, scratched, sprayed, drawn, painted or engraved" (1996, 1). It has two particular characteristics: it is publicly viewable, and it is placed on public or private settings without permission (Zolner 2007). Graffiti marking in public settings has often been linked to the concepts of private property, urban governance (Zolner 2007), and thus, when written without permission, to transgression (Chukhovich 2014).

Graffiti inscriptions or drawings have been studied in a broad range of settings and circumstances, including urban places in the United States (Romotsky and Romotsky 1976; Ley and Cybriwsky 1974; Phillips 1999), correctional institutions (Johnson 2009; Wilson 2008a), sites of natural disasters (Alderman and Ward 2008; Hagen et al. 1999) and zones of political conflict (Hanauer 2004). Research has also examined its use by diverse "marginalized" groups such as gang members, detainees (Constanzo et al. 2013), and sexual and ethnic minorities (Rodriguez and Clair 2009). Studies have found that graffiti is an easily accessible tool (Bass 2006; Kostka 1974) for voicing resistance as well as feelings such as hope and despair. It allows a person to remain anonymous while expressing his or her opinion. This explains why graffiti, as a device for self-expression, is widely used by marginalized groups. As Rodriguez and Clair point out, the plain wall erases social inequalities by "getting past all of the factors – such as social status, hierarchical position, education, access, familiarity with rules, expertise, communication competence – that advantageously privilege and benefit certain members against others" (1999, 2). The art historian Boris Chukhovich suggests that self-expression arises in a context of "isolation, lack of understanding, loneliness, alienation, privation and a state of prostration" (2014, 11), all of which are often experienced by people in exile. Transit migrants constitute a particularly marginalized group due to the increasing criminalization of irregular migration worldwide and the exilic process involved in forced migration.

## Investigating Migrants' Experiences in Transit Migration and Refugee Camps in Europe

In this section, we elaborate on the concept of "transit migration" in order to identify several examples of the settings and camps in which transit migration takes place in Europe. Transit migration first appeared as a concept in policy documents to describe migrants' stay in a given country before seeking durable settlement into a third country (UN/ECE 1993, quoted in Düvell 2006). The term highlighted migrants' intentions to continue their journey as well as the non-linear nature of the migratory process. Thus, "transit countries" referred to the southern countries of the European Union as well as to countries bordering on the EU, be it with a land border (non-EU Balkan States and Ukraine) or a sea border (North African countries and Turkey, for instance). Early policy-oriented definitions emphasized the clandestine character of transit migration and its possible connections with smuggling and trafficking activities (Bredeloup 2010; Düvell 2006); thus, research critically highlighted the diversity of social and legal realities corresponding to transit migration (Hess 2012). Empirical studies focusing on social and contextual factors showed how the tightened policies of destination countries, the lack of social, economic, and legal opportunities (Düvell

2006; Papadopoulou-Kourkoula 2008), and experiences of racism and discrimination (Brewer and Yükseker 2006) produce spaces of transit migration. Several years after arrival, migrants might be forced to migrate again if they lacked legal, social, and economic opportunities to durably settle in their first destination country (Duvell 2006).

## Transit Migration within Europe

Next, we describe the diverse contexts in which transit migration takes place in Europe today. The dearth of comprehensive reception and integration policies and employment prospects, among many other factors, can lead to further mobility among EU countries as migrants seek legal status or better job opportunities (Düvell 2012). Within the European migration system, transit migration is also generated by European migration and asylum policies, such as the Dublin Regulation. As tabled in 1990, that document established an allocation system for asylum applicants whereby the country of first entry into the EU was identified as responsible for the asylum process. Initially, its main goal was to prevent practices of secondary movements within Europe labelled as "asylum shopping," that is, to bar asylum-seekers from submitting asylum applications to several EU countries. Through identification and biometric registration of fingerprints upon arrival, the Dublin Regulation also aims at tracing asylum-seekers' and irregular migrants' onward mobility to control "secondary movements" from a (safe) EU country of first entry toward other European countries. All of this helps track asylum-seekers' mobility, in part by assigning them to camps within their first EU country of arrival. In effect, those countries serve as a "buffer zone" (Bouagga 2017) or as a "precarious transit zone that works as containment area interrupting migratory trajectories within the EU" (Hess 2012, 435). In addition, European migration and asylum policies have produced differentiated "legal spaces of asylum" (Picozza 2017): there are the southern European transit countries, and there are the northern European countries that return migrants to the margins of Europe. As a result, migrants can find themselves caught in transit at several points along their journey: they can experience transit either outside or within EU territory, or they can be kept in restless mobility within the EU as a result of the Dublin mobility restrictions (Picozza 2017; Tazzioli 2019; Schwarz 2018). Some places, such as the

Mediterranean islands and border areas like Calais and the Strait of Gibraltar, have been migratory gateways from ancient times. Moreover, since 2015, urban transit hubs – such as the big cities through which migrants pass during their journey (Paris, Athens, Rome, Brussels, Berlin) – have become visible elements on this new map of mobility in Europe as a result of the flourishing of self-organized transit migrants' camps. These micro-settings, especially camps and border areas where transit migration is often experienced, provide researchers with valuable empirical insights into migrants' trajectories and daily experiences.

## Micro-Scale of Transit: The Camp Setting

The literature on refugee camps in the global south is deep and broad, in contrast to recent literature developed in the European context of migration and asylum policies (Agier 2013; Bouagga 2017; Migreurop 2012; Picozza 2017). Refugee camps and pre-removal and detention camps have become a core element of European migration and asylum policies in terms of identifying, controlling and removing foreigners from EU territory – (Migreurop 2012). In his anthropological work on refugee camps, Michel Agier (2010a) examined various types of migrant and refugee camps: (1) refugee camps organized by international organizations and UN agencies; (2) self-organized camps run by the migrants themselves, often in hostile political environments; (3) camps for internally displaced persons; and (4) detention centres preventing migrants from entering or leaving a state territory. Researchers have pointed to the continued use of camps as temporary measure to keep a particular population under control or at a distance from the host society (Agier 2013; Grabska 2014; Rahola 2007; Turner 2015). Marginalization is reinforced when surveillance, separation, and migration control considerations prevail over socialization and integration practices (Clochard et al. 2004; Rahola, 2007, Lietaert et al., forthcoming). In these settings, migrants experience a temporal and spatial limbo, with no place to settle and no certainty about the future (Bissell 2007; Brun 2015; Horst and Grabska 2015). Such camps are understood as "non-places," designed solely for transit, circulation, or holding purposes, where people have no choice but to cohabit (Augé 1995). Besides, refugees can find themselves transferred repeatedly from one camp to another as their administrative status evolves (Rodier and Saint-Saëns 2007). Several studies have highlighted the detrimental impact of past trauma and camp-life-related stressors (insecurity, isolation, daily hassles) on refugees' and migrants' mental health (Mollica et al. 1993; Crisp 2000; Rasmussen and Annan 2010). As migrants confront these difficulties and the stress often related to their situation, they adjust their daily practices to these neutral spaces (Agier 2013).

Scholars from the Babel research group on migrant camps in Europe point out that infrastructures designed for diverse functions, such as humanitarian protection and control of migration flows, often coexist in the same space (Bouagga 2017). Given the specific features of camp settings and migrants' life experiences in transit migration, this chapter suggests that graffiti analysis be used to investigate how transit migrants relate to these settings as infrastructures.

### Graffiti and Exile: Graffiti Analysis in Migration Studies

Given its nature and functions, graffiti offers insights into people's migration and transit experiences. Migrants distrust both officials or researchers, and the journeys they have undertaken are both hidden and unpredictable. Graffiti is a means for migrants to safely voice their thoughts on their own terms. Yet this topic remains largely underexplored in migration studies. In a context of highly politicized debates on migration policies, a growing number of researchers are investigating how visualizing methods convey an alternative discourse on migration (Buhr and McGarrigle 2017; Mekdjian 2017). Sarah Mekdjian (2017) extends the concept of "artivism" (Lemoine and Ouardi 2010) as a means to exert migration activism through urban artistic productions. Together with migrants' mental maps and other artistic displays, graffiti are used to temporally weaken the "established urban order" (9). Migration and exile have also inspired street artists, who, after refugee arrivals peaked in 2015 in Europe, expressed their solidarity with refugees and migrants throughout the urban landscape (Tulke 2013, 2015). Graffiti in urban landscapes, then, is a means to publicly express an alternative discourse on migration policies.

Regarding graffiti placed by migrants, why are they posted where they are, why do migrants feel the need to leave such messages, and how do they use graffiti in transit settings specifically? Few studies have investigated graffiti left by migrants, interrogating migrants' expressions in border spaces and what those messages convey (Derluyn et al. 2014; Madsen 2015; Tsoni and Franck 2019; Soto 2016). Derluyn and colleagues (2014) examined graffiti left by transit migrants held in a police lock-up after being intercepted on their way to England. An analysis of those messages provided unique insights into the experiences of migrants who had been stopped on their way. Among others, they indicated poor mental health while in detention (Derluyn et al. 2014). More recently, Tsoni and Frank investigated graffiti left by both migrants and locals on the island of Lesbos that revealed the presence of political and humanitarian voices in that border space (Tsoni and Franck 2019). Another study examined graffiti left by Central American migrants at resting places under highway bridges that provided insights in migrants' mobility practices. Rest periods were used to share experiences of the journey (Soto 2016). The messages left on the walls indicated that in perilous situations, transit migrants negotiated with their environment to exercise agency and regain a sense of control (Derluyn et al. 2014; Soto 2016). The supposed invisibility and ephemerality of their passage is challenged by their written testimonies, which turn neutral spaces into places of belonging (Madsen 2015) and memory (Soto 2016).

Research on graffiti left by transit migrants offers access to genuine and unbiased narratives about their daily needs and struggles as a community (Derluyn et al. 2014). As an ethnographic method, it offers an effective way to avoid some of the limitations experienced with other qualitative research methods. Moreover, in the general context of displacement, transit migrants may well distrust researchers and other professionals (Derluyn et al. 2014) and thus try to conceal their identity and their migratory journey, as well as how they feel about their current situation. Graffiti's very anonymity allows them to affirm their identity without jeopardizing their invisibility strategies as they transit through Europe. Drawing on the ethnographic approach taken by Derluyn and colleagues to graffiti left by transit migrants in temporary detention (2014), and more recently on Soto's use of graffiti left on highways (2016), we suggest extending the analysis to diverse migrant settings intended for temporary stays, including squats and self-organized camps.

## Functions of Graffiti Research in Relation to Migration and Forced Displacement

We draw on graffiti collected within the ambit of the (ERC-funded) Child-move project, a study on unaccompanied minors' trajectories in Europe to illustrate how graffiti, as an innovative research method, can reveal migrants' narratives of daily experiences and feelings. Our focus will be on its specific uses and on methodological challenges that arise with this method. The research project used a mixed-method design and longitudinal follow-up. Participant observation and graffiti research was applied in the settings investigated. We carried out our data collection in migrant facilities between interviews with unaccompanied minors. Over the course of the study, the researchers interviewed three hundred minors from the Middle East, West African nations, and the Horn of Africa. Drawings and writings left on walls and furniture were collected in migrant camps in Greece and Italy, where we made regular visits between October 2017 and June 2019. Additional inscriptions were found in Libya, in official detention centres where fieldwork took place in 2018, and in Calais in 2019, near the site of the former "Jungle."

## Collecting and Analyzing Graffiti in Multiple Migrant Settings

Graffiti was collected by the field researchers in various migrant camps in Greece and Italy. In Italy, graffiti were mainly found in transit camps for migrants. In Rome, graffiti were found in a self-organized camp managed by the volunteer organization Baobab Experience. Located at the time on a parking lot near an abandoned factory, the camp is a transit hub for settled migrants and irregular migrants on the move within Italy. The camp was dismantled several times, with all tents removed (Ziniti 2018).

Data collection took place in the Italian border city of Ventimiglia near the French border, an exit point for migrants. Graffiti was found at two different campsites: the Roya camp, a government transit camp ran by the Italian Red Cross, and a self-organized camp supported by Italian and French solidarity organizations and professional NGOs. Located near an abandoned industrial area, the Roya camp is composed of container units, which hold men, families, and unaccompanied minors. For access the camp, the police demand facial and fingerprint identification. This poses a considerable challenge: the migrants are hoping to leave Italy, and they assume that giving their fingerprints in the camp will subject them to the Dublin Regulation, which means that if they do manage to leave the country, they will eventually be brought back to Italy. As a result, many migrants refuse to seek shelter at the camp in their efforts to cross the border into France.

The second, self-organized camp was in the city of Ventimiglia, near the Roya River, and was sheltered by a large bridge. Most of the migrants there attempted every day to cross the border, meanwhile experiencing dire living conditions, protracted waiting, frustration, and fatigue. Pushbacks from the French border police significantly lengthened their stay in Ventimiglia. The graffiti collected in Calais were found after The Jungle and the government camp were both dismantled in October 2016. Calais remains a transit hub for migrants on their way to the UK, but at the time of our visit, The Jungle was no longer being used as a visible, transitory place.

In Greece, the second author carried out data collection at a First Reception and Identification centre on the island of Samos, in shelters for unaccompanied minors in Athens and Thessaloniki, in the detention centre of Amygdaleza, and in a drop-in centre in Patras called the "Day Center." In all cases where photos were taken indoors, consent from the minors or the personnel was required. The camp on Samos is government-run and had a capacity of 650; it was first opened as a reception and identification centre (a "hotspot"). Originally, the maximum stay was twenty-five days, but this has been extended to "indefinitely" since the EU-Turkey Agreement of 2016. The camp now hosts more than 4,000 people, both adults and minors (Greek Council for Refugees, Country Report, 2019). The graffiti collected there in November 2017 was found inside and outside containers in the unaccompanied minors' section. Before taking photos of the interior of the containers, we asked for the oral consent of the minors staying there at that time (who were not necessarily the same ones who created the graffiti). The outdoor graffiti was in plain view, so it was considered public. Most of the graffiti at the Samos centre were abstracts from prayers as well as names, linked in some cases with destinations.

The shelters for unaccompanied minors in Athens and Thessaloniki and the Day Center in Patras are run by different NGOs. They normally each host up to thirty minors aged fourteen to eighteen. Some of the graffiti in the shelters related to daily events, such as the food or the wi-fi; other graffiti expressed aspirations, hopes, and disappointments.

The "Day Center" is in the port of Patras, one of the main exit points in Greece for irregular migrants. The centre is open to both minors and adults and offers food, clothing, washrooms, medical services, internet, and places to relax. It is near two abandoned factories, where people wait to embark clandestinely on a boat to Italy. Graffiti was also collected in Amygdaleza, one of the eight pre-removal and detention centres in Greece. It has a capacity of two thousand, though it often holds many more than that. Due to a shortage of suitable accommodation, unaccompanied minors are being detained there (in "protective custody") for periods ranging from a few days to several months. Graffiti was found in the containers in the former minors' section, which was empty at the time. Abstracts of prayers and names were again among the writings on the walls.

Migrants predominantly wrote graffiti in their native languages (Arabic, Tigrinya, Amharic, Farsi/Dari, Urdu, English), in the administrative language of their country (French), and, finally, in the language of transit country (Italian or Greek). Being a global language, English allows people to share thoughts with the larger community of migrants as well as with volunteers and bystanders (see figure 7.1).

Graffiti was found on walls of bridges and containers as well as on furniture. Some migrants "customized" their tents with graffiti (see figure 7.2). Stones from a river (see figure 7.3) were used as tablets, to leave short messages.

Messages were more or less visible depending on where they had been placed inside or outside a building. In the government camps that our field researchers visited, migrants were not allowed to write on the walls. They did it anyway, or they hid their graffiti in their cells or containers (see figure 7.4). In the latter, these messages were often not intended for camp officials or researchers and were addressed solely to other migrants. In the Day Centre in Patras, graffiti were related to the journey itself: maps were annotated with arrows to point out the trip so far and the destination. Also, small "thank you" notes meant for the staff of the organization and the volunteers hung on the walls of the centre. When writing on the walls was not allowed, other strategies were negotiated to allow migrants to express themselves. In

Figure 7.1 "Time goes by so fast. People go in and out of your life. You must never miss the opportunity to tell these people how much they mean to you." Self-organized camp in Rome.

one Greek shelter for minors, the young people used a notebook to write messages to one another or wrote some small comments or names on maps hanging on the walls (see figure 7.5).

Figure 7.2 "Graffiti on a tent." Self-organized camp in Ventimiglia.

Figure 7.3 A) "My name Hassko Im from Sudan Im go Franse." B) "Your colour is like the rosey morning. A promise to meet again. I cannot sleep while you are away." C) "Nadya my love." D) "Send me to you. I will continue to love you." E) "Absence, being far." Arabic and English graffiti on stones in self-organized camp in Ventimiglia.

Figure 7.4 "Ali Sharifi 2017.11 Bad life passed." Graffiti found in a shelter for minors.

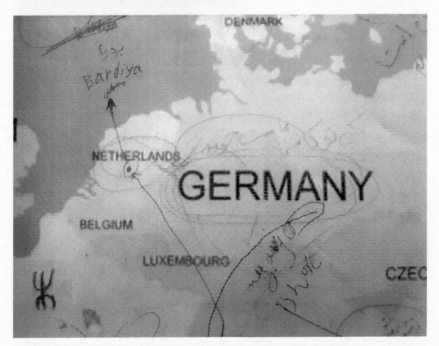

Figure 7.5 "Arrows on maps." Graffiti in the "Day Center" in Patras.

Uzureau observed that in self-organized camps such as the ones in Ventimiglia and Rome, writing on the walls or on the inside surface of a tent was perceived not as a transgression but rather as a way to encourage migrants' self-expression. Graffiti can be written inscriptions or drawings, with the latter often being drawings of country maps, flags, or characters and other topics related to exile and home. Without the author's explanations, these can be very difficult to interpret, which raises methodological challenges for the researcher (see next section).

## Exploring Graffiti Content: The Use of Graffiti by Migrants on Their Way

Graffiti by migrants have different uses and functions. Based on our dataset, we identified four main functions: a communication tool, an expression of agency and control, an expression of memories of the journey, and a means to reclaim identity within anonymity.

### Voicing Feelings with a Direct Self-Expression Medium

In the context of forced displacement and camps, graffiti is an easily accessible means of communication (Bass 2006; Derluyn et al. 2014). In a study of graffiti left after Hurricane Katrina in 2005, Bass found that the landscape served as "a message board" and constituted an "area of communication" (Bass 2006). Refugee camps, even those run by NGOs, are sometimes located on desolate landscapes and are badly under-resourced and understaffed. The staff who provide translation services are often poorly trained and lack support (Translators Without Borders 2017). Our own field observations revealed that access to effective translation services was difficult for migrants and refugees living in large camps; often, only one interpreter or cultural mediator was provided for each linguistic group. Similar observations were made in self-organized migrant camps: interpreters were often only accessible through NGOs offering legal support on a day-to-day basis. Moreover, migrants were often reluctant to share their stories of migration, owing to a lack of trust. According to BenEzer (2002), who worked with Ethiopian Jewish refugees, migrants often experience abuse and betrayal from smugglers or border officers and may well be reluctant to describe to strangers their personal experiences of loss, trauma, and guilt (BenEzer 2002). In this regard, the significance of graffiti as a means of expression and communication is found in two conflicting needs: to share personal suffering and despair, and to stay tight-lipped so as to avoid mockery or betrayal. Migrants also use graffiti to offer advice, warnings, and encouragement to the community of other migrants (Derluyn et al. 2014; Tsoni and Franck 2019). According to the graffitist Fraser, for those in marginalized and vulnerable situations, graffiti allows one to "let the whole world know how you're feeling without giving yourself away" (1980, 260, cited in Rodriguez and Clair 1999). Graffiti inscriptions are not answers to a researchers' interests or questions but rather are spontaneous expressions of feelings and desires.

## Expressing Agency in Times of Precarity and Uncertainty

As previously highlighted, graffiti allows migrants caught along their way to share personal stories and express intense feelings. It thus reveals the impact of irregular migration on migrants' mental health (Derluyn et al. 2014). During and after their journey, refugees and migrants must deal with a variety of stressors, such as squalid living conditions in camps, confinement, lengthy asylum processes (Miller and Rasmussen 2010), restrictive migration policies (Silove et al. 2000), and the invisible impact of time management in a context of uncertainty and precarity (Brun 2015; Horst and Grabska 2015). Schweizer has described the torment of waiting in such migratory settings as "having time without wanting it" (2008, 2). This sort of waiting constitutes a liminal period in a migrant's trajectory: they find themselves excluded from the community of productive citizens (Klein 2006), or else stuck in a border zone, and must find ways to contend with forced idleness while seeking ways to achieve their goals. Graffiti, then, can be viewed as a means to cope visually with a stressful and frustrating present as well as a distant future (Brun 2015), so as to regain a sense of control over one's trajectory and identity (Derluyn et al. 2014). As highlighted by Kohli and Kaukko in their study of time management among unaccompanied asylum-seeking girls in Finland, life still goes on during liminal phases and is enriched by social experiences (2017, 17). Writing graffiti fills in the emptiness of the landscape and the time at one's disposal by allowing expressions of despair, hope, anger, indignation, and solidarity. Thus, it should be interpreted as a way to meaningfully refuse to surrender to boredom (17).

## Marking the Memory of the Journey

Another function of graffiti identified by Soto, who conducted an archaeological study of graffiti left on highway bridges by Central American migrants, relates to processes of memory and remembrance as these relate to death, for instance (Soto 2016). She found that migrants used the wall to recount to newcomers the significant experience of "journeying." A graffiti inscription on a wall serves as an open archive that helps maintain the links between present and past events, besides creating an alternative narrative of them. During our field observation in Calais, nearly three years after The Jungle was dismantled, we found that painted walls were all that was left of the one-time camp. However, migrants who remembered the now deserted site advised us to go there and read the graffiti as a vibrant testimony of European transit migration history (see figure 7.6).

## Managing Anonymity and Safely Reclaiming One's Identity

Finally, migrants engaged in transit migration are a highly vulnerable and hard-to-reach population who at times use graffiti to cope with two different forms of anonymity. First, irregular migrants are denied identity when they lack relevant documents; migration officials often label these people as "clandestines," "illegals," "sans papiers," or "transit-migrants." Identity documents are powerful tools for controlling people's mobility (Noiriel 1991; Vatsa, 2011); they also construct a hierarchical relationship between citizens and immigrants (Vasta 2011), with the latter historically being treated as detainable and removable (Noiriel 1991). Second, migrants develop strategies for remaining anonymous if not invisible to migration control authorities. These strategies include providing fake identity to police (Malkki 1995; Derluyn et al. 2014). In Ventimiglia, migrants encountered French patrols on a daily basis while attempting to cross the border. When intercepted, they systematically gave fake names and nationalities to the border officers. Drawing on the case of Burundi refugees in Tanzania, Gaim Kibreab highlighted the rebellious aspect of these strategies developed by marginalized

Figure 7.6 "France Is Dog Life, England Good Life." Former Jungle of Calais.

groups (1999, 12): "Where people adopt a strategy of invisibility in an attempt to beat a policy that forces them to relinquish their customary lifestyle … they will indeed not give the impression of being submissive masses."

In a similar way, irregular migrants tend to use invisibility strategies to get around the deportability mechanism of the Dublin Regulation. They make themselves physically invisible to avoid detection by border officers – for example, they try to cross borders at night and to hide in cars, trains, or trucks (Bridgen and Mainwaring 2016). Transit migrants may well remain hidden in plain sight as they anonymously inhabit self-organized migrant camps to circumvent the legal visibility produced by government-managed camps as they continue their journey (Bridgen and Mainwaring 2016).

Anonymity is an important protective strategy for irregular migrants. Derluyn and colleagues demonstrated how they reclaim identity through graffiti – which often includes names, places of origin, birthdates, personal narratives, and feelings – while trapped in a situation of anonymity and marginalization (2014, 9). To extend James Scott's (1985) notion of the "everyday forms of resistance" developed by subordinated groups, graffiti serves as a relatively safe medium for migrants to protest and resist migration policies and border controls (Moreau and Alderman 2011, in Derluyn et al. 2014) without directly confronting these authorities and their representatives (Scott 1985, 29).

## Methodological Challenges Encountered in Graffiti Research

Here, we highlight the relevance of applying graffiti research in the context of migration and protracted displacement. When combined with other ethnographic research methods, graffiti analysis provides valuable insights in situations where traditional methods are problematic to implement. However, researchers must carefully consider a number of methodological and ethical limitations to graffiti research, such as degree of access to the campsites and the anonymous – and ephemeral – nature of these data.

### Access to the Camp Settings

Graffiti can be located in settings to which "outsiders" have only limited access, such as detention camps and police cells. To visit these settings, researchers often require authorization from local or national authorities. In the government centres in Greece and in Italy, consent to take pictures of graffiti was granted by the managing authorities. Receiving specific authorization to bring a camera or camcorder can present additional challenges. In self-organized camps, photographing graffiti required the tacit agreement of the people living there, including some explanation as to why. Many migrants in these settings are trying to protect their anonymity and so are highly suspicious and distrustful of journalists and researchers. So we communicated clearly on these matters to the migrants and the local NGO staff. This, and the prolonged time we spent with them, resulted in them accepting that we were not a threat and trusting us to photograph the graffiti. Some graffiti were on private property – for example, painted on a migrant's tent – and as a rule, the field researchers took a photograph after obtaining the owner's oral consent. In one particular case, public graffiti had been written on a wall that expressed hatred of the French anti-riot patrols in

Calais, and the migrants did not allow the field researcher to photograph it. Indeed, worried about the possible impact of the angry message, they immediately tried to erase it. In sum, the mere act of taking a picture required fraught negotiations as well as explanations from the researchers.

Translators play a key role in conveying the message of the graffiti in a language understood by the researcher(s). Working with independent trained interpreters with appropriate linguistic and cultural skills may be of great value here, to check both the accuracy of the translation and the possible (cultural) interpretation of the findings, so as to strengthen the survey's validity (Choi et al. 2012). There were no possibility for us to check interpreters' translations against the actual author's intent, and this presented important limitations. Yet translators' efforts are indispensable in this type of research, for they can provide important cultural frameworks for interpreting the data.

### Durable Marks Still Threatened by Ephemerality

The ephemeral nature of the inscriptions presents an additional challenge for researchers. As reasonably noted by Ross and colleagues (2017), factors such as time, writing over, and placement in a dangerous or illegal location can reduce graffiti's permanence (5). Also, exposure to bad weather can erase the writings or make them illegible. Migrant camps are not built to be permanent; their tents and containers are not meant to last. In addition, graffiti are often painted over, and camps may be shut down and disassembled. The self-organized camps investigated in Rome and Ventimiglia were both dismantled in 2018 shortly after data collection (Ziniti 2018). Ongoing camp evictions and demolitions can result in the removal of all tangible traces of their inhabitant's' collective memory as expressed through graffiti.

Graffiti production is a risky data collection method, since it is both spontaneous and illegal. Researchers have no control over data production. They can only seek out possible places where it might be found; that, or recreate favourable conditions for reproducing spontaneous expression through action research, participatory projects (Mekdjian 2016; Buhr and McGarrigle 2017), or art-based methods (Lenette 2019; Mekdjian and Amilhat Szary 2015).

*Challenges in Exploring Anonymous Data*

Anonymity is a core characteristic of graffiti. It serves as a shield for transit migrants' self-expression, but it also has ambivalent outcomes that are beyond the researcher's control. Researchers have long acknowledged the value of anonymity as a means to protect research participants, especially when conducting research with vulnerable and marginalized populations (Ardévol 2012; Pichardo 2008, in Ardévol 2012; Rodriguez 2003). To ensure safe participation, researchers first need to guarantee participants' confidentiality and anonymity. In most surveys, researchers gather complete demographic information before final anonymization; yet graffiti data are anonymized and incomplete by definition, except – to some extent – in those cases where the graffiti consists of names, dates, and nationalities. So we have very limited information on the writers' profiles and motives. We can assume, though, that they constitute a specific group of agentic migrants who are looking for alternative ways to express themselves.

Moreover, the topics addressed by one language group may be biased if the first writer has channelled the conversation toward a certain topic. Illiteracy can also be a factor, that it reduces self-expression to drawings that are more difficult to analyze and interpret.

Finally, graffiti research does not allow for systematically obtaining the author's consent to use graffiti for research purposes. However, when anonymous writings are left in public places – on walls, buildings, and transit facilities (Rodriguez and Clair 1999) – those data may be treated as part of the "public sphere" and thus accessible for use in research. Graffiti found in semi-public spaces, such as in government or NGO camps, on refugees' tents in transit places, or in police cells, are neither entirely public or nor entirely private (Rodriguez and Clair 1999; Wilson 2008b). However, graffiti of names and dates left in informal transit places (such as self-organized camps) by irregular migrants were anonymized to avoid possible misuse of research data to track their mobility across Europe" (Ross et al. 2017). Navigating this question required a strong ethical reflex in terms of how findings might be (mis)interpreted by the broader political and/or public discourse. Communication about findings should always consider the contexts in which the graffiti was written down and the possible impact of the findings on the wider refugee and migrant community (Vervliet et al. 2015).

## Conclusion

This study set out to explain the relevance of graffiti analysis as a research method and its possible contributions to the field of migration and displacement studies. Graffiti collected in migrant settings provides unique insights into the logics of "journeying" and migrants' experiences of immobility-within-mobility in migratory settings. Focusing on the micro-scale of migrants' experiences allows us to unravel the spatially diverse realities of transit in protracted displacement – realities ranging from identification centres or hotspots for newly arrived migrants to detention and removal centres.

This chapter also emphasizes how irregular transit migrants, a particularly marginalized group, use graffiti to leave messages, voice their feelings, state their biographies, and practise a unique form of agency. It also allows us to examine channels migrants use to speak with their own voices (O'Neill and Harindranath 2006), as well as how those voices are spatially displayed on the landscape, enabling both textual and visual analysis. These muted voices carry political significance and articulate an alternative public narrative on migration (Mekdjian 2018). Anonymity here is approached both as a powerful motivational component for self-expression within self-protection and as an obstacle to further empirical insights.

In terms of Hess's (2012) call for empirical evidence to be used to critically investigate transit migration, graffiti research sheds light on specific elements of transit such as camp settings, the politics of border areas, and how migrants manage space and time in these settings. From a methodological perspective, it opens new fields of research inquiry for the gathering of multi-sited ethnographic evidence in relation to the daily experiences and feelings of individual migrants; as well as to their political engagement with and resistance to migration policies in micro-settings such as camps, border areas, and urban transit hubs.

Graffiti also highlights the relationship between migrants and their immediate environment, thus opening research perspectives on processes of place-making in situations of protracted displacement. Though designed to be "non-places" (Augé 1995), camps become places of residence where migrants develop social practices (Agier 2013; David and Wilson 2002). As such, these places are inhabited by migrants and refugees' social experiences. Linking past and present, the inscriptions work as a "memory trigger" for the viewer (David and Wilson 2002, 6), since "even after the 'original' meaning(s) of an inscription is forgotten, the mark – 'fixed' in the landscape – participates in peoples' constructions of their worlds" (6). In this sense, graffiti research introduces an unexplored area of research linked to place-making (Bender 2001; Parkin 1999) and memory of transit places (Soto 2016).

Possible directions for further research could implement systematic data collection and analysis of graffiti inscriptions in diverse transit and removal camps. This would allow us to list and compare topics and experiences shared by migrants in relation to their migratory journey, their aspirations, and/or their experiences of hardship and support.

NOTE

The data presented in this chapter were collected within the framework of the ChildMove project with the financial support of the European Research Council - Starting Grant no. 714222.

REFERENCES

Agier, M. 2010a. *Gérer les indésirables. Des camps de réfugiés au gouvernement humanitaire.* Paris: Flammarion.

– 2010b. "Humanity as an Identity and Its Political Effects (A Note on Camps and Humanitarian Government)." *Humanity: An International Journal of Human Rights, Humanitarianism, and Development* 1, no. 1: 29–45.

– 2013. "Le campement urbain comme hétéropie et comme refuge. Vers un paysage mondial des espaces précaires." *Brésil(s)* 3: 11–28.

Alderman, D.H., and H. Ward. 2007. "Writing on the Plywood: Toward an Analysis of Hurricane Graffiti." *Coastal Management* 3, no. 1: 1–18.

Ardévol, E. 2012. "Virtual/Visual Ethnography: Methodological Crossroads at the Intersection of Visual and Internet Research." In *Advances in visual methodology*, edited by S. Pink, 74–94. London: SAGE.

Augé, M. 1995. *Non-places: Introduction to an Anthropology of Supermodernity.* London: Verso.

Bass, J. 2006. "Photographic Journal Culture in Nature: Reclaiming Place after Katrina." *Focus on Geography* 48, no. 4: 1–8.

Bender, B. 2001. "Landscapes on-the-Move." *Journal of Social Archaeology* 1, no. 1: 75–89. https://doi.org/10.1177/146960530100100106.

BenEzer, G. 2002. *The Ethiopian Jewish Exodus: Narratives of the Migration Journey to Israel 1977–1985.* London: Routledge.

BenEzer, G., and R. Zetter. 2015. "Searching for Directions: Conceptual and Methodological Challenges in Researching Refugee Journeys." *Journal of Refugee Studies* 28, no. 3: 297–318.

Bissell, D. 2007. "Animating Suspension: Waiting for Mobilities." *Mobilities* 2, no. 2: 277–98.

Bouagga Y., ed. 2017. *De Lesbos à Calais. Comment l'Europe fabrique des camps.* Neuvy-en-Champagne: Le Passager Clandestin, coll. "Babels."

Bredeloup, S. 2010. "Sahara Transit: Times, Spaces, People." *Population, Space, and Place* 18, no. 4: 457–67.

Brewer, K., and D. Yükseder. 2005. "The Unending Migration Process: Survival Strategies of African Migrants in Istanbul 'Waiting' to Leave for Europe." Paper submitted to IMILCO workshop, Istanbul, 1–2.

Brewer, K.T., and D. Yükseker. 2006. "A Survey on African Migrants and Asylum Seekers in Istanbul." MiReKoC Research Projects 2005–6. Istanbul: Koç University.

Brigden, N., and C. Mainwaring. 2016. "Matryoshka Journeys: Im/mobility during Migration." *Geopolitics* 21, no. 2: 407–34.

Brun, C. 2015. "Active Waiting and Changing Hopes: Toward a Time Perspective on Protracted Displacement." *Social Analysis* 59, no. 1: 19–37.

Buhr, F., and J. McGarrigle. 2017. "Navigating Urban Life in Lisbon: A Study of Migrants' Mobilities and Use of Space." *Social Inclusion* 5, no. 4: 226–34.

Choi, J., K.E. Kushner, J. Mill, and D.W.L. Lai. 2012. "Understanding the Language, the Culture, and the Experience: Translation in Cross-Cultural Research." *International Journal of Qualitative Methods* 11, no. 5: 652–65.

Chukhovich, B. 2014. "Le street art, un genre exilique?" Working Paper, series no. 74 – Programme Non-lieu de l'exil. HAL archives ouvertes.

Clochard, O., Y. Gastaut, and R. Schor. 2004. "Les camps d'étrangers depuis 1938: continuité et adaptations. Du 'modèle' français à la construction de l'espace Schengen." *Revue Européenne des Migrations Internationales* 20, no. 2: 57–87.

Collyer, M. 2007. "In Between Places: Trans Saharan Transit Migrants in Morocco and the Fragmented Journey to Europe." *Antipode* 39, no. 4: 668–90.

Collyer, M., F. Düvell, and H. De Haas. 2012. "Critical Approaches to Transit Migration." *Population, Space, and Place* 18, no. 4: 407–14.

Costanzo, B., M. Bull, and C. Smith. 2013. "If These Walls Could Speak: A Visual

Ethnography of Graffiti at Boggo Road Gaol." *Queensland Review* 20, no. 2: 215–30.

Crisp, J. 2000. "A State of Insecurity: The Political Economy of Violence in Kenya's Refugee Camps." *African Affairs* 99, no. 397: 601–32.

David, B., and M. Wilson, eds. 2002. *Inscribed Landscapes: Marking and Making Place*. Honolulu: University of Hawai'i Press.

Derluyn, I., V. Lippens, T. Verachtert, W. Bruggeman, and E. Broekaert. 2010. "Minors Travelling Alone: A Risk Group for Human Trafficking?" *International Migration* 48, no. 4: 164–85.

Derluyn, I., C. Watters, C. Mels, and E. Broekaert. 2014. "'We Are All the Same, Coz Exist Only One Earth, Why the BORDER EXIST': Messages of Migrants on Their Way." *Journal of Refugee Studies* 27, no. 1 (March): 1–20.

Düvell, F. 2006. "Crossing the Fringes of Europe: Transit Migration in the EU's Neighbourhood." Oxford: Centre on Migration, Policy and Society.

– 2012. "Transit Migration: A Blurred and Politicised Concept." *Population, Space, and Place* 18, no. 4: 415–27.

Grabska, K. 2014. *Gender, Identity, and Home: Nuer Repatriation to Southern Sudan*. Melton: James Currey.

Greek Council for Refugees. 2019. *Report on Asylum in Greece*. March. https://www.asylumineurope.org/reports/country/greece.

Hagen, C.A., M.G. Ender, K.A. Tiemann, and C.O. Hagen Jr. 1999. "Graffiti on the Great Plains: A Social Reaction to the Red River Valley Flood of 1997." *Applied Behavioural Science Review* 7, no. 2: 145–58.

Hanauer, D.I. 2004. "Silence, Voice, and Erasure: Psychological Embodiment in Graffiti at the Site of Prime Minister Rabin's Assassination." *The Arts in Psychotherapy* 31, no. 1: 29–35.

Hess, S. 2012. "De naturalising Transit Migration: Theory and Methods of an Ethnographic Regime Analysis." *Population, Space, and Place* 18, no. 4: 428–40.

Horst, C., and K. Grabska. 2015. "Flight and Exile – Uncertainty in the Context of Conflict-Induced Displacement." *Social Analysis* 59, no. 1: 1–18.

Johnson, L. 2009. "Jail Wall Art and Public Criminology." *Research and Practices in Social Sciences* 5, no. 1: 1–21.

Kibreab, G. 1999. "Revisiting the Debate on People, Place, Identity, and Displacement." *Journal of Refugee Studies* 12, no. 4: 384–410.

Klein, S. 2006. *Time: A User's Guide: Making Sense of Life's Scarcest Commodity*. London: Penguin Books.

Kohli, R., and M. Kaukko. 2017. "The Management of Time and Waiting by Unaccompanied Asylum-Seeking Girls in Finland." *Journal of Refugee Studies* 31, no. 4: 488–506.

Kostka, R. 1974. "Aspects of Graffiti." *Visible Language* 8, no. 4: 369–75.

Lemoine, S., and S. Ouardi. 2010. *Artivisme: art, action politique et résistance culturelle.* Alternatives.

Lenette, C. 2019. *Arts-Based Methods in Refugee Research: Creating Sanctuary.* Singapore: Springer Nature.

Ley, D., and R. Cybriwsky. 1974. "Urban Graffiti as Territorial Markers." *Annals of the Association of American Geographers* 64, no. 4: 491–505.

Lietaert, I., M. Rota, M. Behrendt, S. Adeyinka, O. Uzureau, C. Watters, and I. Derluyn. 2020. "The Development of an Analytical Framework to Compare Reception Structures for Unaccompanied Refugee Minors in Europe." *European Journal of Social Work* 23, no. 3: 384–400.

Madsen, K.D. 2015. "Graffiti, Art, and Advertising: Re-Scaling Claims to Space at the Edges of the Nation-State." *Geopolitics* 20, no. 1: 95–120.

Malkki, L.H. 1995. "Refugees and Exile: From 'Refugee Studies' to the National Order of Things." *Annual Review of Anthropology* 24, no. 1: 495–523.

Marcus, G.E. 1995. "Ethnography in/of the World System: The Emergence of Multi-Sited Ethnography." *Annual Review of Anthropology* 24, no. 1: 95–117.

Mavris, L. 2002. "Asylum Seekers and Human Smuggling: Bosnia and Former Yugoslavia as a Transit Region." In WIDER/UNU *Conference on Poverty, International Migration and Asylum.* Helsinki, September, 27–38.

Mekdjian, S. 2016. "Les récits migratoires sont-ils encore possibles dans le domaine des *Refugee Studies*? Analyse critique et expérimentation de cartographies créatives." ACME: *An International E-Journal for Critical Geographies* 15, no. 1: 150–86.

– 2017. "Urban Artivism and Migrations: Disrupting Spatial and Political Segregation of Migrants in European Cities." *Cities* 77: 39–48.

Mekdjian, S., and A.-L. Amilhat Szary. 2019. "*Cartographies traverses, des espaces où l'on ne finit jamais d'arriver.*" https://visionscarto.net/cartographies-traverses.

Migreurop. 2012. "*Les principaux lieux de détention.*" http://www.migreurop.org/IMG/pdf/carte_atlas_migreurop_19122012_version_francaise_version_web.pdf.

Miller, K.E., and A. Rasmussen. 2010. "War Exposure, Daily Stressors, and Mental Health in Conflict and Post-Conflict Settings: Bridging the Divide between

Trauma-Focused and Psychosocial Frameworks." *Social Science and Medicine* 70, no. 1: 7–16.

Mollica, R.F. 1993. "The Effect of Trauma and Confinement on Functional Health and Mental Health Status of Cambodians Living in Thailand-Cambodia Border Camps." *JAMA – Journal of the American Medical Association* 270, no. 5: 581–6.

Nardone, M., and I. Correa-Velez. 2015. "Unpredictability, Invisibility, and Vulnerability: Unaccompanied Asylum-Seeking Minors' Journeys to Australia." *Journal of Refugee Studies* 29, no. 3: 295–314.

Noiriel, G. 1991. *La tyrannie du national : le droit d'asile en Europe (1793–1993)*. Paris: Calmann-Lévy.

O'Neill, M., and R. Harindranath. 2006. "Theorising Narratives of Exile and Belonging: The Importance of Biography and Ethno-Mimesis in 'Understanding' Asylum." *Qualitative Sociology Review* 2, no. 1: 39–53.

Papadopoulou-Kourkoula, A. 2008. *Transit Migration: The Missing Link between Emigration and Settlement*. New York: Palgrave Macmillan.

Parkin, D. 1999. "Mementoes as Transitional Objects in Human Displacement." *Journal of Material Culture* 4, no. 3: 303–20.

Phillips, S.A. 1999. *Wallbangin': Graffiti and Gangs in LA*. Chicago: University of Chicago Press.

Picozza, F. 2017. "Dublin on the Move: Transit and Mobility across Europe's Geographies of Asylum." *Movements: Journal for Critical Migration and Border Regime Studies* 3, no. 1: 71–88.

Pineteh, E.A. 2017. "Moments of Suffering, Pain, and Resilience: Somali Refugees' Memories of Home and Journeys to Exile." *Cogent Social Sciences* 3, no. 1: 1–15.

Rahola, F. 2007. "La forme-camp. Pour une généalogie des lieux de transit et d'internement du présent." *Cultures & Conflits* 68, no. 1: 31–50.

Rasmussen, A., and J. Annan. 2010. "Predicting Stress Related to Basic Needs and Safety in Darfur Refugee Camps: A Structural and Social Ecological Analysis." *Journal of Refugee Studies* 23, no. 1: 23–40.

Rodier, C., and I. Saint-Saëns. 2007. "Contrôler et filtrer: les camps au service des politiques migratoires de l'Europe." In *Mondialisation, Migrations, Droits de l'homme*. Bruxelles: Bruylant.

Rodriguez, A. 2003. "Sense-Making Artifacts on the Margins of Cultural Spaces." In *Expressions of Ethnography: Novel Approaches to Qualitative Methods*, edited by R.P. Clair, 231–40. Albany: SUNY Press.

Rodriguez, A., and R.P. Clair. 1999. "Graffiti as Communication: Exploring the Discursive Tensions of Anonymous Texts." *Southern Journal of Communication* 65, no. 1: 1–15.

Romotsky, J., and S.R. Romotsky. 1976. "L.A. Human Scale: Street Art of Los Angeles." *Journal of Popular Culture* 10, no. 3: 653–66.

Ross, J.I., P. Bengtsen, J.F. Lennon, S. Phillips, and J.Z. Wilson. 2017. "In Search of Academic Legitimacy: The Current State of Scholarship on Graffiti and Street Art." *Social Science Journal* 54, no. 4: 411–19.

Schapendonk, J. 2012. "Turbulent Trajectories: African Migrants on Their Way to the European Union." *Societies* 2, no. 2: 27–41.

Schwarz, I. 2018. "Migrants Moving through Mobility Regimes: The Trajectory Approach as a Tool to Reveal Migratory Processes." *Geoforum* 116: 217–25.

Schweizer, H. 2008. *On Waiting*. Abingdon: Routledge.

Scott, J.C. 1995. *Weapons of the Weak: Everyday Forms of Peasant Resistance*. New Haven: Yale University Press.

Silove, D., Z. Steel, and C. Watters. 2000. "Policies of Deterrence and the Mental Health of Asylum Seekers." *JAMA – Journal of the American Medical Association* 284, no. 5: 604–11.

Soto, G. 2016. "Place Making in Non-Places: Migrant Graffiti in Rural Highway Box Culverts." *Journal of Contemporary Archaeology* 3, no. 2: 174–95.

Tazzioli, M. 2018. "Containment through Mobility: Migrants' Spatial Disobediences and the Reshaping of Control through the Hotspot System." *Journal of Ethnic and Migration Studies* 44, no. 16: 2764–79.

Translators Without Borders. 2017. "Putting-language-on-the-map in the European Refugee Response." https://translatorswithoutborders.org/wp-content/uploads/2017/04/Putting-language-on-the-map.pdf.

Tsoni, I.W., and A.K. Franck. 2019. "Writings on the Wall: Textual Traces of Transit in the Aegean Borderscape." *Borders in Globalization Review* 1, no. 1: 7–21.

Tulke, J. 2013. "Aesthetics of Crisis: Political Street Art in Athens in the Context of the Crisis." MSc diss., University of Berlin.

– 2015. "15 Pieces of Street Art and Graffiti from Europe and Beyond Showing Solidarity in the Ongoing Refugee Crisis." http://aestheticsofcrisis.org/2015/refugees-welcome.

Turner, S. 2015. "What Is a Refugee Camp? Explorations of the Limits and Effects of the Camp." *Journal of Refugee Studies* 29, no. 2: 139–48.

UN/ECE. 1993. International Migration Bulletin no. 3.

Van Impe, K. 2000. "People for Sale: The Need for a Multidisciplinary Approach towards Human Trafficking." *International Migration* 38, no. 3: 113–91.

Vasta, E. 2011. "Immigrants and the Paper Market: Borrowing, Renting, and Buying Identities." *Ethnic and Racial Studies* 34, no. 2: 187–206.

Vervliet, M., C. Rousseau, E. Broekaert, and I. Derluyn. 2015. "Multilayered Ethics in Research Involving Unaccompanied Refugee Minors." *Journal of Refugee Studies* 28, no. 4: 468–85.

Vossoughi, N., Y. Jackson, S. Gusler, and K. Stone. 2018. "Mental Health Outcomes for Youth Living in Refugee Camps: A Review." *Trauma, Violence, and Abuse* 19, no. 5: 528–42.

Willett, R., and M.L. Laws. n.d. "Drafting an Anti-Graffiti Ordinance – Some Essential Provisions." National Council to Prevent Delinquency. www.anti-graffiti.org/legis.html.

Wilson, J. 2008a. *Prison Cultural Memory and Dark Tourism.* New York: Peter Lang.

– 2008b. "Transgressive Decor: Narrative Glimpses in Australian Prisons, 1970s–1990s." *Crime, Media, Culture* 4, no. 3: 331–48.

Ziniti, A. 2018. "Roma, Baobab smantellato: 'Centinaia di migranti in strada.' E Salvini rilancia: 'Altri 27 sgomberi in città. Casapound? Si farà.'" *La Repubblica,* 13 November. https://roma.repubblica.it/cronaca/2018/11/13/news/migranti_sgombero_baobab-211517829/?ref=search.

Zolner, T. 2007. "Concepts of Graffiti: Much More Than Just Art." TAGS – 3: The Anti-Graffiti Symposium, Saskatoon and Vancouver.

# 8

## In Whose Voice? And for Whom?
### *Collaborative Filming and Narratives of Forced Migration*

Katarzyna Grabska

## The Power and Danger of the Visual

The power of the visual in research has now been well-established (Asch 1992; Banks 1992; Banks and Morphy 1997; Banks and Zeitlyn 2015; Crawford and Turton 1992; Pink 2011, 2012). There has also been growing interest in narrative research in forced migration and refugee studies, with particular attention to visual methods, including participatory approaches to narrative-making through video and photography (Aston 2010; Esin 2017; Godin and Donà 2021; Guerrero and Tinkler 2010; Godin and Donà, this volume; Glanville, this volume; Martiniello 2017). The spread of digital technology and low-budget filmmaking allows for "telling a story" or "narrating a life" differently, more immediately, often instantly, thus creating a level of intimacy between the audience and the narrator. Protagonists can use such technologies directly to share their "own story" and thereby subvert the hierarchical relations of power in terms of access to voice (see Godin and Donà 2016; Godin and Donà, this volume). Arguably, this creates new possibilities for capturing refugee and migrant experiences of movement, mobility, and multiplicity. Yet filmmaking and the politics of testimony in individual narratives are located in state, individual, and global public and private spaces. Thus, they have to be understood within these spaces as well as between them. This new focus on narrative, and on narrative and biographical work, is an important development in the "telling of stories" of migrants and refugees. Yet the obsession with visualizing refugees' and migrants' experiences has to be contextualized within the wider politics of storytelling. The visual can be a powerful research and dissemination method, but it can also be a dangerous one, so its ethical dimensions need to be carefully examined.

In this chapter, I describe how two documentary films were created and disseminated: *Time to Look at Girls: Migrants in Bangladesh and Ethiopia* (2015), and its longer version, *2 Girls* (2016). The research project on which these two films are based was carried out collaboratively with Marina de Regt and Nicoletta Del Franco (see below; see also Grabska et al. 2019). They also participated in the filmmaking. For the reflections presented here, however, we decided that it was I who should offer our insights on the filmmaking experiences. This is for two reasons: first, I kept notes throughout the filming and did much of the methodological reflection and analysis, as I was the most experienced and interested in arts-based research methods; and second, I hoped to write a reflective piece on these experiences. That said, the comments and experiences presented here are based on extensive discussions among the three of us. I would note that both Marina and Nicoletta offered extensive comments on the methodological and ethical issues presented here. They also fully endorsed the following analysis and the discussion.

For the filmmaking part of the project, we, the three researchers, decided to work with professional filmmakers: a director and a camera operator, both men. The latter had a PhD in geography and had mainly produced films focused on social issues. Although we had some filming experience, we felt that working with professionals would make for a better-quality film. The collaboration between professional filmmakers and feminist researchers and protagonists led to certain points of tension, as well as reflections on the ethics of using film in research. These sorts of reflections are not new in visual anthropology. In 1975, Margret Mead was already considering the role of visual anthropology in a discipline rooted in words; in 1981, Maurice Godelier wrote down his reflections on the use of audiovisual methods in anthropology; in 1982, Timothy Ash reflected on collaboration in ethnographic filmmaking; in 1993, Peter Loizos commented on the role of film in studying refugees. Guidelines and reflections on collaborative work with research participants and on visual methods as part of transformative action research have also been discussed (Biella 2009; cf. Levine 2003; Englehart 2003, Stadler 2003; Pink 2011, White 2003). Film offers one of many approaches to representing and engaging with subjects' lives. At the same time, it is one of the most contested terrains of "knowledge production."

The protagonists of the two films were young women who had migrated as adolescents under often dramatic circumstances. Their portrayal as "victims" was often favoured by filmmakers as an effective way to captivate audiences. Tensions arose also around how the protagonists wanted to be portrayed and what researchers saw as "appropriate" ways to represent their agency. This chapter focuses on tensions in the co-creation of knowledge and the complex ways in which different knowers need to renegotiate and come to terms with the process of collaborative knowledge creation. This type of collaboration provides insights into the struggle over the interpretative power of narratives and images – a struggle long discussed in feminist writings, but much less so in refugee and migration studies.

I begin by introducing the research project and how it was decided to use film as part of our dissemination strategy. Then I outline our approach to and reasons for collaborative filmmaking, as well as the challenges that process posed to us. The next section addresses some aspects of the messiness related to the collaborative approach to representation. The complexities of the "voice" and "whose voice" are then further discussed. I close with a discussion of ethical dilemmas and challenges facing feminist researchers who use visual methods in research and as dissemination tools.

## The Story of the Project

The collaborative research between three feminist researchers – Nicoletta Del Franco, Marina de Regt, and myself – focused on the experiences of adolescent girls who had migrated, under highly volatile conditions, internally in Bangladesh and Ethiopia, and internationally from Ethiopia and Eritrea to Sudan (see Grabska et al. 2019). The project was funded by the Swiss Network for International Studies and carried out between 2014 and 2016. I was the project's research coordinator as well as the lead researcher for the Sudan case study. Marina was responsible for the research in Ethiopia, Nicoletta for the research in Bangladesh. The study was situated in the field of feminist anthropology, in which difference is the point of departure (Moore 1994) and gender is studied as a social, political, economic, and cultural construct as well as a practice (Ortner 1974). We three were feminist anthropologists with long experience in the countries where we carried out our individual projects. In this particular research, we focused on adolescent girls and adolescence because the years between eleven and twenty are in many respects crucial ones in an individual's life. At the same time, adolescence can be viewed as a "process" characterized by critical transitions during which major life decisions are taken, albeit in context-specific ways (Bucholtz 2002; Del Franco 2012). The spatial shift implied in migration can be read as one such critical transition, one that intersects with other life choices (Crivello 2009; Gardner and Osella 2003; Gardner 2009; Grabska 2010).

We chose feminist methodologies in order to create collaborative, transformative research with a strong focus on making visible the invisible and breaking, to at least some extent, the power hierarchies between researchers and research participants (Harding 1987, 2004). We mainly used life histories, ethnography, observation, and in-depth interviews. We interviewed and followed some sixty young women in each country who had migrated internally (Bangladesh and Ethiopia) or internationally (Ethiopians and Eritreans in Sudan) between the ages of sixteen and twenty-five. We also interviewed policy-makers and practitioners and carried out policy and document reviews for each case study. In each country, we worked closely with a group of young refugee and migrant women, who then became involved in the project, often as research assistants or co-researchers. They helped identify participants and collect, translate, and analyze materials, besides doing some of the writing. The research process was collaborative from the very start; our approach was jointly formulated, discussed, and executed. The narratives collected during interviews and spontaneous conversations were carefully analyzed within the research teams. Given our status as European women who have carried out research with marginalized groups in the respective countries for more than fifteen years, we were aware of the politics of the production of narratives and stories. This was further complexified by the politics of asylum, in general and in Sudan in particular, and by the politics of migration in Ethiopia and Bangladesh. In these contexts, attempts to break hierarchical barriers and build trust were facilitated through the study design. In a collaborative way with research participants in Ethiopia, Bangladesh, and Sudan, we developed a longitudinal research with a small group of young women, many of whom became co-researchers. Together, we agreed on a collaborative approach to the filmmaking in which the research participants would play central roles.

In international human rights, migration, and development discourses and in international media, narratives of migrant and refugee girls' and young women's migration trajectories usually centre on the horrific violence that often accompanies their migration. In these narratives, girls' agency – their reasons, experiences, and aspirations – is often silenced. To break that imposed silence (Ghorashi 2008), and to excavate the meanings of transitions in migrant and refugee girls' and young women's lives, we decided to collaborate with migrant girls in Ethiopia and Bangladesh in producing a documentary film that would break away with the image of young migrants as victims. We also wanted to share the film with a wider public, beyond academia (see below). Even so, the filmmaking and especially its screenings gave us also important insights into the research findings (see below).

## Approach to Filmmaking: A Collaborative Project

Feminist researchers have long tried to minimize the power differentials between the researcher and the researched (Minh-ha 1989; Patai 1991; Scheper-Hughes 2009; Wolf 1996), but the results have been rather unsatisfactory (Wolf 1996). To varying degrees, we experienced this frustration throughout this project, including during the fieldwork and the write-up. This was partly to do with the nature of fieldwork and the process of knowledge production in general. The requirements of maintaining control and distance in social research too often "benefit[] the researcher more than those studied and further[] the gap between the researcher and the researched" (Wolf 1996, 3). Recognizing these pitfalls and embracing the ideals of a more honest and less hierarchical process of knowledge production, we adapted the feminist methodological commitment to care and solidarity in research (see Donà 2007; Fábos 2019; Eastmond 2007). Thus, another aspect of our attempt to break the hierarchies in research and its dissemination was to make a documentary film based on our findings (see also Rollwagen 1996; Elder 1995;

Grabska et al. 2019, chapter 2), while maintaining our commitment to an approach centred on forced migrants (see Fábos 2019). Our method would involve co-producing knowledge through collaborative filmmaking.

Our initial idea when we decided to make a documentary was to break away from the rather fixed parameters of dissemination of academic knowledge, which is dominated by written documents read by a narrow group of people. Our aim was to reach beyond academia toward policy-makers, practitioners, and the general public. In addition, and most importantly, in the spirit of our co-production of knowledge, we wanted to find a way to disseminate the research among the research participants. Film is a much more accessible medium than an academic article or a book. We also aimed at involving the girls as much possible in the process of filmmaking. Our rationale for making a research-based film was thus threefold: it would harness the power of the visual; it would make the visual part of an activist and transformative strategy beyond research; and it would provide a space for the girls to speak in their own voice.

As Sarah Pink (2011) has shown, the power of the visual and the uses that can be made of it are now firmly acknowledged in social research, especially in public and applied anthropology. Visual methods offer a way to reach beyond the discipline's closed circles. As many authors have discussed, images can speak to a broader public – they "tell a story" or "narrate a life" differently, more immediately, and often instantly, thus creating a level of intimacy between audience and narrator. Visual technologies help the research participants tell their own stories of displacement and migration, thereby subverting the hierarchical relations of power (see Godin and Donà, this volume).

Also, visual methods can become part of a transformative strategy for researchers. Freire and his followers offer crucial insights into how images can contribute to an activist/development strategy. Freire (2018, 51) introduces the concept of *codification* when describing the impact that images and films can have and how they can prompt eye-opening conversations among audience members (see Biella 2009). In our project, we showed the film not just to the research participants but also to young migrants and refugees in Ethiopia, Bangladesh, and Sudan as an important means not just to disseminate knowledge but also to learn from how the viewers interpreted the young women's experiences as they were presented in the film. I will comment on this later in the chapter. Freire makes clear – and our experiences in the project confirm this – that a leader or facilitator must direct post-viewing discussions in order to ensure that audiences experience the potential impact of image codification. In this way, the film screenings became a way to open up possibilities for collaborative analysis and transformative action.

Related to this, and key to the idea of feminist co-production of knowledge, our approach to making the film involved providing a platform for the young women to have their voices heard on their own terms. After about year and half of fieldwork in Ethiopia and Bangladesh, we asked several of the research participants whether they would be interested in participating in the film. Some of them expressed interest; others did not. After several discussions, we assembled a small group of young women who were interested. In each country, we filmed four or five young women who had migrated as adolescent girls. Each filming session took between three and five weeks, but those weeks were preceded by at least a year of fieldwork in each location. We developed a slightly different filming strategy for each country. In Bangladesh, Nicoletta del Franco, the main researcher for Bangladesh, developed deep personal relationships with the girls and was also able to film their families in their home villages. In Ethiopia, Marina de Regt, the lead researcher there, worked with local researchers and so was much more detached from the girls' stories. In Ethiopia, I participated in the overall conceptualization, co-design of the script, and editing, and took part in the filming. One of the research participants and assistants in the project in Ethiopia was an extremely powerful character. She took on the role of film coordinator and saw the film as her own project and strategy for expanding her life possibilities.

For political and security reasons, we decided not to film in Sudan. Most of the young Eritrean and Ethiopian refugees and migrants there were vulnerable because of their irregular situation, and we did not want to jeopardize their safety in that country. So the film focused on the lives of sex workers in Ethiopia and garment workers in Bangladesh. In our collaborative film-making experience, we faced moments of tension, compromise, and negotiation that led us at times to question our core ideas about the less hierarchical co-production of knowledge. I turn to some of these next.

## Negotiating Representation: The Messiness of the Process and the Outcome

Representation in research is a highly sensitive subject, and much has been written about this (Guerrero and Tinkler 2010). Addressing questions around who is to be represented in the visual product, and how, entails a complicated and multi-stage process. Such questions encompass the script, the filming, the editing, and the film's overall direction. Thus, in collaborative film-making projects, both the process of representation and the outcome of the representation are subject to intense negotiations and often difficult compromises.

As feminist researchers, we committed ourselves to the primacy of the young women's involvement in decisions involving their own representation. Both films were based on young women's stories of childhood and migration as adolescents, with a focus on the difficult and often constrained circumstances in which they made the decision to move to the city. Our approach involved ensuring that the young women would have a space to tell the stories they wanted to share, the way they wanted to share them, to the degree they wanted to share them. This was carefully negotiated with the filmmakers, who were open to our ideas. This was an important element in ensuring that the girls felt part of and central to the project. These negotiations – in terms of what the final narratives would look like – took place over several stages.

At different moments during the filmmaking, various power dynamics and hierarchies emerged among the professional filmmakers, protagonists, and researchers. Different stages of filmmaking require different skills – that is how power dynamics and hierarchies came about. We all needed to find creative ways to overcome them in order to create a collaborative experience in which power hierarchies would be minimized. During the filming the young women were asked what they wanted to show and talk about in the film. They could also decide whether they wanted their faces to be visible. Ethical issues of how to present the young women in the film were carefully negotiated. Some of the girls refused to be filmed and did not want their faces to be shown. This was accepted, and these young women did not participate in the project. Others, who finally appear in the two films, all agreed to having their faces shown. They saw the film as a way for their stories and struggles to be recognized. Especially in Ethiopia, the issue of showing the faces of girls who work in prostitution was highly controversial and ethically questionable. As researchers, we had our own reservations. Yet the two young women who decided to take part in the film both wanted their faces to be visible. They wanted to confront the marginalization they had suffered, and they saw themselves as advocates for other young women and girls who were going through similar often tragic and traumatic events. After long negotiations between filmmakers, researchers, and protagonists and careful explanations of the possible consequences of revealing their faces, the young women signed ethical release forms.

On-camera filming involved a great deal of decision-making by the girls in terms of what would be filmed and shown, as well as when and how. The editing process was a different experience. That was done in Rome, with the director and an editor largely deciding how to construct the final storyline. Through emails and in-person exchanges, the young women – in collaboration with us researchers – chose the segments from the transcripts that we all thought would best represent their migratory trajectories. The girls were shown rough cuts and were consulted on what should be included in the film. All of them made comments, which the editorial team took into account during the final cut. In general, the young women were happy with how their lives were being portrayed. As researchers and filmmakers, we wanted to ensure that the girls were presenting "their own take." But at times, this clashed with the vision of the filmmakers, especially the director and the editor. The editor wanted essentially to make victims of the girls and proposed rather dramatic music for the shorter film's soundtrack. As researchers, we were against using that particular music, finding it far too sad and dramatic, yet the young women were all in favour of it. Clearly, the filmmaking process had brought to the surface another set of power hierarchies, as well as questions of whose voice counts and when.

The process resulted in two versions of the film. The shorter one was meant for education and awareness-raising purposes, by us as well as by the NGOs with which we had collaborated. And it was used by the protagonists themselves, especially one of the young women in Ethiopia, who on several occasions screened the film and talked about the challenges faced by adolescent girl migrants in the country. The longer version was screened around the globe at more than thirty festivals and received high recognition, including several prizes. The financial benefits went to the film's protagonists. The longer version was able to convey its message and the research findings to a much wider audience, one that might not have been interested in the academic side of the research.

## In Whose Voice? Experiences of Collaborative Filmmaking

The collaboration between researchers, filmmakers, and migrant girls revealed different visions as well as different priorities among the participants. This was motivated to some degree by their different positionalities and personal agendas.

### Different Priorities for Researchers, Film Participants, and Filmmakers

As researchers, our intention was to show the complexities of the migration experience for adolescent girls. But those girls involved in the project had to contend with multiple vulnerabilities and violences, and as researchers, we believed strongly that we had to protect them. So questions such as whom to film, whose faces to show, and how things should be portrayed were crucial for all three of us.

Yet we did not always share equal enthusiasm about the film-making process. Marina de Regt found it a very oppressive process from the beginning. She had had fraught experiences with filmmaking in the past, during her research among domestic workers in Yemen, and she felt that the visual approach would amount to a violation of the girls. She felt very strongly that she needed to protect them to the point that she missed the agendas and own priorities and voices of the girls. Nicoletta Del Franco was much more hopeful about the film's potential impact. She came from a more practitioner background and felt that visual dissemination would open the research to a broader audience. As for me, I had used visual methods in my previous research projects (see Grabska 2014). I was rather critical of participatory filmmaking as carried out by many development and humanitarian organizations, but I also felt that we could develop a collaborative project that would closely heed protagonists' ideas. These differences in experiences – and, at times, tensions – were resolved through extensive discussions among the three researchers, the filmmakers, and the protagonists. These involved resolving all of our serious ethical concerns related to representation. Eventually, we all agreed to proceed in a way that felt acceptable to everyone. Marina's excellent working relations with the two Ethiopian protagonists and their active role in voicing their own preferences also helped resolve these tensions. Through careful listening, and by addressing each other's concerns, we were able to forge an ethical and respectful collaboration.

The young women who chose to participate in the film were not passive – they had their own agendas as well. For example, Tigist, one of the migrant girls who participated in the research, wanted to be the main protagonist of the film:

> I want to show my life story to be an example for others [so that] the violence against the girls can be stopped, and that others will learn about the dangers. We do not want to show our faces because we do not want our parents to know what happened to us and what type of life we are living; we could have done something better with our lives. But we didn't. (February 2015, Addis Ababa)

Tigist felt very strongly about participating in the film and visualizing her story. At first, the sex workers did not want to show their faces, but eventually they agreed, after intense negotiations with the filmmakers to find solutions that would respect the girls' views. In the end, for Tigist, the project became her own empowerment strategy and an attempt to change her life. She later used the screenings of the film in local communities to advocate on behalf of migrant girls (see below).

The filmmakers had their own priorities as well. They work in an intensely competitive industry in terms of marketing their films. They also use different tools than researchers and ethnographic filmmakers. However sensitive they are to their subjects' needs and circumstances, they still must ensure they have enough high-quality visual material to tell a powerful story. There is also a creative element of the filmmaking process in which filmmakers use their own sensitivities and creativity to tell a story. Moreover, good research is not always compatible with a good film. As the cameraman commented, "Good research is not enough ... There is a need for a story, a narrative, and this is where the director or a filmmaker play an important role. He [she] knows how to do this" (February 2015, Addis Ababa).

All of this means that researchers who decide to work on a collaborative film project with professional filmmakers need to learn how to let go to certain extent and not insist on controlling the process. In collaborative projects, one must be able to trust the filmmakers to not abuse the process and to be sensitive to the research participants' needs and goals as well as to the requirements and complexities of the project itself. The numerous discussions that we, as researchers, had with the director in the pre-production, production, and post-production phases were key to developing mutual trust. Also, the good working and personal relationships between Nicoletta del Franco, the Bangladesh research coordinator and principal researcher, and the filmmakers, as well as the positive experiences from Bangladesh, influenced the filmmaking process in constructive ways. The needs and priorities of the young women who had agreed to participate in the film were placed at the project's centre.

At the same time, the filmmakers needed to listen to the film's protagonists, as well as heed the researchers' findings and the overall messages of the film and those findings.

## Research, Filming, Editing, and Postproduction

As the preceding discussion has revealed, during each stage in the collaborative process different people held different decision-making power. As the cameraman pointed out, "There are different people involved in the filmmaking process, but there is only one director. And it is his responsibility for the overall product, the film." This goes to the heart of the hierarchical process of knowledge production when the visual methods are taken up.

Each of the people involved in the project had their own situated knowledge that was recognized during the project's various stages. The protagonists could decide what stories they wanted to tell, and how, as well as what they wanted to reveal or hide. They chose how to dress, where to film, and what to film. The researchers guided the process with their focus on the girls' migration trajectories and, hence, the overall direction of the film.

Our idea that these young women needed to be shown in a complex way beyond victimization drove the process. But it was the director who discussed with the cameraman which images should be filmed for the purpose of presenting the girls' stories. And it was the director who had the final say in how the stories would come together in the cutting room, and the editor who would advise the director on which images to combine and how. Finally, the cameraman played a key role in portraying visually the girls, their surroundings, and the cities and the neighbourhoods in which they lived. While it was a negotiated gaze, the cameraman and the director did much to shape the film's visual outcome. Their way of seeing was crucial to the way the girls were represented in the film. The choice of colour schemes and framings was greatly a function of their own creative sensitivities.

In the cutting room, the director has the final say in how a film comes together. This responsibility may entail negotiation and collaboration, but in the end, his interpretation of the stories told and how they should be visualized is the final one. Multiple knowledges come together during filmmaking, but those knowledges are in a hierarchy, with different ones taking the lead depending on their value at different stages of production.

Different stages of filmmaking require different skills, and this is where power hierarchies emerge. One needs to find creative ways to overcome them in order to create a truly collaborative experience. Hierarchies of power and control over narrative also demonstrate the complex ways in which the "story" emerges. The preceding quotation from the cameraman shows clearly that the hierarchies of power and control are embedded in the knowledge and tools related to how to tell a "story." A powerful narrative is not enough to keep the audience engaged.

The filmmakers did not find it easy to work with feminist researchers who were deeply concerned about the ethics and politics of representation, and who took seriously the principles of care and solidarity in research and dissemination (see Donà 2007; Fábos 2019). We, the researchers, tried to make sure that the filmmakers did not abuse the girls' trust or misrepresent their stories. The filmmakers sometimes found this oppressive and complained about our interventions. But most of the time they respected our suggestions and inputs, as well as those of the protagonists, and found ways to combine them with their own visual and technical skills.

The filmmakers themselves sometimes perceived the process as violent. In Ethiopia, one researcher suggested that they film domestic workers, many of them young teenagers, and include their stories. It was extremely difficult to reach out to this group and to make them visible in their highly invisible worlds. Finally, the researcher managed to access some domestic workers, young girls, at an evening school. The girls were very young and felt extremely stressed during filming. After the interview, the filmmakers decided not to use this footage. The director said that "filming these young girls who were so scared and so shy felt like a real violence. We could not go on with this. It felt wrong" (February 2015). This indicates that the filmmakers themselves had enough sensitivity and empathy to know when their work was doing violence toward their subjects. It also speaks to the ethical responsibility of the researcher and the filmmaker toward those whose stories they are portraying and visualizing.

## When Dissemination Becomes Part of the Research

The shorter documentary was released in June 2015. We intended to show the film in each of the countries in which we carried out our research, and beyond. *Time to Look at Girls*, which had been made for educational and advocacy purposes, showed the stories of four young women, two from Bangladesh and two from Ethiopia, who had migrated under duress from their places of origin in their early teens. The film was first screened for the research participants in each of the countries, then for policy-makers, practitioners, and activists in each of the settings. It was also shown to the wider public at conferences, in cultural and research centres, and at local organizations. At each of the screenings, the protagonists and sometimes the researchers were present to discuss the film with the audience. Over the next six months, the film was shown in Ethiopia, Bangladesh, and Sudan more than forty times. Since then, the film has been shown in educational, advocacy, and general settings more than 200 times in some thirty countries.

The longer version of the film, *2 Girls*, intended for wider screening at festivals and for a more general audience, was released in 2016. It was shown at more than thirty film festivals worldwide and received ten first prizes for best documentary. This film follows two young women who were featured in the shorter version, but it tells their story in a fuller and more biographical way. Both films had been subtitled in several languages, including Amharic and Bangla.

When we started showing the films, we quickly realized that the screenings and the reactions to them could be part of the research process itself, not simply an outcome of it. For the researchers, the discussions that always followed the screenings provided important insights into how the migratory trajectories of the adolescent girls were understood by their peers, parents, activists, and policy-makers as well as the general public. We recorded these conversations and used them as part of our analysis (see Grabska et al. 2019). Sharing these visual stories with a wider and more diverse public allowed us to access the viewers' various situated knowledges. Their reactions and comments offered us a unique view of what we as feminist anthropologists yet coming from very different cultural settings (Italy, the Netherlands, and Poland/Switzerland) had not been able to fully grasp.

These discussions became an important source as we interpreted our findings, which we did collectively with the protagonists, other adolescent migrants, and the general public. The screenings and discussions allowed us to "decode" (following Freire 2018) the different knowledges and meanings that were associated with the experiential meanings attached to the migratory trajectories of adolescent girls. Codification is a way of gathering information in order to build up a picture (codify) around real situations and real people and their lived experiences. As researchers, we did that in the process of conducting the fieldwork. Migrant and refugee young women and adolescent girls were involved in the fieldwork in an active way, and we took in their own interpretations and meanings that they attached to their experiences. The codification appeared clearly in the film, as a collective reconciliation of different interpretations (by protagonists, researchers and filmmakers) of the girls' experiences. These codes embedded in the visual were then decodified during the post-screening discussions. The most meaningful venues for decodification were discussions with other migrant and refugee girls and young women, who shared their own understanding the experiences presented in the film. These forums, then, allowed for a collective decodification.

Freire's concept of decodification is explained as "a process whereby the people in a group begin to identify with aspects of the situation until they feel themselves to be in the situation and so able to reflect critically upon its various aspects, thus gathering understanding. It is like a photographer bringing a picture into focus."[1] Here, the viewers – other migrant and refugee girls and young women – became active creators of knowledge. The film allowed us as researchers to tap into this knowledge and to create a platform of co-creation of knowledge: the ways in which the migratory trajectories portrayed in the film were criticized, commented on, and re-formulated allowed other stories of migration and displacement to appear. Documenting these responses and exchanges was important to knowledge co-creation. For us as researchers, the visual method allowed us to reach wider audiences and thereby rectify to some degree some of the hierarchies inherent in the research and interpretative process.

The film made it possible for the protagonists to share the findings of the research with wider audiences. All of the young women who participated in the two films received copies of them. One of them, Tigist in Ethiopia, be-came very active, screening the film in several venues in Ethiopia. For ex-ample, she participated in a screening and debate at an Orthodox Church centre in Addis Ababa, where she had been invited after a public screening I had organized at the French Research Centre in that city. Tigist took on the role of an advocate and was invited to other events; one of these had been organized by an NGO working with young sex workers in South Africa; another was part of a conference in Switzerland. Unfortunately, because of strict visa regulations, she was unable to attend these events.

Documenting our findings on film rather than in a written report enabled us and the research participants to reach out to audiences beyond the narrow circles of academia. In this way, as researchers, we were able to achieve more fully the objective of Freire's *Pedagogy of the Oppressed* and the feminist methodologies of co-creation of knowledge while fully including research participants in the research and dissemination process. As Freire (2018) writes, "Attempting to liberate the oppressed without their reflective partic-ipation in the act of liberation is to treat them as objects that must be saved from a burning building" (65). Within its limitations, the film became part of an emancipatory agenda of the young women and migrant girls, while keeping to the principle of migrant-centred approach (see Fábos 2019).

The critique that we, as researchers, faced during the different film screen-ings allowed us to tap into a de-colonial reading of voice and narrative and analyze different layers of the visual and the creation of the visual. Because we had worked with Italian filmmakers who were men, we were at times ac-cused of depicting the girls through a male colonial gaze. However, by dis-cussing and presenting the complexities behind the production of the narratives and the negotiated approach to the visualization, we were able to "de-colonize" the gaze. We received different reactions to both films, with those reactions depending in part on the audience. Other migrant and refugee adolescent girls and young women, their parents and relatives, their peers, other academics, policy-makers, activists, and the general public read and understood the films in different ways. Their own situated knowledges, linked to their gender, class, ethnic, age, national backgrounds, and geographic locations, and the diverse ways in which they experienced the migration narratives in the films, both visually and sonically, provoked often heated debates. This demonstrated for us, as researchers, the extent to which filmmaking and the politics of testimony in individual narratives are located in state, individual, and global public and private spaces. They are located in the global economy, global discourses about migration, and global politics of controlling migration, all of these reflecting the gendered dimensions of controlling young girls' bodies.

## The Visual as a Powerful and Dangerous Method

The key question that emerges from collaborative filmmaking with young marginalized women and girls in volatile positions, feminist yet privileged researchers, and professional filmmakers, is that of ethics. All who were involved in the process grappled with this central dilemma in different ways. The cameraman put it succinctly:

This is a strange activity that mixes job [research and filmmaking], life and emotivity together. But it is a serious thing, because it deals with the more sensitive sides of the human person and also with money, schedules, contracts and results. Its effects can be good but can also be very harmful …

Ethics in research and documentary is a very tough [sensitive and delicate] issue. I reflect on that since years and I admit that I'm still working on my point of view, refining it at any new experience. But what I learned is always to question[] myself about that and be[] wary of those that want to teach others about it. They are usually the ones that create troubles. I hate this attitude when it comes from the academic environment. (Cameraman, June 2016)

The ethical aspects of making a film were carefully debated among the researchers involved, and we sometimes had heated discussions about how to reconcile the various positionalities in the collaborative process. We were acutely aware of the power hierarchies that underpinned our positionalities. We were privileged European women researchers working with young marginalized women and adolescent girls who had gone through a lot of traumatic experiences and who had to negotiate their vulnerable positions as young migrant female factory workers in Dhaka and as sex workers or domestics in Addis Ababa. The commitment to "do no harm" was constantly on our minds. We therefore carefully negotiated and discussed these issues with the film protagonists and other research participants.

Visual and film methods in particular can be problematic for feminist researchers. Combining research with visual media can be a very powerful way to show and share research findings. Yet some key issues must be addressed. Visual methods have greater interpretative power and impact, but at the same time, they can be interpreted in diverse ways. Thus, visual dissemination requires more accompanying commentary than a report. Furthermore, collaboration on a visual production means having to reconcile different standards and perspectives. The researchers are compelled to address ethics issues much more closely in order to protect the respondents and safeguard their anonymity. Can we truly guarantee anonymity and confidentiality when we conduct this type of research and dissemination? To what extent is collaborative filmmaking truly collaborative when the participants hold a variety of knowledges and skills? How can we ensure that our collaborations are ethical and do not place those in vulnerable positions at risk? How much control do we have as researchers and filmmakers over the visual products of our research? And in what other ways are we exposing our respondents and research participants to risks and dangers when we use this type of medium?

The filmmakers, researchers, and film protagonists need to share the same frame of mind, or at least their ideas about what it is they want to do with the film. But is this at all possible, given the different worlds in which researchers and filmmakers operate, not to mention the protagonists? It is key to listen to one another, to be open-minded and non-judgmental. It is also vital to stay true and close to the story – but which story is the "real" story?

Which narrative will prevail? Whose voices are being heard through visual media? Is this really an ethical and correct way of making other voices heard, of making them visible, when they had made themselves invisible in their lives and jobs in order to protect themselves from further violence and abuse?

Maintaining the feminist methodological commitment to care and solidarity in research (see Donà 2007; Fábos 2019), and ensuring that the protagonists were kept informed about the various aspects of the filmmaking process, allowed us to overcome some of these pitfalls. We continuously reminded ourselves to stick to an approach that focused on the girls and young women (see Fábos 2019). Some audiences' interpretations the young women's lives were outside of our control, but having the young women take a central role decisions about how they would be represented and how the film would be disseminated somewhat ameliorated these pitfalls. This proved to be a rather challenging and ethically difficult process, always a delicate balancing act.

## The Struggles over Interpretative Power

Jean Rouch (2003) was correct that film and the visual are among the most contested terrains of knowledge production. This chapter has shown how collaborative filmmaking that involves research participants, researchers, and professional filmmakers can be a powerful tool for research, interpretation, and dissemination. Yet the tensions that emerge during a filmmaking project are many, and all who are involved have to address them collectively. That experience provided me with insights into the interpretative power of narratives and images. That power has been discussed in feminist writings, much less so in refugee and migration studies. In collaborative filmmaking, who has the power to interpretation the research? Is it the filmmaker? The protagonists? The researchers themselves? Or is it the public? During our project, all of these involved themselves the "struggle for interpretive power" (see Cornwall et al. 2007).

Knowledge is socially constructed and situated. During our project, we paid attention to the knowledge and experiences of those who had been marginalized and whose voices had not been recognized. While collaborative filmmaking opens up some possibilities of overcoming the power hierarchies in knowledge production, its execution needs careful ethical and reflexive consideration. It is about an emphasis on and commitment to dignity and recognition in the film-making research process.

NOTE

1  https://www.freire.org/paulo-freire/concepts-used-by-paulo-freire.

REFERENCES

Archer Mann, S., and A.S. Patterson. 2015. "Intersectionality Theories." In *Feminist Theory: From Modernity to Postmodernity*, 218–98. Oxford: Oxford University Press.

Asch, T. 1988. "Collaboration in Ethnographic Film-making: Personal View." In *Anthropological Perspectives on the Production of Film and Video for General Public Audiences*, edited by J.R. Rollwagen, 1–30. New York: Hardwood Academic.

– 1992. "The Ethics of Ethnographic Film-Making." In *Film as Ethnography*, edited by P.I. Crawford and D. Turton, 196–204. Manchester: Manchester University Press.

Aston, J. 2010. "Spatial Montage and Multimedia Ethnography: Using Computers to Visualise Aspects of Migration and Social Division among a Displaced Community." *Forum Qualitative Socialforschung/Forum: Qualitative Social Research* 11, no. 2.

Banks, M. 1992. "Which Films Are the Ethnographic Films?" In *Film as ethnography*, edited by P. Crawford and D. Turton, 116–29. Manchester: Manchester University Press, in association with the Granada Centre for Visual Anthropology.

Banks, M., and H. Morphy, eds. 1997. *Rethinking Visual Anthropology*. New Haven: Yale University Press.

Banks, M., and D. Zeitlyn. 2015. *Visual Methods in Social Research*. London: SAGE.

Biella, P. 2009. "Visual anthropology in a time of war: Intimacy and interactivity in ethnographic media." https://www.researchgate.net/publication/265031075_Visual_Anthropology_in_a_Time_of_War_Intimacy_and_Interactivity_in_Ethnographic_Media.

Bosswick, W., and C. Husband. 2005. *Comparative European Research in Migration, Diversity, and Identities*. Bilbao: University of Deusto.

Bucholtz, M. 2002. "Youth and Cultural Practice." *Annual Review of Anthropology* 3, no. 1: 525–52.

Cornwall, A., E. Harrison, and A. Whitehead. 2007. "Gender Myths and Feminist Fables: The Struggle for Interpretive Power in Gender and Development." *Development and Change* 38, no. 1: 1–20.

Crawford, P.I., and D. Turton. 1992. *Film as Ethnography.* Manchester: Manchester University Press, in association with the Granada Centre for Visual Anthropology.

Crivello, G. 2009. "'Becoming Somebody': Youth Transitions through Education and Migration in Peru." Young Lives Working Paper no. 43. Oxford: Young Lives, University of Oxford.

Del Franco, N. 2012. *Negotiating Adolescence in Rural Bangladesh: A Journey through School, Love, and Marriage.* New Delhi: Zubaan Books.

Donà, G. 2007. "The Microphysics of Participation in Refugee Research." *Journal of Refugee Studies* 20, no. 2: 210–29. https://doi.org/10.1093/jrs/fem013.

Eastmond, M. 2007. "Stories as Lived Experience: Narratives in Forced Migration Research." *Journal of Refugee Studies* 20, no. 2: 248–64. https://doi.org/10.1093/jrs/fem007.

Elder, S. 1995. "Collaborative Film-Making: An Open Space for Making Meaning, a Moral Ground for Ethnographic Film." *Visual Anthropology Review* 11, no. 2: 94–101.

Engelhart, L. 2003. "Media Activism in the Screening Room." *Visual Anthropology Review* 19, nos. 1–2: 73–85.

Esin, C. 2017. "Telling Stories in the Pictures: Constituting and Processual and Relational Narratives in Research with Young British Muslim Women in East London." *Forum Qualitative Sozialforschung/Forum: Qualitative Social Research* 18, no. 1. http://www.qualitative-research.net/index.php/fqs/article/view/2774/4063.

Fábos, A. 2019. "A Refugee-Centred Perspective." *Forced Migration Review* 61: 58–60.

Freire, P. (1968) 2018. *Pedagogy of the Oppressed.* 50th anniversary edition. New York: Bloomsbury Academic.

Gardner, K. 2009. "Lives in Motion: The Life-Course, Movement, and Migration in Bangladesh." *Journal of South Asian Development* 4, no. 2: 229–51.

Gardner, K., and F. Osella. 2003. "Migration, Modernity, and Social Transformation in South Asia: An Overview." *Contributions to Indian Sociology* 37, nos. 1–2: 5–28.

Ghorashi, H. 2008. "Giving Silence a Chance: The Importance of Life Stories for Research on Refugees." *Journal of Refugee Studies* 21, no. 1: 117–32.

Godelier, M. 1981. "Le travail et ses représentations." *Journal des anthropologues* 5: 10–14.

Godin, M., and G. Donà. 2016. "'Refugee voices': New Social Media and the Politics of Representation." *Refuge: Canada's Journal on Refugees* 32, no. 1: 60–71.

– 2021. "Rethinking Transit Zones: Migrant Trajectories and Transnational Networks in Techno-Borderscapes." *Journal of Ethnic and Migration Studies* 47, no. 14: 3276–92.

Grabska, K. 2010. "Lost Boys, Invisible Girls: Stories of Marriage across Borders." *Gender, Place, and Culture* 17, no. 4: 479–97.

– 2014. *Gender, Identity, and Home: Nuer Repatriation to Southern Sudan.* Oxford: Boydell and Brewer. James Currey edition.

Grabska, K., M. de Regt, and N. del Franco. 2019. *Transitions into Adulthood: Adolescent Girls' Migration in the Global South.* New York: Palgrave Macmillan.

Guerrero, A.L., and T. Tinkler. 2010. "Refugee and Displaced Youth Negotiating Imagined and Lived Identities in a Photography Based Educational Project in the United States and Colombia." *Anthropology and Education Quarterly* 41, no. 1: 55–74.

Harding, S. 1987. "Introduction: Is There a Feminist Method?" In *Feminism and Methodology*, edited by S. Harding. Bloomington: Indiana University Press.

– 2004. "Introduction: Standpoint Theory as a Site of Political, Philosophical, and Scientific Debate." In *The Feminist Standpoint Reader: Intellectual and Political Controversies*, edited by S. Harding. New York and London: Routledge.

Levine, S. 2003. "Documentary Film and HIV/AIDS: New Directions for Applied Visual Anthropology in Southern Africa." *Visual Anthropology Review* 19, nos. 1–2: 57–72.

Loizos, Peter. 1993. *Innovation in Ethnographic Film: From Innocence to Self-consciousness, 1955–85.* Manchester: Manchester University Press.

Martiniello, M. 2017. "Visual Sociology Approaches in Migration, Ethnic, and Racial Studies." *Ethnic and Racial Studies* 40, no. 8: 1184–90.

Mead, M. 1928. *Coming of Age in Samoa.* Ann Arbor: Morrow.

Minh-ha, T. 1989. *Woman, Native, Other: Writing Postcoloniality and Feminism.* Indianapolis: Indiana University Press.

Moore, H. 1994. *A Passion for Difference.* Cambridge: Polity Press.

Ortner, S. 1974. "Is Female to Male as Nature Is to Culture?" In *Woman, Culture, and Society,* edited by M. Zimbalist Rosaldo and L. Lamphare, 67–87. Stanford: Stanford University Press.

Parkin, S., and R. Coomber. 2009. "Value in the Visual: On Public Injecting, Visual Methods, and Their Potential for Informing Policy (and Change)." *Methodological Innovations Online* 4, no. 2: 21–36.

Patai, D. 1991. "U.S. Academics and Third World Women: Is Ethical Research Possible?" In *Women's Words: The Feminist Practice of Oral History,* edited by B. Gluck and D. Patai, 137–53. New York: Routledge.

Pink, S. 2011. "Images, Senses, and Applications: Engaging Visual Anthropology." *Visual Anthropology* 24, no. 5: 437–54.

– ed. 2012. *Advances in Visual Methodology.* London: SAGE.

Rollwagen, J.R., ed. 1996. *Anthropological Perspectives on the Production of Film and Video for General Public Audiences.* 4th ed. New York: Hardwood Academic.

Rouch, Jean. (1973) 2003. "The Camera and Man." In *Cine-Ethnography Jean Rouch,* edited by S. Feld, 29–46. Minneapolis: University of Minnesota Press.

Scheper-Hughes, N. 2009. "Making Anthropology Public." *Anthropology Today* 25, no. 4: 1–3.

Stadler, J. 2003. "Narrative, Understanding, and Identification in Steps for the Future: HIV/AIDS documentaries." *Visual Anthropology Review* 19, nos. 1–2: 86–101.

White, S.A. 2003. *Participatory Video: Images That Transform and Empower.* Thousand Oaks: SAGE.

Wolf, D.L. 1996. "Situating Feminist Dilemmas in Fieldwork." In *Feminist Dilemmas in Fieldwork,* edited by D.L. Wolf. Boulder: Westview Press.

# 9

## Methodological and Ethical Reflections on the *Displaces* Participatory Photographic Project in the "Calais Jungle"

Marie Godin and Giorgia Donà

Interest in innovative arts-based approaches to research with displaced populations and refugees has increased in recent years, as has the awareness that creative methodologies can be powerful tools for people on the move to increase the visibility of their experiences of displacement, transit, migration, and belonging. This chapter examines methodological, relational, and ethical issues in participatory photography, an arts-based method we used to portray (im)mobility through the gaze of displaced people in transit. Writing about narratives, Marita Eastmond (2007) suggested that "they can tell us about how people themselves, as 'experiencing subjects', make sense of violence and turbulent change. From personal accounts, we may also glean the diversity behind over-generalised notions of 'the refugee experience'" (249). While many people on the move share the condition of displacement, their individual stories are qualitatively diverse. Visual storytelling methodologies allow researchers, artists, and migrants themselves to portray both the singularity and multiplicity of their stories and voices.

Visual methodologies were first used in the field of migration, ethnic, and racial studies (Martiniello 2017) to describe residential segregation, inequality and discrimination, labour market segmentation, processes of racialization and ethnic formation, and citizenship and belonging (Ball and Gilligan 2010). Although visual methodologies are relatively new in forced migration and refugee studies (see for instance Esin 2017; Martiniello 2017; Ní Raghallaigh 2013; Vecchio et al. 2017), they can be innovative approaches to research and practice and help advance knowledge about displaced people's visual cultures. However, in contexts of "transit displacement" in border zones, specific methodological and ethical challenges are involved in this approach, and some opportunities remain underexamined.

Drawing on the participatory photo-project *Displaces,*[1] a collaboration with people on the move at Calais on the UK-France border, this chapter examines participatory photography as a research and pedagogical methodology created with and by individuals moving across borders. *Displaces* was part of a broader civic engagement project run by the University of East London, which included a university short course called *Life Stories.* The course used a multi-modal narrative methodology – written, oral, arts, photographic, and multi-media – that enabled forced migrants in transit in Calais to directly represent their stories and co-produce narratives of displacement at the border (Esin and Lounasmaa 2020). We begin by briefly reviewing the literature on visual (photographic) methodologies in migration and refugee studies to provide context for the *Displaces* photo-project and our reflections on its methodology.

Visual methodology is an umbrella term that captures a multitude of practices such as photovoice, *fotonovela*, digital storytelling, and quilting (Vecchio et al. 2017). All of these provide participants with a visual means "through which to express themselves, their community and their knowledge" (Vecchio et al. 2017, 135); thus they are well-suited to refugee communities. Gold (2004) advocates for integrating visual methods into fieldwork with migrant communities on the basis that "visual methods are shown to be useful for learning about the research context, generating rapport with respondents, analysing findings, and sharing research with students and colleagues" (1551). Visual methodologies are increasingly popular in forced migration and refugee studies, where they are most often a part of research, pedagogy, and praxis involving refugees in contexts of resettlement (Brigham et al. 2018; Godin and Donà 2016; Gold 2004; McBrien and Day 2012), as well as in studies of refugee youth (McBrien and Day 2012; Vecchio et al. 2017). Visual methodologies have also been chosen for their role in facilitating newcomers' integration (Martiniello 2019; McGregor and Ragab 2016), supporting therapeutic care (McBrien and Day 2012), and fulfilling pedagogical functions. An example of the latter is photography based education that provides a strategy for communication with migrant and refugee students learning in an unfamiliar language (Guerrero and Tinkler 2010).

Because of the power of visual cultures, these methodologies are often used to raise public awareness (Brigham et al. 2018; Lenette 2016). That is, they are representational devices that may reproduce or problematize mainstream representations of migrants and refugees and, in doing so, expose the politics of representation. For instance, Wilmott (2017) highlights the politics of photography by critiquing stereotypical visual portrayals of Syrian refugees in UK online media, while Mannik (2012) draws attention to the politics of public and private portrayals of refugees. To counter essentialist representations of forced migrants, critical photography provides nuanced portrayals of refugees' lived experiences over time (Lenette 2016) that reveal intimate negotiations of imagined and lived identities (Guerrero and Tinkler 2010) and unpack gendered dynamics (Gold 2004). By depicting the plurality of migrant and refugee stories, critical photography contributes to broader social analyses of what it means to be an immigrant or refugee (Brigham et al. 2018).

Participatory photography represents a departure from the use of photography as a representational device. In this chapter's context, it serves as a social change tool for articulating the politics of representation. This method is situated within critical pedagogical and methodological frameworks of knowledge production that call into question existing power relations between, for example, teachers and students or researchers and participants and advocates for greater participant engagement in decision-making processes (Donà 2007). McBrien and Day (2012) explain their choice to use participatory photography with resettled refugee youth as a way to "help newcomer refugee students express themselves beyond their current capacities in English, and we used the students' photographs as catalysts to interview them about their resettled lives in the United States" (546). Brigham and colleagues (2018) use participatory photography as a reflexive methodology; in their work, ten immigrant and refugee women took and shared photographs and engaged in self-reflexive practice through writing and dialogue over a two-year period. They produced photo-stories – a process of storytelling through photography – to illustrate the plurality of their life journeys and highlight the importance of relationships in women's migration experiences.

This literature review points to increased use of visual (photographic) methods with migrants and refugees to achieve various cultural, educational, political, therapeutic, and empirical outcomes across different cultural and geographical contexts, and especially in contexts of migrant and refugee resettlement. The recent "European refugee crisis" has led to the formation of new migratory spaces of transit within which people on the move are forced to face (im)mobility at the border. In these new European interior borderlands, a new genre of visual photographic practice has emerged. Grassroots and communal, this arts-based practice adopts a position of open solidarity with people on the move, a position of criticality of mainstream representations of the figure of the migrant/refugee, and an activist standpoint of resistance that calls for shifting the gaze away from people on the move so as to launch a critique of borders. This approach became prominent in the context of the UK-France border at Calais.

## Visual Representations at the Calais Border: From Disposable Photography to Anti-Photography

Borders were once understood as sites of crossing; today they are perceived as sites of (im)mobility where people on the move are stuck in temporal, geographical, and socio-political transit (Donà and Godin 2019). The border zone around Calais is a transit space of precarity and ongoing (im)mobility; people on the move have been gathering there in informal camps for more than two decades. These spontaneous congregations fluctuate over time: they expand, are demolished, and reconstitute themselves. Before the official closure of the informal settlement known as the Calais "Jungle" in October 2016, and subsequent eviction of its residents, around eight thousand individuals resided in The Jungle (Help Refugees 2016). Though it has been dismantled, people on the move continue to informally congregate around Calais before attempting to cross the English Channel into the UK.

The "European refugee crisis" has produced many representations of migrants and refugees crossing the borders of Fortress Europe. As migrants and refugees continue to approach, enter, and cross European countries, the mainstream media produce visual portrayals of the phenomenon that are often ambivalent, oscillating between two common representations of people on the move: the migrant/refugee-as-threat-to-host-society, and the migrant/refugee-as-powerless-victim-in-need-of-protection (Chou-liaraki and Stolic 2019). In both cases, people on the move are being dehu-manized and silenced. In fact, until now, refugees themselves have rarely been the narrators of their own stories (Georgiou 2018). At the Calais bor-der, however, photojournalists, humanitarians, activists, and researchers have attempted to present nuanced portrayals of life in transit.

For example, the photojournalist Sean Smith visited The Jungle and got to know its people before producing the photo-essay "Migrant Life in Calais' Jungle Refugee Camp" (2015),[2] described in *The Guardian* as an attempt at "capturing a flavour of life in the settlement, alongside the risks many take trying to get across the border to the UK." However, the journey is often cen-tral to portrayals of migrants and refugees on the move (Collyer and King 2016); in the European context, there has been particular emphasis on the crossing but less emphasis on the transit spaces, which are often represented as a "meaningless in-between phase" (Schapendonk 2012, 30). Most impor-tantly, there are many examples of "counter-witnessing the borderwork of Calais" (Hicks and Mallet 2019). As volunteers and ordinary citizens from across Europe congregated in Calais, new "pop-up art-projects" – pop-up theatre, poetry, dance, music, and photographic projects, most of them tem-porary and volatile – sprang up in the Calais settlement to offer alternative visual representations of life at the border. Among the myriad photo-based projects developed, we would like to draw attention to the "Citizen Photog-raphy Project,"[3] initiated in March 2016 by the UK-registered charity Refugee Info Bus. It opened up visual spaces for migrants and refugees to tell their stories, a counterpoint to the journalists, filmmakers, and art students who were constantly arriving in The Jungle to take snapshots of life at the border before quickly departing. The Refugee Info Bus distributed disposable cameras to fifty residents, providing them with the possibility of becoming citizen-journalists who could report the events unfolding in the camp on the ground; this became particularly poignant during the evictions from the camp in October 2016. The project aimed to challenge dominant represen-tations of the "refugee crisis" – in particular, the dehumanizing mainstream media reporting on the migrants and the camp – as well as to raise funds for the charity. Shifting the gaze from the migrants to the ordinary citizens volunteering in the camp, other projects similarly captured overlooked elements of everyday life at the border. As an example, Danny Burrows[4] photographed volunteers working for the grassroots NGO Refugee Community Kitchen in Calais and used the photographs to raise awareness of the work of the organization through social media channels.

In addition to photojournalists, professional photographers, and volunteers-turned-photographers, researchers have used photography to document the daily lives of camp residents and depict the camp through their gaze. Signe Sofie Hansen, Tara Flores, Ishita Singh, and Layla Mohseni – all students at King's College London – created a photo-essay called "Humans of Calais." They distributed fifteen disposable cameras to migrants and asked them to take photos of their lives in the camp, as a means to document Calais through the eyes of its residents. The cameras were collected one day later and follow-up interviews were conducted. The students described this method, which they called auto-photography, as "a visual method, which is rarely used in the social sciences, despite its potential for retrieving different information through the use of photos rather than just words" (Singh et al. 2016, 5).

This brief and non-exhaustive overview of photographic projects at Calais indicates that images of, with, and by migrants can disrupt the mainstream tropes of migrants and refugees as victims or threats. In so doing, such images can reveal the human intricacies of everyday life in transit. Hicks and Mallet (2019) argued that "la Lande" (The Jungle) became something close to what Judith Butler has called a "sphere of appearance" of collective performativity (2016, 58; Koegler 2017, 78–9). However, some residents of The Jungle expressed a certain degree of fatigue and mistrust toward these photographic projects. For instance, when Hagan (2018) first considered distributing disposable cameras to capture the politics of visibility on the ground, residents were not interested in engaging in this form of predefined visual narrative. As she spent time in the camp, however, some of them started to share images with her "on their own terms" and "in their chosen form" of digital visual materials captured with mobile phones and shared through messaging applications. Hagan noticed that migrants and refugees in transit at the border were more interested in documenting the human rights violations they endured, and that making and sharing visual political statements provided them with a sense of agency over their absurd living situation.

Given the overwhelming volume of reproductions of images of people in the Calais camp, some photographers even questioned the use of photography to represent people on the move. Photographer Gideon Mendel responded by instead collecting objects – clothing, children's toys and books, furniture, and personal hygiene products – which constituted the remnants of the lives that once animated the camp. He wanted to capture the "unstructured archaeology" that had been left behind after the demolition of The Jungle. He described his anti-photo-project "Dzhangal"[5] as focusing on the "politics of the site" rather than "its residents." In so doing, he offered a "counter-aesthetics" of the experience of displaced people (Malaquais 2017). The 2,189 objects collected were stored in the Museum of London Archaeology Archive, and a selection of photos of them was published in the "Dzhangal" catalogue (Mendel 2017).

These visual (photographic) projects at the border are often temporary and volatile. Although they adopt stances of solidarity and activism, some of them appear to use migrants and refugees as visual subjects to evoke empathy among the general public, potential donors, or both. Migrants and refugees continue to be "spoken about" rather than "speaking themselves," thus often losing control of their visual narratives (Chouliaraki and Stolic 2019).

The *Displaces* project was conducted at the informal camp in Calais, where political engagement and power relations intersected with migrants' everyday lives and political subjectivities. *Displaces* is situated within and has developed from the existing tradition of participatory and pedagogical photography with migrants and refugees as outlined at the start of this chapter. Like Guerrero and Tinkler (2010), we use photography based education to fulfill pedagogical functions, and like Brigham and colleagues (2018), we adopt participatory photography as a reflexive methodology. The *Displaces* photo-project also draws upon a tradition of critical and activist photography (Lenette 2016; Wilmott 2017) that challenges essentialist representations of forced migrants and offers nuanced portrayals of their lives, thus exposing the politics of representation. In the transit space of the UK-France border at Calais, our *Displaces* project belongs to a growing body of visual projects of "counter-witnessing the borderwork of Calais" (Hicks and Mallet 2019).

*Displaces* was developed as part of a civic engagement project, not as a research project as such. The stories and photographs shared by residents were not those of "research participants" but rather of "authors of their own work" (Lounasmaa et al. 2019, 12). Still, the methodological and ethical issues associated with engaging with refugee–residents in Calais through the use of photography as a storytelling tool are, we believe, pertinent to research with refugees in transit spaces. The methodological and ethical reflections on the *Displaces* participatory photographic project presented in the rest of this chapter focus on the distinctive features of the project that set it apart from most other visual projects carried out at the border. Three key issues in participatory visual research are discussed: ownership and copyrights, sustained relationships, and the representation and voice of migrants and refugees.

## The *Displaces* Project

*Displaces* is a participatory photo-project and one component of a broader civic engagement initiative run by the Centre for Narrative Research at the University of East London (UEL), which delivered accredited university short courses, under the name Life Stories, to migrants in transit in Calais between November 2015 and September 2016.[6] The aim of the project was to bring the experience of British higher education to the heart of The Jungle in the context of the University for All framework. A team of academics and students from across the university collaborated with visual artists to deliver oral, written, arts, and media workshops. Residents of the Calais camp who took part in the Life Stories courses were asked to write a piece that reflected their own life story. Upon completing this assignment, they received a university certificate in the short course Life Stories in Higher Education in Europe. Of the sixty students who completed the course, twenty-two continued the collaboration with the UEL team, which led to the publication of their life stories in the co-authored book *Voices from the Jungle* (2017), published by Pluto Press (see Squire 2017; Lounasmaa et al. 2019). While the writing of a book – one that would include visual materials – was not originally envisaged for the project, the proposal developed organically after course participants expressed a desire for their life stories to reach a wider audience (Calais Writers 2017). As with other migrant-centred arts-based projects derived from the new humanitarianism at the border, the Life Stories project was situated within the emerging spaces of political solidarity challenging the politics of the border; in the case of the *Displaces* photo-project, that challenge was articulated through the visual. *Displaces* is more specifically located within an emerging "subversive humanitarianism" (Vandevoordt 2019) that has characterized the wave of civic initiatives supporting displaced people during the European "refugee crisis." This new form of spontaneous humanitarianism marks a shift from professional humanitarianism, that which views migrants and refugees as recipients of aid, toward new forms of citizen volunteerism and humanitarianism enacted through gestures of solidarity that foreground migrant and refugee socio-political subjectivities (264). Thus, this participatory photo-project adopts the political strategy of counter-representation in its documentation of the border and those who inhabit it.

The *Displaces* project's visual methodology grew out of the collaborative photo-storytelling project *Through Positive Eyes*, which featured 130 people living with HIV and AIDS in ten cities around the world, led by South African photographer Gideon Mendel and photo-educator Crispin Hughes in collaboration with David Gere, director of the Art and Global Health Center at the University of California in Los Angeles. The method was adapted for the Calais context. Photography workshops were held between October 2015 and October 2016. Mendel Hughes facilitated four one-day photography sessions. Marie Godin, one of the authors of this chapter, was involved with the UEL team to deliver the photography workshops and help students write their coursework.

Between twelve and fifteen migrants – all men – attended the workshops. The participants were from Afghanistan, Ethiopia, Eritrea, Iran, Iraq, Pakistan, Sudan, and Syria. All of them had lived in The Jungle for days, weeks, or, in some cases, many months between 2015 and 2016. The photography workshop was advertised at the Jungle Books Calais Migrant Library, an informal setting where camp residents could access books and teaching materials and where the workshops were conducted. Residents visited the library because it had generators, gas stoves, and lighting. It was also a school, with French and English classes provided for adults and children. Camp residents passed by to charge their mobile phones, read, attend classes, and receive information about available workshops. In the photography training workshops, participants were taught conceptual approaches and practical techniques to help them respond to their lives and surroundings in a deliberate, thoughtful, and emotional way. Participants had a week to practise the techniques they had learned and produce personal visual narratives. During follow-up visits, students were taught to edit the photos they had taken. The editing process focused on the needs of the individual photographers and their personal views of the world. Individual and group activities were conducted with the migrant- and refugee-photographers, professional photographers, and facilitators; the photos were then rated from one to five stars based on the criteria of artistic gaze, subject, and the story behind each photo. The editing process led to critical discussions about the visual materials produced, with students being the ones always making the final decision about the selection. The workshop sessions were interspersed with tutorials and one-to-one conversations during which refugee participants were encouraged to "tell, share and make sense of their life stories using multimodal narratives" (i.e., visual, verbal, written and processual narratives) (see Esin and Lounasmaa 2020, 392).

In the *Displaces* participatory photo-project, participants often worked in their mother tongue, with their contributions translated into English by other participants. Some participants had sufficient knowledge of English and could, therefore, discuss the creation, production, and dissemination of their visual materials directly with facilitators. The *Displaces* photo-project aimed to foster a space for communal reflexivity in which the voices of residents could be foregrounded, and where, even amid asymmetrical teacher–student and volunteer–migrant/refugee power relations, power dynamics could be unpacked and discussed as part of the participatory approach. Following the official conclusion of the *Displaces* project, exchanges with a group of former residents continued after they left the camp to reach the UK or settle in France. These sustained friendships have led to ongoing artistic collaborations with the authors of this chapter that continue at the time of writing.

## Methodological and Ethical Reflections on *Displaces*

Research carried out with migrants and refugees in vulnerable settings needs to take into account their specific positionality, characterized by their precarious legal status and unequal power relations, situated within broader contemporary geopolitical frames, which tend to criminalize migration

(Clark-Kazak 2017). It is thus imperative that when working with individuals living at the border, methodological and ethical approaches move beyond standard guidelines and processes to embrace a broader set of political stances, care, and solidarity. Like others (Hugman et al. 2011), we believe that researchers who collaborate with refugees and migrants have the responsibility to think beyond techniques and procedures to adopt a people-centred perspective (Fábos 2019) that is guided by the ethics of care (Taggart 2016). We align ourselves with feminist methodologies, which strive for more reciprocal relationships and to address power imbalances between researchers and the people who are being researched (Liamputtong 2007). We situate *Displaces* within the broader environment of "political listening" (Bassel 2017); our aim is to hear multiple voices of knowledge and allow people on the move to challenge knowledge hierarchies as well as hierarchies of credibility. The following sections on ownership and copyrights, sustained engagement, and voice and representation offer a reflexive account of the challenges and possibilities that arise during creative research collaborations that use photography to present counter-representations of the border and those who inhabit it.

## Ownership and Copyrights

The distinctive methodological and ethical stance adopted in *Displaces* empowered migrants and refugees at the border to take control not only of their visual representations but also of the tools and processes involved in creating critical responses about life in Calais. Central to this approach was giving learners ownership of the cameras as well as the copyright to the images they produced. They received not only a short course on photography, which enhanced their multimedia skills, but also the tools to practise their photography beyond the duration of the project. Good-quality cameras were donated to migrants and refugees for them to keep (as opposed to loaning them cameras or providing disposable ones). Participants were very positive about owning cameras with a memory card rather than having cameras on loan or temporarily, which was the common practice of other participatory photographic projects in Calais (as described above). Haris,[7] originally from Pakistan, explained the benefits of giving cameras to residents:

It is a very good idea to give cameras to different people in the camp. Each of them take hundreds pictures in a day or in a week. For one person it is very hard to cover the whole "Jungle" … Creating this programme is a very good idea so we can cover a lot about the "Jungle." Journalists come to show the world the condition in the "Jungle" and to show that people need help: "Please help these people, they are living in the 'Jungle.'" When someone hears the name "Jungle," they think about animals, not human beings. Here in Calais there is a jungle, yes, but humans are living in the "Jungle," so if you want to show that, you show the toilet conditions of the "Jungle," the food conditions, the tents, clothes and shoes. You show them the people who are living in here. You show them the human life. (Calais writers 2017, 253)

Having cameras at one's disposal, he elucidated, allowed migrants to depict the variety and richness of everyday life at the border and challenged outsider-essentialized representations of the condition in The Jungle. This approach is indicative of the shared political stance among facilitators, educators, and collaborators and student photographers to articulate the politics of (in)visibility in migrants' terms. Giving residents of the camp ownership of the cameras also reduced unequal power relations: it relinquished control of the visual tools and gave the students control of the modalities of present and future use; they could employ the cameras as they saw fit. To our knowledge, most of them kept their cameras. A few returned them or transferred them to others when they thought they could not use them anymore. Some participants saw the cameras as currency, recognizing their economic value, and sold them to have the cash to pay for essentials, such as food, clothes, or mobile phone credits in the camp. Since the cameras were of good quality, there was a risk that they would be stolen in the transient and precarious environment and that the owners would become targets of attack while they were carrying the cameras around. A group discussion was held, which led to a group decision not to use cameras at night and to ensure that the migrants could use them in safe spaces. Possession of the cameras increased migrants' engagement with the project and led to the production of a large, rich, and diverse display of 3,716 images (see Godin et al. 2019).

Another innovative component of *Displaces* was that students held the copyright to their images. They could make them available to the group to be discussed collectively during the project, but they could also choose not to return or share them. The decision to share or not share the photos was made on the ground. While a few of the students abandoned the project (they had crossed the border, or they had other priorities), most of them completed the training and chose to share their photos. Following a participatory approach, the images were made available in print form or on the computer to be collectively examined and discussed. The conversations took place at different times and in different communal spaces around the camp, such as in community areas and local restaurants.

The fact that these migrant photographers held the copyright to the pictures they had taken altered the conventional understanding of informed consent. We extended the informed consent process to include "a renewal of informed consent," applicable each time we wished to make use of the participants' photographic material. Most participants gave us informed consent to use their visual outputs at the beginning of the training while in transit, but we respected their freedom to change their mind in light of their shifting vulnerabilities related to changes in immigration status and with the understanding that some ex-residents might prefer not to be associated with The Jungle once they left it. Consequently, requests for informed consent to use the photographs evolved into an ongoing process that would be constantly (re)negotiated after the project ended. This meant that some of the photographs could not always be shown and that some of them were lost. We did not encounter a participant who did not want us to present their visual outputs, but we lost contact with some of the students/photographers, and as a result, we stopped using their photographs. Recently, we asked some participants for the right to use a selection of their pictures for a presentation, and one of them replied positively but also told us that he had lost all of his pictures while on the move. Getting back in touch with him, we told him we could send him the pictures he had taken for the *Displaces* project. The renewal of informed consent to use their work meant that migrants/ authors continued to be kept updated and engaged in the process of researchers' knowledge production about migration, transit, and visual cultures. Such long-term relationships, beyond the duration of the project, are another distinctive – ethical and methodological – feature of *Displaces*.

## Sustained Engagements, Friendships, and Collaborations

Research with migrants in transit can be challenging because of the volatile and transient nature of their life at the border, where, for many, the main goal is to leave and cross the border. For the purpose of migration control, the authorities engage in an active usurpation of time. There is an overall battle over time between migrants and border agents. However, while migrants at the border want to reduce the time they spend in transit, little is known about what they do in their struggle regarding the passing and loss of time. The photos that students in the *Displaces* project took offer a novel portrayal of the struggle over time; they also display how waiting at the border is not about "wasting time and being stuck" but rather should be referred to as "active waiting" (Grabska 2020, 33): some migrants did business, some used their time to gain information to decide whether to move across the border or apply for protection status in France, and others took a break before resuming the crossing. The latter's sense of waiting consequently differed from that of those who kept attempting to cross the border. The *Displaces* participatory photo-project was, for many participants, a "passing distraction" (Lounasmaa et al. 2019, 15). However, this distraction was highly valued, and they engaged with the visual project very seriously.

In such a volatile ecosystem, our ethics of care approach was guided by respect and flexibility. Facilitators, forced migrants, and practitioners had a verbal agreement that there would be ongoing participation for those who could, with the understanding that some would not be willing or able to complete the training in a context of high uncertainty. In comparison with other photo-projects in the camp, the *Displaces* photo-project was considerably longer, taking place over several months. The transitory nature of The Jungle presented a challenge in terms of sustained engagement with participants. Working within the ethics of care and respect, we tried to maintain contact with former camp residents after the *Displaces* project ended. In that regard, relationships that began in 2015 continue with a subgroup of former students to the present day. Smart phones, social media platforms, and apps have been mobilized to "access information, resources and news; for purposes including communication, emotion-management, establishing intercultural relations, identification, participation, political protest and sending/receiving remittances" (Leurs and Smets 2018, 2); they have also become new methodological tools for participatory engagements during and after the termination of the *Displaces* project. Social media platforms facilitate ongoing relationships, the continuity of conversations, and the formation of less unequal relationships that break down conventional facilitator-participant boundaries to create more collaborative partnerships and friendships.

Long-lasting engagement among migrants, refugees, professional photographers, and academics/facilitators became a key feature of the project. This allowed us to reflect together on the visual materials produced at a particular point in time and collaboratively shape the dissemination of knowledge. Besides informally sharing their visual outputs with family and friends and collating them for the university certificate, the migrants participated in discussions about how to reach a wider audience. With the support of the UEL team, which included the authors, migrants' visual portrayals of everyday life at the border were exhibited at the Barbican Centre in London (UK) in 2016 and at UEL (UK) during Refugee Week in 2018. The authors of this chapter curated a selection of *Displaces* images, which were shown in the arts section program at the International Association for the Study of Forced Migration (IASFM) conference held in Thessaloniki, Greece, in 2018. A few *Displaces* participants took part in an exhibition titled "Calais – Témoigner de la 'Jungle'" (Calais – Witnessing the "Jungle," our translation), curated by Bruno Serralongue at the Pompidou Centre in Paris, which opened in October 2019 and closed in February 2020. Among the works presented there were photographs by Riaz Ahmad, Zeeshan Haider, Ali Haghooi, Babak Inanlou, and Arash Niroomand, all former residents of The Jungle who had participated in the *Displaces* project. Niroomand, an Iranian now living in London, travelled to Paris for the opening and was extremely proud to have his work exhibited.

In Calais, some migrants and refugees had an interest in learning a new visual skill such as photography, and others seized the opportunity to express their artistic skills. Some of the participants in *Displaces* had been creative arts professionals in their home countries. This was the case with the young Iranian multimedia professional and Calais camp resident Babak Inaloo, who produced a short film, *The Bridge*, with another Calais resident, Ali Haghooi. The film, which was made with the support of UEL staff to encourage audiences to rethink The Jungle, was shown in the recent Paris exhibition. Majid Adin was a professional cartoonist when he fled to Europe following persecution in Iran; he spent six months in the Calais camp before reaching London in the back of a refrigerator lorry. While in the Calais camp, Adin took part in the Life Stories program. Since arriving in the UK, he has continued to collaborate with the UEL team and other volunteers he encountered in Calais and has established new professional connections in the media industry. A talented cartoonist, he successfully resumed his career in animation. Recently, he won an international competition to produce an animated video available on YouTube[8] for Elton John's 1970s Hit *Rocket Man*, which beautifully reinterpreted the lyrics of the song with images of migrants' journeys toward Europe. Majid Adin collaborated with Giorgia Donà to reproduce a still from the animated video for the book cover of the 2019 co-edited collection *Forced Migration: Current Issues and Debates*.

Arash Niroomand and Majid Adin took part in the *Displaces II* project, titled Beautiful Swarm,[9] which continued after the closure of the Calais camp at the University of East London's Open Learning Initiative program, which helps migrants, asylum-seekers, and refugees access higher education in the UK. Both are also members of the Ostran Group (i.e., Refugee photographers defamiliarize the UK), with photo-educator Crispin Hughes. The Ostran Group[10] created a series of visual reflections not only about immigration but also about Brexit, nationalism, and the broader concepts of permanence and fragility. Niroomand and Adin, with curatorial support from Donà and Godin, were preparing to show their recent images at the Richmix exhibition space in London in the spring of 2020; that plan was suspended due to the coronavirus pandemic. Moving imaginatively between spaces and places, the visual artists plan to showcase images of the city of London (i.e., rather than Calais), where they currently live, and show the city from the perspective of a newcomer.

These life experiences and trajectories show that transit zones are not just "in-between" spaces; they are also transformative and transforming spaces (Godin and Donà 2021). The *Displaces* project created an apparatus for students to engage in a critical and creative process. In doing so, it allowed migrants and refugees to move away from a "performed refugeeness" (Georgiou 2019, 663) and express themselves, at least temporarily, as visual artists. The use of creative methodologies for the co-production and co-dissemination of migrants' and refugees' stories can be both constraining and liberating. As long as people on the move, researchers, activists, and practitioners engage with one another in transient and often precarious conditions, there is a need for flexible and renegotiable processes to be embedded in the ethics of care and respect. Migrants and refugees involved in the project, and in the legacy collaborations that emerged after the official conclusion of the project, played an active role in the ongoing interpretation and dissemination of the visual materials. However, we also acknowledge the messiness that operates in collaborative endeavours when contacts are lost, priorities differ, deadlines diverge, unequal power dynamics have not disappeared, and intersectional identity markers of race, age, gender, and class play a role in collaborations.

## Representation and Voice

Engagements with the students led to different types of participation, from telling their stories to reflecting with the facilitators on the visual materials produced and collaboratively shaping the representation of their voices over time. The visual narratives of displacement were the product of interactional, relational, and contextual relationships. We engaged in a dialogical process of relationality that, although never perfect or idealized, shifted power relations and gave migrants a stronger representational voice, besides repositioning facilitators in supportive roles. The "subjects" can challenge researchers and professional photographers, who may misrepresent them, and hold them to account.

As stated by Clark-Kazak (2019), "'Doing no harm' in forced migration research means proactively prioritizing the dignity, safety and well-being of participants, partners, research assistants, interpreters and researchers" (14). Within the *Displaces* project, the principle of anonymity needed to be reconsidered in practice in the context of precarity at the border. For instance, some of the student photographers wanted to take selfies of themselves in front of houses or cars, or at the beach in Calais, instead of images of the transit camp; this would have concealed the reality of their circumstances for family members back home (Godin et al. 2019). However, taking selfies or taking photos of other camp residents and posting them online could endanger these people's chances of claiming asylum once they had crossed the border (see Dublin Regulation 604/2013 of the European Parliament and the Council). It is currently acknowledged that immigration authorities scrutinize asylum-seekers' social media profiles to cross-check the stories told by refugees when their claims are being processed (Brekke and Balke Staver 2019, 9). Many of our participants had not claimed asylum in France at the time of the workshop, which meant that showing pictures of them could have jeopardized their asylum claims in the UK at a later stage. The process of anonymizing can be complex when migrants at the border are being visually represented. It may even appear to contradict the aim of the *Displaces* project, which is to amplify migrants' and refugees' representational agency and voice. Yet within the ethics of care, the safety of participants was paramount. We as facilitators were careful to avoid disseminating pictures of the project on websites and Facebook public pages. Social media and mobile technology give migrants more tools for exercising action, having a voice, and navigating highly securitized borderscapes. However, when states invest resources in technology for securitization, those same media jeopardize migrants' safety. Facilitators as well as many residents were often aware of what they should or should not put on Facebook, and this was discussed in depth during workshops with all students. As the legal situation of each participant changed over time, with the majority being able to secure their stay in their chosen country of residence, changes in terms of what to make visible and what to keep invisible were made in dialogue with ex-residents.

Migrants and refugees represent themselves differently than governments, humanitarian organizations, or legal organs represent them. The visual narratives produced in *Displaces* contributed to a rethinking of visual narratives at the border; those narratives were transformed into representations of everyday life about, in, and beyond displacement. The visual representations that emerged from the *Displaces* project, and its legacy, indicate that refugees' aspirations and migration trajectories are undeterred by border regimes. They also reveal visual forms of resistance to the politics of the border. Migrants and refugees in the Calais camps were often aware of the "border spectacle" (De Genova 2013) in which they were embedded and of being "forced" to play a specific role. That is why *Displaces*'s participants enacted visual resistance to the border spectacle and parodied the border regime through what we call visual border performances, a form of improvised visual, poetic, and political satire. Instead of using the concept of voice, we introduced the concept of "visual interferences," in reference to different ways of being political and exposing the politics of the border (Godin et al. 2019). In this way, forced migrants became narrating subjects who challenged portrayals of people on the move as passive, vulnerable, needy victims or as threats to outsiders. In so doing, they shifted the gaze away from the migrant toward the border, thus enabling politically reflexive accounts of the border spectacle. At the same time, visual records of everyday life in transit showed the hidden beauty of life at the border. The photos that migrants and refugees created in *Displaces* serve are intimate images of daily life in the camp, celebrations of momentary "togetherness" in transit, and snapshots of the beauty that migrants uncovered in The Jungle and its landscape. And even as migrants' images portrayed life in displacement, they also showed their interest in visual representations that went beyond displacement. The camp represented everything that they were not, a place through which they were forced to transit but that did not define them. Providing cameras to migrants and refugees risked pushing them to create images that reinforced negative stereotypes about the Calais camp or that forced them to associate with a place they wanted nothing to do with, a place where they did not belong and from which they wanted to dissociate. That is why students/photographers/migrants took photos that had nothing to do with displacement or their life in the Calais camp. They took selfies in which they represented themselves as tourists, lying on the beach in Calais, doing shopping, wearing nice clothes, or standing in front of new cars and houses. They also shared photos that captured their aspirations. These distancing/avoidance narratives reveal stories of personal aspirations, produce reassuring pictures that life can be good, and shift the transit camp somewhere into the distance, spatially and temporally. To create a space for refugees to produce their own visual narratives is critical if we are to challenge stereotypical images of the border migrant/refugee. Researchers can contribute to these discussions by focusing on exploring self-definitions and constructions and by acknowledging that no experience is the same, or the same at different points in time, or in different settings.

## Conclusion

This chapter has provided a reflexive account of the use of participatory photography as a research and pedagogical methodology created with and by people on the move at the border. It has examined the challenges and possibilities arising from creative research collaborations that use photography to present counter-visual representations of the border and of those who inhabit it. Drawing from the participatory photographic project titled *Displaces*, methodological, relational, and ethical reflections revolved around three key issues in participatory visual research: ownership and copyright, sustained relationships, and the representation and voice of displaced people. The reflexive account contributes to the analysis of the emerging genre of visual (photographic) practice at the border by calling for the foregrounding of the ethics of care within the emerging spaces of political solidarity and for challenging the politics of the border through the visual.

Within the ethics of care and respect, giving learners ownership of the cameras and copyright to the images they produced was central to the approach adopted by the project. Providing participants with cameras mitigated unequal power relations by relinquishing control of the visual tools and modalities of present and future use to the displaced persons themselves. The migrant-photographers' copyright ownership of the pictures they took altered the conventional understanding of "renewal of informed consent" whenever we – as researchers – made use of the photographic material produced by participants. Cognizant of the micro-politics of collaboration among academics, practitioners, and migrants, we attempted, through this project, to generate a safe working space in which we could sustain collaborative conversations over time both offline and online. Within an extremely volatile and securitized "borderscape" (Rajaram and Grundy-Warr 2007), this safe space was created to alter the "process of knowing about Others" while acknowledging these "Others" as thinking and knowledge-producing subjects (Mbembe 2016, 36). Co-production calls for continuity amid uncertainty and for finding time when time is ticking as forced migrants – often, but not always – wait to cross the border. And it requires a desire to build long-lasting relationships to sustain creative co-dissemination.

Critical creative methodologies conducted in transit spaces at the border have become political projects that problematize the border and challenge the objectification of displaced people. *Displaces* gave refugees in transit the opportunity to depict "moments" of their everyday lives and make the invisible visible; it also enabled them to highlight the politics of the border by visually documenting how people on the move experience and view borders. The *Displaces* project shows that visual narratives produced in a context of displacement cannot be conceptualized exclusively through the storytelling lens of displacement; better if we understand them as visual interferences depicting different ways of being political that are about, in, and beyond displacement. Migrants in transit spaces are constrained by the border but they also subvert it. Finally, the project fostered visual narrative engagements and knowledge co-production in support of the creative agency of migrants and refugees.

As part of a decolonial approach to knowledge production (Tuhiwai Smith 1999; see also Taha, this volume), participatory arts-based methodologies at the border enable migrants and refugees to re-politicize the narratives of people in transit and reconfigure relations of power between them and the researchers/academics/facilitators and visual artists with whom they work. Long-lasting engagement allows researchers and migrants to reflect jointly on the visual materials produced at a particular point in time and to collaboratively engage with the politics of representation and dissemination of displacement and transit over time. In the context of work with individuals living at the border, methodological and ethical approaches need to move beyond standard guidelines and processes to embrace a broader set of political stances, care and solidarity.

NOTES

1  For more information about the *Displaces* project, visit "Educating without Borders: UEL and Friends in Calais and Beyond" at https://educatingwith outborders.wordpress.com/displaces-a-project-by-gideon-mendel-and-calais-jungle-residents.

2  *Migrant life in Calais' Jungle Refugee Camp*, a photo essay by Sean Smith, Guy Lane, and Matt Fidler. *The Guardian*, 10 August 2015. https://www.

theguardian.com/media/ng-interactive/2015/aug/10/migrant-life-in-calais-jungle-refugee-camp-a-photo-essay.

3 Visit "Citizen Photography Project by Refugee Info Bus" album on Facebook: https://www.facebook.com/media/set/?set=a.1799939456908141&type=3.

4 See Danny Burrows's project "Photographing Volunteers in Calais with Refugee Community Kitchen: http://dannyburrowsphotography.com/tag/refugee-community-kitchen.

5 More information on the project *Dzhangal* (2017) can be found at: https://gostbooks.com/product/dzhangal. A short video on the project "The Act of Collecting" (2017) shows some of Gideon Mendel's process.

6 The *Life Stories* project, https://educatingwithoutborders.wordpress.com/university-for-all-2, was put in place by the Centre for Narrative Research at the University of East London and is part of the broader project "Educating without Borders," https://educatingwithoutborderswordpress.com. The "university for all" project was supported by UEL's civic engagement strategic fund. In Calais, teaching involved photography, art, and poetry workshops, in addition to life story work. As explained by Esin and Lounasmaa (2020), it consisted of "five credits at level 3 in Social Sciences for those who attended three teaching sessions and completed assessment in the form of their own life story" (393). Students could opt for writing a life story, through oral presentation, a recording, a visual life story, or a combination of these.

7 Some authors have used their own names for the book project; others have adopted pseudonyms for a variety of reasons (see Calais Writers 2017, ii).

8 Majid Adin's "Rocket Man": https://www.youtube.com/watch?v=DtVBCG6ThDk. As of the time of writing, it has had more than 67,374,514 views. The winning video was shown to the public during an exhibition about refugee experiences held at the House of Illustration in London between 9 November 2018 and 24 March 2019.

9 Work after the Calais "Jungle" with ex-students includes a further *Displaces* (*Displaces II*) project titled "Beautiful Swarm": https://displacesblog.wordpress.com.

10 For instance, see *Arash: Coast Series* (accessed 10 June 2020): https://ostrangroup.wordpress.com/2019/04/24/arash-coast-series.

REFERENCES

Ball, S., and C. Gilligan. 2010. "Visualising Migration and Social Division: Insights from Social Sciences and the Visual Arts Forum Qualitative *Sozialforschung.*" In *Forum: Qualitative Social Research* 11, no. 2.

Bassel, L. 2017. *The Politics of Listening: Possibilities and Challenges for Democratic Life.* London: Palgrave Macmillan.

Brekke, J.-P., and A. Balke Staver. 2019. "Social Media Screening: Norway's Asylum System." *Forced Migration Review* 61: 9–11.

Brigham, S.M., C. Baillie Abidi, and Y. Zhang. 2018. "What Participatory Photography Can Tell Us about Immigrant and Refugee Women's Learning in Atlantic Canada." *International Journal of Lifelong Education* 37, no. 2: 234–54.

Butler, J. 2016. *Notes Toward a Performative Theory of Assembly.* Cambridge, MA: Harvard University Press.

Calais writers. 2017. *Voices from the "Jungle": Stories from the Calais Refugee Camp.* Edited by M. Godin, K. Møller Hansen, A. Lounasmaa, C. Squire, and T. Zaman. London: Pluto Press. https://doi.org/10.2307/j.ctt1n7qkpb.

Chouliaraki, L., and T. Stolic. 2019. "Photojournalism as Political Encounter: Western News Photography in the 2015 Migration 'Crisis.'" *Visual Communication* 18, no. 3: 311–31.

Clark-Kazak, C. 2017. "Ethical Considerations: Research with People in Situations of Forced Migration." *Refuge* 33, no. 2: 11–17.

– 2019. "Developing Ethical Guidelines for Research." *Forced Migration Review* 61: 1–14.

Collyer, M., and R. King. 2016. "Narrating Europe's Migration and Refugee 'Crisis.'" *Human Geography: A New Radical Journal* 9, no. 2: 1–12.

De Genova, P.N. 2013. "Spectacles of Migrant 'Illegality': The Scene of Exclusion, the Obscene of Inclusion." *Ethnic and Racial Studies* 3, no. 7: 1180–98.

Donà, G. 2007. "The Microphysics of Participation in Refugee Research." *Journal of Refugee Studies* 20, no. 2: 210–29.

Donà, G., and M. Godin. 2019. "Mobile Technologies and Forced Migration." In *Forced Migration: Current Issues and Debates,* edited by A. Bloch and G. Doná, 126–44. London: Routledge.

Eastmond, M. 2007. "Stories as Lived Experience: Narratives in Forced Migration Research." *Journal of Refugee Studies* 20, no. 2: 248–64.

Esin, C. 2017. "Telling Stories in the Pictures: Constituting and Processual and Relational Narratives in Research with Young British Muslim Women in East

London." *Forum Qualitative Sozialforschung/Forum: Qualitative Social Research* 18, no. 1. http://nbn-resolving.de/urn:nbn:de:0114-fqs1701155.

Esin, C., and A. Lounasmaa. 2020. "Narrative and Ethical (In)action: Creating Spaces of Resistance with Refugee-Storytellers in the Calais 'Jungle' Camp." *International Journal of Social Research Methodology* 23, no. 4: 391–403.

Fábos, H.A. 2019. "A Refugee-Centred Perspective." *Forced Migration Review* 61: 58–60.

Georgiou, M. 2018. "Does the Subaltern Speak? Migrant Voices in Digital Europe." *Popular Communication: International Journal of Media and Culture* 16, no. 1: 45–57.

– 2019. "City of Refuge or Digital Order? Refugee Recognition and the Digital Governmentality of Migration in the City." *Television and New Media* 20, no. 6: 600–16.

Godin, M., and G. Donà. 2016. "'Refugee Voices': New Social Media and the Politics of Representation: Young Congolese in the Diaspora and Beyond." *Refuge* 32, no. 1: 60–71.

– 2021. "Rethinking Transit Zones: Migrant Trajectories and Transnational Networks in Techno-Borderscapes." *Journal of Ethnic and Migration Studies* 47, no. 14: 3276–92.

Godin, M., G. Donà, and C. Hughes. 2019. "Reversing the Gaze on Fortress Europe: Visual Interferences Produced by Migrants ino Transit at the France-UK Border." Paper presented at Digital Fortress Europe: Exploring Boundaries between Media, Migration and Technology, Belgium, 30 September–1 October.

Gold, S.J. 2004. "Using Photography in Studies of Immigrant Communities." *American Behavioral Scientist* 47, no. 12: 1551–72.

Grabska, K. 2020. "'Wasting Time': Migratory Trajectories of Adolescence among Eritrean Refugee Girls in Khartoum." *Critical African Studies* 12, no. 1: 22–36.

Guerrero, A.L., and T. Tinkler. 2010. "Refugee and Displaced Youth Negotiating Imagined and Lived Identities in a Photography-Based Educational Project in the United States and Colombia." *Anthropology and Education Quarterly* 41, no. 1: 55–74.

Hagan, M. 2018. "Capturing the Invisible: The Challenges of Using Photography as Method with Asylum Seekers Living in Calais, France." https://www.law.ox. ac.uk/research-subjectgroups/centre-criminology/centreborder-criminolo gies/blog/2018/10/capturing.

Help Refugees/L'Auberge des Migrants. 2016. *Census Report.* October. http://

www.helprefugees.org.uk/news/new-calais-census-released-568-children-calais-74.

Hicks, D., and S. Mallet. 2019. *Lande: The Calais "Jungle" and Beyond.* Bristol: Bristol University Press.

Hugman, R., E. Pittaway, and L. Bartolomei. 2011. "When 'Do No Harm' Is Not Enough: The Ethics of Research with Refugees and Other Vulnerable Groups." *British Journal of Social Work* 41, no. 7: 1271–87.

Koegler, C. 2017. "Precarious Urbanity: 'The Jungle' (Calais) and the Politics of Performing the Urban." *Postcolonial Text* 12, nos. 3–4: 1–15.

Lenette, C. 2016. "Writing with Light: An Iconographic-Iconologic Approach to Refugee Photography." In *Forum Qualitative Sozialforschung/Forum: Qualitative Social Research* 17, no. 2.

Leurs, K., and K. Smets. 2018. "Five Questions for Digital Migration Studies: Learning from Digital Connectivity and Forced Migration in(to) Europe." In *Social Media + Society,* guest-edited special edition, "Forced Migration and Digital Connectivity" (January): 1–16. https://doi.org/10.1177/2056305118764425.

Liamputtong, P. 2007. *Researching the Vulnerable: A Guide to Sensitive Research Methods.* London: SAGE.

Lounasmaa, A., T. Hall, and C. Squire, eds. 2019. "From Margin to Centre? Practising New Forms of European Politics in the Calais 'Jungle.'" In *Challenging the Political across Borders: Migrants' and Solidarity Struggles,* edited by C. Cantat, E. Sevinin, E. Maczynska, and T. Birey. Budapest: Center for Policy Studies, Central European University.

Malaquais, D. 2017. "Forensics (Photography in the Face of Failure)." In *Dzhangal,* edited by G. Mendel, 73–4, http://gideonmendel.com/art-historian-text.

Mannik, L. 2012. "Public and Private Photographs of Refugees: The Problem of Representation." *Visual Studies* 27, no. 3: 262–76.

Martiniello, M. 2017. "Visual Sociology Approaches in Migration, Ethnic, and Racial Studies." *Ethnic and Racial Studies* 40, no. 8: 1184–90.

– 2019. "Introduction to the Special Issue 'Arts and Refugees: Multidisciplinary Perspectives.'" *Arts* 8, no. 3: 98–9.

Mbembe, A.J. 2016. "Decolonizing the University: New Directions." *Arts and Humanities in Higher Education* 15, no. 1: 29–45.

McBrien, L.J., and R. Day. 2012. "From There to Here: Using Photography to Explore Perspectives of Resettled Refugee Youth." *International Journal of Child, Youth, and Family Studies* 3, no. 4.1: 546–68.

McGregor, E., and N. Ragab. 2016. "The Role of Culture and the Arts in the Integration of Refugees and Migrants." European Expert Network on Culture and Audiovisual (EENCA). https://migration.unu.edu/publications/reports/the-role-of-culture-and-the-arts-in-the-integration-of-refugees-and-migrants.html.

Mendel, G. 2017. *Dzhangal.* GOST Books.

Ní Raghallaigh, M. 2013. "The Causes of Mistrust amongst Asylum Seekers and Refugees: Insights from Research with Unaccompanied Asylum-Seeking Minors Living in the Republic of Ireland." *Journal of Refugee Studies* 27, no. 1: 82–100.

Rajaram, P.K., and C. Grendy-Warr. 2007. *Borderscapes: Hidden Geographies and Politics at Territory's Edge.* Minneapolis: University of Minnesota Press.

Schapendonk, J. 2012. "Turbulent Trajectories: African Migrants on Their Way to the European Union." *Societies* 2: 27–41.

Singh, I., T. Flores, L. Mohseni, and S.S. Hansen. 2016. "Humans of Calais: Migration from the Perspective of Migrants," research report, King's College London.

Squire, C. 2017. "Scattered but Hopeful: Stories of Life after the Calais 'Jungle' Refugee Camp." *The Conversation,* 9 March. https://theconversation.com/scattered-but-hopeful-stories-of-life-afterthe-calais-jungle-refugee-camp-73009.

Taggart, G. 2016. "Compassionate Pedagogy: The Ethics of Care in Early Childhood Professionalism." *European Early Childhood Education Research Journal* 24, no. 2: 173–85.

Tuhiwai Smith, L. 1999. *Decolonizing Methodologies: Research and Indigenous Peoples.* London: Zed Books.

Vandevoordt, R. 2019. "Subversive Humanitarianism: Rethinking Refugee Solidarity through Grass-Roots Initiatives." *Refugee Survey Quarterly* 38, no. 3: 245–65. https://doi.org/10.1093/rsq/hdz008.

Vecchio, L., K.K. Dhillon, and J.B. Ulmer. 2017. "Visual Methodologies for Research with Refugee Youth." *Intercultural Education* 28, no. 2: 131–42.

Wilmott, A.C. 2017. "The Politics of Photography: Visual Depictions of Syrian Refugees in UK Online Media." *Visual Communication Quarterly* 24, no. 2: 67–82.

# 10

## Memories, Stories, and Material Traces:
### *Exploring Displacement through Collaging and Participatory Art Installation*

Nihal Soğancı

Displacement in any form implies a disruption of our understanding of time and space. In Cyprus, on an island and in a century in which the mourning of displacement can be traced across generations, the healing, resisting, and creative power of artistic expression offers new ways to understand the experience of displacement, the role of memory and home-making. In this chapter, I elaborate methodologically and conceptually on two arts-based methods – collage workshops and a participatory art installation – that I designed and employed during my doctoral research in social anthropology. My doctoral research focuses on how home is collaged in the context of dispossession and displacement in North Cyprus. I began my doctoral studies in February 2016 and I am currently writing my thesis. The arts-based methods were carried out from June to October 2019. Through these interdisciplinary practices, which combined anthropological approaches with contemporary artistic practices, I hoped to create a reflexive space that would allow "reading in-between the lines" of mobility and confinement, home and abroad, past and present, and peace and rupture. In this chapter, I explain the guiding principles of my fieldwork in North Cyprus as well as the methodological and ethical questions raised by my approach. I then describe the two methods I followed and the stories that emerged as a result of those methods. In exploring the links between memories, stories, and material traces (in this case, everyday objects), the project has been inspired by the work of Walter Benjamin, for whom things and memories form a junction with our past.

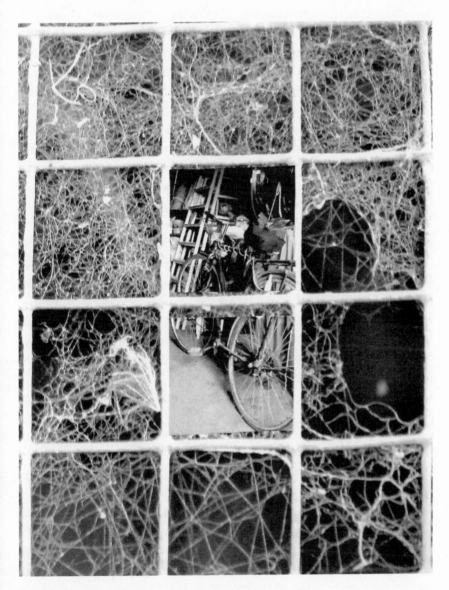

Figure 10.1 Memories and material traces.

## Ethics and Location

This chapter reflects on the fieldwork I carried out as part of my doctoral research. I started fieldwork in North Cyprus in February 2016, focusing on how home is collaged in the context of dispossession and displacement in North Cyprus post-2003, the year that crossing points opened for travel between Northern and Southern Cyprus. My fieldwork started with participant observation and open-ended interviews; my intent was to understand the participants in the research as "actors" of the study. Following Wilson (1993), I conducted my research not "on" displaced people, but "with" them. Along the way, I sought a methodology that would allow the participants more agency. Hence, I decided to employ arts-based methodologies, which I found very helpful though not unproblematic.

To locate myself in the study, I myself am from Cyprus, from the northern part of Nicosia. However, I was away from "home" studying abroad for about six years before starting my PhD. In 2016, I started fieldwork "back home" and actually *about* "home." The particularities of "anthropology at home" (Jackson 1987) have long been discussed. Seymour-Smith (1986, 19) refers to the "anthropological study of a social cultural system by a member of the society concerned"; Strathern (1987, 17) describes "anthropology at home" as the "anthropology carried out in the social context which produced it." But what does home actually mean? When are we at home? Is home the country one comes from or the country one lives in? Is language a home, as Barbara Cassin and colleagues (2016) suggest, and does speaking the same language as the community in which you live mean that you are at home? Conversely, could home describe a deeper interrelation between the part of the world a person considers as the "self" and the part of the world considered as the "other," as Michael Jackson (1995) proposes?

Since I come from North Cyprus, it was certainly easier for me to engage with certain communities. Speaking Turkish, being familiar with the context, and knowing people who would introduce me to others all played a facilitating role in my research; people who knew my family or friends happily opened their doors to me and talked about their lives. However, among the communities that had migrated to North Cyprus from Turkey after 1974, I had a very different level of familiarity owing to my personal background, on which I will further elaborate below. Age, gender, and political affiliation also influenced my relations with different participants. So, rather than focusing on whether I was at "home" or "abroad," I will take specifically into account how I related to the study's participants, my changing familiarity with them, and the particularities of the fieldwork itself, which was collectively constructed by relations, events, and experiences.

To expand connections with people outside my circle, during the first year of my fieldwork, I worked as a volunteer, helping with cleaning jobs, volunteering at shops, and conducting free language classes. My aim was to balance the power dynamics as much as I could, which then enabled me to have the familiarity to ask people to take part in the participatory workshops and the art installation. Confidentiality and anonymity were important aspects of this research, given that it was a sensitive research being carried out with people who had been through hard times. Any information that might place anyone in danger was not written down and was not mentioned directly in the research. From the very start, I thought it crucial to clearly explain the focus and aim of the research. I was always eager to explain my perceptions of the study, and my findings, and even to share readings whenever a participant showed interest. I refrained from asking rigid questions and instead conducted informal, open-ended interviews over coffee, tea, and food. I allowed people the time and space to touch upon topics that were important to them. One cannot assume that the researcher is free of all bias: we can only analyze and observe the world through the lens of our pre-existing perceptions and ideas, and those are situated and never neutral. The self is very much part of the fieldwork process; that said, one must guard against egocentricism, which is not always easy.

Narayan (1993) points out that "we might more profitably view each anthropologist in terms of shifting identifications amid a field of interpenetrating communities and power relations. The loci along which we are aligned with or set apart from those we study are multiple and in flux" (671). I understood what Narayan meant a few months after I started fieldwork. Each fieldwork encounter was unique and encompassed multiple identities with particular ethical and moral dilemmas that reached beyond carrying out "anthropology at home" (Jackson 1987) or being a "native anthropologist" (Narayan 1993). It involved changing relationships and a changing self along with the new understandings that followed. The fieldwork itself was at times intuitive, messy, and emotional. Especially early in the research, I juggled between the professionalism required by the discipline and certain norms expected from me as someone coming from the community. I felt that I should keep a certain professional distance, but after some time, deeper bonds formed between me and some of the participants that made it problematic to simply refer to them as participants, given that a reciprocal process of sharing and understanding had taken shape that blurred the boundaries between the private realm and the fieldwork. People knew from the beginning about my research and studies, but after four years of passing by a shop, if one day a person tells you all about their personal problems, how do you as a researcher distinguish what becomes part of writing? Can we really separate fieldwork clearly and rigidly from everyday life? According to Shore (1999), this is not possible, for personal bonds and mutual communications make it very difficult to draw precise boundaries between the researcher and the participants. The arts-based methodologies offered an alternative, as they created a temporal and a spatial break from everyday relations, thus allowing a clearer separation between the personal and the academic. I had already developed close relations with a number of people which then made it possible to ask them to participate in the workshops and the installation. I had by then informed them that the stories they would be sharing during these meetings would become part of my research.

At the same time, during fieldwork from February 2016 to February 2019, I had also realized that participants had difficulty engaging with topics related to displacement and the trauma of war. So I sought alternative methods that might foster that engagement. I wanted to achieve an active, participatory research method in which participants would become part of the creative thinking process and actors of the study. Embedding creativity into a social process while separating research from everyday life, the methods lead us to think critically about agency, creativity, art and art-making. In the following sections, I will elaborate on the artistic, experimental and improvisational approaches to ethnographic research that I developed and on what we can learn from them in collective contexts.

## The Background and Context

We should now examine the historical context. As British colonial rule over Cyprus was coming to an end in the late 1950s, Greek and Turkish Cypriots were already becoming polarized. In 1960, the Republic of Cyprus was founded, uniting Turkish and Greek Cypriots within a single sovereign state. However, Greek Cypriots endeavoured unification with Greece, and Turkish Cypriots with Turkey, which along with economic and representation problems, led to violent conflict in 1963 that continued until 1974. After the Turkish intervention/invasion/peace operation[1] in July 1974, a ceasefire was negotiated, through which the island, including the capital city Nicosia, was divided by the Green Line. According to Zetter (1994), 180,000 Greek Cypriots, and according to Ozersay and Gurel (2006), 142,000 Greek Cypriots, had to migrate to the southern side of the Green Line, while 65,000 Turkish Cypriots had to migrate to the northern side.

Meanwhile, migration of "agricultural labour" from Turkey to North Cyprus was incentivized; policies encouraging settlement on the island through Turkey continued from 1975 to 1979. Communities that had demanded internal relocation within Turkey – mainly due to socio-economic and environmental problems – were compelled to migrate to North Cyprus. At the same time, people of different ethnic backgrounds, such as the Kurdish and Pontians, who had long faced discrimination and violence in Turkey, found homes in North Cyprus too. This second stage of migration began around 1985. A third stage began in the 2000s, driven by economic factors, and these communities settled mainly in the old town of Nicosia.

Over the past ten years, Nicosia's old town has rapidly transformed. New cafes and bars have opened, and buildings marked with bullet holes have been painted over with colourful images, attracting "multicultural" individuals from both sides of the divide. At this point, it is important to note that after 1974, following a decade and a half of violent conflict, Turkish Cypriot inhabitants of the area had moved to more spacious houses in other districts of Nicosia as the Greek and Armenian Cypriot inhabitants were forced to empty their homes and to move to the southern part of the island. According to Navaro (2012), "the border area (and the old town of Nicosia) had become, for the Turkish-Cypriots, something they wanted to abject out of themselves as it represented to them the originary violence (in Walter

Benjamin's sense) at the foundation of their system, in which they were also involved" (158). Navaro states that Turkish Cypriots knew of the corpses and the violence beneath their system, so, if they were to establish homes after the war, certain spaces had to be associated with ruination. Elaborating on Butler's theory of gender melancholia, Navaro argues that when the loss belongs to the community of the "enemy," it is not perceived as loss and is hence not mourned; this leads to melancholia, where the source of the loss remains unknown.

In 2003, the crossing points that had been closed since 1974 were opened. Many Cypriots visited their old homes, and Turkish Cypriots individually acquired EU citizenship. After that, existential questions arose among the community, consolidating perceptions that the war was not actually over. What would happen now? Who was the Other? Who were we? What would happen to people who had come from Turkey after 1974? Would the exclusion of the people who had migrated from Turkey to cross to the southern part of the island further complicate matters? All of these questions fuelled internal ruptures in the Turkish Cypriot community after 2003 and are the main focus of my PhD research.

## Interactions

As we sat with a few friends in the old town of Nicosia in April 2019 at a bar that had opened a few years earlier, a song called "Torn" by Natalie Imburglia played. It was as if the lyrics of the song were describing the old town of Nicosia. War debris from the 1960s and 1970s was still scattered throughout this part of the city. On the building across the street from us, gunshots had been painted with colourful images, just like wound dressings. The barrels that had been used during the conflict had been turned into bar stools, and the almost abandoned street was lit by dangling lights. As the conversations continued at the bar where we were sitting, I saw a Kurdish friend who was also a research participant at the opposite table. He had migrated to North Cyprus from Turkey ten years earlier. Farther back, uneven gentrification was staring us in the face: barefoot children across the street were living in a building decorated by gunshots, and beyond, I could see the border wall, the very embodiment of the Cypriot crack – which was also recently painted with colourful images. The paint was also on the people, covering up the division as if trying to hide an internal wound. All had come from different backgrounds, by themselves or with their parents or grandparents, having left a home somewhere else to make a new life in North Cyprus. They had attempted to "collage" homes by bringing together various fragments of the recovering city. As the strings of my research came together, my four years of fieldwork started to make sense.

As it turned out, the topic I had first wanted to research and with which I had started my fieldwork was actually an important indicator of my positionality at the beginning of the study. I wanted to study the forced/non-forced migration from Turkey to North Cyprus after 1974. I was critical of the prejudices and stereotypes that these people were being subjected to by Turkish Cypriot "natives," but I had failed to consider the broader context. What did internal displacement *mean* for the community? What did settling in houses abandoned by Greek Cypriots *mean*? What were the socio-psychological implications of establishing a *de facto* state that was not recognized by any country except Turkey? What did the categories "settlers" and "natives" signify post-2003? What was enabling increasing feelings of homelessness? Was it a new EU citizenship, or was it the identity that came with the postwar state?

"Native Cypriots" had attached several stereotypes to those who had come from Turkey – that they were dirty, uneducated, and cultureless. During my first fieldwork encounters with people who had come from Turkey, I was struck by how often people who had come from Turkey tried to assure me they were clean. People who lived outside the old town of Nicosia would say that the Turks of the old town were dirty, and the ones from the old town would say how the people from Hatay[2] were dirty, and the people from Hatay would say how the students from Nigeria were making the city dirty. It was an endless cycle of blaming, although I never asked anything about dirtiness or cleanliness. They were clearly trying to send me the message that they were not the dirty people whom "Cypriots" often complained about. The concepts of Orientalism (Edward Said, 1978), the abject (Julia Kristeva, 1984), and pollution and taboo (Mary Douglas, 1966) provide crucial explanations for these categorizations, but I haven't the space to provide more details in this chapter.

While I was thinking about how I could go beyond this positionality, I interviewed a participant whose parents had migrated from Turkey. She invited me to her engagement party so that I could gain more insight into their traditions. As I danced through the night with the bride and their relatives, the rigidity of our previous conversations disappeared. That night, my love for dancing changed my relations with that particular community. Weddings and engagement parties are important events in North Cyprus, just as they are in many other cultures. However, these celebrations in North Cyprus are judged first by how many people attend and second by the number of people who dance. The people who dance at your wedding are viewed as the people who love and respect your family. Clearly, my dancing that night shifted my positionality and enabled me to be perceived in a different light than that of a "Cypriot" researcher to whom they needed to prove their cleanliness. This is one example of a changing fieldwork identity and relationship, and it led me to ask several ethical questions. I was doing professional research, but where could I place something as personal as dancing in the fieldwork experience? Did I dance because I wanted them to trust me, or did I dance because I simply wanted to? From childhood, I have danced at almost every wedding and engagement party I attend. Making sense of this experience and its implications for my fieldwork required thorough questioning.

My relations with some of the people I met during the fieldwork have turned into friendships. The debate over friends as participants in anthropological research advances different points of view related largely to the blurred boundaries between the personal and the professional. According to Hendry (1992), friendship during research may lead to a disorientation of roles and also limit extensive writing. But according to Tillmann-Healy (2003), friendship can enable empathy and understanding. Van der Geest (2015) emphasizes, however, how hard it is to arrive at a term for "informants" that embraces the reciprocal relationship that has formed during the fieldwork and suggests that the term "friend" can be useful in this regard. When I refer to a friend in my writing, it is indeed an intentional reference to a mutual and reciprocal communication that goes beyond asking questions to acquire information or knowledge. The participants in my study were not merely informants whom I valued solely for their ability to provide information. This certainly carries ethical implications: how do you analyze the information you get from someone whom you consider your friend?

Figure 10.2 Collaging displacement.

On a similar note, who was I to give voice to their experiences? I could approach with empathy but I could only make sense of these experiences and thoughts through my own subjectivity. This tells us much about why the alternative arts-based methods changed the course of my research. Through the collage workshops and the participatory garage, participants had much more agency than they would have had had I used more conventional methods such as participant observation and interviews. At the same time, the temporal and spatial disjunction inherent in these methods made possible a separation between the everyday and research as well as between the personal and the professional. The affective stories elicited through these alternative methods helped answer the question of what role alternative art practices can play in making sense of the experience of displacement. In the next parts of this chapter, I discuss the role these methods played in processes of remembering, deconstructing, and reconstructing experiences as well as in allowing the participants to become the actors of the process.

## Cutting and Stitching: Collaging a Home

Collage workshops invited participants to analyze and use different fieldwork visuals in teams of ten to deconstruct and reconstruct images and ideas through a creative process during which people shared stories during cutting and gluing. These workshops were held over the course of four months; one workshop was organized for each month from June 2019 to September 2019. Each workshop had ten participants (five men and five women), ranging in age from eighteen to seventy-five. Two workshops took place in Nicosia, one in Hamitkoy, a suburb of Nicosia, and one in the central walled city of Nicosia. The other two took place in Iskele, a town in the eastern part of North Cyprus that has a high number of internally displaced people. The workshops took place in cafés with outside spaces that provided a calm environment where people could feel comfortable. To make up the teams, I contacted people I already knew from my fieldwork; with those who agreed, we set a time and place that suited everyone. In this chapter, the real names of the participants are not used. During workshops, I first explained the aim, and then the method, making it clear that the stories they would share during these workshops would become a part of my PhD research. During all stages, I reminded the participants that they were the actors of the study and that the exploration was not *on* them, nor was it *about* them; rather, it was *with* them.

I wanted to bring my anthropological work into dialogue with art, so as to render it more participatory and collaborative. I got the idea for these workshops from Max Ernst's (1936) thinking of collage as the combining and reshuffling of different elements on an unexpected plane with non-perfect cuts and stitches relating to the "surrealist element of ethnography" in Clifford's (1981) terms. I was inspired to organize collective collage workshops at the Hisar Art Collective, run by Turkish Cypriot Artist Asik Mene, where I have been involved for several years. At the collective, a group of amateur artists come together at the art studio to work in a friendly environment. I was doing collages myself at the studio, and one afternoon we met with a few friends who are artists to work together. As we continued, stories that I had not heard from them despite their being long-time friends started to bubble up, and this gave me the idea of organizing collage workshops. I collaborated with a Turkish Cypriot artist, who helped with the process and invited participants to join as well.

Images come with meanings attached. So, can tearing that image help deconstruct the rigid understandings we associate with it? During collage workshops, I provided people with photographic materials from my fieldwork as well as newspapers, magazine clippings, and other materials such as threads and stones. To eliminate researcher's bias, I also asked them to bring any visual materials or items they wanted to use for collage making. They were then invited to cut, montage, and glue what home meant to them. During these workshops, we worked together at making collages; afterwards, we all shared our feelings. This helped overcome the distancing power dynamic between participants and researcher – a matter of core importance, for it lent voice to the unspoken words.

As one of the participants began cutting around an image of the border, putting a big rock right in front of it, she started to explain:

> I feel Turkish Cypriot, but Cypriots consider me as the Turkish one from Turkey. On the other hand, when I go to Turkey, people consider me as the Cypriot one. I was actually born in North Cyprus but my parents had come from Turkey in 1975, I am not familiar with all the local traditions in Turkey. When the borders were first opened, I was curious and excited to pass to the other side; however, when I went to the Greek borders, the woman took my ID, examined it well and then threw it back at me shouting that my parents were from Turkey so I had no right to pass since I was not a true Cypriot. I felt very unwanted and I am afraid of what will happen to us if a solution is ever reached.

When a Kurdish friend, also a participant, who had moved to North Cyprus from Diyarbakir in eastern Turkey, saw an image of eyes in one of the magazines, he suddenly stopped and asked if I knew why Kurdish people talk with their eyes:

> After the coup in 1980, it became forbidden to talk in Kurdish in public, however for my mom it was the only language she ever knew. As we grew up and started school, at first we could speak very little Turkish but our teachers were constantly warning us [against] speaking in Kurdish among each other. Afterwards, our Turkish did improve and I accompanied my mother at every public institution or hospital so that I could translate for her. So, what do you do – when you are forbidden to express yourself in your own language, you start to speak with your eyes.

The above is an example of Kurdish experiences of exclusion – of struggling for recognition. Most Kurdish participants emphasized that in North Cyprus, they do not feel any discrimination, the way they do in Turkey.

Hayriye was a child who had migrated internally in Cyprus during the violent conflict. As she began cutting blankets from a magazine, she started telling this story:

> I remember nights where we were putting blankets over windows and closing down all the lights in order not to become a target of bombing. We were four siblings with our mother, we would usually sleep on the floor or under the beds for extra protection, in order for us to relax and fall asleep, my mother used to tell us fairy tales, she would gather us around, put on a very small candle and tell us about injustices that would happen to ordinary people and how a "force" would come and always find a way around it.

Others joined in the conversation, and it became apparent that fairy tales had been used during the conflict as a means to keep hopes high and to calm children on nights they could not go out, and also as a promise of protection. The presence of a protective force that would eliminate "the bad power" was central to these stories. Taussig (1992, 132) writes that in the lives and beliefs of ordinary people the idea of the state finds its place; thus, I believe that by exploring these fairy tales we can also catch a glimpse of what this war-torn population expected from their state. The cutting out of images led the participants to voice stories, which in turn allowed access to fragments of their memories. Cutting, in this sense, became a way to foster engagement and interaction between the mind, hand, and social context.

Cengiz cut out an image of a green barrel from the border and glued it over a chair hanging randomly on a house. I was very curious why, and he explained:

> When I was a child we lived right near a barricade which is right at the border now. On one side of the building there were barrels that were on top of each other and they had soil and cotton inside. After our parents were leaving for work, we were collecting the cotton from the bar-

rels and selling it to the quilt maker right around the border. I did not know why they were there but for us it meant buying a few extra sweets.

A few days later, we went together to the house that Cengiz had mentioned in Nicosia. Its inhabitants had moved there from Turkey after 1974. They had found it very difficult at first to live so close to the border, but they got used to it. As Ayse recounted:

The first thing we did when we came here was to remove those barrels. My son cut them into [pieces] and we gave all the bullets and the metal to the soldiers. We used the soil to make a garden and I grow vegetables there ever since. They want to throw us out of here if a resolution in the island is reached but until then, we will live here.

In a world where everything is more rushed than ever and on an island where liminality seems everlasting, uncertainty regarding where home is marks the existences of individuals and collectivities. The collage workshops were meant to be a space where each individual could reflect, construct, and deconstruct what home meant to them.

Figure 10.3 A moment at *The Affective Garage.*

## *The Affective Garage*: A Collective Junction

The participatory installation *The Affective Garage* was an open-air garage made from wooden pallets and pebbles. It contained objects from the garages of the participants. It was situated in the Buffer Zone in Nicosia as part of the Buffer Fringe Performing Arts Festival 2019, organized by the Home for Cooperation. The installation had been inspired by a personal story. I first experienced the buffer zone when I was ten years old, during a school picnic that had been organized to visit the village of Pyla. Pyla is the only village in Cyprus where Greek and Turkish Cypriots live together under UN control. Our picnic spot was considered part of the buffer zone. At the same time, for me, Pyla was a buffer zone because it was the nearest point of contact we could have with the "other" side of the island. When my brother heard that I was going to Pyla, he asked me to bring him back pebbles from there. So after our picnic I filled up my picnic bag with pebbles from all around the picnic area. It neither mattered nor did we realize that these pebbles looked exactly the same as the pebbles we could find around where we lived, as Pyla was only a forty-minute drive from Nicosia. Encountering Pyla was a moment of questions, a moment of uncertainty that materialized as we exhibited these pebbles on our balcony in the months to come. They came from a place that had contact with the part of the island we always heard about yet could not visit. For us, Pyla was a mystical place that could fuel and also help curb our curiosity about the "other" side.

The people of Cyprus harboured various perceptions of the buffer zone. As the crossing points opened, encountering that zone activated past memories. Every time we passed through the buffer zone with my parents and grandparents, memories emerged that reached far back to before the conflict. These conversations often reminded me of a visit to a garage. For most people in Cyprus, a garage is a place to store objects that cannot be used but neither can be thrown away because of their emotional value, which means that visiting the garage often leads to the telling of stories about the past. So when I saw the open call for the Buffer Fringe 2019, which was seeking contributors to artistically explore what the buffer zone meant as an in-between space, I decided to conceptualize that zone through the garage as a third space.

Through this interaction with the in-between space, and through the audience's participation, I hoped to re-create a space that would emphasize new potentials the buffer zone held. I also wanted to create a space where individuals could reflect on how the buffer zone echoed through their own existence. In *The Affective Garage*, the buffer zone would function as a third space in Bhabha's (1994) terms, one that produced a disjunctive temporality: the past interrupted the present, in this way forming a liminality between memory and perceived reality. It took me four months to collect the objects that would make up the garage. During those months, I visited people I knew from my fieldwork. I visited more than thirty homes of people from different backgrounds to ask what they would be willing to give me from their garage. I made sure that the objects were from different generations, and in the end they ranged from the 1920s to the 1990s. This collection process was as important as the actual day that people would encounter the installation. Many participants were part of this process, asking, thinking, and questioning how *The Affective Garage* related both to the buffer zone and to the objects in their garage. It became a way to remember, to forget, and to engage. The participants who donated objects from their garages, the Buffer Fringe Festival audience, and people passing by visited the installation on the 26 October 2019 and shared their stories and what they felt upon seeing these objects in a highly unconventional setting. The ages of the people who gave objects to the garage ranged from thirty to ninety. The people who found out about it on the day it took place were mainly between their twenties and their sixties. Similar numbers of men and women from both northern and southern parts of the island participated in the installation.

Building the walls of *The Affective Garage* and placing the objects took about two days. That is how long we had before our UN permit expired. I was there to observe and talk to people during and after their encounter with the installation. I invited them to interact with it: they could move objects around, leave any objects they had brought, write what they felt, share their memories, or talk about the objects that were most meaningful to them. I told them that the stories they shared would become part of my doctoral fieldwork. They were also invited to paint on a collective canvas, using a variety of painting materials I had made available. Also available was a notepad so that people could jot down their thoughts and memories. I especially wanted to know which objects meant the most to them. As the spectators became participants, they reimagined their perceptions and associations with the buffer zone.

### Stories from The Affective Garage

The first people I approached to discuss *The Affective Garage* and to ask if they would like to participate were a close friend's grandparents. They had two garages but no cars. They also had two storage rooms in the garden, and the garden itself was full of objects, old, new, torn, and usable. It seemed that from the day they moved into the house, in 1974, they had never thrown anything away. Their house was a "rum evi" as they said – that is, a house that had been abandoned by Greek Cypriots. Then Emine recounted her story:

> We were tenants in another area in 1963, then conflict broke out and we became hostages. I had just given birth to my eldest daughter, they put the women and children separately. We did not know what was going to happen to us. From stress my milk stopped coming and I was wetting biscuits to feed my child. Then, they [Greek Cypriot soldiers] came and chose the youngest girls, they said that they were taking them to cook for us, at the end of the day they were coming but no food ever came. We were asking where the food is, they never replied. After this period, we understood that they were not being taken to cook but they were taken to be raped. After a few weeks, they set us free but our house was in a Greek Cypriot area, all our things, our clothes were there. My husband tried to find a van to go back and to pick them up, eventually someone accepted to take the risk so we managed to get whatever we could. We stayed in other houses after and after the division they gave us this house, so the house of the "Greek" became our home. You can see here, this wardrobe is from the "Greek," this bread toaster too but that clock you see over there is mine, I had bought it in 1950, it broke down a bit but it still works.

After our conversation, I was left with many questions. What was the relationship between the experience of leaving home and all these objects they were storing in their garages and garden? What do all these objects mean to them? Were they a way to connect with the past? According to Navaro (2009), Turkish-Cypriot refugees' melancholy has two facets: first, they have lost their people, homes, and belongings; and second, they have become part of the violence meted out against Greek Cypriots by making homes over their homes and objects which they continue to live with. After several hours at this couple's home, I couldn't ask them to give me anything. They seemed tightly bonded with their objects; if I took one away, something would go missing from their life.

The mere fact that I could not touch or move any object that was a part of their world speaks to core ethical considerations attached to these two methods. I felt that their attachment to these objects served to maintain a link between their past and present. They had no need to talk to each other about what they had been through; to remember, they only needed to look around themselves. It was as if the objects consoled them by bearing the weight of their memories. Homi Bhabha (1994) points out in *The Location of Culture* that "remembering is never a quiet act of introspection. It is a painful remembering, a putting together of the dismembered past to make sense of the trauma of the present" (63). I think that this in a way shows how these methods can place people in vulnerable situations, for it involves entering into a very intimate space. I see this as a core problem for most studies that aim to understand human experience: the more you try to understand certain experiences, the more likely you are to touch on memories and feelings that people may not want to summon. But at the same time, voicing these stories also seems to have a healing effect for some, for it can help people face aspects of the present. I felt that most participants were happy that someone had shown interest in objects and memories that were dear to them. So, it is important to set aside rigid aims and procedures and to pay attention to small cues in conversations; in this way, one gives the participants the necessary space to express themselves. I emphasize again that presenting myself not just as someone doing research but also as someone from Cyprus who wanted to understand more about her own community helped greatly to foster intimate conversations. As I began to understand the participants better, I began to understand more about myself too.

Marios, in his seventies, arrived at the garage and studied the objects one by one, then wrote on the notepad "the world is a lie" and drew a coffin. He said he had spent his youth fighting for Cyprus and his adulthood thinking and discussing the Cyprus issue and waiting for it to be solved. He believed it never would be solved. It seemed that *The Affective Garage* was serving as a space for contemplating displacement, one that allowed visitors to think about where they came from and where they were now. This notion can perhaps help develop a framework for exploring how "home" is remembered, imagined, and re-created. Displacement is painful, but not necessarily the act itself. Rather, what causes the pain of displacement is not knowing what will happen next, and the fear of losing one's feelings for what had once been home. As the crossing points opened, homes that had been left behind were revived through the objects that could still be found there. Maria, a Greek Cypriot participant in her fifties, wrote after encountering the garage:

> When the checkpoints opened, we went back to our house and most of our items were stored in a cupboard. In that cupboard, we found many things that we had left behind, we brought back whatever we could.

Many people went back to their old homes and tried to bring back whatever object still remained. These objects carried their past, their memories. Later, Maria added:

> After seeing these objects in the buffer zone, I realize that we do not actually need a buffer zone in this country to separate us, we can leave all these old objects where they belong and look ahead.

Other visitors to the garage and its objects expressed feelings of nostalgia. Metin recounted:

> When my parents had just broken up, I used to listen to "Manga" [a Turkish rock band from the 2000s]. I have the same cassette that I saw here. It reminded me of my childhood and how much I loved to listen to Manga to escape from reality. It was like a gift to me. I think the only cassette that I still keep is my Manga cassette.

On a similar note, Sifa wrote down:

The blue pyjamas reminded me especially of times when my mom would make me and my siblings go to bed at 7 o'clock to sleep. Of course we would not sleep, we would talk in low tones so that my mom would not hear us and we would also frighten each other. My mother would come to check on us occasionally and of course we would act as if we have slept but I have even missed that feeling of fear. How I would love to feel like I did at those times.

According to Boym (2001), in the twentieth century, nostalgia was privatized and internalized transforming longing for home into longing for one's own childhood. This seemed to be the case with the above narratives. Many people in their forties, fifties, and sixties remembered their childhood through the Chopper bicycle. Some remembered having a red one, some a gold one. Gül looked at the Chopper in the garage and sighed:

We left our house in the south, we couldn't bring back our bike with us to the north but I remember once my mother had gotten on the bike together with me and I fell; I still have a scar here on my waist from that fall.

According to Boym (2001), nostalgia may seem like longing for a place, it is actually a longing for another time – the time of our childhood, when life's pace was slower. The nostalgic is a displaced person occupying an in-between place between the local and the global, the collective and the individual memory.

Before the installation opened, I drove with Salih and his family, all of whom were research participants, to the village where Salih was born and raised. He explained how his mother liked to store everything. No one had lived in their house in the village for the past ten years, so their garage was beginning to fall apart. I saw a tractor a few metres away, and as I approached it, I came across innumerable items that had been stored in the garage for many years: farm equipment, luggage full of university notebooks, school uniforms, onion buds to be planted one day, a child's bathtub, pillows, kitchen equipment. Salih had not been there ever since his mother died, and although the garage was falling apart he had not wanted to touch any of the objects. They were what remained of his parents and his old village life. He was still reluctant to touch them, yet he knew that the garage was about to collapse and that he had to take some things back with him. He chose a few kitchen items, luggage, and a child's bath. As he lifted the bathtub, he sighed, saying that his mother had used to wash him in it. He was travelling back to his childhood, and his memories of that time now surfaced. He remembered his mother not as an old woman who had to be taken care of but as herself, the caregiver. As Boym argues (2001), reflective nostalgia carries components of mourning and melancholia. Although loss is not fully known, it is linked with the loss of collective frameworks of memory, which carries out a deep mourning that works through reflection of pain toward the future. It seems that while the actual trauma is at no time fully recollected, the element of nostalgia in the process of remembering in this context is linked to the loss of collective frameworks of memory.

## In Retrospect

The participatory collage workshops and the installation brought to the fore new forms of remembering that underscored the role improvisational creativity could play in homemaking after a rupture. The stories and creations became a space of contemplation on displacement that allowed thinking about how "home" is imagined. The question that guided the collage-making was how abstract understandings of home can be expressed. It is perhaps impossible to express the imaginary manifestations of home through verbal utterances, but they can find expression as images are cut and montaged so as to reflect the depths of memory where one can reach beyond the confines of time and space. Memories that resurged through *The Affective Garage* helped evoke historical trauma even while allowing a working through of the ruins and remnants of the past. Rendered visible in this way was a past that had not truly been pondered and that could help with peacebuilding and homemaking. An elderly man whom I later learned was Armenian, ninety-four years old, entered the garage installation, walked around, touched almost every item, made a few phone calls, sat down, pointed toward the Venetian walls, and started talking to me:

I used to live in that house over there, my family was forced to migrate from Turkey during the Armenian genocide and we had to move again in 1960s because of the conflict in Cyprus to the south of the island. I have lived for 25 years in that house you see there, I got married and had my kids there, it was especially difficult to leave for my family as they had had to leave Turkey too. I [knew] this area when there was no buffer zone, not even this Ledra Palace Hotel. There used to be a sausage maker here and he used a cupboard to store meat just like the one you have in [the] garage. Most of the surrounding area belonged to the Armenians who all had to migrate. I have lived through times where I used most of these objects, including the times when there was no electricity and what they remind me is that I have lived in both sides of the divide in harmony with Greeks, Turks and Armenians and to see all of them coming together in the Buffer Zone makes me happy.

Just like him, thousands of people were forced to move from the area. Since the buffer zone cannot be resettled, it now stands as an embodiment of the rupture created by displacement and disposition, one that is present in the memories of the people of Cyprus and of every war-torn region, creating a discontinuous sense of being.

Fieldwork has been a transformative experience for me, unexpectedly so at times. It has been instinctive and filled with ethical questions and constant moral negotiations that actually became turning points of the study. These challenges guided my search for alternative ways to explore displacement. Arts created a deeper and more reciprocal connection, one that went beyond the ethical dilemma of "the self and scientism" in Okely's (1975) terms while still respecting the disciplinary codes of research. The interdisciplinary approach created space for critical and creative thinking. It allowed the participants to become guides and creators, thus blurring the boundaries and power dynamics between the researcher and participants. With any research on sensitive topics such as displacement, the deeper you try to understand certain experiences, the more you are likely to touch upon memories and feelings that are very sensitive and that people may never want to recall again. So I found it especially important to give participants space to deconstruct and reconstruct their experiences on their own terms and in their own time.

These methods, however, required building a prior relationship and familiarity with the participants, as mutual trust and understanding take time to form. Arts-based methods enabled me to explore the intersection between art and anthropology and to reimagine displacement as a reflexive process. The methods also created a temporal and spatial rupture to understand the intersections in-between mobility and confinement, home and abroad, past and present and peace and rupture showing us that home is more than a place you come from and go to; it is also a collage of displaced memories scattered around the world inside us and outside us.

NOTES

1 Different actors have different discourses regarding the military operation.
2 Hatay is a province of southern Turkey with borders on Syria. It is a particularly multicultural region with a large Arab community. A sovereignty dispute over the region continues between Turkey and Syria.

BIBLIOGRAPHY

Benjamin, W. 1935. *The Work of Art in the Age of Mechanical Reproduction.* Somerset: Prism Key Press.

Berger, J. 2003. *The Shape of a Pocket.* Reprint edition. London: Vintage.

Bhabha, H.K. 1994. *The Location of Culture.* London and New York: Routledge.

Boym, S. 2001. *The Future of Nostalgia.* New York: Basic Books.

Butler, J. 1990. *Gender Trouble: Feminism and the Subversion of Identity.* New York: Routledge.

– 2015. *Notes toward a Performative Theory of Assembly.* Cambridge, MA: Harvard University Press.

Byrne, E. 2009. *Homi K. Bhabha (Transitions).* New York: Palgrave Macmillan.

Cassin, B., P. Diagne, and S. Brault. 2016. *Nostalgia.* New York: Fordham University Press.

Clifford, J. 1981. "On Ethnographic Surrealism." *Journal of Comparative Studies in Society and History* 23, no. 4: 539–64. https://doi.org/10.1017/S0010417500013554.

Davis, H. 2004. *Understanding Stuart Hall.* London: SAGE.

de Certeau, M. 1988. *The Practice of Everyday Life.* Berkeley: University of California Press.

Douglas, M. 1966. *Purity and Danger: An Analysis of Concepts of Pollution and Taboo*. London: Routledge and Kegan Paul.

England, K. 1997. "Getting Personal: Reflexivity, Positionality, and Feminist Research." In *Reading Human Geography: The Poetics and Politics of Inquiry*, edited by T. Barnes and D. Gregory. London: Hodder Education.

Ernst, Max. (1936) 2009. *Beyond Painting*. Washington: Solar Books.

Gürel, A., and Özersay, K. 2006. "Cyprus and the Politics of Property." *Journal of Mediterranean Politics* 11, no. 3: 349–69. http://doi.org/10.1080/13629390 600913957.

Hendry, J. 1992. "The Paradox of Friendship in the Field: Analysis of a Long-Term Anglo–Japanese Relationship." In *Anthropology and Autobiography*, edited by J. Okely and H. Callaway. London: Routledge.

Jackson, A., ed. 1987. *Anthropology at Home*. London: Tavistock.

Jackson, M. 1995. *At Home in the World*. Durham: Duke University Press.

Kristeva, J. 1984. *Powers of Horror: An Essay on Abjection*. New York: Columbia University Press.

– 2001. *Hannah Arendt: Life Is a Narrative*. Toronto: University of Toronto Press.

Narayan, K. 1993. "How Native Is 'Native' Anthropologist?" *American Anthropologist* 95: 671–86. http://doi.org/10.1525/aa.1993.95.3.02a00070.

Navaro, Y. 2009. "Affective Spaces, Melancholic Objects: Ruination and the Production of Anthropological Knowledge." *Journal of the Royal Anthropological Institute* 15, no. 1: 1–18. http://doi.org/10.1111/j.1467-9655.2008.01527.x.

– 2012. *The Make Believe Space: Affective Geography in a Post-War Polity*. Durham: Duke University Press.

Okely, J. 1975. "The Self and Scientism." *Journal of the Anthropological Society of Oxford* 6, no. 3: 171–88.

Said, E.W. 1978. *Orientalism*. New York: Pantheon Books.

– 1994. *Culture and Imperialism*. London: Vintage.

– 2002. *Reflections on Exile and Other Essays*. Cambridge, MA: Harvard University Press.

Seymour-Smith, C. 1986. *Macmillan Dictionary of Anthropology*. London: Macmillan.

Shore, C. 1999. *Fictions of Fieldwork: Depicting the "Self" in Ethnographic Writing*. In *Being There: Fieldwork in Anthropology*, edited by C.W. Watson. London: Pluto Press.

Strathern, M. 1987. *The Limits of Auto-Anthropology*. In *Anthropology at Home*,
    edited by A. Jackson, 17–35. London: Tavistock.
Taussig, M. 1992. *The Nervous System*. New York: Routledge.
Tillmann-Healy, L.M. 2003. "Friendship as Method." *Qualitative Inquiry* 9, no. 5:
    729–49.
Van der Geest, S. 2015. "Friendship and Fieldwork: A 'Retrospect' as Foreword."
    *Curare* 38, nos. 1–2: 3–8.
Wilson, K. 1993. "Thinking about the Ethics of Fieldwork." In *Fieldwork in
    Developing Countries*, edited by S. Devereux and J. Hoddinott. Boulder:
    Lynne Rienner.
Young, R. 1990. *White Mythologies: Writing History and the West*. London and
    New York: Routledge.
Zetter, R. 1994. *We Are Strangers Here: Continuity and Transition – The Impact Of
    Displacement and Protracted Exile on the Greek-Cypriot Refugees*. Headington:
    Oxford Brookes University.

# SECTION THREE
## Crossing Methodological and Disciplinary Boundaries

Christina R. Clark-Kazak

One of the opportunities – and challenges – of documenting displacement is the interdisciplinary approach to research. Creative interdisciplinarity attends to the multi-faceted nature of displacement and unsettles discipline-specific knowledge production and ways of knowing. At the same time, as a field, refugee and forced migration studies has not until recently benefited from in-depth methodological and epistemological discussions about how to facilitate this interdisciplinary collaboration while attenuating some of its challenges. Moreover, our field has been dominated by particular disciplines, especially law, anthropology, and political science. In this section, we bring together examples of creative, interdisciplinary methodologies that challenge other researchers to think seriously about how to innovate within and across disciplines. This section also highlights disciplines that have historically been underrepresented in refugee and forced migration studies.

### Interdisciplinary Enrichment and Questioning

The researchers in this section reach beyond their disciplinary comfort zones – and, in some cases, their own disciplinary training – to enrich displacement research. Banki and Phillips adopt and adapt the cultural probe technique used in design studies. Frydenlund and Padilla's chapter demonstrates how simulation and modelling methods from computer science can further research in migration studies, which has been dominated by social sciences disciplines and law. Goheen Glanville brings in interdisciplinary insights from communication studies, cultural studies, and literary studies. Gamage and Jayatilaka combine geographic mapping with narrative techniques from memory studies.

The interdisciplinary collaborations highlighted in this section expand the methods, theories, and epistemologies of refugee and forced migration studies. Indeed, one of the critiques of our field has been its lack of attention – until recently (see the introduction to this volume) – to these foundational methodological questions. In this section, Gamage and Jayatilaka demonstrate how interdisciplinary methods can lead to "broader understandings of the social, economic, and cultural conditions of displacement." Frydenlund and Padilla challenge the situatedness of knowledge by showing how migration is part of dynamic, complex systems.

However, a danger of interdisciplinary work is a "pick-and-mix approach," where researchers (mis)apply methods without adequate training or reflection. Authors in this section have taken seriously the importance of deep engagement with methods across disciplines, and demonstrate in their chapters how they adapted these methods to documenting displacement contexts. For example, Frydenlund and Padilla clearly outline the ways in which modelling and simulation can be applied in forced migration contexts, but also how different terms can be interpreted differently across disciplines, which "can lead to slight misunderstandings that compound over time" (303). They, and other authors in this section, also show how these methods do not provide all answers, but rather complement our ways of knowing. Collaboration across disciplines thus requires continuous communication, learning, reflection, and the courage to question taken-for-granted methodological and epistemological training on what is counted and valued as knowledge.

## Ethical Opportunities and Challenges of Mixed Methodologies

The authors in this section also demonstrate how innovative mixed methodologies can be used to respond to some of the ethical challenges raised in Section 1 and throughout this book. For example, Banki and Phillips argue that the multimedia package (MMP) approach can partly address problems of over-research. Similarly, modelling proposed by

Frydenlund and Padilla builds on existing data. Gamage and Jayatilaka (348) were conscious of potential traumas in retelling stories, opting for "the mobility video format allowing participants to narrate their stories, in ways that allow silences." Goheen Glanville (363) argues for an ethical praxis that goes beyond ethics protocols and is embedded in ways of doing research that "remain[] responsible to the communities being represented."

On the other hand, researchers have to be aware of how data can be used to undermine migration rights and protection. For example, Frydenlund and Padilla are conscious of the risk that modelling can be used to prevent asylum. Gamage and Jayatilaka used creative methods to ensure the anonymization of stories without undermining the importance of the personal experiences. Goheen Glanville attends to the politicization of discourses about refugees. She deliberately titled her project "worn words" to demonstrate the overuse of certain words in "simplifying and homogenizing a vast array of diverse experiences" and "the way those words have been worn by diverse people – often in ways that wear people down" (362).

## Multimedia and Digital Technologies within Participatory Approaches

As Goheen Glanville (369) argues, to change the discourse about displacement, "alternative forms and processes of storytelling—not just new data—are needed." All chapters in this section explicitly engage with creative methods and multimedia technologies as innovative ways to narrate, represent, and interpret displacement. Gamage and Jayatilaka produced "mobility videos" by integrating life-story narratives, memory mapping, and video documentation. Banki and Phillips (309) adapted the cultural probe technique to develop a MMP that allowed participants to "share their ideas through observations, video, objects, jokes, songs, and other non-traditional commentary." Frydenlund and Padilla demonstrate how simulation and modelling allow for different ways of thinking about complex, dynamic systems of migration.

However, this focus on technological innovation is intimately tied to human experiences through the participatory and collaborative underpinnings in each chapter (see also section 2). As Gamage and Jayatilaka state, "we grappled to resolve the digital divide that existed between participants and the media producers" Similarly, Banki and Phillips creatively explored ways to engage participants, through whimsical drawings and methods specifically adapted to their cultural and geographic context. Frydenlund and Padilla "challenge modeling teams to also include voices from those communities, systems, and entities that are included in the model, such as migrants and migrant-led initiatives and organizations" (302). Indeed, Goheen Glanville prioritized participatory processes throughout the research, from "an ethics protocol ... that positioned interviewees as experts whose knowledge I was mobilizing" (371) to soliciting feedback on the storyboard. In each chapter, authors show how they prioritized participation without romanticizing it – they were keenly aware of the ways in which uncritical "participatory" methods can reinforce power inequalities. Moreover, authors in this section show how collaboration extends beyond participatory methods, to how research findings are presented and stories are narrated.

## Conclusion

The chapters in this section inspire researchers to reach across disciplines and engage in meaningful research through innovative methodologies. This often requires an adaption of methods to the specific contexts of (im)mobilities, including through deep engagement with the communities with whom we are working, and attention to the ethical opportunities and constraints the research poses. The creative approaches in this section not only expand the methodological possibilities in documenting displacement, but also challenge researchers to reimagine their ways of thinking and doing.

# 11

## Opportunities and Challenges of Using Computer-Based Simulation in Migration and Displacement Research: *A Focus on Lesbos, Greece*

Erika Frydenlund and Jose J. Padilla

In the early months of 2020, as the world was slowly waking up to the realities of what would become a global pandemic, the Moria Reception and Identification Center on the island of Lesbos, Greece, was well beyond its capacity. A notoriously overcrowded "hotspot" for processing displaced persons into Europe from Turkey, Moria had nearly twenty thousand occupants in a camp built to hold only a few thousand. Migrants stranded in Lesbos awaiting results from bureaucratic procedures that would allow them to move to the mainland lived in makeshift shelters with little access to water, sanitation, nutritious food, and personal safety. How many more would come? How would the novel coronavirus, Covid-19, spread through a population that was living so tightly packed and without the resources to implement effective public health precautions? Little did we know that, in the midst of a pandemic lockdown later in the year, Moria would burn to the ground, leaving humanitarian responders scrambling to set up a new site for more than twelve thousand people while testing and quarantining those exposed to the virus. Prior plans and data snapshots suddenly became obsolete as the island shifted to its new reality.

Traditional computational methods, from data dashboards to statistical models, can provide an instantaneous picture of a situation at a moment in time. Some questions, however, do not lend themselves well to static models; instead, they require tools that allow dynamic exploration of "what-if" scenarios. Computer-based simulation models can add to the research and planning tools that complement existing empirical methods, allowing exploration of alternative policies and scenarios, as well as virtual experimentation that can provide insights into the effectiveness of theories and policies in a given situation. These tools can help us plan for unexpected events or respond to changing conditions, and thus they have a role to play in research on displaced persons and humanitarian operations. In this chapter, we summarize the role of computer simulation in displacement research by focusing on the various questions that can be asked about the refugee and migrant situation on Lesbos.

## M&S in Migration and Displacement Research

Modelling and simulation (M&S) has been accepted as a research approach for decades in disciplines such as computer science, engineering, and health care studies (Roberts and Pegden 2017). Social science has been slower to adopt this research approach, but it has been gaining some traction. The use of M&S in migration and displacement research dates back to the early 2000s, when government agencies began looking at models of people's movements (Bailey 2001). By the late 2000s, applications of simulation to migration and displacement issues such as health care and safety were beginning to appear (Anderson et al. 2007), with implications for scenario and policy development. The following year, Scott Edwards (2008) introduced the notion of M&S – specifically, agent-based modelling – to the refugee studies community. His paper presented a convincing argument for using M&S in forced migration research. Even so, the growth in subsequent papers using modelling for migration and displacement research topics has fallen largely outside the migration scholarship, specifically within engineering and computer science.

After 2011, the volume of migration and displacement modeling increased, though it was presented mainly in computational and environmental journals and at related conferences. Following the trend of the earlier papers, M&S-based studies focused on spatial distributions and population flows (Gulden et al. 2011; Kniveton et al. 2011; Hassani-Mahmooei and Parris, 2012; Sokolowski et al. 2014; Collins and Frydenlund 2017; Suleimenova et al. 2017) and on health care and safety (Hailegiorgis and Crooks 2012;

Frydenlund and Earnest 2015). Beyond these two areas, researchers have attempted to use M&S to model durable solutions related to Syrian refugees (Vernon-Bido et al. 2017), the economic impacts of refugees on host countries (Taylor et al. 2016), and the impact of protracted stays on encamped refugees' attitudes toward host community members (Frydenlund and Padilla 2017), further expanding the potential applications of M&S.

Most of these studies, however, continue to be published outside of the migration and displacement literature, and this has limited the potential collaboration between modellers and migration and displacement scholars, in terms of both policy and practice. One possible reason for this unbalanced use of M&S approaches has to do with perceived barriers to entry (in terms of computer coding skills, for instance). Also, M&S in most educational programs is not widely presented as a methodological option, particularly in the social sciences as far as we have seen, so the field suffers from a lack of awareness on the part of other disciplines and their methodologies. The weak representation of M&S in migration and displacement research, and in social science research more broadly, may reflect a lack of understanding about the potential benefits of these methods, as well as some hesitation related to how simulation actually works.

To understand how M&S fits into social science, it is important to understand that it involves a systems (or even system of systems) approach to thinking about phenomena. In particular, M&S is appropriate when thinking about *dynamic* systems that capture complex, often adaptive, interacting entities (Zeigler et al. 2000). To make the case that M&S is an effective means of researching migration and displacement,[1] we begin by describing what is meant by the term "complex adaptive system" and how this lends itself to social science research methodologies in the context of migration and displacement. After providing an overview of the usefulness of an M&S way of thinking, we illustrate three major paradigms in simulation – system dynamics, discrete event simulation, and agent-based modelling – using the case of the increase in migrant arrivals on Lesbos, Greece, in 2015. We conclude with a discussion of the methodological and ethical challenges of using M&S to study migration and displacement.

## Migration as a Complex Adaptive System

There is a difference between "complicated" and "complex." Complicated systems can be reduced to component parts, and those parts can be analyzed and understood separately to build a more complete picture of the entire system (Mitchell 2009). An example of this might be a pre-computer-era car engine. That engine can be disassembled, and each part examined and understood separately to comprehend how it contributes to the car being able to move. This type of deconstruction underlies much of how many disciplines address research questions. Social systems are far more complex than this, and social phenomena often represent "more than the sum of their parts." The phenomenon of xenophobic violence against migrants, for instance, might be traced back to many factors, from macro-level economic conditions to individual-level cultural differences and personal coping mechanisms. Each factor contributes to xenophobia by affecting other factors in non-linear and often unpredictable ways – much like the idea of the "butterfly effect."

A complex system can be defined as "a system that exhibits nontrivial emergent and self-organizing behaviors" (Mitchell 2009, 13). In these systems, there are often entities that can learn and adapt to their environment and circumstances, thus changing the very system in which they exist. While this does not characterize all research topics related to migration and displacement, the vast majority of social systems are difficult to disaggregate and investigate because learning and adaptation, and often self-organizing behaviours, together create a dynamic system that is more than the sum of its parts. If we can agree that many, if not most, social systems are complex and not merely complicated, then traditional methodological tools including mathematics and statistics can no longer fully capture the essence of the phenomenon we seek to study. To borrow from the study of complex adaptive systems (Miller and Page 2007, 26), "the usual bounds imposed by our typical tools, such as the need to keep the entire model mathematically tractable, are easily surmounted using computational modeling, and we can let our imagination and interests drive our work rather than traditional tools."

This thinking also applies to qualitative research that is not constrained by keeping the research "mathematically tractable." Though it has quantitative origins, M&S is not inherently quantitative and can have a profound impact on the way we explore qualitative data and develop theoretical insights. In this sense, M&S might be characterized as a means of reconciling mixed methods approaches to address research questions about complex, dynamic phenomena. M&S is of value in the mixed methods approach as it can open up a new way to explore the connections between other research methods, theoretical developments, and ways that we communicate research findings to others.

## M&S Paradigms, Data Types, Research Questions

Modeling and simulation draws on theory, mathematical and statistical models as well as qualitative insights about the dynamics of the systems and phenomena of interest. Some have called simulation a "third way" of doing science that is neither inductive nor deductive (Axelrod 1997). Simulation models are created by translating the social phenomenon under study into computer code and then executing that code to observe qualitative or quantitative outcomes of the model's dynamics as they have been "set in motion." Like other types of modelling, M&S depends heavily on the driving research question. Models can be under- or (more often) over-specified as researchers try to capture all the elements of a complex social system – essentially recreating a virtual world – without considering the specific research question at hand. Tolk and colleagues (2013) present an iterative framework for developing simulation models that attempts to balance this risk by first listing all assumptions and known factors in a reference model, which then informs the modelling question. That modelling question then bounds a conceptual model that can be converted into computer code for simulation.

M&S is composed of a multitude of modelling paradigms. This section is not a comprehensive discussion of them, but rather an overview of the three main modelling paradigms. Additionally, modelling paradigms can be combined to span multiple levels of analysis. The modelling paradigm that will prove most appropriate to a study should be chosen based on the research question, intended level of analysis, and types of data available.

Table 11.1 describes the three main M&S paradigms: system dynamics, discrete event, and agent-based modelling. Note that these are generalizations,

Table 11.1  Three major modelling and simulation paradigms

|  | Level of analysis | Data types | Question type |
| --- | --- | --- | --- |
| *System dynamics* | Macro/systemic | Mainly quantitative; some qualitative | System-level questions about many interacting factors |
| *Discrete event* | Meso/processes | Mainly quantitative; some qualitative | Procedural/queuing questions |
| *Agent-based* | Micro/individual | Both quantitative and qualitative | Individual interactions that generate macro-level phenomena |

and each can be used to explore other levels of analysis, including multi-paradigm modelling approaches that combine model types.

Modelling and simulation methods are not necessarily separate from traditional or more familiar methodologies found in social science research. Rather, they constitute a framework through which to unite disparate methods, theories, and concepts and potentially advance the state of the art. These methods rely on other methods, such as ethnographic field notes, policy analysis, qualitative interviews, and statistical analysis, to build simulation models that reflect the combination of many data sources and data analyses. The translation of a conceptual model into computer code presents some barriers to entry, so that many social science simulations are the product of multidisciplinary teams of social scientists and computer programmers. So for any model to be effectively constructed and run, the computer modeller and the social scientist must work together to specify the available quantitative and qualitative data, analyses, and theory in reference to the research question. They must also arrive at a consensus about how those data and theories are best represented in the computer simulation environment. A simulation constructed in the absence of social science subject matter experts and real-world data is potentially a dangerous research artifact that may contain significant researcher bias and have very little to do with the real-world phenomena.

## The Usefulness of an M&S Way of Thinking

Computer simulation has barriers to entry. Learning to develop a qualitative or statistical analysis requires a time investment to understand the required techniques, principles, and software; simulation has a similar learning curve. However, software advances are changing the entry point into this field, making way for researchers without computer coding skills to conceptualize, build, and execute computer simulations through graphical user interfaces. Complex models, however, still require the ability to develop computer code in languages such as C, C#, and Java, which can pose substantial barriers to entry for some researchers.

Even without the computer simulation model as an output, an M&S way of thinking can be beneficial to any research agenda. Much of this value comes from the practice of thinking about problems *as if* they were to be instantiated as computer code. For those familiar with statistical modelling, M&S adds the requirement that the model include the dynamic relationships between variables, which, when simulated, reflect the real-world phenomenon. Additionally, since simulations are eventually "set in motion," the researcher must consider the passage of time and dynamic change in the relationship between actors and variables. Indeed, M&S may be similar to how qualitative researchers approach their studies. In our work with ethnographers, we have found that the iterative, observation-driven process of doing qualitative research aligns quite naturally with the iterative, factor-elicitation-driven processes of simulation model design (Padilla et al. 2018). Like many qualitative studies, models require observation of the real-world phenomenon, including the environment, actors, and variables and the relationships between these.

Qualitative researchers such as ethnographers may not think of themselves as modellers, and this can pose a barrier to multidisciplinary collaboration with simulationists. While qualitative researchers in our experience often focus on individual actors and behaviours, frequently citing specific field observations to explain the larger phenomenon, many of the elements in their work align closely with simulation design and development. In particular, qualitative researchers are adept at identifying specific actors and their relationships with one another – for instance, how the founder of a small aid organization sees and interacts with UNHCR during a humanitarian response – and can convey how this relationship is (or is not) indicative of larger phenomena. Of course, adding to the disciplinary language barrier, qualitative researchers and simulationists tend to live on different ends of the methodological spectrum, with the former focused on contextualized, time-bound observations and the latter on some aspect of extrapolation and generalization. Simulationists try to capture generalized behaviours and interactions between actors, often stress a need for quantitative data, and require a specificity from data and theory that seems incompatible with qualitative researchers' interpretations and goals. While these end goals can seem at odds with each other, it is important to note that simulations are not necessarily for *prediction*; they can fill many other roles that can greatly benefit social science research of all kinds. In our experience, focusing on common, non-predictive end goals can often bridge the divide between simulationists and qualitative researchers, allowing for fruitful collaboration.

M&S offers at least four major benefits to social science researchers (figure 11.1). First, it facilitates discussion and understanding of a problem or research question. Since simulation requires concepts and ideas to be coded into a computer program, discussion of model design necessitates that concepts be defined explicitly, whether the research is top-down or bottom-up in its approach. During the model design phase, as we prompt the social science subject matter experts for more specific information, it often becomes clear that even within the research team, definitions and perceptions of a given concept (for instance "solidarity" or "integration") actually are different. This on its own can prompt deep discussions about concepts that not only illuminate a path for the model but also advance the team's ability to name and explain the phenomena of interest. Likewise, when working with various types of research stakeholders – from NGO and government representatives to local citizen organizations and migrants – the model design can highlight conceptual differences between parties or missing links that motivate more questions, future research, and data collection. For this reason alone, researchers we have modelled with in the past have found thinking in terms of M&S to be highly useful for developing a more robust approach to their research design, questions, and future data collection strategies (Padilla et al. 2018). Essentially, the act of trying to build a computer simu-

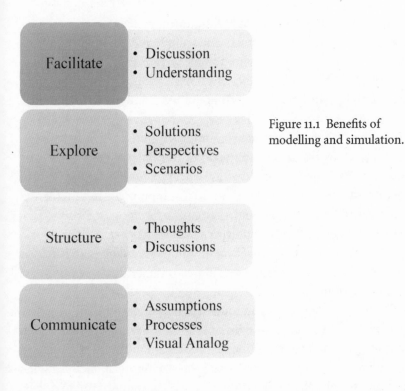

Figure 11.1 Benefits of modelling and simulation.

lation forces researchers to examine existing research and prior methodologies through a different lens, and this may highlight inconsistencies or areas in which more data are necessary in order to better define nuanced relationships and other dynamics related to the phenomenon.

Second, a completed model can serve as a space for exploring scenarios and solutions. For migration and displacement research, this is a particularly intriguing feature. Unlike statistical models, simulation models can be "set in motion"; that is, they allow scenarios to play out based on varying input factors. For theoretical insights derived from small-n, deep ethnographic analyses, for instance, M&S provides the opportunity to put those insights into a model and experiment with the robustness of theoretical insights.

If we increase the population size, for example, does the observation or theory hold? What if we change the underlying assumptions about family structure or economic impact? How reliant is the observation or theory on context and assumptions? While we can never have a definitive answer, a

simulation model provides a means to experiment with our insights and assumptions in order to test the robustness of observations and theories generated even from highly contextualized studies. Again, the new and dynamic
lens of a simulation may afford the researcher a vantage point to see their
data and analytical insights in ways that did not stand out before. Rather
than being used for prediction, these insights may shape future studies or
help identify new data requirements to improve on the research findings.
Additionally, for work that impacts policy as much as migration and displacement research does, computer simulation provides the opportunity to
consider future scenarios based on a variety of inputs. For instance, given
that a refugee settlement has been largely stable for the past twenty years,
what would happen if its food supply were cut by 50 per cent? What would
happen if there were a drought? These questions would be impractical or
unethical to explore with a real-world population, but they can be asked
through simulation.

Finally, M&S is a powerful communication and teaching tool. A completed model can structure thoughts and discussion on particular topics.
This has the potential to centre the discussion among academics, practitioners, and policy-makers with differing vantage points. Simulation models
can be presented visually so that people can gather around them to discuss
their assumptions, the compounding ramifications of certain policies, or
environmental changes. Because they are visual, these models can communicate researchers' assumptions about the phenomenon/system and serve
as a foundation for stakeholder input to refine those assumptions, point to
data sources that may be available, and contribute to developing the next
iteration of the model. As we tried to model the humanitarian response in
Lesbos, Greece, we quickly learned that volunteers, professional aid workers,
political representatives, locals, and migrants all had very different views of
how the humanitarian system was functioning. A model makes clear the
actors' assumptions, factors, and links to one another, and this helps to keep
their dialogue focused on the challenge at hand by serving as a visual analog
for the real-world phenomenon.

These features of M&S and an M&S way of thinking do not sit at one end
of an imagined quantitative/qualitative continuum; rather, they are additional tools that allow further experimentation and visual representation.
The development of social science simulation models is often a multidisci-

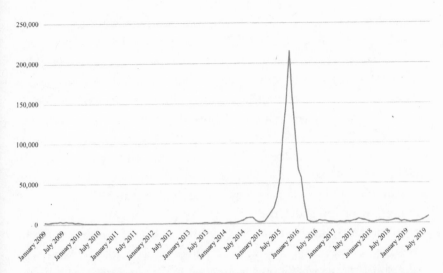

Figure 11.2 Monthly migrant apprehensions at the borders along the Eastern Mediterranean Route sea crossings (Greek islands) according to Frontex data from August 2019. *Source*: https://frontex.europa.eu/along-eu-borders/migratory-map.

plinary endeavour, in at least the sense that it brings together computer programmers and social scientists. This poses the same challenges as any other interdisciplinary collaboration, such as communication barriers related to terminology and world views; even so, M&S has the potential to facilitate communication between disciplines and stakeholders through its visual representation and experimental capabilities.

## The Humanitarian Response in Lesbos, Greece

In 2015, the Greek islands in the Aegean Sea experienced a dramatic increase in migrants,[2] mainly Syrians, crossing from Turkey. Migrants had been arriving on their shores for decades, but never before had they seen thousands of people arriving in tiny, dangerously overcrowded boats every day. Lesbos, just 5.5 kilometres from Turkey, was landfall for most of the migrants crossing to the Greek islands in the hope of continuing on to Europe (see figure 11.2). As more migrants arrived on the Aegean islands (long a tourist destination), local governments and citizens struggled to address their needs. Before humanitarian assistance arrived, and in the days and years that followed its arrival, island citizens found their infrastructure and resources stretched beyond capacity and their own tolerance for migrants beginning to fray.

Dozens of small charitable organizations attempted to provide some relief to the migrants on Lesbos. Meanwhile, governments and the UNHCR scrambled to bring the situation under control and provide an adequate humanitarian response. In May 2017, the authors attended the Lesbos Dialogues. This small initiative, held on the island itself, brought together qualitative and quantitative academic researchers, city government officials, NGO workers and representatives, and local citizens' organizations such as the tourism board to discuss the impacts of the increased migrant arrivals and humanitarian response and to determine ways to move forward in this and possible future humanitarian situations. The idea was to learn from the many witnesses on the beaches in 2015 so as to strengthen local policies. We also hoped to develop best practices for other communities that found themselves facing unprecedented humanitarian challenges. During this meeting and subsequent visits to the island, we spoke with local residents, government officials, and NGO workers, as well as camp managers, to try to find a place for simulation research that might improve the humanitarian response on the island. This is an ongoing project, but from the insights gathered so far, we can speculate about how simulation could be used to study migration- and displacement-related issues. In the next sections, we present three possible questions, each of them framed in terms of our knowledge of the unprecedented situation on Lesbos. They are provided here in order to demonstrate more concretely what simulation research might look like in a migration and displacement context. The models are only for illustrative purposes and include some insights about where more collaboration with social scientists would improve the model's insights.

## How Many People Are Coming? A System Dynamics Example

It cannot be predicted precisely how many migrants or displaced persons will arrive in a given community on a given day. There is some information we can derive from the common routes people may take to reach their transit and destination countries, and there are some data on what percentage of people tend to take different routes. In our qualitative interviews and discussions with local residents, organizational leaders, and government representatives on Lesbos, this question has always been at the forefront of their minds, because, while they regained control of the situation in the year following the summer of 2015 and managed to increase humanitarian relief, they constantly worry that Turkey will reopen its borders and they will be caught unprepared again. In fact, this scenario was unfolding while we were writing this chapter: there was a new upswing in migrant arrival numbers at the end of the summer of 2019, and Turkey reopened its borders in the spring of 2020.

Figure 11.3 shows a system dynamics model of the movement of migrants into Greece. It is based mainly on quantitative data from government and NGO datasets; these are combined with qualitative analysis of policy documents and migrant reception procedures to build the causal structures shown in the figure. As an illustrative model, it lacks more significant insight from social scientists and humanitarian practitioners that would increase the granularity of the processes.

In the model, a starting migrant population has left their country of origin at some rate. The *outflow rate* captures some percentage of the people who have left their respective countries. In this scenario, those migrants either go to Turkey (to begin the route we are following in this example) or follow a different route to a different transit/destination country. In the Syrian case, for instance, a portion of people go to Turkey, but others may go to other host countries such as Lebanon or Jordan. Of those in our model who go to Turkey, some percentage pay smugglers to help them cross the Mytilene Strait to Lesbos (on the Eastern Mediterranean Sea Route). Upon arrival in Greece, migrants are processed at the Reception and Identification Center (RIC) Moria. In fact, before it burned to the ground in September 2020, most migrants awaiting processing that would allow them to travel to mainland Greece, and possibly farther into Europe, would either stay in Moria or, if deemed "vulnerable," can be placed in one of two other smaller camps on Lesbos (all of which have now been condensed into one central RIC). A small number are provided with apartments instead of camp accommodations. This level of granularity is not captured in our sample system dynamics model, but could be if the question were about the allocation of individuals to various accommodation sites.

Once processed in the RIC, migrants await a status determination. Some individuals, faced with the dire conditions in the RIC and now realizing that

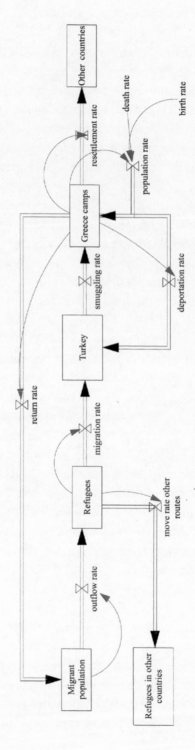

Figure 11.3 Example of a system dynamics model of migrant movement into Greece.

their asylum claims are very likely to be rejected, return voluntarily to their country of origin (*return rate*). Others have their claims rejected and await deportation to Turkey (*deportation rate*). Those whose asylum claims are accepted are moved to mainland Greece and, they hope, to other countries of Europe (*resettlement rate*). The *population rate* in the model captures the "circle of life" that goes on in the camps as migrants await their asylum claim outcomes; namely, some migrants are born in that time span, and some die, resulting in minor fluctuations in the model's count of how many people are likely to be in the camp at any given time. These respective rates are calculated based on quantitative data about monthly births, deaths, returns, claim rejections, and individuals moved off the island as published by the UNHCR. When run, the simulation will generate data representing the number of people in the camp at any given time given the inflow rate, outflow rates, and birth and death rates. For policy-makers and humanitarian planners, this will give some insight into what types of arrival numbers to expect under different scenarios, such as a reduction in the smuggling rate (for instance, as a result of the March 2016 EU-Turkey Statement [European Commission 2016]) or an increase in the outflow rate from countries of origin.

Visually assessing the example simulation model, it is easy to imagine how one might add more granularity based on a particular context or research question. This type of granularity would benefit from collaboration with social scientists – and, depending on the research question, government, NGO, and intergovernmental organization representatives – in order to accurately capture the details that would make the system more closely reflect the phenomenon at hand. For instance, perhaps we are monitoring specific situations such as the political stability in Syria and Afghanistan, which are the main origin countries for migrants arriving in Greece. The model could be expanded from "Migrant Population" to model specific countries with specific outflow rates, which would provide a more realistic picture of the potential numbers of migrants attempting to journey to Greece. We could also provide more granularity about camps or other accommodations to assess when and for how long these options will be at or beyond capacity. The smuggling rate could also feed into separate Greek islands instead of just one *Greek Camp* variable to track how many migrants might arrive to specific islands.

Using this type of model, various scenarios could be run to anticipate different flow rates at each point in the model in order to anticipate future humanitarian needs. As discussed at the end of this chapter, scholars and practitioners would then play a critical role in interpreting the model's output in order to determine what is informative or actionable for the real-world situation. The model can produce scenario-based output for interpretation, but without proper context these data and the model could potentially be used to block arrivals or (more likely) to implement policies that are unfavourable to the human rights and basic needs of migrants on the island (see below). The system dynamics model is well-suited to these types of questions, particularly when it comes to understanding how changes in one part of the system (a closure of borders to the other country routes, for instance) might ripple through and create impacts in other parts of the system (e.g., Greek camp overcrowding).

## How Can Migrants be Transported? A Discrete Event Simulation Approach

A serious problem that arose with the first increase in migrants arriving on Lesbos was that they landed on the northern part of the island and had to travel 59.9 kilometres over mountainous terrain to reach the municipal capital of Mytilene for processing in RIC Moria (e.g., medical check-up, registration with the Greek government, housing assignment if available). There simply was not enough transportation to accommodate the large numbers of arrivals. Initially, a few buses ran every day from one side of the island to the other, and some locals used their personal vehicles to transport migrants to Mytilene. Many had no choice but to walk. In the first few weeks, with hundreds of new people arriving on the island each day, transportation became a logistical issue. Simulation might have been able to provide some insights.

Discrete event simulations are useful for understanding queueing systems of this type. We produced this example of a discrete event simulation to show how M&S might be useful for allocating enough transportation resources to quickly and effectively help migrants reach the municipal capital for asylum claim processing. This is an illustration model, but it is based on qualitative, semi-structured interviews we conducted in 2016 with ten NGO workers and local volunteers who were working on the beaches in 2015 during the first increase in arrivals on Lesbos. Figure 11.4 shows the transportation of migrants as a queueing system with three different modes of transport: a small vehicle for five people, a large vehicle for fifty people, and walking.

In this model, migrants arrive on the beach and wait to be processed. That processing takes a certain number of personnel. You can think of these personnel as the ones who direct the migrants regarding where to go and what to do and who provide them with dry clothes and some food and water. After that, the migrant must decide which transportation option to take, depending on availability. This model accounts for the time it takes the vehicle to reach Mytilene and return for those still waiting in the queue.

While this is a simple model of the transportation situation during the first sudden increase in arrivals, a queueing model such as this could help government officials and humanitarian workers determine the best way to meet the transportation needs of those arriving at a border so that they can reach a camp, urban centre, or other location. A higher-fidelity model would require more qualitative and quantitative input – for instance, interviews with NGO workers in the field at the time, who could recount how migrants were received there, how long the initial process took, and how long people had to wait for transportation to the capital. It is also possible to imagine extending the model to include more granularity, such as the option of using locals' personal vehicles, which carry fewer people but may be available more frequently than buses. Including this option would also allow decision-makers to understand the consequences of establishing rules that forbid local citizens from transporting migrants in their personal vehicles.

## Disease Spread in an Overcrowded Camp: An Agent-Based Modeling Example

The Greek islands had once been merely a pathway to mainland Greece and, from there, deeper into Europe. But since the implementation of the EU-Turkey Statement on 20 March 2016, migrants have found themselves waiting indefinitely on the islands for their claims to be processed and decided. The EU-Turkey Statement was meant to be a mechanism for sending back

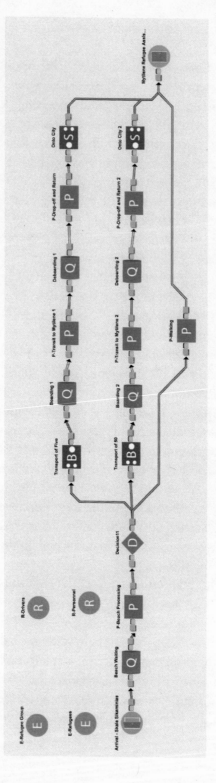

Figure 11.4 Example of a discrete event simulation of migrant transport.

to Turkey those who did not qualify for refugee status. But "hotspots" established on the Greek islands no longer function as centres for processing migrants for the mainland; now they are extended detention centres, and they have become increasingly overcrowded.

RIC Moria, the former hotspot on Lesbos, was one such place. It was originally a military barracks built to hold between 2,000 and 2,500 people. The dramatic slowdown in the processing of migrants' claims, together with the continued arrival of new migrants, resulted in anywhere between 4,500 (Smith 2017) and 6,500 people living in RIC Moria (aid workers in RIC Moria, personal communication, November 2017). By 2019, RIC Moria's population had reached 14,000, around 460 per cent over capacity. Recent reports indicate that by early 2020, that number had risen to 20,000.

To understand the conditions in RIC Moria and their implications for public health, over the course of four two-week trips between 2016 and 2018 we conducted semi-structured interviews with local residents, humanitarian aid workers, refugee and migration organization spokespersons, RIC Moria residents, and researchers working and residing on Lesbos. Many had witnessed the first increase in arrivals in 2015 and/or had provided assistance; some had experience with earlier upticks in arrivals on the island dating back to the 1980s. These interviews, as well as hand-drawn maps of the facility, formed the basis of the model, which was supplemented by aerial images of RIC Moria over time and a qualitative assessment of global news coverage of the site. These sources helped establish the public health risks and the residents' generalizable routine (e.g., visiting offices to check asylum claim status, medical tents, latrines, food distribution sites, or town). While illustrative rather than predictive, this model is the most granular of the examples here and as such points to opportunities for multidisciplinary collaboration to develop insights for further study.

According to the interviewees, there is no available housing at RIC Moria. When migrants arrive, they are told to find their own spots at the site, for the barracks and shipping containers are all full. Residents must live packed closely together, often crowding the walkways and occupying every available space. When those spaces are completely filled, they must find camping places in the olive groves beyond the site walls. This has resulted in infrastructural and social challenges. The sanitation facilities are only designed to accommodate a certain number of people, so septic tanks and related infrastructure must be maintained several times a day; our informants indicated that this was not happening as frequently as it should have been. Social challenges include tensions with local Greeks about migrants' encroachment on the olive groves and nearby villages.

The site layout was such that women and children had to pass through poorly lit areas housing single men. Aid workers speculated that this resulted in a high incidence of gender-based violence. RIC Moria residents reported that earlier in 2017, two or three people mysteriously died within a relatively short time, and the camp management's only response was to douse the deceased persons' tents with sanitizing chemicals in the hope of preventing further outbreaks. Scabies and respiratory diseases were reported to be common in the camp. Residents could leave the contained area during the day, but when they did, the police often harassed them, so many chose to stay in the camp. The catering services that provided food aid reportedly serve a gruel/porridge made of rice and lentils, but the residents said it made them sick and that they preferred to buy their own food with the cash assistance provided by the Greek government and European Union.

The situation in RIC Moria was dire. As a result of the conditions they faced there and the lack of knowledge about the status of their asylum claims, migrants' rates of suicide and severe psychological distress were high (Human Rights Watch 2017). A similar hotspot on the neighbouring island of Chios found that one in three migrants there had witnessed a suicide (Bulman 2017). Additionally, when winter approached there was inadequate preparation. Migrants died from the freezing weather in tents designed for summer (2017).

A number of organizations have decried the conditions in hotspots on the Greek islands (Lovett et al. 2017; Council of Europe 2017; Human Rights Watch 2017). Until ways are found to process migrants' asylum claims more quickly, places like RIC Moria will continue to be bottlenecks. That will mean continued problems providing health care and other services to migrants on Lesbos. NGO workers we interviewed reported that medical services lack even basic medicines, such as aspirin, nor are there enough doctors and hospital beds. In a recent news report, a representative of the Greek Center for Disease Control declared that understaffing is not the biggest problem: "In a place that is made for 2,000 people and holds 6,000, no matter how many doctors you put in service, they won't be able to make a difference" (Fotiadis and Howden 2017).

Figure 11.5 shows an agent-based model of the spread of a hypothetical communicable disease in RIC Moria. The pattern follows a standard SIR epidemiological model for contagious disease. When this model was developed, the world did not yet know about Covid-19 and how it would disproportionately affect those without access to basic health and sanitation services. At the time, the Moria camp was still standing. In September 2020, it burned to the ground, and new accommodation schemes are now being planned. A similar agent-based model could have helped uncover how a fire would spread through a camp as crowded as RIC Moria. Perhaps that knowledge would have made it possible to develop a fire containment plan.

The layout in the model is based on aerial imagery as well as on sketches (pre-fire) that interviewees drew during our fieldwork in Lesbos in 2017 that indicate the purpose of specific buildings. To develop the algorithms for the model, we have relied on qualitative descriptions of the housing situation in RIC Moria, as well as on qualitative descriptions of migrants' daily activities and necessary tasks. In this model, individual people ("agents," in modelling terms) arrive to the camp, are processed in various medical and administrative areas, and then find living spaces for themselves. Interviewees recounted that when the people cannot locate a space in a building or container, they look for a space to put their tent. If there is no such space in the open areas, they begin raising their tents in and around the walkways without entirely blocking foot traffic. In the model, each "person" follows his or her own daily routine – for example, visit food distribution site, visit medical tent, go to the bathroom, check on asylum claim status. At the end of the day, they return to their home tent or building. As people go about their daily tasks, they encounter others in close proximity. If those people carry a communicable disease, they can catch that disease. Some people leave the camp during the day for shopping; some leave permanently as their asylum claims are approved.

Note that the description of the context for the agent-based model is much richer and leads to some qualitatively derived algorithms (for instance, about how agents decide where to set up their home in the camp) that are necessary to specify the model. This is both an advantage and a disadvantage of agent-based modelling. On the one hand, qualitative research can tell us

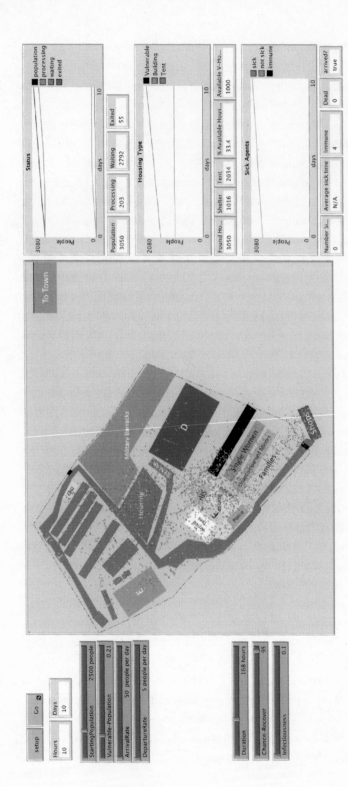

Figure 11.5  Example of an agent-based model of disease spread in RIC Moria.

a great deal about how individual actors or people ("agents") interact with one another and the environment. Their interactive algorithms do not have to be described using mathematical equations, but can arise from narrative descriptions of real-world people's actions, behaviours, and decisions. On the other hand, these models can easily become highly complex, and because the relationships are not visually obvious, the underlying model assumptions and algorithms can be difficult to describe to someone who has not worked closely with the model.

System dynamics models show flows of individuals through feedback loops that entail little decision-making. Discrete event simulation adds more granularity in terms of providing decision points and allowing for allocation of resources to meet demands. Agent-based modelling provides the finest level of granularity: individual agents in this case represent individual people (though they could easily represent groups of people or even institutions). A critical difference is that agents are heterogeneous and make decisions based on their own unique needs. As a result of their repeated interactions at the micro, individual level, macro, systems-level patterns begin to emerge, such as the massive overcrowding of camps to the point that people start sleeping on the walkways. Frydenlund and de Kock (2020) provide a comprehensive summary of agent-based modelling in forced migration research. From this level of granularity, in the case of the disease model we can see clear extensions for decision-makers such as maintaining sufficient medical infrastructure to meet the needs of the population, and possibly planning a vaccination campaign. In terms of the 2020 Covid-19 pandemic, such a model could have helped us find alternatives to social distancing that would have minimized the spread of the disease in a situation beset by overcrowding, poor food, and under-resourced medical facilities. To develop this model, however, would require collaboration between scholars, NGO practitioners, RIC Moria residents, and government representatives for the purpose of creating a more accurate picture of the challenges in RIC Moria and of the resources available for addressing public health needs there.

There is always a benefit in watching modelled phenomena "run" and observing the outcomes. For models based on social science theories, setting a theory in motion in a simulation allows one to see in what scenarios the theory holds, as well as when the theory might "break" or produce unexpected results. Models are an effective tool for decision-makers and policy-makers;

they also have the potential to advance social science theory by providing an experimental space for evaluating and "watching" the insights in motion.

## Challenges and Cautions

The prior sections indicated what simulation models might look like in migration and displacement research and how better social science collaboration would improve these models' fidelity. It was by no means an exhaustive discussion, but it did illustrate the many possible ways that M&S might help us look more closely or through a different lens at existing research questions in migration and displacement, even for addressing challenges in the same context, like RIC Moria. Like all research methodologies, M&S has its own challenges and concerns. Regarding cautions, while M&S is gathering some momentum in migration and displacement research, it is important to understand the team that constructed those models and their intended research questions. Given that M&S is so interdisciplinary, it is crucial that teams constructing models that can have direct real-world implications be composed of both computer modellers and migration and displacement scholars. The authors have learned from experience that on-the-ground context is vital for developing models that are relevant to the real-world phenomena we are trying to grasp. The models outlined were meant to structure problems and communicate ideas, which means that the model must be built firmly on a foundation of existing theories and knowledge as well as on data drawn directly from migration and displacement scholars, NGO practitioners, and government representatives. This could be taken one step further: we challenge modelling teams to include voices from those communities, systems, and entities that are included in the model, such as migrants and migrant-led initiatives and organizations. This means there are opportunities to use simulation to bridge the divide between community-based practices and academic research. The visual components of computer models lend themselves well to this enterprise, since the research assumptions, data, and findings are illustrated in ways that others may be able to add to and explore.

Another challenge that arises from the inherently multidisciplinary nature of model design and development is team communication. While software advances are changing the entry point to M&S, advanced models will likely continue to involve both subject matter experts and modellers (such as computer coders). This presents challenges regarding interdisciplinary communication. Currently, this is an area of ongoing research for many interdisciplinary teams working on complex real-world problems. Translating concepts, goals, and values across disciplinary lines is not a trivial task, particularly in an endeavour as time-consuming as model-building. We often find that terms like "conceptual model" and "agent" have similar meanings but different nuances across disciplines, and this can lead to slight misunderstandings that compound over time. Additionally, computer modellers and social scientists may expect different outcomes from the model – for example, advances in algorithm designs versus tools to help policy-makers make more informed decisions. These differing outcomes and investments in the approach can take a toll on the modeling team dynamic, which must be addressed early on.

One final caution is that this approach is not designed to answer all types of research questions. For those of us familiar with modelling – particularly in a context like migration and displacement, which is tied so closely to policy and practice – some organizations really just need a statistical analysis or data dashboard. Certain highly nuanced situations for which we have very little understanding or data still rely entirely on qualitative research. The time and effort required to construct a simulation model would go well beyond a given project's needs. Models require months, if not years (depending on the complexity), to develop and test for validation. They can be very powerful for certain types of research questions and in certain contexts, particularly if built in advance of their need (such as the next humanitarian situation), but they cannot fit all research questions or timelines.

As with any research method, it is important to think about the ethical implications of the design and one's intentions. Recently, we have seen a strong push toward modelling for the purpose of putting scenario exploration tools in the hands of policy-makers. As discussed earlier, there are many other (perhaps better) reasons to model (Epstein 2008), but it is worth a serious discussion that has yet to be had about whether models should ever be placed in the hands of the public or policy-makers. As with other aspects of research – field notes, and statistical models, for instance – not all models are meant for general consumption. Scenarios are agnostic in terms of the user's understanding of context, ethical boundaries, and practical limitations. They can therefore be framed in ways that defy their intention. A system dynamics model of refugee and migrant arrivals, for example, can become an experimentation tool for blocking those arrivals or developing encampment policies. Certain scenario outcomes of a disease-spread model might be used to justify not having a vaccination campaign. A model of transportation across the island could instead be turned into a model for policing drivers and enforcing rules against assisting migrants using one's own vehicle.

Given that models can have so many nuances and interconnections, an experimental tool that lacks a subject matter expert to explain the outcomes and temper the expectations could be very dangerous. M&S can be useful for research in many ways, but there are more discussions to be had about this emerging approach to migration and displacement research and the practical and ethical implications of openly providing models for others to use and interpret. Models are simply computer algorithms assembled under particular theoretical and data specifications. They do not provide context or informed insight; rather, they are tools for helping one develop informed insights. One would not let a statistical model speak for itself; in the same way, simulation models require context and a human interpreter to avoid advancing simulation outcomes that are unreasonable or unethical. A computer cannot make the decision that one outcome is culturally inappropriate or ethically wrong (Molnar 2019); to interpret simulation results, human intervention is necessary. So it is important that the researchers consider in what ways the model can and should be shared. We would not recommend that simulation models, particularly regarding issues of migration, displacement, and humanitarian decision-making, be released into the world for those who do not understand the data, assumptions, and context.

It is also important to consider who should own simulation models with a specific shelf life. Simulation models are built on current data and theories and must be revisited and refined to stay relevant. A model that goes unused for five years may produce drastically different results than the current data and theoretical knowledge would suggest. Similarly, a model shared on a website for anyone to interact with may fall out of date and could mislead a potential user. A model can be "finished" when the research question at hand has been answered sufficiently and satisfactorily, but a model can also live on indefinitely as a researcher revisits and refines it based on updated knowledge and data.

With those challenges and concerns in mind, however, M&S can provide an excellent mixed methods tool for merging theories, data, and varying perspectives into one research artifact. Even a model that does not "run" can contribute by facilitating discussion about a research topic and structuring dialogue about potential solutions, future research directions, and data collection efforts. A simulation model that is executable in computer code can also be useful for exploring scenarios and policy options, besides serving as a visual analogue for theory and data in order to communicate findings to wider audiences.

NOTES

1 The terms "migration" and "displacement" here are purposely broad to encompass the many different types of voluntary and involuntary movement of people.

2 We use the term "migrant" here to reflect the complex circumstances that led people to make the journey to Lesbos, without speaking to the legal status they may or may not be able to acquire upon arriving to Greece.

REFERENCES

Anderson, J., A. Chaturvedi, and M. Cibulskis. 2007. "Stimulation Tooks for Developing Policies for Complex System: Modeling the Helath and Safety of Refugee Communities." *Health Care Management Science* 10, no. 4: 331–9. http://doi.org/10.1007/s10729-007-9030-y.

Axelrod, R. 1997. "Advancing the Art of Simulation iin the Social Sciences." In *Simulating Social Phenomena*, edited by R. Conte, R. Hegselmann, and P. Terna, 21–40. Berlin and Heidelberg: Springer Verlag.

Bailey, P. 2001. *The Diamond Model of Peace Support Operations*. Hampshire, UK.

Bulman, M. 2017. "One in Three Refugees on Greek Island of Chios Has Witnessed Suicide Since Arriving, Report Finds." *The Independent*, 29 May. https://www.independent.co.uk/news/world/europe/refugees-chios-suicide-greece-rights-data-project-report-migrant-crisis-a7761931.html.

Collins, A., and E. Frydenlund. 2017. "Strategic Group Formation in Agent-Based Simulation." *SIMULATION: Transactions of the Society for Modeling and Simulation International* 94, no. 3: 179–93. http://doi.org/10.1177/0037549717732408.

"Concern over Spate of Deaths in Greek Refugee Camps." 2017. *Al Jazeera*,

30 January. https://www.aljazeera.com/news/2017/1/30/concern-over-spate-of-deaths-in-greek-refugee-camps.

Council of Europe, Committee for the Prevention of Torture. 2017. *Report to the Greek Government on the Visits to Greece Carried Out by the European Committee for the Prevention of Torture and Inhuman or Degrading Treatment or Punishment (CPT) from 13 to 18 April and 19 to 25 July 2016.* https://rm.coe.int/pdf/168074f85d.

Edwards, S. 2008. "Computational Tools in Predicting and Assessing Forced Migration." *Journal of Refugee Studies* 21, no. 3: 347–69. http://doi.org/10.1093/JRS/FEN024.

Epstein, J.M. 2008. "Why Model?" *Journal of Artificial Societies and Social Simulation* 11, no. 4: 12.

European Commission. 2016. EU-Turkey Statement: Questions and Answers.

Fotiadis, A., and D. Howden. 2017. "Greece Faces a Rerun of Its Refugee Winter of Discontent." *Refugees Deeply,* 10 October. https://www.newsdeeply.com/refugees/articles/2017/10/10/greece-faces-a-rerun-of-its-refugee-winter-of-discontent.

Frydenlund, E., and C. de Kock. 2020. "Agent-Based Modeling within Forced Migration Research: A Review and Critique." *Refugee Review* 4. https://espminetwork.com/wp-content/uploads/2020/06/Refugee-Review-IV.pdf.

Frydenlund, E., and D.C. Earnest. 2015. "Harnessing the Knowledge of the Masses: Citizen Sensor Networks, Violence, and Public Safety in Mugunga." In *World Politics at the Edge of Chaos: Reflections on Complexity and Global Life,* edited by E. Kavalski. Albany: SUNY Press.

Frydenlund, E., and J.J. Padilla. 2017. "Modeling the Impact of Protraction on Refugee Identity." SBP-BRIMS, Washington, DC.

Gulden, T., J.F. Harrison, and A.T. Crooks. 2012. "Modeling Cities and Displacement through an Agent-Based Spatial Interaction Model." Computational Social Science Society of America Conference, Santa Fe.

Hailegiorgis, A., and A.T. Crooks. 2012. "Agent-Based Modeling for Humanitarian Issues: Disease and Refugee Camps." Computational Social Science Society of America Conference, Santa Fe.

Hassani-Mahmooei, B., and B.W. Parris. 2012. "Climate Change and Internal Migration Patterns in Bangladesh: An Agent-Based Model." *Environment and Development Economics* 17, no. 5: 763–80.

Human Rights Watch. 2017. "EU/Greece: Asylum Seekers' Silent Mental Health

Crisis." 12 July. https://www.hrw.org/news/2017/07/12/eu/greece-asylum-seekers-silent-mental-health-crisis.

Kniveton, D., C. Smith, and S. Wood. 2011. "Agent-Based Model Simulations of Future Changes in Migration Flows for Burkina Faso." *Global Environmental Change* 21: S34–40. https://doi.org/10.1016/J.Gloeanvcha.2011.09.006.

Lovett, A., C. Whelan, and R. Rendon. 2017. "The Reality of the EU-Turkey State-ment: How Greece Has Become a Testing Ground for Policies That Erode Pro-tection for Refugees." International Rescue Committee, Norwegian Refugee Council, and Oxfam.

Miller, J.H., and S.E. Page. 2007. *Complex Adaptive Systems: An Introduction to Computational Models of Soccial Life*, edited by S.A. Levin and S.H. Strogatz. Princeton: Princeton University Press.

Mitchell, M. 2009. *Complexity: A Guides Tour.* New York: Oxford University Press.

Molnar, P. 2019. "New Technologies in Migration: Human Rights Impacts." *Forced Migration Review* 61: 7–9.

"Moria Migrant Camp on Lesvos Breaks New Record with Nearly 14,000 Resi-dents." 2019. *Ekathimerini*, 15 October. https://www.ekathimerini.com/news/245523/moria-migrant-camp-on-lesvos-breaks-new-record-with-nearly-14-000-residents.

Padilla, J.J., E. Frydenlund, H. Wallewik, and H. Haaland. 2018. "Model Co-Creation from a Modeler's Perspective: Lessons Learned from the Collabora-tion between Ethnographers and Modelers." In *Social, Cultural, and Behavioral Modeling*, edited by R. Thomson, C. Dancy, A. Hyder, and H. Bisgin, 70–5. SBP-BRIMS. Lecture Notes in Computer Science. Heidelberg and Berlin: Springer International.

Roberts, S.D., and D. Pegden. 2017. "The History of Simulation Modeling." Proceedings of the 2017 Winter Simulation Conference, Las Vegas.

Smith, H. 2017. "Surge in Migration to Greece Fuels Misery in Refugee Camps." *The Guardian*, 29 September. https://www.theguardian.com/world/2017/sep/29/surge-in-migration-to-greece-fuels-misery-in-refugee-camps.

Sokolowski, J.A., C.M. Banks, and R.L. Hayes. 2014. "Modeling Population Displacement in the Syrian City of Aleppo." Simulation Conference (WSC), 7–10 December, Savannah, Georgia.

Suleimenova, D., D. Bell, and D. Groen. 2017. "A Generalized Simulation Devel-opment Approach for Predicting Refugee Destinations." *Nature.* http://doi.org/10.1038/S41698-017-13828-9.

Taylor, J.E., M.J. Filipski, M. Alloush, A. Gupta, R.I. Rojas Valdes, and E. Gonzalez-Estrada. 2016. "Economic Impact of Refugees." *Proceedings of the National Academy of Sciences* 113, no. 127: 7449–53. http://doi.org/10.1073/PNAS.160 4566113.

Tolk, A., S.Y. Diallo, J.J. Padilla, and H. Herencia-Zapana. 2013. "Reference Modeling in Support of M&S: Foundations and Application." *Journal of Simulation* 7, no. 2: 69–82.

Vernon-Bido, D., E. Frydenlund, J.J. Padilla, and D.C. Earnest. 2017. "Durable Solutions and Potential Protraction: The Syrian Refugee Case." Spring Simulation Multi-Conference, April, Virginia Beach.

Zeigler, B.P., T.G. Kim, and H. Praehofer. 2000. *Theory of Modeling and Simulation*. 2nd ed. Amsterdam: Elsevier Science.

# 12

## Overcoming Over-Research:
### *The MMP Approach*

Susan Banki and Nicole Phillips

It is perhaps a harsh truism, but we state it unequivocally: refugees owe researchers no favours. To the contrary, refugee researchers generally benefit (through career advancement and/or discipline recognition) more than the populations they study. Particularly regarding those who collect data directly from refugee populations, we argue that there is an obligation not only to "do no harm" but also, where possible, to create experiences for study populations that are meaningful and offer reciprocity.

This chapter describes one such approach. The method, which we call "multimedia package" (MMP), is an adaptation of the cultural probe method used in design studies. The MMP allows respondents time to share their ideas through observations, video, objects, jokes, songs, and other non-traditional commentary. Given the oft-cited problem of imbalance between researchers and respondents, the approach aims not only to gather information from participants but also explicitly to develop a process that is, at its best, enjoyable and/or whimsical. Furthermore, the MMP encourages deep reflection by refugees, but it does so in a meaningful way, yielding data on refugee identity that are rich and dynamic.

This chapter presents the MMP approach. It begins by discussing the problems of over-researched populations. It then introduces one study population with whom we worked in order to pilot the MMP approach, the Bhutanese Nepali "triple diaspora." We then describe MMP implementation in detail. Without delving too deeply into the results of the research (a topic for a separate paper), the chapter then discusses the merits and drawbacks of this non-traditional approach, focusing on, among other elements, design and preparation, the potential for participant involvement, and possibilities for large-scale research of this nature in this exceptionally resource-intensive context.

## Overcoming Over-Research of Liminal Populations

As a justification for carrying out field research on liminal populations, some argue that it has the potential to increase our understanding of said populations and thus contribute to their betterment (Krulfeld 1998). In the case of refugee populations in particular, it has been argued that illuminating refugee movements can bring attention to their humanitarian needs as well as highlight the abuse, persecution, and neglect in the home country that first caused the refugee flows. We ourselves have offered this justification – for example, when studying refugees from Myanmar living in Thailand (Banki and Phillips 2017b). The accuracy of these claims notwithstanding (and it is difficult to draw direct causal links between academic research and positive outcomes for liminal populations), it is widely accepted that research fatigue, or "over-research," is an issue of concern, perhaps especially in the context of refugee populations that are located in artificial collectives that allow humanitarian organizations to deploy new technologies to collect massive amounts of data – technologies such as biometric registration and new experimental techniques such as iris testing (Jacobsen 2015).

Research fatigue, assessment fatigue, and over-research are all terms that describe the reluctance of individuals or groups to participate or continue their involvement in research projects after researchers have saturated communities with questionnaires, evaluations, interviews, and field observations. The phenomenon can occur when research is undertaken during long-term ethnographic field research or via short-term visits or survey distribution. It is worth noting that these terms do not describe the reluctance that emerges from research conducted in communities that have not been over-researched; in those cases, the reluctance may have other causes, such as fears about safety or a lack of time or inclination. With over-researched populations, the reluctance stems from previous experiences with research – the barriers rise because of participants' negative attitudes based on repetition, frequency, and redundancy of the research (Clark 2008, 955–56). Over-researched populations also complain that they are neither informed of the research results, nor do they benefit from them (Sukarieh and Tannock 2013). Responding to all this (i.e., developing sound research methods in over-researched communities) can be difficult when "the notion ... appears to accommodate conflicting ethical concerns ... [It can reflect] a concern that any benefit in research is an undue inducement, and ... a concern about a lack of benefit to participants and communities. Furthermore, 'over-research seems to be a highly subjective and variable assessment of a community's involvement in research, which may be advanced to achieve various ends" (Koen et al. 2017, 8).

In refugee research specifically, a great deal of commentary has emerged on the relationship between researchers, their research, and the subjects of their research. Safety concerns are paramount. Risks faced by refugees from various research projects include "those of intimidation and discrimination within camps and also threats to physical safety, from security forces, camp managements and even from other refugees" (Hugman et al. 2011, 1277). Despite time-consuming and picayune applications that researchers are required to undertake in order to conduct refugee research, ethics review boards (ERBS) remain insufficient for protecting refugees from harm (Hugman et al. 2011). Thus, ERB procedures can work against the ethical researcher, who, not being able to guarantee a "no risk" environment that the university prefers, may stop the research, leaving it to others who do not understand the risks or who fail to mention them in their ethics applications. Or they may modify their research to gain approval in ways that may actually increase the risk of harm. For example, Beyrer and Kass (2002) note that standard procedures requiring ERB-approved procedures to seek consent of the host government risk exposing refugee populations to breaches of confidentiality or deportation.

Disconnection from the research process is another common issue and can contribute to research fatigue. Even when participants provide information willingly, their willingness may be a result of their lack of understanding of the research process. The purpose of the research, its possible outcomes, the steps that will be taken to protect participants, and the long-term moral relationship between the researchers and researched must be laid out clearly to avoid such disconnection. "In particular, refugees report

312                                        SUSAN BANKI AND NICOLE PHILLIPS

that they have provided information in good faith, seeing this as part of a
relationship with researchers that might benefit their condition, only to find
that their information is treated like a commodity" (Hugman et al. 2011,
1277). This is why Mackenzie and colleagues (2007) argue that researchers
need to further their standard of ethical research in a way that goes beyond
the minimization of harm and instead focuses on shared benefits for participants and their communities in the research design (300). This can take
the form of reciprocal research in which the entire research experience is
decolonized and equalized (Taha, this volume) and/or trying to create narrative transitional spaces for refugees whose stories may not otherwise find
homes (Aziz, this volume).

While ethical problems concerning safety, disconnection, and potential
harms/lack of benefit to a community are not unique to refugee research,
those with ongoing exposure to researchers are more likely to raise these
problems when they emerge because of the repeated return of researchers
to whom they can make complaints or offer feedback. This is another way
of saying that addressing problems of research fatigue or over-research are,
in fact, important for all populations, not only over-researched ones that
have the ability to easily communicate with researchers. And this aligns with
those who assert that the concept of "over-research" is not, in fact, useful,
because the issue is not the continuation or repetition of research, but poor
design and unreflexive methodologies (Pascucci 2016).

Given such complaints, there has been an understandable call for research
that eschews poor design and considers the experiences of the participants
themselves. In the discipline of mental health, for example, it has been argued that the likelihood of research fatigue may diminish if the purpose of
the research project is clear to the participants, the need for the research is
understood, and the same questions are not asked to the same people (Peterson 1999, 8).

## Bhutanese Nepali Diaspora

We have conducted research using the MMP approach on resettled Bhutanese Nepali refugees, who are what we might call a "triple diaspora": as residents in Bhutan, their collective identities were solidified around their

common ethnic Nepalese heritage. Then, having been expelled from Bhutan because of that ethnicity, they lived in Nepal and/or India for twenty years. Since the mass resettlement of more than 100,000 of these refugees to countries of the global north beginning in 2008, the Bhutanese Nepali diaspora have been reconstructing their identities for at least a third time. The multiple stages of migration have complicated Bhutanese Nepali refugee identity, as does the fact that relatives and friends now possess transnational links all over the globe. We were interested in evaluating whether the MMP approach would be an effective means to explore these complicated identities as well as address issues of overcoming over-research. To begin, we offer a short account of the Bhutanese Nepali refugee issue.

The Bhutanese Nepali history is little known. It has its roots in struggles for representation and citizenship in a country ruled by a monarchy unaccustomed to being challenged. Bhutan's ethnic Nepalis left Bhutan due to a "suite of social, political and ethno-cultural pressures" (Banki 2013, 125). These included an insistence that they drop their Nepalese identity as well as policies that eschewed their language, dress, and customs (*Driglam Namzha*). It also included the singling out of ethnic Nepalis as "anti-nationals." As many as 80,000 Bhutanese Nepalis – as much as one-sixth of the country's entire population – fled between 1989 and 1992. An unknown number, estimated at 10,000, disappeared into India. Another 75,000 moved to Nepal, where the vast majority lived in refugee camps for many years waiting for a durable solution while growing into a population of more than 100,000. In 2008, resettlement to countries in the global north became an option, and now, more than a decade later, most Bhutanese Nepalis live in those resettlement countries, with many of them now citizens of those countries. As of 3 December 2020, there were 6,365 Bhutanese Nepalis remaining in camps and more than 113,500 had been resettled (Shrestha 2020), with more than 96,000 resettling to the United States (US Department of State 2019).

There are compelling reasons for seeking out innovative research methods on the Bhutanese Nepali diaspora in particular. Until resettlement, the community in Nepal was, if anything, *under*researched. A Google Scholar search of articles about this population (using the term "Bhutanese refugees") prior to 2008 yielded 711 articles. However, as the population has resettled to the global north, where researchers can undertake research more easily and refugee resettlement is a topic of great interest for practitioners and government officials, the exposure of researchers to this population has grown significantly. The total number of articles on the population through 2020 has increased to 3,330.[1]

## Discussion of the Multimedia Package

The MMP implicitly acknowledges the power dynamic between liminal and researched populations and explicitly aims to improve the relationship through a creative, somewhat whimsical, no-frills self-documentary multimedia package. The package is given to participants, who complete whatever portion of the package they want, when they want, and where they want. In this way, the participant has control over the data they want to share, exclude, and elaborate on. After a pre-established amount of time, the researcher then interviews the participant, using the information from the MMP to prompt interview responses.

### History and Design of the MMP

The MMP is an adaptation of the cultural probe method designed by Gaver and colleagues (1999) and first used in the field of design with the elderly community. These probes were described as "collections of evocative tasks meant to elicit inspirational responses from people – not comprehensive information about them, but fragmentary clues about their lives and thoughts" (Gaver et al. 2004, 53). Like the MMP, the cultural probe method was designed to reduce power imbalances between the researchers and the participants as well as to address differentials arising from differences in language, culture, and age. Gaver and colleagues note: "To establish a conversation with the elder groups, we had to overcome several kinds of distance that might separate us, some endemic to most research, some particular to this project. Foremost was the kind of distance of officialdom that comes with being flown in as well-funded experts. Trying to reduce this sort of distance underlay a great deal of the tone and aesthetics of the probe materials" (1999, 25).

Since then the method has been adapted to many disciplines such as health, immigration, social media studies, and technology innovation. Mattelmäki and Battarbee (2002) studied health and exercise habits and thoughts for non-heart monitor users. Horst and colleagues (2004) used the probes to understand how families stay in touch. Thomas and colleagues (2017) sought to understand young people's social media usage. Robertson (2008) examined the migrant experiences of foreign students in Australia. Given the method's emphasis on mixed media, it is perhaps not surprising that the study of technology (its uses and consequences) looms large in cultural probes' widespread use, from the intersection of human intimacy and technology (Kjeldskov et al. 2004), to the use of technology in health care and assisted living (Hassling et al. 2005; Crabtree et al. 2003), to the use of integrated technological systems in the home (Arnold 2004).

Researchers have labelled it many other things, such as "mobile probes" (Hulkko et al. 2004), "design probes" (Goikhman et al. 2016), "technology probes" (Hutchinson et al. 2003), "self-documentary kit" (Hassling 2005) and "domestic probes" (Arnold 2004). All these alternative names have made it challenging to know whether this is an exhaustive list, but it is clear that adaptations have expanded beyond the original design intention and beyond liminal populations as well. "Multimedia Package" is a working name for our approach, but it is based on the principle of epistemic equality: we wanted a descriptive title that could be easily understood by our participants and that did not carry invasive connotations, as the word "probe" may do. While some researchers may call their approaches by a different name when describing it to participants and when writing about the approach in peer-reviewed work, we consciously chose to keep these terms the same, thereby insisting on consistency and transparency as a way of continuing to lessen the distance between the researcher and the researched.

In Gaver and colleagues' (1999) original design, the materials given to participants were postcards (prompting cards), maps, a disposable camera, and a diary (logbook). Adaptors have considered the location and needs of the participants in their modifications, as well as the materials' ability to elicit responses specific to their research questions. On the former point, Crabtree and colleagues' (2003) adaptation of the cultural probe method for innovation in technologies for assisted living consisted of further materials such as a Polaroid camera in addition to the regular camera and a voice dictaphone instead of a physical notebook diary. The adaptation by Thomas and colleagues (2017) for young people's social media usage used Pinterest collages.

Arnold's (2004) adaptation for learning about domestic technologies con-sisted of a digital camera (on loan) rather than the disposable one in the original design.

On the latter point, adaptors (including we two authors) began to shift the emphasis from inspiration (the original purpose of the probe) to infor-mation. Crabtree and colleagues (2003) explicitly point to information-gathering as their primary goal. Robertson (2008) used the cultural probe approach as a tool to explore the nature of daily interactions of foreign stu-dents turned migrants and their transnational connections. She explains that using the cultural probes method in sociology automatically changes its approach. "No longer intended to inspire a design project, they are in-stead intending to provide extra layers to the 'thick description' of partici-pants' lives and experiences" (2008, 5).

This repurposing is concerning for the original designers of the method. Gaver and colleagues (2004) expressed appreciation that their approach was being used across different disciplines, but they equally expressed concern that a focus on the collection of scientific data misunderstands the original intent of the method. Centred as it was on a methodology and epistemology that values ambiguity and uncertainty, the original design was certainly not intended to be used to analyze the kind of data that one might collect from a Likert-scale survey instrument, for example. Yet for sociological and an-thropological questions that recognize the intersubjective nature of much qualitative data, the probes have the potential to provide meaningful and rich data that would not otherwise be collected. Such data, we will argue, al-lows researchers to supplement, but not replace, data collected in more tra-ditional ways. But rather than being understood – as described in Gaver and colleagues' (1999) original description – as "fragmentary" (a charge that could reasonably be made of any data collected in an open interview, and thus less useful as a descriptor), we find that the adapted method provides layers of information that allow for deep analysis.

## MMP Adaptations

In adapting the cultural probe method, we had three central goals. First, we aimed to explore the changing identities of the Bhutanese Nepali triple di-aspora and how the themes of persecution, displacement, and home (all aspects of classic diasporas) were reflected in those identities. This chapter sets these questions aside, although a work-in-progress on diaspora Bhutanese Nepali publications will explore that theme (Banki, in progress). Second, like Gaver and colleagues (1999), we wanted to reduce the distance between researcher and researched, both in terms of the power differential and in terms of life circumstances and experience; and as a corollary to that goal, we wanted the participants to enjoy the process. Third, we wanted to evaluate the MMP as a research tool, assessing its potential to serve as something other than an inspirational set of prompts. In the next section, we describe in detail the original model and the materials used, their purposes, and some adaptations, and then discuss our own modifications.

*Postcards* with a question and image on the front and a space for the participant's response on the reverse side replaced standard questionnaires in the original model, This was meant to encourage a casual and friendly research environment (Gaver et al. 1999). Robertson (2008) used them "to encourage participants to express feelings regarding significant events in their migrations journey" (13). Arnold's (2004) postcards featured open-ended questions and statements.

In our package, we included eight prompting cards with the following questions: "1. Write how you feel when you think about your homeland." "2. During what times/when do you miss your homeland the most?" "3. What do your family members do that reminds you of your homeland?" "4. What food reminds you of your homeland?" "5. What things do you like to talk about in English?" "6. What things do you like to talk about in Nepali?" "7. What things do you like to talk about in Dzongkha (the dominant language of Bhutan)?" "8. Draw a doodle of your earliest memory." Each question was written in both English and Nepali.

Regarding the design of the cards, like the original creators, we approached this (and the entire package) a means of personal communication, hoping that the designs would encourage participants to be forthright and share personal thoughts in their return communications (Gaver et al. 1999). We used a light green colour for the cards, to make them easily identifiable in the package and also to lend the package a personal, non-professional hue. We included a small, line-drawn image on each card for the same reason. One challenge noted by Robertson (2008) was to obtain (non-copyrighted) images that were visually appealing but would not influence participant responses. We looked

# What things do you like to talk about in Dzongkha?
तपाई के बारेमा बोल्दा जोन्खा भाषा को प्रयोग गर्न रुचाउनु हुन्छ?

*Please write your answer on the back*

# What do your family members do that reminds you of your homeland?
तपाईको परिवार को सदस्यले के गर्दा तपाईलाई आफ्नो मातृभूमीको याद आउँदछ?

*Please write your answer on the back*

# What things do you like to talk about in Nepali?
तपाईं के बारेमा बोल्दा अड्रेजी भाषा को प्रयोग गर्न रुचाउनु हुन्छ?

Please write your answer on the back

Figure 12.1 *Opposite top* The front side of a blank prompting card: "What things do you like to talk about in Dzongkha?"

Figure 12.2 *Opposite bottom* The front side of a blank prompting card: "What do your family members do that reminds you of your homeland?"

Figure 12.3 *Above* The front side of a blank prompting card: "What things do you like to talk about in Nepali?"

for a part-time illustrator to volunteer to draw a few whimsical images un-related to each card. These creative drawings, we hoped, would inspire open and "out-of-the-box" responses.[2]

*Maps* (local and international) were used in the original design along with coloured stickers to help us understand how the elderly interacted within their own environments. The interactive maps ranged from straight-forward tasks (preferences for locations to be social and locations to be alone) to tasks with a playful nature – for example, asking participants to place New York–themed stickers on their city maps (Gaver et al. 1999). De-pending on the adaptation, the map portion can look very different. In Gaver and colleagues' (1999) design, about seven maps were included in each package. Robertson's adaptation was a single map of the world, so that

participants could create a visual representation of their networks and connections around the world (2008, 10). Crabtree and colleagues (2003) also
used a local map to gather information on local routines and to understand
areas where the participant felt unsafe (3). Arnold instead used people's actual homes as the maps, asking participants to put different-coloured stickers on devices when they used them in the home.

In our adaptation, we used a world map and different coloured/shaped
stickers and asked participants to identify the following: where they were
born; where they had lived; where they had family; where they had friends;
where they knew people with whom they communicated regularly; where
they had visited; where they would like to go; where they would like to live
in the future; places about which they felt mixed emotions; and where they
considered their homeland to be. These instructions were included in both
English and Nepali.

These are, of course, questions that can be asked directly in a survey instrument. But the use of the map aligns with Gaver and colleagues' (1999)
desire to create a personal communication channel with the participants. In
addition, placing stickers on a world map allows participants to view places
and distances geographically and by scale. Also, seeing certain places on the
map may remind them of locations that might not have cropped up initially.
It also allows them, in their own time, to think about what it means to have
relationships with locations that are near one another or farther apart.
Rather than simply saying, for example, "Most of my friends are in Australia
and my family is in the US. I consider Nepal my home," participants, in placing stickers on the map, can see the entire world and begin to ponder what
these connections mean, in advance of being prompted.

In the original probe, a disposable *camera* fostered user-centred inspiration, as did other probe materials. Some specific photographs were requested;
the rest of the film was available for participants to take photographs of whatever they wanted (Gaver et al. 1999). Similarly, Robertson (2008) asked participants to take photographs of sites and objects of significance as a "means
for nonverbal expression, and to gain a deeper understanding of the significance of places and objects in participants' lives" (8). By removing or covering
all brand names on the cameras and including instructions for what to photograph, both Gaver and colleagues (1999) and Robertson (2008) intended
to separate the instrument from its "commercial origins" (Gaver et al. 1999,

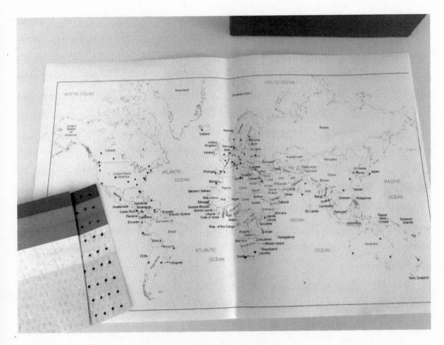

Figure 12.4  A blank MMP map and coloured stickers.

23) and to make it match the other package materials (Robertson 2008, 8).
Robertson also established a "playful" tone by asking participants to take a
photograph of their favourite meal (8). Adaptations of the camera include
Arnold's use of a digital camera to allow participants to make short videos;
those videos, when combined with photographs, were intended to help participants create an "autobiographical montage" (Arnold 2004, 184). Graham
and Rouncefield (2005) used a Polaroid camera instead, adding Post-It notes
to ask participants to create a photo diary.

Instead of providing disposable cameras, we chose to include memory
sticks in our package, and requested that participants upload items such as
articles, songs, and videos. This allowed for a wider range of material that
participants could upload, besides being cost-effective. We asked participants (in both English and Nepali) to add ten items to the memory stick: "1.
A photograph of an object or place that makes you proud of your heritage."
"2. A recording of a song or music that represents your homeland culture."

"3. A video of you or someone else telling a joke that represents your home-land culture, or a joke that is especially funny to your friends or family from your homeland." "4. A newspaper article about your homeland." "5. A pho-tograph of a place that represents your homeland." "6. A photograph of an object that represents your homeland." "7. A "selfie" that shows how you feel when you think about your homeland." "8. A photograph of a gift that you have given or received that reminds you of your homeland." "9. A photo-graph of beautiful nature in your homeland." "10. A photograph of some-thing (costume, artefact, ritual object) that you have brought to a cultural event that relates to your homeland." Beyond this, we did not provide further directions for the memory sticks, as we did not want to limit what partici-pants could include. Because we intended to publish neither images nor text from the MMP without the explicit permission of the creator, and were only going to use the materials as prompts for further questions, we had no copy-right or trademark concerns.

The inclusion of the memory sticks did broaden the type of imagery and visual data available for analysis. However, it also carried certain assump-tions about the technological know-how and possessions of participants. As we discuss below, this can present a problem for certain populations (for ex-ample, elderly participants and/or those with no computer), either because they cannot complete this task or because they must rely on family members to help them, injecting outside influences into the responses.

A *diary* in the original package was labelled a "media diary." It asked re-spondents to record their television and radio use as well as incoming/out-going calls, their relationships to the caller, and the subject of the call. In her adaptation, Robertson (2008) went one step further, asking participants how they felt when they spoke to family/friends/colleagues overseas. She did this to gain immediate emotional responses to various interactions or events. As a tool for self-documentation, diaries are useful in permitting us to analyze personal experiences and occurrences in an unforced manner, close to the time of the event, thus reducing distant reflections (Bolger et al. 2003, 580). Indeed, Robertson (2008) notes that a diary's immediacy means that par-ticipants do not have to recollect their responses in an interview setting; ar-guably, though, a method with even more immediate results would be direct observation. Crabtree and colleagues' (2003) adaptation of the diary included a voice-activated dictaphone as well as a diary for recording and re-flecting on daily activities. Graham and colleagues (2005) divided the log-book section into three distinct parts: a photo diary, a "message book," and an "ideas book."

Along with traditional diary methods, Hutchinson and colleagues (2003) used a technology probe in which family members could commu-nicate through digital message and video boards. Schouten and colleagues (2017) gave people voice recorders instead of logbooks for recording in-formation. Another adaptation, this one by Thomas and colleagues (2017), was to have participants create a digital pinboard through Pinterest over a six-week period.

In our adaptation, participants were asked to write down in a logbook ac-tivities related to the homeland. While we provided some suggestions of what that meant (communications, news, cultural activities, sporting events, po-litical activities), we left the instructions intentionally vague so that partici-pants could interpret homeland activities as they wished. As we discuss below, this ambiguity may have led to confusion or a lack of clarity about the pur-pose of the logbook, as participants did not use it as directed or requested.

## Creation, Distribution, and Collection of the MMP

Creating and sending out the multimedia packages was time- and resource-intensive. The process included designing the materials, translating them into Nepali, purchasing the materials, and collating each individual packet with all the directions included. This raised the question of whether this model could be replicated with greater numbers, which we cover below.

Gaver and colleagues (1999) had met with the participants beforehand and explained the materials, creating a collective experience that, they claim, improved completion rates. In a modification of that design, we sent the materials by mail to a community leader, who explained them to each par-ticipant. Then participants were given two weeks to complete the MMP. While Robertson's (2008) adaptation included a training beforehand and a provision of examples from her own life (further personalizing the probe), we chose against this model because we neither wanted to influence the re-sults (particularly in relation to the word "homeland") nor to over-explain the package. In our view, having the MMP explained by a community leader gave the package credibility.

We did not have the materials sent back to us before the interviews for early analysis, as had been done by Robertson (2008) so that she could then modify the interview questions (8). Rather, we went through the packets with the participants with fresh eyes, as it were. Besides being more time-efficient, this strategy lessened the burden on participants (they did not have to send anything back to us). We believe it may also have encouraged completion, in much the same way that people want to come prepared for a meeting or interview. Finally, having us open the packages with the participants personalized the interview process and helped underscore the project's whimsical nature.

### Recruitment and Community Involvement

We recruited our participants through a leader in the Bhutanese Nepali diaspora community. Mirroring methodologies that seek to find topics of mutual interest and benefit between researchers and the researched (Pittaway et al. 2004), we approached a leader of the Bhutanese Community of Central Ohio in Columbus. Central Ohio has the highest population of Bhutanese Nepalis in the world outside of Bhutan due to secondary and tertiary migration from their initial resettlement cities (Bhutanese Community of Central Ohio, n.d.).[3] We discussed our general themes of interest with the community leader, who, without prompting from us, offered his own hypotheses about the relationship between diaspora and home, having to do with generational differences. We took this into account in our recruitment, making efforts to recruit participants from a range of ages. Community involvement can be, of course, a double-edged sword, possibly injecting its own biases into the design method. We believe that our approach largely mitigated this concern, for the separate and individual interviews allowed us to ask in-depth questions, including about people's feelings about their "home." Throughout the process, we adhered to our institution's ERB guidelines when addressing issues of coercion, anonymity, and consent. All the MMP response material was reviewed only by us two researchers, and no recordings or drawings were made public. Any transcribed materials would have been de-identified, had this been necessary, although in the end it was not.

In consultation with the community leader, we recruited ten participants. We had hoped for an even distribution of age and gender: five males and five females, as well as three age brackets (18–30, 31–50, 51+). In this, we were only partly successful; our final recruits included eight males and two females, ranging in age from their thirties to their seventies. The elderly respondents required help completing the package and during interviews (as neither of us speaks Nepali). This was a design flaw we would like to address in this project's next iteration.

We had hoped, at this initial stage, to get at least a 50 per cent response rate, which would have yielded five packages and interview responses. This would have been on par with other adaptors of the cultural probe method, whose participant completion sets ranged from 33.3 to 50 per cent. Robertson (2008) had ten out of twenty participants complete the packets; Graham (2005) sent packages to three people, received back two, and only interviewed one. So we were pleasantly surprised that all ten participants completed at least part of the MMP.[4] This 100 per cent response rate perhaps represents our previous experience of employing non-traditional refugee research methods and reflects a strong level of trust engendered with this community in particular. Interviews took around two hours and took place in Columbus, either in people's homes or at the community centre. They were conducted in either English or, with the help of translators, in Nepali. Our interview script was used as a guideline; we adapted it depending on responses to the package.

## Participant Responses

As noted, 100 per cent of the participants completed some part of the package, but there was variation in terms of which items were completed. Table 12.1 shows that variation.

Table 12.1 reveals that the cards were the most popular items in the packet. We believe that this is because they were straightforward and easy to complete for the participants, either in one sitting or on one's own time. The maps were the second most completed item in the packages. One question (about a place with "mixed emotions") was left unanswered by several participants, reflecting a lack of clarity on our part. We had intended this question to be a prompt for people to discuss the mixed emotions they might

Table 12.1 Participants and their response rates

| Gender | Age range | Map | Cards | USB | Logbook |
|---|---|---|---|---|---|
| Male | 35–44 | Y | Y | I | N |
| Female | 55–64 | Y | Y | I | I |
| Male | 75–84 | Y | Y | N | I |
| Male | 55–64 | Y | Y | N | N |
| Male | 45–54 | Y | Y | N | N |
| Male | 35–44 | I | Y | I | N |
| Male | 35–44 | I | Y | N | N |
| Male | 35–44 | Y | Y | I | N |
| Male | 55–64 | Y | Y | Y | I |
| Female | 35–44 | Y | Y | N | N |

Y = Yes, complete or nearly complete (one answer missing)
N = No
I = Yes, but only partially complete

have about Bhutan or Nepal. Instead, some admitted they didn't understand this (Columbus09), and another placed stickers on the Democratic Republic of Congo and Russia, reflecting a concern about current events.

Only one person completed the memory stick section in its entirety; however, we were able to effectively prompt all the people who added items to it during the interview section. It is clear from the completion rates that the logbook was our weakest item; those who wrote in it only answered the questions about whom they contacted in a general sense, rather than in a diary form. This reflects either participants' limited completion time, or our poor instructions, or both.

*Experiences of Participants*

In this section, we ask whether the MMP reduced the distance between researcher and researched, potentially overcoming over-research. In our experience, the MMP significantly improved the research experience for the participants. Our 100 per cent response rate is a partial indication of this. Having conducted various forms of data collection with refugee groups in a variety of settings, we are able to compare the openness of our participants in diverse settings. We can assert that the MMP, like other participatory methods, facilitated a level of trust and openness between us and our participants. The response by one participant is perhaps emblematic of the general experience for our participants: "It was a joy. When I happen to talk to you I reached to Bhutan, Nepal and different persons, so thank you for coming" (Columbus09). While this quality is difficult to measure, the thoughtfulness of responses, as well as the time that participants took during the follow-up interviews, tells us much about their enjoyment. We also point to the eagerness of the community leader to be a part of the process (more so than other community liaisons with whom we have worked in other settings) as an indication of his appreciation of the MMP process.

The enjoyment the participants experienced helped reduce – although not eliminate – the distance between the researcher and the researched. In our view, significant trust was built throughout each interview. Invitations to dinner (not a regular occurrence for "regular" interviews in this population) were extended. Interview responses reflected trust regarding the sensitive subject of memories about Bhutan, as participants were comfortable expressing deep emotions. One participant (Columbus07) said about Bhutan: "I would like to go there. Walk there and no matter what, I don't care about my study or my job. I want to be with that" (Columbus07). Furthermore, the rhythm of the follow-up interviews was different from what we as interviewers had experienced in the past. The back-and-forth between handling material expressions of home and answering questions allowed the participants to shape the conversation in an unforced manner. Perhaps this is because the small silences that punctuated a switch from looking at objects to discussing questionnaire responses were frequent and long enough that broader thoughts about homeland, flight, and diaspora connections could emerge.

## Disaggregation

While the participants' experiences were generally favourable, the fact that some elements of the package were completed less than others suggests that each item has the potential to engender its own outcomes, both from a data point of view and from the perspective of participant experience. While we consider the MMP approach (and its predecessor, cultural probes) to be a method that works most effectively when all segments of the package are

offered, below we offer some thoughts on each element, separately considering in greater detail participant enjoyment and whether the MMP element
effectively brought out other kinds of data.

The prompting cards, with their offbeat questions and whimsical images,
seemed to facilitate an enjoyable experience. Nine participants completed
these cards in full. One participant (Columbus08) visibly opened up when
asked about one drawing. Earlier, he had grown quiet when he admitted that
he remembered so little of Bhutan, having departed at such a young age. But
his attitude shifted when he reviewed the "draw a doodle of your earliest
memory" prompting card. The image was of a school building. The participant then proceeded to share his childhood memories from Bhutan. He described the school in detail and pointed to the field where they played soccer.
The ball was made of "cloths" and wasn't a real ball. Remembering the school
and his fear of his very strict teacher, the participant laughed genuinely and
joked that "I was lucky enough to avoid those situations. To leave the country." He then continued to tell stories about his cheeky childhood in Bhutan.
While we do not delve into the substantive findings here, we note that the
cards were effective in bringing out emotive data, encouraging participants
to discuss feelings of pride and nostalgia, as well as moments that connected
them to the physical landscape of Bhutan and Nepal.

The world maps were easily recognizable for all participants and thus created an effective feeling of familiarity. The generally simple instructions and
associated to-do task that accompanied the maps were well-heeded. While
a few participants did not place all stickers on the maps, the experience appeared to be a positive one. The maps allowed the participants to speak
about their refugee journey and their diaspora experience, and many participants used the maps in unexpected ways, telling the interviewer about
various vacations they had taken since arriving in the United States. One
participant spoke enthusiastically about going on a cruise ship to the Ba-
hamas (Columbus10). During follow-up interviews, the data yielded complex ideas about the refugees' role in the world and as part of a transnational
community: "There's a global Bhutanese platform they have created now
and that platform actually provides an opportunity for the Bhutanese
Nepalis living in different parts of the world to communicate, to share ... I
mean even when we didn't have that platform we kept on communicating,

but creating a platform like that brings us together and then share something of value, something of cultural importance." (Columbus06)

Our memory stick was enjoyable for those who completed it. In particular, those who recorded a person telling a joke displayed amusement and laughter when playing the video during the follow-up interview. One participant (Columbus08) was delighted about the content of the joke, a joke he recalled from elementary school in Bhutan about finding/not finding pieces of gold, the punch line of which was slightly lost on the interviewer but rendered the participant supremely happy. Another participant (Columbus09) beamed with pride while showing the recording of his young niece telling a joke in perfect English. Just to repeat: the only material we might publish would be the (de-identified) participant's *reflection* of his niece's joke telling, not the video of her itself.

Only five of ten participants returned the USB to us with items, and only one had completed it. We attribute this to poor instructions, which we described earlier and offer suggestions to correct for below. The information that did emerge, however, was rich and varied. For example, it showed that connections to homeland were tied up not just with personal persecution, but with collective trauma, cultural practice, and family responsibility.

The logbook was the least successful of our items. Only three people used it, and they answered the questions we posed only in part. We view this not as a negative experience but rather as one that participants chose to ignore if it was not appealing. Where we did obtain information from prompting after discussing the logbook, participants generally discussed cultural activities within the central Ohio community, reflections that were generally enjoyable. We did find that more controversial issues were avoided in follow-up questions to logbook use; when we asked about potential political activism, many participants said they were too busy working while living in the camps to participate in any political activity. This is less a commentary on the enjoyable/unpleasant nature of the interview experience and more a reflection on participants' choices. A summary of our disaggregated findings is provided in table 12.2.

Table 12.2 M M P items: enjoyment and effectiveness

| Item | Participant experience | Effective prompt? |
| --- | --- | --- |
| Prompting cards | Easy for participants to complete; enjoyable. 9/10 completed the cards fully. | The cards brought out emotive data, particularly about connections to the land. |
| Maps | Easy for participants to complete. 6/10 fully completed and 4 others missed 2–3 questions. | Yes, participants viewing the maps with the researchers yielded rich DATA. |
| USB | Enjoyable for those who participated, but directions confusing or overwhelming for some participants. 1/10 completed fully. 4 other participants did it, but did not properly follow direcions. | USB data prompted wide-ranging types of information. |
| Logbook | Too burdensome for participants; none followed instructions entirely. 3/10 answered the questions partially. | Despite incomplete responses, speak about homeland events, connections and conversations about their homeland. |

## Drawbacks and Future Potential

Our data demonstrate that the MMP is an appealing approach, particularly for over-researched populations such as refugees. Given that community leaders were involved in its design, it effectively includes questions of relevance and importance to the community itself. And, in improving the research experience for participants, it also improves the richness and quantity of the data. However, we note several drawbacks.

First, the MMP is a time- and resource-consuming approach. We estimate that we spent 110 hours and approximately US$90 on the design, preparation, and distribution of packages to ten participants. Compared to the time and cost of preparing interview questions, this represents a significant draw on resources for generally under-resourced researchers. Having completed the design, we might well be able to reduce the "overhead" in the time and financial cost of the MMP, but given the importance of providing materials to the participants, there would still be a significant unit cost per participant.

Second, and relatedly, and as flagged by Celikoglu and colleagues (2017), because of its high resource requirements, there are concerns about whether the MMP and related approaches can reach large numbers of participants. This is a common concern for methodologies that delve into individual narratives (such as ethnography). The MMP will not appeal to researchers who prefer questions more easily answered by large *n*-sets.

Third, the MMP approach makes some assumptions about the literacy and technological know-how of its participants. A memory stick requires a computer and experience with downloading and uploading internet content. Also, the instructions in the package and on the prompting cards, and in the request to use a logbook, assume literacy.

Fourth, we are pessimistic about the large-scale replicability of the MMP as an approach. As with all open questionnaires, the prompts that any one participant offers will change the exact way that the interview is collected, and the data will therefore be different for different populations. Additionally, and importantly, the MMP, for all its creativity and innovation, would, we believe, quickly become yet another tool creating research fatigue if pressed upon the same population multiple times. This is, of course, an admission that the newness of the approach is part of its appeal. If that is so, and if participant experience continues to be a priority, then the MMP approach may not be useful in longitudinal studies. Or it would need to be modified so that each follow-up interview was much shorter.

These drawbacks aside, we believe the MMP to be a respectful and enjoyable approach for participants. Having engaged in this pilot study, however, we would make some amendments in our next MMP study:

1. While two weeks between the time of receiving the package and conducting the interview kept the project "fresh" for participants and encouraged them to complete the package without delay, the disappointingly minimal responses in the logbook (which, we believe, would have been a rich source of data) leads us to conclude that a one-month lead time would facilitate greater responses.
2. If reaching out to different generations is a priority, the MMP should provide an alternative to asking for multimedia responses on a memory stick. Polaroids, digital cameras, collage materials, and the like would be useful as a way to involve all generations.

3. With some adjustments, the MMP could lend itself to creative responses that require even less reliance on translators. In our case, one could, for example, show photographs of obvious locations (Bhutan, refugee camps, a resettlement country's airport) and ask participants to write, draw, or photograph their emotional responses. Reflecting on the importance of homeland, for example, without having to use a word to assign this, would be useful, if we could develop appropriate imagery.

4. To further lessen the distance between researcher and researched, and to provide clarity for some instructions, interviewers could provide their own personal examples of how to respond to certain items. Like Robertson (2008), for example, we could provide our own versions of a map or logbook. And for items that were deemed confusing, such as telling a joke about one's homeland, we could provide an example. Such examples would most effectively be carried out in a pre-package workshop, which could also mitigate concerns that only literate populations could complete the MMP. A workshop like this would add significant resource requirements to the project. Therefore, this aspect is aspirational for us.

5. In the case of our research, some unique elements remain unexplored, and the MMP approach allows for a wide-ranging set of issues to pursue further, allowing participants themselves to highlight what is important. These issues include caste, elite versus grassroots members of the community, and intra-group fragmentation at the political level.

## Conclusion

Our research topic, an investigation into the narratives and symbols to which "triple diasporas" cling and the ways they understand their homelands, lends itself to the MMP approach.

First, the project's combination of creative expression and its optional nature reduces the potential for research fatigue, at least in the small doses in which we have carried it out. Second, the creativity encouraged by the MMP facilitates both participants' enjoyment of the process and also a levelling of the playing field in terms of field research dynamics. Rather than seeing the information collected as a one-way experience, the approach allows participants to think about objects and stories of importance and share these, both at the MMP completion phase and during interviews.

Finally, the MMP's "gentle guidelines," as they may be called, allow participants to highlight issues of importance to them, alleviating concerns about the approach's time-intensive nature, as participants both enjoy the process and consider the topics important. The resulting rich and divergent data we view not as a design flaw but rather as a signal that there is complexity in the attitudes, narratives, and emotions of participants as regards to their homeland. We believe that the ability to express oneself through sound, objects, and imagery exponentially increases the possibilities for other ways of thinking about and understanding the refugee experience or, in our case, the triple diaspora experience. This suggests not only that the MMP is an effective approach for gleaning information, but also that in situations where researchers are collecting information that is a complex mix of attitudes and emotions, there may be an epistemological impetus to use methods that allow for a collection of nuanced information. Perhaps especially in the field of refugee studies, we owe this to our participants.

NOTES

1 This increase in interest contains a bitter irony for those refugees who wanted nothing more than to return to Bhutan; when they wanted the attention that might have wrought change in Bhutan, it was not forthcoming. Now that return to Bhutan is an even more remote possibility, the focus on their community has increased.

2 We thank Shanthi Robertson for this suggestion.

3 The City of Columbus City Council (n.d.) notes: "Central Ohio's Bhutanese-Nepali refugee population has increased by nearly 400% in the last eight years. Currently, The Ohio State University estimates there are 23,437 Bhutanese-Nepali people in Central Ohio and projects this population to increase to 30,000 over the next five years."

4 Only two out of the ten people who received the multimedia package completed it fully. Everyone completed the prompting cards and map sections with varying degrees of enthusiasm; 50 per cent added items to the memory sticks, and 30 per cent wrote in their logbooks.

REFERENCES

Arnold, M. 2004. "The Connected Home: Probing the Effects and Affects of Domesticated ICTs." In *Proceedings of PDC2004*, Toronto, 27–31 July, 183–6.

Banki, S. 2013. "The Transformation of Homeland Politics in the Era of Resettlement: Bhutanese Refugees in Nepal and the Diaspora." *European Bulletin of Himalayan Research* 43: 120–43.

– Forthcoming. "The Home/Work Relationship: An Analysis of Two Bhutanese Nepali Diaspora Publications."

Banki, S., and N. Phillips. 2017a. "Leaving in Droves from the Orange Groves: The Nepali-Bhutanese Refugee Experience and the Diminishing of Dignity." In *Human Dignity: Establishing Worth and Seeking Solutions,* edited by E. Sieh and J. McGregor, 335–52. London: Palgrave Macmillan.

– 2017b. *"We are not emergency people": The Voices of Young Women from Myanmar.* Unpublished.

Beyrer, C., and N. Kass. 2002. "Human Rights, Politics, and Reviews of Research Ethics." *Lancet* 360, no. 9328: 246–51.

Bhutanese Community of Central Ohio. n.d. "Who Are We?" https://www.bccoh.org/about.

Bolger, N., A. Davis, and E. Rafaeli. 2003. "Diary Methods: Capturing Life As It Is Lived." *Annual Review of Psychology* 54: 579–616.

Celikoglu, O.M., S.T. Ogut, and K. Krippendorff. 2017. "How Do User Stories Inspire Design? A Study of Cultural Probes." *Massachusetts Institute of Technology Design Issues* 33, no. 2: 84–98.

City of Columbus City Council. n.d. "Council to Provide $45K in Funding to Bhutanese Service Center." https://www.columbus.gov/Templates/Detail.aspx?id=2147506056.

Clark, T. 2008. "We're Over-Researched Here! Exploring Accounts of Research Fatigue within Qualitative Research Engagements." *Sociology* 42: 953–70.

Crabtree, A., T. Hemmings, T. Rodden, K. Cheverst, K. Clarke, G. Dewsbury, J. Hughes, and M. Rouncefield. 2003. "Designing with Care: Adapting Cultural Probes to Inform Design in Sensitive Settings." In *Proceedings of the 2004 Australasian Conference on Computer-Human Interaction (OZCHI 2004)*, 4–13. Brisbane: Ergonomics Society of Australia.

Gaver, B., T. Dunne, and E. Pacenti. 1999. "Design: Cultural Probes." *Interactions* 6, no. 1 (January): 21–9.

Gaver, W., A. Boucher, S. Pennington, and B. Walker. 2004. "Cultural Probes and the Value of Uncertainty." *Interaction* 11, no. 5: 53–6.

Goikhman, A., R. Theron, and E. Wandl-Vogt. 2016. "Designing Collaborations: Could Design Probes Contribute to Better Communication between Collaborators?" In TEEM '16 *Proceedings of the Fourth International Conference on Technological Ecosystems for Enhancing Multiculturality*, Salamanca, 2–4 November, 1219–22. New York: ACM.

Graham, C., and M. Rouncefield. 2005. "Whose Probe Is It Anyway?" Workshop on Appropriate Methods for Design in Complex and Sensitive Settings at OZCHI.

Hassling, L., S. Nordfeldt, H. Eriksson, and T. Timpka. 2005. "Use of Cultural Probes for Representation of Chronic Disease Experience: Exploration of an Innovative Method for Design of Supportive Technologies." *Technology and Health Care* 13, no. 2: 87–95.

Horst, W., T. Bunt, S. Wensveen, and L. Cherian. 2004. "Designing Probes for Empathy with Families." In *Proceedings of the Conference on Dutch Directions in HCI*. Amsterdam: ACM.

Hugman, R., E. Pittaway, and L. Bartolomei. 2011. "When 'Do No Harm' Is Not Enough: The Ethics of Research with Refugees and Other Vulnerable Groups." *British Journal of Social Work* 41, no. 7: 1271–87.

Hulkko, S., T. Mattelmäki, K. Virtanen, and T. Keinonen. 2004. "Mobile Probes." In *Proceedings of the Third Nordic Conference on Human-Computer Interaction, Tampere*, 43–51. Finland: ACM.

Hutchinson, H., W. Mackay, B. Westerlund, B.B. Bederson, A. Druin, C. Plaisant, M. Beaudouin-Lafon et al. 2003. "Technology Probes: Inspiring Design for and with Families." In *Proceedings of the SIGCHI Conference on Human Factors in Computing Systems*, 17–24. ACM Press.

Jacobsen, K.L. 2015. "Experimentation in Humanitarian Locations: UNHCR and Biometric Registration of Afghan Refugees." *Security Dialogue* 46, no. 2: 144–64.

Kjeldskov, J., M. Gibbs, F. Vetere, S. Howard, S. Pedell, K. Mecoles et al. 2005. "Using Cultural Probes to Explore Mediated Intimacy." *Australasian Journal of Information Systems* 11: 102–15.

Koen, J., D. Wassenaar, and N. Mamotte. 2017. "The 'Over-Researched Community': An Ethics Analysis of Stakeholder Views at Two South African HIV Prevention Research Sites." *Social Science and Medicine* 19 (December): 1–9.

Krulfeld, R.M. 1998. "Exploring New Methods for Collaboration in Ethnographic Research: An Attempt at Overcoming Exploitation and Violation of Informant Rights." In *Power, Ethics, and Human Rights: Anthropological Studies of Refugee Research and Action*, edited by R.M. Krulfeld and J.L. MacDonald, 21–56. Lanham: Rowman & Littlefield.

Mackenzie, C., C. McDowell, and E. Pittaway. 2007. "Beyond 'Do No Harm'": The Challenge of Constructing Ethical Relationships in Refugee Research." *Journal of Refugee Studies* 20, no. 2: 299–319.

Mattelmäki, T., and K. Battarbee. 2002. "Empathy Probes." In *Proceedings of the Participatory Design Conference*, Malmö, 266–71.

Pascucci, E. 2016. "The Humanitarian Infrastructure and the Question of Over-Research: Reflections on Fieldwork in the Refugee Crisis in the Middle East and North Africa." *Area* 49, no. 2: 249–55.

Peterson, D. 1999. "Encouraging Ethical and Non-Discriminatory Research with Mental Health Consumers." *Mental Health Commission Occasional Publications*, no. 1. Wellington: Mental Health.

Pittaway, E., L. Bartolomei, and C. Shaw. 2004. *Reciprocal Research: Human Rights and Gender Training in a Burmese Refugee Camp in Northern Thailand*. Sydney: ANCO.

Robertson, K.S. 2008. "Cultural Probes in Transmigrant Research: A Case Study." *InterActions: UCLA Journal of Education and Information Studies* 42, no. 2.

Schouten, D.G.M., R.T. Paulissen, M. Hanekamp, A. Groot, M.A. Neerincx, and A.H.M. Cremers. 2017. "Low-Literates' Support Needs for Societal Participation Learning: Empirical Grounding Theory- and Model-Based Design." *Cognitive Systems Research* 45: 30–47.

Shrestha, D.D. 2020. "In Nepal, a Refugee Changemaker Drives Forward the Inclusion of Refugees with Disabilities." UNHCR. https://www.unhcr.org/asia/news/stories/2020/12/5fc8b12a4/in-nepal-a-refugee-changemaker-drives-forward-the-inclusion-of-refugees.html.

Sukarieh, M., and S. Tannock. 2013. "On the Problem of Over-Researched Communities: The Case of the Shatila Palestinian Refugee Camp in Lebanon." *Sociology* 47, no. 3: 494–508.

Thomas, L., P. Briggs, A. Hart, and F. Kerrigan. 2017. "Understanding Social Media and Identity Work in Young People Transitioning to University." *Computers in Human Behavior* 76: 541–53.

US Department of State, UNHCR. 2019. "Press Statement: US Ambassador Randy Berry visits Bhutanese Refugee Settlements." Relief Web. https://reliefweb.int/report/nepal/press-statement-us-ambassador-randy-berry-visits-bhutanese-refugee-settlements.

# 13

## Life Story Narratives, Memory Maps, and Video Stories: Spatial Narratives of Urban Displacement in Sri Lanka

Shashini Gamage and Danesh Jayatilaka

Civil wars create precarious journeys of displacement, emplacement, return, and recurrent movement, disrupting the sense of "home" as an immobile entity. For those displaced by civil wars, "home" becomes a conceptual, affective, and variable space rather than a geographical entity alone (Hammond 2004, 10). Protracted civil wars create "in flux" lives of displacement, shaped by experiences of exclusion in one's own environment, substantial alterations to cultural practices while living in welfare camps, and the complexities of life after resettlement (Grabska 2014, 5). Displacement by civil war throws spatial and temporal boundaries of place off course, and this makes the lived experiences of the displaced essential to any understanding of place-making (Castles 2003; Chatty 2014; Clark-Kazak 2017; Collyer 2012; Grabska 2014; Grabska et al. 2019; Lenette and Miskovic 2018; Wallace 2018; White 2017).

The material goods of everyday life in the "home" tend to be destroyed or abandoned during civil wars, and it is the cognitive mode of memory that helps the displaced to hold on to their past under such circumstances. More importantly, memory enables those who are fleeing violence to record their journeys, which in civil wars are never from point to point. For those in exile, memories of a home that is no longer accessible must be constructed and retold, and memory-based stories of mobility contain vital information on the social, political, and cultural contexts that created the conditions for displacement (Creet 2011, 3, 10–11).

Pierre Nora's (1989, 7) seminal work on memory, situated in a field of study now known as memory studies, tells us that there are no "real environments" of memory and that "sites of memory" exist "where memory crystallizes and secretes itself." Nora's conception of memory is particularly tied to place. He argues that while place remains the "most natural" embodiment of memory, it is also artificial, as remembering and eliciting such memories requires a deliberate effort (cited in Creet 2011, 4). If, as Nora writes, artificial efforts are required to elicit memories affiliated with place, in research on conflict-induced displacement these efforts become a question of methods. To reflect the fluidity and nuances of lives in exile, researchers have had to reconfigure ways of doing research on displacement.

Sociological and anthropological methods have been central to under-standing such contextual experiences of displacement (see Brun 2005; Castles 2003; Chatty 2010; Hammond 2004; Harrell-Bond 1986; Lenette et al. 2013; Malkki 1995). These studies position displacement within lived realities of agency, movement, deterritorialization, and dispossession. Arts-based research that takes a bottom-up approach utilizing methods such as moving images (Haaken and O'Neill 2014), artwork (Knowles and Cole 2008), virtual patchwork quilts (Koelsch 2012), narratives (Lafrenière and Cox 2013), short stories and novellas (Leavy 2013), visual ethnography (Lenette and Boddy 2013), digital storytelling (Matthews and Sunderland 2017), and participatory photography (McIntyre 2003) is gaining prominence in studies that examine displacement, in particular in the field of forced migration research. Such methods have contributed to producing narratives that situate agency, gender, and the strengths of participants at the centre of analyses of displacement (Lenette 2019, 32).

In our study, conducted in Colombo, the commercial capital of the South Asian island nation of Sri Lanka, we developed a video storytelling method to digitize narratives of displacement shaped by civil war and development activities. We call these "mobility videos." These narratives existed primarily in the memories of a group of displaced people then living in urban slum settlements in the city. The participants produced these videos in collaboration with researchers and video producers. They contain oral life-story narratives and visuals of participants hand-drawing maps of their memories of displacement. In this chapter, we examine how these videos enabled the elicitation, retelling, and recording of memories. Such videos would help others better understand the social, economic, and cultural conditions of displacement. We have used these videos in a blog, a working paper series, and exhibitions to connect macro-level development practitioners with grassroots displaced communities in urban contexts.[1] Rapid infrastructure and development projects created the conditions for haphazard evictions and the poorly planned relocation of underserved communities in Colombo during the postwar years, when the videos were produced. Our intent was to use these mobility videos for community engagement and as a means to articulate the broader findings of our work with displaced communities in underserved neighbourhoods in Colombo, in this way educating development practitioners and policy-makers about the need for community-informed approaches during eviction and relocation processes.

## Narratives, Life Stories, and Digital Storytelling

In our study, we resorted to life stories and digital storytelling when producing the mobility videos. In research on displacement, narrative inquiry has long been a key method for data gathering, analysis, and representation. Narratives enable researchers to situate participants as "collaborators" (Mead 1969, 13), "knowledge holders" (Lenette 2019, 23) and "experiencing subjects" (Eastmond 2007, 249) in ways that acknowledge them as experts in their own lives. In this sense, narratives are constructions produced through cognition and memory (Lambert and Hessler 2018, 6). Life stories retold in contexts of displacement fuelled by civil war are framed through memories of violence, trauma, and movement to produce complex, contextual, and nuanced narratives rather than fixed or localized accounts (Clark-Kazak 2011, 43). For instance, Hutu stories of displacement found in Malkki's (1995, 49) work in Tanzanian refugee camps indicate to us how memories of dispossession and violence constantly intersect with historical subjectivities and national identity to produce narratives of exile and return. For many who live through displacement, migration histories themselves become their life-stories; that is, movement turns into an essential way of life in terms of finding work and land to support families (Hammond 2004, 29).

Life stories provide opportunities to understand broader ideological and historical frameworks. These in turn expose asymmetries in gender, reflecting different experiences of displacement for women and men living through civil wars, as Grabska's (2014, 16) work with South Sudanese Nuer refugee women in Tanzania shows. Life stories open windows onto "intersectional inequalities" that shape women's experiences in situations of displacement driven by civil war and political oppression (Grabska et al. 2019, 90). Feminist ethnographers have been central to recognizing such nuanced experiences of women's lived realities, presenting those narratives in ways that challenge positivist tendencies to research women through a masculine gaze (Behar and Gordon 1995, 429; Visweswaran 1994, 23).

Feminist ethnographers (Malkki 1995; Bolak 1996; Grabska 2014; Oakley 2005; Okely 1992; Parameswaran 2001; Visweswaran 1994) have taught us to seek out nuances and diversities, reflexivity and narratives, deconstructions and reconstructions, expressions and silences, that can place participants at the centre of the research. Given the complexities of relationships and the overlaps that exist within movement in displacement (O'Neil 2010, 4; Grabska 2014, 22), such a conceptualization of research – be it about women or men or gender-diverse contexts – is especially applicable in the contexts of our participants, whose experiences have been shaped by civil war, displacement, economic migration, trauma, and return or relocation. We sought to digitize their memories of displacement through life-story narratives.

The digitizing of such life stories follows a long tradition in visual anthropology (Biella 2009; Mead and Bateson 1952). Health research and social work also utilize digital forms of storytelling, such as videos, documentaries, exhibitions, and screenings, devising mechanisms that bridge researchers, communities, and policy-makers (Gubrium et al. 2014, 1607). In the 1980s, digital storytelling methods, pioneered by (among others) Dana Atchley of the Centre for Digital Storytelling in California, further merged digital media technologies with oral storytelling, combining "old" and "new" narrative worlds (McLellan 2006, 26). In digital storytelling, non-professional participants are trained in workshops to produce two-minute videos composed of personal narratives and photographs; these allow participants to tell their own stories (Dreher 2012, 160). Similarly, our mobility videos draw from narrative inquiry and digital storytelling. We extend the digital storytelling format beyond its roots in "first-person digital content creation" (Salazar 2010, 74) to include collaborations among participants, researchers, and video producers. These collaborations provide opportunities for these three groups to contribute already existing knowledge and expertise instead of having to acquire new skills of storytelling.

## Situating Displaced Urban Migrants in Colombo

The 1983–2009 conflict in Sri Lanka was driven by ethnic identities and associated causes. Tensions that had been brewing between the Sinhala and Tamil communities since colonial times erupted in ethnic riots, which triggered even greater violence. The Liberation Tigers of Tamil Elam (LTTE), representing the Tamil community, waged war against the government for an independent state in the north and east of the island. As the fighting escalated, large-scale internal displacement became a major feature of the conflict.

The war had dire consequences for Sri Lanka's economy, with many Sri Lankans choosing to leave their country to seek employment in the Middle East, Europe, Australia (Gamage 2019), Canada, and the United States. As well, more than 800,000 people were internally displaced during the three-decade war, with many moving into hundreds of IDP camps in the north and east of the country (Jayatilaka et al. 2018; Jayatilaka and Amirthalingam 2015). Thousands more migrated to Colombo, where they squatted in underserved neighbourhoods, which over the decades developed into generational housing (Lakshman et al. 2016, 2019).

Our mobility videos are produced in Colombo. Underserved communities in Colombo took root over the decades as internal migrants flocked there (and to other urban centres) for resettlement, jobs, marriage, and educational opportunities (Amirthalingam and Lakshman 2012; Brun and Lund 2009; Jayatilaka and Amirthalingam 2015). These neighbourhoods in the capital are also home to those who have been evicted or relocated within Colombo or who have migrated from plantations in central Sri Lanka. In 2014, it was reported that around 900 acres of government land in Colombo were now occupied by slum dwellers; that land included unused railway land, canal banks, and swamps (Jayatilaka et al. 2018, 82). Low-cost housing attracts displaced people to these slum areas, where overcrowding, flooding, and social problems such as drug abuse, alcoholism, crime, and poor health create challenging living conditions (Lakshman et al. 2016, 2019). Nevertheless, these slum communities are close-knit, with members of all religions and ethnicities forming vital support networks (Gamage 2018). Forced evictions in post-conflict Colombo have become a recurring reality for these residents, especially now that state-led postwar urban development projects have begun to unfold with the end of the war in 2009 (Collyer et al. 2017; Samaratunga and O'Hare 2014).

## *The Unknown City* research project

The mobility videos were produced in the final year of a two-year umbrella study, *The Unknown City: The In(visibility) of Urban Displacement*, carried out in Colombo between 2016 and 2018. This project was launched by the Centre for Migration Research and Development (CMRD) in Colombo, in partnership with the University of Sussex. It was part of a broader comparative research project on mobility in low-income settlements in the cities of Dhaka in Bangladesh, Harare in Zimbabwe, and Hargeisa in Somaliland. Colombo was selected due to its rapid urban development, post-conflict environment, and South Asian location. The research was conducted in four key underserved settlements in Colombo; the participants were a simple random sample of five hundred residents; fifty of them were selected for in-depth inquiry because of their dynamic mobility histories. In the settlements where the project was carried out – Sammanthranapura, Lunupokuna, Wadulla, and Kirulapone – around 37,000 people were living as squatters. Each community faced a slew of challenges: poor housing, drug use, crime and violence, overflowing canals, annual floods, and the risk of forced relocation. Three researchers at these field sites applied immersive methods, such as oral histories, in-depth interviews, walks, photography, community profiles, graphical accounts, and social, historical, resource, and infrastructure mapping. The study's objective was to change the way we think about migrants to the city. The research also attempted to understand how migrants perceived their world and why and when they chose to be invisible (or visible); it was hoped that this would allow new theoretical understandings of urban displacement and generate recommendations for housing policy and urban planning.

## Mobility Videos: Digitizing Life Stories and Memory Maps

Eight mobility videos were produced for this study during its final year. We called them mobility videos because they digitized the participants' narratives of movement during displacement. The videos were produced as a collaboration between a group of participants, a team of researchers from *The Unknown City* project, and video producers in the development communication sector. Three researchers and four video producers (including a videographer, a sound recordist, and a lighting technician), led by the two authors, were involved in the production. After a series of consultations between the researchers and the video producers, a mobility video format was developed for the purpose of digitizing the memory-based narratives of the participants. We drew on digital storytelling and memory mapping formats in the repositories Topological Atlas (https://topologicalatlas.net), StoryCentre (Lambert and Hessler 2018, 37), and Photobus (McLellan 2006, 26). The participants contributed their oral life stories as well as hand-drawn maps that traced their memories; the researchers coordinated the production of the videos; the video producers facilitated the technical aspects of production.

Producing the mobility videos involved several important phases: pre-production, production, and post-production. This reflected standard practice in media production. The pre-production phase included visits to the homes of participants. A series of these visits took the video producers and researchers into the participants' homes, where they provided information about the production. In media jargon, this is known as a "recce" (short for reconnaissance). The participants were already affiliated with the umbrella study and known to the researchers. During the recce, the video producers explained the technical aspects of production to the participants, who, at this point, gave their informed consent.

Eight participants (six male, two female) who had already been interviewed for the overall study were invited to participate in the mobility videos. They had volunteered to do so, and they had the time for it and felt comfortable with the video documentation method. During the production phase that followed pre-production, the participants were filmed over two days in a studio as they drew memory maps and narrated their stories of displacement. The researchers engaged with them, providing instructions

Figure 13.1 Screenshot from a mobility video of *The Unknown City* project – a participant's journey of displacement during civil war in Sri Lanka, narrated through memory, compiling a map.

about how to compile the memory maps, drawing on discussions exchanged during field visits. The participants were asked to (1) draw a geographical map; (2) mark their entry and exit points; (3) narrate their journeys; and (4) include any other drawings they wanted. Art paper and markers were provided. The instructions offered a framework for participants to recount their life stories of displacement in digital format.

Each video was between eight and ten minutes long and showed the participants completing their memory maps and narratives. In the videos, they traced their memory-based narratives by drawing a map on art paper. They marked points of displacement, emplacement, and recurring movement on their maps using pictures, dates, arrows, words, captions, and dots. While drawing, they explained the maps, retelling their journeys of displacement from birth to the present. Their drawings and narrations were recorded in a single shot. To de-identify them, only their hands were filmed. The use of one long take meant that the participants were able to narrate their journeys from beginning to end without intervention by the researchers or the camera crew. Each video contained the following: (1) the participant's hands drawing a geographical map; (2) the participant marking the map with significant memories from his or her journey; (3) the participant's narration; (4) a montage of general shots at the beginning of the video, accompanied by music; and (5) subtitles in English.

All of the participants in the mobility videos were minority Tamils whose experiences of movement had been strongly shaped by the civil war. They were between thirty-four and sixty years of age and had lived in underserved neighbourhoods with their families since arriving from the central and northern parts of the country. They work as labourers or conducted small businesses from their homes. Those who arrived from the central provinces had once been estate workers, whose parents had been brought to Sri Lanka from southern India as indentured labourers during British colonial times (see Jayawardene and Kurian 2015). Some participants had arrived from northern or eastern Sri Lanka – areas that had experienced the impact of armed conflict. Many of them possessed a T-Card (Temporary Card) instead of deeds to their houses and did not hold permanent land rights. The houses, which were constructed adjoining each other, amounted to "2-perches land pieces" (approximately fifty square metres), and this had resulted in slum conditions. Overview shots of the participants' communities were taken after the memory maps had been completed, to insert as evidence of the environments in which they resided.

During post-production, a professional editor prepared the final videos, supervised by the authors and the research team. The Tamil-language narrations were translated into English, and subtitles were inserted. The videos were later included in exhibitions and conferences in Colombo, and this facilitated community engagement as well as an exchange of knowledge with the policy and development sectors. Also, the videos have been included in a series of working papers published in the form of a blog and digital archive by CMRD (www.cmrd.lk). The videos have helped link communities at the grassroots level with policy-makers and development practitioners at the macro-level. Data from the videos have been included in analyses by the researchers to interpret patterns of displacement, housing policy, gender, and living conditions in underserved settlements in Colombo.

## Ethics, Challenges, and Limitations

It had been nine years since the civil war ended in Sri Lanka when we began filming the mobility videos in 2017–18. Sectarian violence against yet another ethnic minority – the Muslim community – had spread into several areas in March 2018, two weeks before we were scheduled to begin filming. The civil war and ethnic tensions that had resulted in the displacement of the Tamil minority group with whom we were collaborating to produce the mobility videos were very much alive even then. A sudden mistrust in digital communication had arisen with the revelation that social media were being used to mobilize violence against minorities. As researchers and media producers who were outsiders to this community, how could we ensure that the participants would be protected? Preliminary field visits facilitated a two-way information exchange with the participants about the expectations and outcomes of the mobility videos. Setting up the digital component as part of the umbrella project assisted in this. Through long-term immersion in the communities for the umbrella project, the researchers had been able to win the community's trust and acceptance. This in turn helped the media producers exchange information with participants about the technicalities of the production process and to obtain informed consent. Including Tamil-language conversant researchers from ethnic minority backgrounds facilitated these information exchanges in culturally appropriate ways.

Our participants had grappled with traumatic memories of displacement, including arrests, jail time, loss of loved ones, financial hardship, and illness. By asking them to retell their stories, we were in effect asking them to relive these memories. The mobility videos had been designed to acknowledge that trauma was at the core of their previous experiences and present lives and to create a "culturally safe, trauma-informed and community-engaged forms of collaborative inquiry" (Lennet 2019, 15). This was reflected in the mobility video format, which gave the participants room to narrate their stories in ways that would allow silences. Removing the interviewer and an interview schedule, and instead providing a set of simple instructions to participants, helped place them in charge of retelling their narratives of mobility.

It was a struggle to bridge the digital divide between the participants and the media producers. The educational and media backgrounds of the researchers and video producers generated inequalities and power imbalances in the field. As other have noted (Burgess 2006; Couldry 2008; Dreher 2012; Fairey 2017; Polk 2010), this problem often arises in digital storytelling projects. Digital divides result in hierarchical relationships when participants are being taught to use digital communication methods (Biella 2009, 5–7). Our project was the first time the participants had experienced the process of recording a digital story in a studio environment. We sought to harness the drawing and storytelling expertise they already possessed. Engaging their skills in a collaborative production meant they did not have to acquire new skills, besides recognizing the skills they already had.

Filming in a studio, away from their own households, helped reassure the participants that their identities would be protected, but this created further concerns. The studio was in a modern house in Colombo, and this accentuated the disparity with their own living conditions in the slums. However, de-identification was an important aspect of the production, given that the participants were minority Tamils who had been profoundly affected by conflict and persecution. The resulting videos do not show faces, nor do they provide names or addresses. (However, the participants did not object to us using their real voices.) The mobility videos showed only hands drawing memory maps, and this made the participants feel comfortable with sharing their stories.

One limitation to the format we developed was that it standardized the participants' life stories by sticking to a particular layout. The mobility videos compressed their life stories into concise ten-minute narratives. We attempted to mitigate the limitations arising from this standardization by creating political listening (Matthews and Sunderland 2017, 6), incorporating the stories into an exhibition, a workshop, and working papers, as well as a blog series that linked development practitioners with the participants. These ethical, technical, and social challenges shaped our video project, and we could not fully eliminate the resulting limitations. However, our project could not avoid them, and the end result was community engagement and dissemination of results at the macro and grassroots levels.

## Retelling Life Stories of Displacement

For all participants, their journeys of displacement include complex entry and exit points – within, from, and to Sri Lanka. In this section, we examine these complexities by analyzing the narratives they retold for the mobility videos. The participants followed different strategies when remembering their journeys of displacement. These included remembering locations, incidents, family members, and milestones on their journeys. Varunan, a fifty-three-year-old male participant, laid out his journey in chronological order, from one milestone to the next. He remembered the years and recalled his travels accordingly, using the years to transition between his experiences of mobility.

He loses both his parents as a child, and the war in Kilinochchi causes him to lose his livelihood from agriculture, compelling him to migrate to the Middle East in search of manual labour work. In 1989, the Indian peace-keeping forces that are assisting the Sri Lankan government with the war arrest him in his town, but he does not tell us why. He also tells us that his father "worked for the army" but leaves out the details of which side he was employed in. This silence is important, as it reflects his fear of expressing sensitive information related to the persecution, fear that remains even decades later.

In 1990, he is displaced by the war and abandons his job as a field assistant with a cooperative society in Kilinochchi. He moves to Colombo, to an underserved neighbourhood, and finds work as a day-labour mechanic. In 1998, he travels to Saudi Arabia, where he works as a labourer, returning to Sri Lanka after ten years there. He is unable to secure visas to return to Saudi Arabia. He then journeys to France, without a visa, and is arrested while travelling on foot to Switzerland by way of Yugoslavia. After being deported

from Europe, he is imprisoned in Sri Lanka for a month. He is released in
2011 after a court hearing. Thus imprisonment is a recurrence in his journey
of displacement, in both host and home countries.

Another participant, Raja, was born in 1975. He drops out of school after
grade six because of financial difficulties in his family. In 1988, when he is
thirteen, he moves to the small town of Koslanda in the central hills of the
island to work on the estates there for a salary of 750 rupees (US$4) to sup-
plement his family's income. In 1990, he moves to Maradana, a hub of informal businesses in Colombo, where he works in a textile shop for a slightly
higher salary of 1,100–1,500 rupees (US$6–8). He stays there for five years,
until 1995. In 1995, he finds work at a printer's in Pettah, the commercial
centre of Colombo, where there is a network of wholesale markets and
transportation hubs offering day-labour. He works at the printer's for eight
years. In 2003, he joins a newspaper shop, delivering newspapers in Pettah,
working part-time to supplement his income. He is able to open a small-
scale eatery during that time, but must close that business after three years
due to lack of profits. Next he moves to Nuwaraeliya, in the central estates,
to work with his uncle on a vegetable farm. Lack of profit in that business,
too, leads him to return to the underserved settlements of Sammanthranapura in Colombo, where he still lives, working as a day-labourer.

Participant Arun ties his movements to poverty and a war-ravaged economy – a common plight for Sri Lanka's estate workers. They are mostly engaged in informal labour on tea plantations and face the challenges of low
wages, poor living conditions, deteriorating housing, and limited education
opportunities. Arun's parents had been forced to migrate to Sri Lanka from
South India as indentured labourers during British colonial times, thus
demonstrating the cyclical nature of displacement. He moved frequently between Colombo and his home village of Hatton in the estate region of central
Sri Lanka, following opportunities for informal employment.

Arun's sister, who migrated to Colombo from the central estates, has influenced his movements. In 1996, she took him to the city for the first time.
"Colombo was wonderful," he says. He returned to Hatton after a short stay
with her. He moved to Colombo in 1997 and found work in an apparel factory
there. "But I was not very happy about the work I did. I also felt bored in
Colombo. I worked there for about six months and moved back to Hatton."
So he says, reflecting on his sense of belonging to both the city and the village.

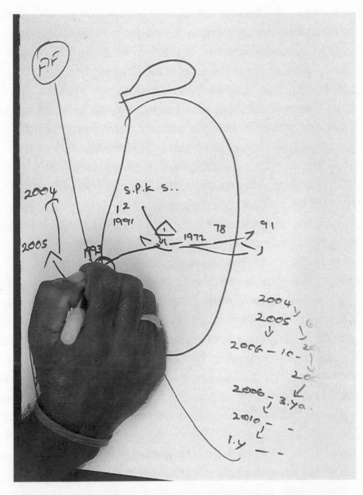

Figure 13.2 Screenshot of Ananthan's memory map in the mobility video with complex displacement, emplacement, and recurring movement, internally and externally to Sri Lanka.

After returning to Hatton in 1998 to work on the estates, he learned of a vacancy at a shoe shop in Colombo through an acquaintance. He moved back to Colombo to work at the shop. His low salary and issues about employment standards at the shop caused him to return yet again to Hatton, in 2000. In 2001, he moved back to Colombo to work at a hardware store. During this time, the death of his mother required him to return to the estates to care for his father. His marriage brought him back to Colombo in 2002, where he now lives with his three children. Meanwhile, his wife has taken a job overseas to support their family; clearly, movement is a constant in his life.[2] "We bought a house from the money she sent," he says. "We are living happily now." He talks about his present life with a sense of fulfillment.

Priya, a female participant, marks the years her two children were born on her hand-drawn map of Sri Lanka. She includes these childbirths as important milestones on her journey of mobility. Rani, another female participant, does the same. Thus, men emphasize journeys of passage in their narratives, especially in terms of the work they are able to find; women, by contrast, emphasize childbirths and mark those events on their maps as inseparable from their personal narratives.

Priya was born in 1972 in the central hills around Kandy and had seven siblings. She received a scholarship to a school in Colombo after earning high marks in the government's grade five scholarship exams. Anti-Tamil ethnic riots in 1983 compelled her to move back to her hometown for safety, leaving her education behind in Colombo. "I was caught up in the July riots during that time. We lost everything. So in the same year, we returned to Kandy. I began to go to school in Kandy again." In 1991, she returned to Colombo and began conducting Hindu religion classes for children. In 1995, she moved to a compound in a *kovil* (Hindu mosque) in the underserved neighbourhood of Wadulla in Colombo, where she still lives. Priya married in 1997. She says, "In 1998, we moved to another house in Wadulla Waththa and I gave birth to my first son." She marked that milestone in her map.

Like Priya, Rani was born in the central estates in Hatton, in 1981. In 2001, after completing her secondary education, she moved to Colombo to work in an apparel factory. She then found a better-paying job as an accounts assistant in Pettah. She got married in 2005 and in 2009 took maternity leave from her job to give birth to her son. In 2012, she found work at a vehicle spare-parts shop in Dehiwala, Colombo. Again she found a better-paying job, this time at a vehicle repair company. A turning point in her life was the death of her husband in 2017. Her husband by then had given her 2,000 rupees (US$11) to start a food business: "In 2017, my husband died. I lived alone with my son at home and continued the business. When my husband was alive, I got 2,000 rupees from him to start my food business. My husband hoped to expand this business. At that time, I did not have an income and

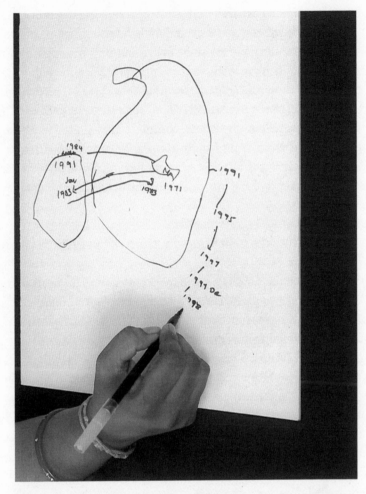

Figure 13.3 Screenshot of Priya's mobility video marking childbirth as a milestone in her journey of displacement.

had plenty of time. That is why I agreed to do the business. It is very useful to me now."

The men in the videos had travelled overseas; in the women's videos, migratory journeys were mostly internal. Leaving Sri Lanka to work overseas was not an option for these women, who had taken on the role of primary carer in their families. That said, Sri Lanka is an important source of female labour for the Middle East and Southeast Asia, and female labour is a key export commodity for Sri Lanka (Handapangoda 2012, 559). The women featured in the mobility videos were providing important care in their homes, facilitating men's movements, which entailed life-threatening journeys in search of economic advancement. Women also supplemented the family's income by conducting small businesses. Priya and Rani both operated food businesses from the home, commercializing their skills in preparing traditional foods. All of their household contributions are easily overlooked in dominant narratives of labour and employment. In Sri Lanka, too, women's unpaid care and informal work are not well-represented in fiscal statistics.

## What the Mobility Videos Tell Us about Displacement in Sri Lanka

The participants in the mobility videos reflected several patterns of movement. Some were from the northern and eastern parts of the island – the war zones; the rest were from the tea estates of the central highlands, and their forebears were indentured labourers imported from South India during British colonial times. They had been displaced by the civil war, ethnic riots, economic instability, and job losses. Both men and women had acquired a primary and secondary education through the island's public school system. Whether they had completed their formal schooling or not, they were employed in the informal sectors. This was largely because they lacked the resources to supplement their schooling with a trade certification, English language, higher education, and professional development.

Participants' migratory experiences are situated within and outside Sri Lanka – at times both. A common pattern was to migrate to Colombo's commercial hubs, where markets and small businesses offered informal and insecure low-paid jobs. Such places include Pettah, Maradana, and Wellawaththe in Colombo, where small groceries, hardware stores, shoe shops, eateries, factories, and textile businesses are concentrated. They live in slums near these commercial hubs, where the rents are low. Low wages and job insecurity drive them or their husbands to migrate to overseas labour markets in the Middle East, South Asia, and Europe. This often involves shady immigration brokers, illegal pathways, and precarious journeys, often on foot across borders. Some participants experience persecution, detention, and deportation along the way. On returning to Sri Lanka after their visas expire, or after being deported, they return to their informal jobs in Colombo, and to the slums. Their narratives reflect the insecurity of their employment and poor work prospects, which require them to move constantly in search of work. Significant here is that their journeys of displacement started with the civil war, either as a direct result of violence or due to the staggering economy.

## Conclusion

The mobility videos that were produced in collaboration with participants, researchers, and video producers were used in exhibitions, workshops, a working paper series, and a CMRD blog. These platforms helped connect grassroots communities in underserved neighbourhoods, where people's life stories are shaped by displacement from civil war, with macro-level development practitioners and policy-makers in Sri Lanka. The digitization of displacement narratives enabled the communication of key patterns from the overall study of displacement and living conditions in underserved communities.

A key message delivered to development practitioners and policy-makers was the need to better manage evictions and relocations affecting underserved communities, at a time when the city of Colombo was launching rapid and unplanned postwar development projects. The links the videos created between development practitioners and participants living in underserved communities generated useful discussion about the nuances of participants' experiences.

The mobility videos helped elicit the participants' memories of their displacement. Drawings and oral narratives served as opportunities for the participants to share their knowledge despite the differences in their education levels, cultural backgrounds, gender, age, and social status. The videos also amounted to an archive of memories of civil war and displacement in Sri Lanka.

NOTES

The authors thank Professor Michael Collyer, Principal Investigator for the
*Migrants on the Margins* project, and other research members, including
Mohideen Alikhan, Sakeena Alikhan, and Abdhullah Azam, along with the
Arts and Humanities Research Council (AHRC), the Economic and Social
Research Council (ESRC) and the Royal Geographical Society (RGS).

1  See http://cmrd.lk/en/publications/blogs/blog2020_01.php for mobility
   videos.

2  This is different from the women featured in the mobility videos, who remained in Sri Lanka, where they provided unpaid care in the home and conducted micro-businesses while their husbands took overseas employment.

REFERENCES

Amirthalingam, K., and R.W.D. Lakshman. 2012. "Impact of Displacement on
   Women and Female-Headed Households: A Mixed Method Analysis with
   a Microeconomic Touch." *Journal of Refugee Studies* 26, no. 1: 26–46.
Behar, R., and D.A. Gordon, eds. 1995. *Women Writing Culture*. Berkeley: Univer-
   sity of California Press.
Biella, P. 2009. "Collaboration in Conflict: The *Maasai* Migrant Film Project."
   http://userwww.sfsu.edu/biella/biella2009f.pdf.
Bolak, C. Hale. 1996. "Studying One's Own in the Middle East: Negotiating
   Gender and Self–Other Dynamics in the Field." *Qualitative Sociology* 19, no. 1:
   107–30.
Brun, C. 2005. "Women in the Local/Global Fields of War and Displacement in
   Sri Lanka." *Gender, Technology, and Development* 9, no. 1: 57–80.
Brun, C., and R. Lund. 2009. "'Unpacking' the Narrative of a National Housing
   Policy in Sri Lanka." *Norsk Geografisk Tidsskrift/Norwegian Journal of Geogra-
   phy* 63, no. 1: 10–22.
Burgess, J. 2006. "Hearing Ordinary Voices: Cultural Studies, Vernacular Creativ-
   ity, and Digital Storytelling." *Continuum* 20, no. 2: 201–14.
Castles, S. 2003. "Towards a Sociology of Forced Migration and Social Transfor-
   mation." *Sociology* 37, no. 13: 13–34.
Chatty, D. 2010. *Displacement and Dispossession in the Modern Middle East*.
   Cambridge: Cambridge University Press.
– 2014. "Anthropology and Forced Migration." In *The Oxford Handbook of
   Refugee and Forced Migration Studies*, edited by E. Fiddian-Qasmiyeh, G.
   Loescher, K. Long, and N. Sigona, 74–85. Oxford: Oxford University Press.

Clark-Kazak, C. 2011. *Recounting Migration: Political Narratives of Congolese Young People in Uganda*. Montreal and Kingston: McGill-Queen's University Press.

– 2017. "Ethical Considerations: Research with People in Situations of Forced Migration." *Refuge* 33, no. 2: 11–17.

Collyer, M. 2012. "Migrants as Strategic Actors in the European Union's Global Approach to Migration and Mobility." *Global Networks* 12, no. 4: 505–24.

Collyer, M., K. Amirthalingam, and D. Jayatilaka. 2017. "The Right to Adequate Housing Following Forced Evictions in Post-Conflict Colombo, Sri Lanka." In *Geographies of Forced Eviction: Dispossessions, Violence, Resistance*, edited by K. Brickell, M. Fernández Arrigoitia, and A. Vasudevan, 47–69. London: Palgrave Macmillan.

Couldry, N. 2008. "Mediatization or Mediation? Alternative Understandings of the Emergent Space of Digital Storytelling." *New Media and Society* 10, no. 3: 373–91.

Creet, J. 2011. "Introduction: The Migration of Memory and Memories of Migration." In *Memory and Migration: Multidisciplinary Approaches to Memory Studies*, edited by J. Creet and A. Kitzmann, 3–26. Toronto: University of Toronto Press.

Dreher, T. 2012. "A Partial Promise of Voice: Digital Storytelling and the Limits of Listening." *Media International Australia* 142: 157–66.

Eastmond, M. 2007. "Stories as Lived Experiences: Narratives in Forced Migration Research." *Journal of Refugee Studies* 20, no. 2: 248–64.

Fairey, T. 2018. "Whose Photo? Whose Voice? Who Listens? 'Giving,' Silencing, and Listening to Voice in Participatory Visual Projects." *Visual Studies* 33, no. 2, 111–26.

Gamage, S.R. 2018. "Soap Operas, Women, and the Nation: Sri Lankan Women's Interpretations of Homegrown Mega Teledramas." *Feminist Media Studies* 19, no. 2: 873–87.

– 2019. "Sri Lankan Migrant Women Watching Teledramas in Melbourne: A Social Act of Identity." In *The Handbook of Diaspora, Media, and Culture*, edited by R. Tsagarousianou and J. Retis, 401–14. Hoboken: Wiley-Blackwell.

Grabska, K. 2014. *Gender, Home, and Identity: Nuer Repatriation to South Sudan*. Oxford: James Currey.

Grabska, K., M. De Regt, and N. Del Franco. 2019. *Adolescent Girls' Migration in the Global South: Transitions into Adulthood*. Cham: Palgrave Macmillan.

Gubrium, A.C., A.L. Hill, and S. Flicker. 2014. "Situated Practice of Ethics for

Participatory Visual and Digital Methods in Public Health Research and Practice: A Focus on Digital Storytelling." *American Journal of Public Health* 104,
no. 9: 1606–14.

Haaken, J.K., and M. O'Neill. 2014. "Moving Images: Psychoanalytically Informed
Visual Methods in Documenting the Lives of Women Migrants and Asylum
Seekers." *Journal of Health Psychology* 19, no. 1: 79–89.

Hammond, L.C. 2004. *This Place Will Become Home: Refugee Repatriation to
Ethiopia.* Ithaca: Cornell University Press.

Handapangoda, W.S. 2012. "Can Money Buy Them Power? A Re-evaluation of
Women's Transnational Labor Migration and Their Household Empowerment
in Sri Lanka." *Women's Studies* 41: 558–82.

Harrell-Bond, B.E. 1986. *Imposing Aid: Emergency Assistance to Refugees.* Oxford:
Oxford University Press.

Jayatilaka, D., and K. Amirthalingam. 2015. "The Impact of Displacement on
Dowries in Sri Lanka." Brookings LSE Project on Internal Displacement.
https://www.brookings.edu/wp-content/uploads/2016/06/The-Impact-of-
Displacement-on-Dowries-in-Sri-Lanka-Feb-2015.pdf.

Jayatilaka, D., R.W.D. Lakshman, and I.M. Lakshman. 2018. "Urban Community
Profiles: Safe Relocation and Resettlement in Post-War Sri Lanka." In *Social
Theories of Urban Violence in the Global South: Towards Safe and Inclusive
Cities,* edited by J.E. Salahub, M. Gottsbacher, and J. de Boer, 79–94. London:
Routledge.

Jayawardena, K., and R. Kurian. 2015. *Class, Patriarchy, and Ethnicity on Sri
Lankan Plantations: Two Centuries of Power and Protest.* Hyderabad: Orient
BlackSwan.

Knowles, J.G., and A.L. Cole, eds. 2008. *Handbook of the Arts in Qualitative Research: Perspectives, Methodologies, Examples, and Issues.* Thousand Oaks: SAGE.

Koelsch, L.E. 2012. "The Virtual Patchwork Quilt: A Qualitative Feminist Research
Method." *Qualitative Inquiry* 18, no. 10: 823–9.

Lafrenière, D., and S.M. Cox. 2013. "'If you can call it a poem': Toward a Framework for the Assessment of Arts-Based Works." *Qualitative Research* 13, no. 3:
318–36.

Lakshman, I.M., M.M. Alikhan, and A. Azam. 2019. "Finding 'Reasons to Stay'
amidst Issues of Well-Being: A Case Study of Two Underserved Communities
in Colombo." *CMRD Working Papers.* Colombo: Centre for Migration and
Research Development.

Lakshman, I.M., D. Herath, A. Mohammad, and A. Ekanayake. 2016. *Experiences of a Relocated Community in Colombo: Case Study of Sinhapura, Wanathamulla.* International Centre for Ethnic Studies, Colombo. https://ices.lk/publications/6002.

Lambert, J., and B. Hessler. 2018. *Digital Storytelling: Capturing Lives, Creating Community.* New York: Routledge.

Leavy, P. 2013. *Fiction as Research Practice: Short Stories, Novellas, and Novels.* Walnut Creek: Left Coast Press.

Lenette, C. 2019. *Arts-Based Methods in Refugee Research: Creating Sanctuary.* Singapore: Springer.

Lenette, C., and J. Boddy. 2013. "Visual Ethnography: Promoting the Mental Health of Refugee Women." *Qualitative Research Journal* 13, no. 1, 72–89.

Lenette, C., M. Brough, and L. Cox. 2013. "Everyday Resilience: Narratives of Single Refugee Women with Children." *Qualitative Social Work* 12, no. 5: 637–53.

Lenette, C., and N. Miskovic. 2018. "'Some viewers may find the following images disturbing': Visual Representations of Refugee Deaths at Border Crossings." *Crime, Media, Culture: An International Journal* 14, no. 1, 111–20.

Malkki, L. 1995. *Purity and Exile: Violence, Memory, and National Cosmology among Hutu Refugees in Tanzania.* Chicago: University of Chicago Press.

Matthews, N., and N. Sunderland. 2017. *Digital Storytelling in Health and Social Policy: Listening to Marginalised Voices.* Oxford: Routledge.

McIntyre, A. 2003. "Through the Eyes of Women: Photovoice and Participatory Research as Tools for Reimagining Place." *Gender, Place, and Culture* 10, no. 1: 47–66.

McLellan, Hilary. 2006. "Digital storytelling: bridging old and new." *Educational Technology* 46, no. 5: 26–31.

Mead, M. 1969. "Research with Human Beings: A Model Derived from Anthropological Field Practice." *Daedalus* 98, no. 2: 361–86.

Mead, M., and G. Bateson. 1952. *Trance and Dance in Bali.* https://commons.wikimedia.org/wiki/File:Trance_and_Dance_in_Bali.web.

Nora, P. 1989. "Between Memory and History: Lesles lieux de mémoire." *Representations* 26, special issue, *Memory and Counter-Memory*: 7–24.

Oakley, A. 2005. *The Ann Oakley Reader.* Bristol: Policy Press.

Okely, J. 1992. "Anthropology and Autobiography: Participatory Experience and Embodied Knowledge." In *Anthropology and Autobiography*, edited by Judith Okely and Helen Callaway, 1–28. New York: Routledge.

O'Neil, M. 2010. *Asylum, Migration, and Community*. Bristol: Policy Press.

Parameswaran, R. 2001. "Feminist Media Ethnography in India: Exploring Power, Gender, and Culture in the Field." *Qualitative Inquiry* 7, no. 1, 69–103.

Polk, E. 2010. "Folk Media Meets Digital Technology for Sustainable Social Change: A Case Study of the Center for Digital Storytelling." *Global Media Journal* 10, no. 17, art. 6.

Salazar, J. 2010. "Digital Stories and Emerging Citizens' Media Practices by Migrant Youth in Western Sydney." 3CMedia, 6 August. http://fairfieldstories.net/documents/digital_stories.pdf.

Samaratunga, T.C., and D. O'Hare. 2014. "'Sahaspura': The First High-Rise Housing Project for Low-Income People in Colombo, Sri Lanka." *Australian Planner* 51, no. 3, 223–31.

Visweswaran, K. 1994. *Fictions of Feminist Ethnography*. Minneapolis: University of Minnesota Press.

Wallace, R. 2018. "Contextualizing the Crisis: The Framing of Syrian Refugees in Canadian Print Media." *Canadian Journal of Political Science* 51, no. 2: 207–31.

White, J. 2017. "The Banality of Exclusion in Australian Universities." *International Journal of Inclusive Education* 21, no. 11: 1142–55.

# 14

## The Worn Words Project:
## *Narrative Mobilization, Refugee Discourse,*
## *and Digital Media Production*

Erin Goheen Glanville

Despite the swell of concern for Syrian refugees in 2015 and 2016, public opinion about Canada's responsibility to forced migrants continues to be polarized as well as haunted by misinformation. The question of how to recalibrate simplistic debates through collaborative analysis has been the concern of a number of recent public-facing research projects.[1] Beyond misinformation, discourse – and language itself – can be a barrier to listening and dialogue across the political spectrum. Thus the need exists for stories that can re-narrate entrenched ideological tropes. This chapter outlines the methodology of "Digital Storytelling as a Method for Refugee Dialogue in Canada" (hereafter, "Digital Storytelling"), an applied media research project I developed and conducted at the School of Communication at Simon Fraser University from 2017 to 2019.[2] "Digital Storytelling" explores the narrative mobilization of refugee discourse for public dialogue. In conversation with refugee claimant communities, the project produces educational multimedia narratives about ordinary words in refugee discourse. These multimedia narratives bring together cross-sector expertise to assess and interrupt cultural narratives that are regularly used to frame refugee claimants. This research is an experiment, then, in breaking the patterned narrations of refugees' lives, through ethical praxis that combines creative media-making practices with critical refugee theory.

Given the project's theme and its digital dissemination, my methodology and methods deeply engage the dilemma of how to do ethical community-involved research with vulnerable populations. Going beyond establishing and following ethical principles in a research protocol, "Digital Storytelling" embeds questions about ethical refugee research in and across two years of production practice. The project represents a methodological shift in my own research on forced migration narratives. It builds on previous theoretical interventions in the field of postcolonial studies (Glanville 2013; Coleman et al. 2013) and on community workshops I developed to popularize critical analyses of refugee representations (Glanville 2018a). "Digital Storytelling" continues that analytical work but embeds it in a narrative arts project. It takes up an applied critical-creative question: what might critical refugee research look like as praxis in creative media production? A secondary question that may guide a follow-up research project is whether the narratives produced through this kind of praxis can be useful in prompting deeper dialogue in educational contexts.

I have called the public face of the project "Worn Words," which points to three things: (1) the way a few overused words are doing a lot of heavy lifting in debates about refugee claimant policy, simplifying and homogenizing a vast array of diverse experiences; (2) the way those words are losing their ability to communicate, to support learning, to arouse compassionate curiosity, and to accurately describe those experiences; and (3) the way those words have been worn by diverse people – often in ways that wear people down. With the help of activist and support service networks, I chose six ordinary "worn" words to reanimate through critical narrative mobilization: *refugee, welcome, border, security, humanitarian*, and *trauma*. In my media production praxis, I focus on how these ordinary words, as building blocks for refugee discourse, signify within the broader cultural context, asking which stories have become attached to them in the present day, how we might diversify those stories, and what happens when we hold the popular use of these words accountable to the people who wear them. By "refugee discourse" or "asylum discourse" I am referring to a set of terms that normatively delineate social practices and policy around seeking refuge. The public discourse that supports and is enacted by the practice of asylum (or refuge) is my object of study.

Worn Words' method of research is outlined below, but in broad strokes, it comprises cross-sector research interviews (prioritizing people with either a lived experience or a family history of migration), a partnered process of storyboarding, animation, and illustration, experimental video editing, and educational website design. The creative work of producing digital multi-media narratives has served as a living method of inquiry into refugee discourse and not as a method for producing data on people seeking refuge. The first completed video is a non-stylized montage of interview footage on the significances of "listening" for refugee dialogue.[3] The second video, *Borderstory*, uses interview footage, animation, and illustration to tell the story of securitization, in which "border" is the shape-shifting main character.[4]

The potential public and long-term aim of this praxis is to re-narrate refugee discourse in uncommon ways and thereby mobilize it for constructive public dialogue that cultivates deep listening. The ethical challenge of making media that resists being subsumed into prevalent frames for refugee cultures and that also remains responsible to the communities being represented has salience intellectually, relationally, and politically.

Intellectually, the project is asking, what does a critical refugee studies approach look like in the *process* of ethical media-making and in the *form* of creative digital narratives? Critical theory makes us curious about knowledge that is taken for granted; it also articulates categories for knowing differently. My journey into critical refugee theory began with studying refugee literature and media through the lens of diaspora theory and cultural studies. Diaspora studies reframed the significance of refugee cultures beyond and in tension with the nation-state and raised the question for me of the relationship between theoretical analysis and communities with lived experience of displacement. Constructivist approaches to political theory, tracing back from the work of Peter Nyers to Giorgio Agamben and then Hannah Arendt, connected cultural theory to political institutions and offered vocabulary specific to forced migration. Worn Words, dreamed up out of this series of scholarly conversations, aligns with the recent development of critical refugee studies, a critical-creative approach to participatory research.[5]

Relationally, the project is asking, how can researchers and media-makers remain responsible to refugee claimant communities – put plainly, can I remain in good relationship with my community networks once this project is completed and disseminated? This is especially important because I have never been a refugee. A number of relationships and experiences have shaped my research ethic. One branch of my family tree traces its story back to refugee roots. Frequent uprooting throughout childhood, parents who migrated to Canada as children, and an emigration experience in adulthood have made me aware of different kinds of migrations. These have both fed my commitment to solidarity with close friends who are former refugees and also produced a visceral sense of the differences in migration experiences. Volunteer work and community education in the support sector have given me many opportunities to hear snippets of people's refugee experiences. While much of this may seem peripheral to research, these relationships and experiences have been vital for engendering relational responsibility over the course of this project.

Politically, as assaults on global asylum rights intensify, so does the urgency of constructively engaging humanitarian storytelling traditions rather than simply critiquing them. I address this further in a discussion of what knowledge the project mobilizes. This chapter outlines the methodology of Worn Words and narrates what I have learned thus far putting it into practice.

## An Integrative, Emergent Methodology

In their introduction to *Going Public: The Art of Participatory Practice*, Elizabeth Miller, Edward Little, and Stephen High (2017) note the "strong 'public turn'" in universities "that is rekindling interest in multimedia knowledge production, new kinds of cross-disciplinary alliances, and participatory approaches to research-creation" (4). "Digital Storytelling" can be situated as part of this emergent public turn. Engaging critical media-making praxis for refugee knowledge mobilization has been a complex and creative research experience, and its integrative methodology is not easily articulated. Patrick John Lewis (2014) acknowledges the difficult nature of researching narrative: "Narrative research is complicated, complicating, and never easy ... Though a story may seem to move in a linear fashion the research work never does" (163). So "it is useful to accept that the job will be 'messy and emergent' ... Be patient with yourself" (174–5). To adequately locate my praxis in scholarly conversations, I use the following section to delineate three methodological approaches I have drawn on as the project has progressed: decolonial cultural studies, knowledge mobilization via narrative inquiry, and literary studies.

At an analytic level, the interdisciplinary approach of cultural studies draws out historical and cultural contexts of contemporary phenomena that are often ignored or distorted in dominant media. Cultural studies has its roots in post–Second World War Britain. It attends to culture's discursive formation, focusing on popular images and narratives used across society, from policy documents to everyday language. The construction of meaning through texts and images embedded in material relations constitute the data that cultural studies observes in order to understand power relations at work in ordinary structures. Tracing the path of cultural studies as a discipline, John Hartley (2011) notes that "cultural studies has included the study of: Popular culture and the emancipatory potential of popular media [and l]anguage as a sense-making system or network as well as an evolving historical artifact" (40). Noting the critical innovation of its beginnings, Hartley explains that "experience, identity, and reflexivity — the politics of the personal — were part of [cultural studies'] important challenge to positivism and scientism" (41). Following in this tradition, I chose the keywords of the project for their common use in popular discourse and then invited people from different sectors and backgrounds to give their personal perspectives on these ordinary words in open-ended qualitative interviews, in order to draw out the obscured contexts of each term. I also approached the words as part of larger discursive communities and attempted to disentangle those discourses to understand the significance they hold when embedded in narratives.

The intersection between decolonial research and cultural studies as a discipline is of particular interest to this project. Yasmin Jiwani's (2011) article on the production and forms of media offers useful insight into anti-colonial interventions in culture. "Anti-colonial frames," she writes, permeate "a broad spectrum of interventions but have, as their starting point, a contestation of power aimed at dismantling and/or disrupting dominant hegemonic ways of seeing and apprehending existing power constellations" (334). Raka Shome's (2009) analysis of the recent disciplinary shift toward internationalizing cultural studies explores decolonial approaches to cultural studies. The central question currently facing decolonial cultural studies, Shome offers, is not "how can research decentre Western contexts" but rather "how do we cross borders and barriers in a *downward movement* even within the same nation/region?" (715). Shome's words echo the critique of humanitarianism made by some of this project's interview participants, who answered the question about how to act ethically as a global citizen with another question: what are you doing about local issues of displacement and inequality – situations that are within your sphere of influence? Culture, in the era of globalization, is decolonized not by those with privilege extending humanitarian reach. Decolonization can happen when we/they simultaneously implicate ourselves in unequal relations and limit ourselves to undoing inequality in close, ordinary spaces of belonging. Worn Words attempts then to connect research with the politics of the personal in order to produce an inversion of power within a local space of belonging – specifically, Canadian refugee discourse as it is understood and used in Vancouver, BC.

The project's integrative methodology also includes the relatively new area of knowledge mobilization via digital narrative inquiry. Knowledge mobilization has at least three parts: producing knowledge, increasing the "desire and capacity for its use," and "mediating [the] processes" by which that happens (Levin 2008, 8). Ben Levin's discussion paper suggested that extant explorations of this methodology have focused more on the production of knowledge and less on disseminating it well or finding an interested audience. By contrast, Worn Words is particularly interested in collecting knowledge used by academic and non-academic experts and adapting it for dissemination to a public audience in a way that increases their desire to learn and to live and to think differently in response. One strategy for disseminating well and finding an interested audience is the use of narrative as the core communication tool. As well, both the choice to produce online videos and the choice to include animation respond to a growing method in knowledge mobilization methodologies. Online video is quickly becoming "a key means for people to satisfy their information ... needs" (Trimble 2014), and video has strong advocacy capabilities, for it reaches a diverse international audience through social media and serves as a pedagogical tool in academic and popular education (Cisco 2015).

"What" the project mobilizes is re-narrations of refugee discourse. While the practice of offering refuge has existed in societies for millennia, today's Western NGOs work with a practice of asylum that was established in Europe following the Second World War as a way of standardizing and globalizing "key techniques for managing mass displacements" (Malkki 1995, 497; see also Marfleet 2007). Contemporary refugee discourse is centred in the UN's 1951 definition of refugees as people who "owing to a well-founded fear of being persecuted for reasons of race, religion, nationality, membership of a

particular social group or political opinion, is outside the country of his nationality and is unable or, owing to such fear is unwilling to avail himself of
the protection of that country" (UNHCR). The international right to asylum
remains the legal foundation for defending refugee welcome, despite an increasingly complex context. Contemporary complexities include record
numbers of people displaced by war and environmental disasters, challenges
to national sovereignty and borders by indigenous nations, human smugglers, and protracted conflicts, to name only a few. The United Nations High
Commissioner for Refugees (UNHCR) describes the current refugee crisis as
an erosion of the commitment to the practice of asylum (UN n.d.; see also
Woolley 2014, 10). Pleading with nation-states to honour international agreements, the UNHCR, advocates, and NGOs are met with backlash through a
variety of discourses: securitization, conflating terrorists with refugees,
xenophobia, and cultural nationalism. As these phenomena become increasingly entangled discursively, the international community's commitment to
the practice of asylum is further challenged by protracted conflicts and pro-
tectionist politics. Refugee discourse is losing its power to communicate effectively and persuasively at a global level; a rights-based humanitarianism
has neither the flexibility to respond to modern global complexities nor the
social purchase necessary to convince skeptics. Worn Words sees potential
for re-narrations of refugee discourse in storytelling and analysis by local,
grassroots communities.

A knowledge mobilization project that uses narrative inquiry gathers,
organizes, analyzes, curates, and/or disseminates peoples' stories in various
creative forms to provide research-based support to the work of communities and community organizations. Narrative inquiry emerged in the
1980s as a qualitative research method that listens to the stories people tell
to understand the significance research subjects give to certain phenomena.
The aims of narrative researchers include understanding the way narrative
makes meaning for particular subjects and also the way a reconstruction
of those narratives produces knowledge for the researcher. Notably, though
narrative inquiry has been recognized largely as a social science method, it
has been influenced by the work of key narratology theorists in the humanities (Pinnegar and Daynes 2007, 6) and by literary and cultural methods
of narrative analysis (Squire et al. 2013, 9). Over the past two decades, a
number of interdisciplinary researchers have engaged the ethical issues that

plague storytelling projects related to refugee and forced migration experiences. Liisa Malkki's (1995) analysis of anthropological research offers a
warning against the essentializing power of stories that contribute to a singular and universal "refugee" category, "quite irrespective of the different
historical and political conditions of displacement and of the individual
differences between people who become refugees" (253). Julie Salverson's
work in theatre has addressed the relationship between refugee storyteller
and non-refugee audience and the way it turns stories into spectacle; instead
of attempting mimesis, she asks what translation and refused expectations
might do to open up how audiences relate to the story. A number of scholars
have tackled the tensions "between reality and its representation" to understand "'narrative truth'" as "the inescapably imperfect and fluid work of
memory, organization and meaning" and to distinguish among narratives
relating to life as lived, to life as experienced, and to life as told (Eastmond
2007, 260; see also Jackson 2002; Grabska 2014). A number of collaborations
at Concordia's Centre for Oral History and Digital Storytelling (COHDS)
have responded to the problem of refugee narratives becoming anecdotal
evidence for disciplinary conversations by using research to collect and cu-
rate stories that support the work of relevant communities, not only academic ones (High 2013).

Narrative inquiry research on forced migration tends to assume that
forcibly displaced people are the subjects of its study. Responding constructively to the ethical challenges of refugee representation in narrative, one of
Worn Word's foundational commitments is to explicitly delineate the subject
of narrative research as refugee discourse rather than people seeking refuge.
This project engages not only in methodological innovation but also in a
renegotiation of the domain of knowledge for narrative methods in forced
migration research. At every stage of the research – during the project's ethics
protocol, through the interview process, and while editing outputs – I have
struggled to keep the scholarly gaze off people seeking refuge. At each point
I have recast the vision of the project (for me and for others) as the use of
experiential, historical, and intersectional knowledge to re-narrate the ordinary words of public discourse about refugees.

Resisting narrative's magnetic pull toward personal, affective story remains an ongoing struggle as I explore a different role for narrative in refugee
research. The metaphor I use to visualize this objective is that of a spotlight.

Where traditional refugee research might train a spotlight on refugee lives and experiences to answer disciplinary or policy-oriented questions, this project's interview process intends to turn off that spotlight in order to better see what the flashlights of people with refugee experience are illuminating as pertinent knowledge. As an application of Marita Eastmond's (2007) call to "relate [stories refugees tell] to the social and political contexts that have shaped and continue shaping the circumstances of their lives and which engage their commitments" (252), the subject of my research then is the systems that people inhabit and the work those systems do to publicly demarcate the subjectivity of people seeking refuge. The system-as-research-subject this project analyzes is that of language.

Literary studies has a rich scholarly tradition of close and detailed analysis of language and narrative. As questions about the possibilities and limits of narrative forms emerged in this project, literary theory has given me categories for exploring this intersection of aesthetics, rhetoric, and ethics. The relevance of literary studies for knowledge mobilization was obvious to me when, in 2018, I facilitated a day-long professional development workshop for humanitarian workers on the ethics of an organization's storytelling. Together we articulated the difficulty of "changing the narrative" around refugee claimant lives. Their experiences affirmed that, despite having ethical concerns related to narrating refugee realities, when a humanitarian or support worker stands up to educate or raise funds, they find themselves using familiar narrative forms, in other words imposing external patterns onto dynamic lived realities. They wanted to know about the formal elements of story and how they might rework those elements in their storytelling to better reflect their realities. Changing a narrative requires consideration of the formal details of the narrative as well as transformation of the process of telling a narrative. For example, in popular digital cultures humanitarian discourse is equated with refugee representation. Lilie Chouliaraki (2010) has described the history of humanitarian storytelling as a history of its critique both of the hierarchical "social relationships that the imagery of suffering establishes" and of its didactic use of story to call for immediate action (4). In order for research to support communities in changing the narrative about refugee claimants as recipients of humanitarian charity, alternative forms and processes of storytelling – not just new data – are needed. Concretely, where humanitarian storytellers might take personal anecdotes about refugees and narrate them through the voice of a humanitarian worker to raise awareness about a crisis, a decolonial approach to narrative might be multi-voiced, without an overarching narrator. Such a shift has implications both for narrative form and for the process by which the narrative is produced and disseminated.

## Methods: Ethics and Interviews

Worn Words consisted of three overlapping stages. The first was developing my research ethics protocol and my method of collection for media assets. The second was designing and completing semi-structured research interviews and collecting interview footage. The third included working with a videographer, an animator, and musicians to create educational media materials using animation and interview footage. I address the first two stages here and elaborate on the third stage in the following section on media outputs.

If Worn Words develops an integrative methodology that attends to the formation of narrative discourse through a downward movement in a particular context, then the particular context for this project was Vancouver, Canada, and the interrogation of refugee discourse took place through interviews with fourteen participants, mostly local and many with experiential expertise. I produced experimental narrative media out of the participants' reflexive analyses of the ordinary building blocks in refugee discourse, in dialogue with the videographer, animator, and musicians and with regular feedback from local practitioners. The critical refugee studies praxis that resulted from moving between theorization and practice grappled with the complexities of research ethics.

The research ethics the project enacted included: prioritizing relationality over productivity in response to the history of refugee research as exploitative (i.e., mining a community for data and using those data to enrich academic conversations); prioritizing the perspectives of people with lived experience of forced migration in response to the way academics without experience can silence refugee voices by taking up too much room in the conversation or by "dissecting the lives of refugees as if they were a caged animal";[6] finding aesthetic forms to mobilize different modes of communication, as a response to the way hierarchies of knowledge have disadvantaged people with experience (e.g., the rejection of emotion as subjective, or the way some conversations require mastery of academic jargon); focusing on the ordinary rather than the extraordinary in response to the exoticization and spectacle that drive many popular representations of refugees; integrating personal storytelling and systemic critique as a response to the depoliticization of refugee realities in many research projects; and slowing down to do research that aims to produce a listening community rather than produce media for influence (i.e., an approach that differs from the urgent and prolific production of research in moments of "refugee crisis").

I began by developing an ethics protocol that incorporated participatory steps throughout the process and that positioned interviewees as experts whose knowledge I was mobilizing rather than as research subjects. Sources that I found helpful for formalizing my protocol included two edited volumes: *Values and Vulnerabilities: The Ethics of Research with Refugees and Asylum Seekers* (Block 2013) and *Oral History at the Crossroads* (High 2014).[7] To position interviewees as experts rather than sources for data extraction, my protocol limited me to approaching people who already had some sort of public or work-related profile that related to refugee discourse. They were approached not as people with personal experiences that could be translated into research data but rather as expert commentators in the field. Furthermore, open-ended interview questions focused on the definitions, significances, theorizations, and cultural narratives of specific terminology; people were approached for and interviewed about their expertise in refugee or migration discourse. The protocol also stipulated that transcripts of the interview would be sent to interviewees, who were then given an opportunity to suppress any part of the interview they desired. Video footage related to the portions of transcriptions that interviewees requested us to delete was permanently deleted from the devices we were using to edit. The protocol's inclusion criteria were as follows: persons nineteen years of age or older, those with either permanent residency or citizenship in Canada, and people who are (a) scholars researching in refugee and related studies, (b) employees of organizations with a mandate to support refugee or refugee claimant populations, or (c) artists or activists with a public profile on refugee issues.

In conversation with videographer Flick Harrison, I considered how to capture footage that would support the project's knowledge mobilization concern so as to increase people's desire to listen across difference. Mode of address – the way video speaks to its imagined audience and invites them into relationship – was a key consideration (Ellsworth 2008). We wanted viewers to feel warmly addressed by the video, to experience a winsome invitation to listen to and engage with different perspectives. So we first experimented with Harrison interviewing me to find a creative way of framing and positioning the interviewers that would invite careful listening. We decided to film the participants using a homemade version of Errol Morris's Interrotron. It is a box made of cardboard, cloth, and glass taped together and placed in front of the camera lens. The angled piece of glass allowed the interviewee and me to see each other's reflection and to speak to each other through the glass, but the camera captured only their side of the conversation. The warmth and ease of the interviewees' address markedly increased when they spoke to my listening reflection in the mirror rather than to the gaze of the camera lens. In this way we could materialize an invitational mode of address and immerse viewers in the original conversation. With the interviewer removed from sight and the interviewee looking straight into the camera, the viewer takes the place of listener and enters a friendly engagement with a series of voices on a polarizing topic.

In order to choose the keywords for the project (and before funding was confirmed), I had emailed my network of refugee activists, settlement workers, and community educators and asked them to each give me the top five everyday words in English they feel are misunderstood or commonly misused in debates about asylum rights and Canada's responsibility to refugees. From a list of around fifty words, I chose six reoccurring words to work with: "refugee," "welcome," "border," "security," "humanitarian," and "trauma." In addition to being words whose meaning is often taken for granted, they each corresponded to a body of critical research. For the interviews, then, I imagined the kinds of questions asked by critical theory that could unearth the inequalities, histories, contexts, oversimplifications, and homogenizations latent in these words. I adjusted these theoretical questions to serve as interview questions. For example, in your experience, whose "security" does the "border" protect? Or, how do you see people using the word "refugee" and what do you think about the way they use it? What other terms get repeatedly associated with that term? If you could tell everyone in Canada something about the word "refugee," what would you like them to know? What do you think of the word "trauma?" Is there a word that fits such experiences better? Would you call yourself a humanitarian? If not, how do you describe your work?

The second stage of research was interviewing and was funded by the Dragon Fire Fund held at the Vancouver Foundation. Interviews were conducted in English. Interviewees were given the choice to opt into an audio-only recording or a video recording. One interview was audio-recorded rather than filmed. With the help of Harrison, I filmed in-depth interviews with fourteen experts in refugee discourse: twelve were based in British Columbia, one was based in Montreal but had studied in Vancouver, and one was based in Sydney, Australia, but was visiting Vancouver. In addition to the fourteen participants, two people chose not to be recorded at all but allowed me to interview them for the project. Their perspectives have influenced the project, but their interviews are not included in it. As well, one participant asked to interview me, so we booked an interview with flipped roles and recorded this as well. I approached an additional ten people who declined to be interviewed or who could not interview within my timeframe.

Interview participants were selected to provide cross-sector perspectives. Some people identified with more than one sector: a mental health counsellor, two activist-authors, an indigenous rights defender, a community-based artist, five academics working variously in the disciplines of history, sociology, communications, political science, and health sciences, a city councillor, four settlement and service providers, and a lawyer. To generate a cross-section of people that could invite and model attentive dialogue, interviewees were invited from two umbrella refugee organizations in Vancouver, including frontline workers and managers; two grassroots refugee support organizations; five academic institutions; two organizing networks; a law firm; and municipal government. When selecting people to approach, I prioritized those with personal experience navigating the refugee claim system in Canada, those with a family history of displacement, and those who were personally embedded in refugee and refugee claimant communities. That said, my selection process remained dependent on who agreed to be interviewed. In keeping with a cultural studies focus on the ordinary in popular culture, I prioritized people with experiential expertise even when this meant, for example, approaching frontline workers over an Executive Director or interviewing a city councillor rather than a Member of Parliament. Future projects would benefit from a longer timeline; having one for

this project would have allowed the flexibility to include the important perspectives of individuals who were unavailable during the period I was interviewing. Given more resources, these interviews could have been done
with an interpreter and included perspectives of advocates in languages
other than English.

Before each interview and again at the start of each interview I made explicit to interviewees that they were invited to speak in broad terms about
their knowledge and to only offer personal information or examples as necessary and as they were comfortable. As an interviewer, I was aware that in
complex ways, the positions of interviewees within their organizations or
in their line of work produced certain kinds of knowledge during the interview process, including differing levels of freedom to be critical of a rights-
based refugee discourse. Relatedly, my own positionality intersected with
those I was interviewing differently in each interview. Following each interview, I reflected on this and adjusted my questions or preparatory instructions or affect for the next interview encounter.

Related consultation on the project more broadly and on specific phases
of media production was undertaken variously through conversations with
employees of Mosaic, ISS of BC, Canadian Council for Refugees, Kinbrace
Community Society, Journey Home Society, and VAST. Crucially, informal
relationships and unstructured community involvement guided the development of my methods and continue to provide me with direct and indirect
feedback on the educational media production.

## Methods: Editing Media Outputs

As I have attempted to pull on the thread of a single, ordinary English word
in asylum discourse, I have experienced the tensions of entanglement within
the weave of the discourse and the tensions of entanglement with other issues. The act of pulling on a single discursive strand (for example, "border")
has brought to the surface the large and complex cultural narratives anchor-
ing tropes that currently structure popular dialogue in Canada.

Our first editing step was to compile footage from the interviews in files
corresponding to each of the six keywords. I then uploaded the interview
transcript texts to the qualitative data analysis software NVivo. Using that
software, I began the work of coding, which determines the concepts that are

relevant to the research question and identifies passages where they appear in order to discover the relationships among data points. However, given the length of the interviews and the subtlety of recognizing when an intervie-wee's comment was relevant to a word even when it did not mention the word directly, I realized that watching and re-watching the footage was a more reliable way of coding the interviews according to our key terms. The first rough assemblage we watched through was an hour and a half of footage on the word "refugee." Without reordering the clips, we put them into a sin-gle file to see what the footage was capable of doing independent of our orig-inal vision. After watching it straight through with the videographer, we took some time to articulate what we had just experienced. While themes emerged, a storyline certainly did not. Furthermore, listening to multiple, cross-sector voices offering critical and constructive readings of a single term felt cacophonous. The videographer described it as a boxing match, with ev-eryone engaged in different skirmishes – sometimes even with one another. The discourse produced by the footage was experienced as contradictory and conflicting, and the result for us as viewers was a sense of doubt as to whether each interviewee's opponents actually existed. Contributing to the cacophony were clips seemingly addressing concerns from both the political right and left in North America, clips addressing issues in other global con-texts, clips using institution-specific language, clips with conflicting social aims, and clips reliant on divergent forms of communication, such as lists of facts, theory, historical anecdotes, personal examples, and political cri-tique. Each person, in the context of his or her own interview, provided thoughtful, multi-faceted answers to the questions I posed; each interview had provided powerful answers to questions about discourse and had ad-dressed the significance of a single ordinary word; each person was respond-ing to the misunderstandings of refugee discourse that they had observed regularly in their own work; and each offered clear alternative language or action for people within their spheres of influence. But brought together, they lacked a coherent addressee highlighting the appeal of a single narrator.

Determined to hold the tension productively, I initially made sense of this disjointedness as the result of interviewees imagining different audiences or participating in separate communities of conversation. The cross-sector na-ture of the project meant we were discussing discourse embedded in insti-tutions with varying and even oppositional missions, so a keyword carried a multitude of significances for all the subcultures and communities they represented or were in conversation with. As well, the reckless, radical shifts in political contexts meant that even across six months of interviewing, people interviewed near the end were aware of new policies that earlier interviewees were not contending with and felt the urgency of particular media events or of explosive rhetoric recently detonated by political communication. In addition to the challenges of cross-sector dialogue and shifting contexts, interviewees were addressing a lithe and powerful discourse. At least two people refused the stated project of defining or re-narrating words for this reason. The impulse to define *is* the ethical problem, they said. Colonial discourse cannot be reworked without being reinforced. Language from the field of discourse analysis confirms my assessment of this experience: a "discourse strand" is a thematically uniform discourse process though it is in practice always entangled with other discourses. Each research interview cut across the discourse strand of asylum rights in order to draw out and challenge the limits their discourse community has placed on the significance of an individual word. Yet as the interviewees critically analyzed key terms in asylum discourse, they also participated in the discourse on different discursive planes, defined as "the societal locations from which 'speaking happens'" (Siegfried 2001, 49). They participated variously on the linked but separate discursive planes of politics, education, administration, activism, and – very likely – additional planes that were less obvious to me. With some disquiet, I held this problematic in mind as we continued interviewing. What digital narrative form could hold the various voices together without conflating heterogeneous perspectives? What would allow for equality and cohesion amid differing kinds of communication (e.g., a personal anecdote and cultural analysis or a historical fact and a poem) collected in the footage?

One solution was to notice what additional keywords were emerging from the interviews. As we watched and re-watched the footage, we noticed many of the interviewees speak about the importance of listening. So, though we were only halfway through the interviews, we created a simple video montage of interview footage on the theme of "listening" in refugee dialogues.[8] While it was not meant to be a formal output, I have used it since, in classrooms and public talks, to prompt conversations about the ethics and particularities of entering dialogue on forced migration. In those contexts, the multi-voice, conversational style of the video raises peoples' curiosity and interest. I have uploaded it to my website for others to view and use, and I screen it regularly in my own classes to elicit conversations about what listening might look like in the specific context of refugee dialogue.[9]

A second answer to this problematic arrived with a return to Sara Ahmed's Introduction to *The Cultural Politics of Emotion* (2014). Her careful work on the intangible "familiar narratives" that shape the exchange of emotions taking place on national and personal planes around immigration gave me an opening for imagining a retelling of those familiar narratives. Her analysis was a reminder that the interlocutor that made the interviews meaningful in relationship with one another was not an audience – demographic, sectoral, geographic, or otherwise; rather our shared interlocutor *was* the familiar narrative, or buried story. Asylum discourse in popular culture depends on a partly submerged or hidden narrative shaping the connotations of the word in question, and that narrative needed to be dug up and addressed. In other words, when we tried to extract and re-narrate a word for the purpose of discursive revision, we found that interviewees' critiques of the words lacked coherence because they were responding to the complexity of the narratives in which that word had been embedded. I believe this is, in part, a genuine limitation of critical research. While a series of personal stories from a single community might be able to rework discourse creatively, a series of cross-sector voices, challenging a persistent cultural narrative, is less able to construct something new. It responds to an external narrative rather than communicating something innate. With the help of an animator and feedback from service providers and activists, I began writing and visualizing a cultural narrative about nation-state borders that might prompt curiosity about the breadth of critical insight collected in the interviews. Put simply, that familiar narrative is that the nation-state border is an essential source of security and protection.

For this stage in the research, I have worked with Andrea Armstrong, a local animator, to tell the story in an experimental form. Armstrong designs media for programs related to refugee claimant support, including the READY Tours and Kinbrace Community Society, as well as volunteering with them. She has shared a home with refugee claimants for some years and was able to quickly understand the nuances of the stories I shared with her. We worked together to embed the project's methodology in the narrative and visuals of *Border Story* in the following ways.

1. We aimed to animate the story of securitization in a way that might create cognitive dissonance, or to put it differently, an animation that might de-familiarize the word "border" in the tradition of decolonial cultural studies. One way of creating dissonance has been embedding contradictions in the relationship between the voice-over and the animation. As a simple example, when the narrator says the border keeps people safe and secure, the animation shows figures being knocked over by the drawing of a new border.

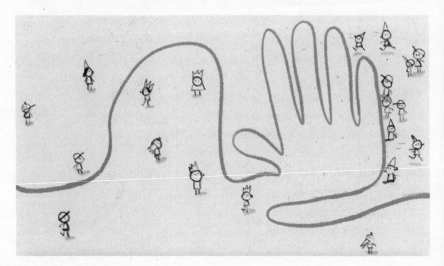

Figure 14.1 "Handstill."

2. Drawing on literary studies' approach to understanding genre and genre's power to construct knowledge and interpellate audiences differently, I asked, what is the genre of a cultural narrative like securitization: is it a fairy tale? A fantasy? A ghost story? In this case I have used a fairy tale aesthetic to reference subconscious tropes, comfortable familiarity, and the unreality of securitization narratives. So, crowns mark citizens, and dragons overlay people's imagined fears, and the intended effect is strange familiarity.

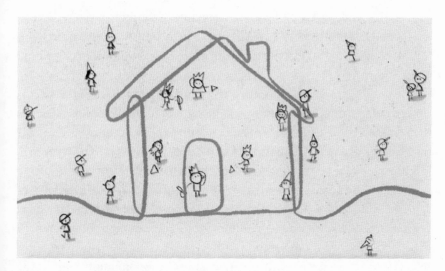

Figure 14.2 "Housestill."

3. Because ordinary English words in refugee discourse are the subject of the research narrative, the "main character" of the animation is the border. It is animated as a shapeshifter, demonstrating the flexibility of discourse. As the border changes shapes across a minute and a half, viewers see the complexity of a single word's meaning spotlighted and hear a series of voices responding to it.

4. To visualize the border as the main character, the film uses the central metaphor of a ball of yarn; the border arranges itself in different shapes to allude to theories of discourse. Discourse has been described as a "knitting together" of language for the use of particular communities. In addition, the yarn metaphor demonstrates both the malleability and the dishonesty of the securitization narrative.

5. At several key stages in the storyboarding process, I returned to a participatory process and took the storyboard to groups of activists and support workers to get feedback on the script and the visuals. Additional layers have resulted from these consultations. For instance, one group was adamant that the script needed at some point to step out of

the fairy tale to list the very real difficulties of the refugee claim process. Another group expressed dislike for an early storyboard's happy ending and suggested it finish instead with a question that invites storytelling.

The animation is also embedded in a longer film to address the ethical concern of personal stories of asylum being turned into anecdotes that are then framed by institutional mandates. The one-and-a-half-minute animated story could stand on its own as a discussion starter in a classroom. But because of the susceptibility of short-form narrative media to unsuitable framing, we are producing a twenty-five-minute version as well. In this version, the animation is placed within a longer multi-media film that includes rewinds and interruptions of the animation. These interruptions are produced with interview footage and still illustrations. The diversity of perspectives that are represented in the interruptions to the animation support the project's aim of cultivating a culture of listening rather than pushing for urgent action. Interruptions of the animation allow speakers to reject or nuance parts of the story. In tandem with the multi-voice narration of the animation, the film models listening, disagreement, multiple perspectives, and energized dialogue.

## Research Challenges

Worn Words has faced several challenges. First, cultural studies methodologies focus on ordinary instances of culture and are critical of exoticism and spectacle. But media-making often depends on exotic and spectacular material to claim space in an oversaturated digital environment. Because I want to experiment with un-patterning familiar forms of storytelling, I find myself in a productive but challenging creative space where what is familiar needs to be critiqued without depending on the showiness of the alternatives. The commitment to the process of this methodology has led me to simplify my hopes for the impact of this project's media and to trust instead the process of engaging thoroughly in an ethical praxis.

Second, applied media research is more costly than traditional research. I found community funding for the videography, but the remainder of the funding had to come out of my SSHRC postdoctoral salary. This inevitably limited the number of outputs and my ability to hire former refugees, who often find themselves in precarious financial situations as well. The emergent nature of applied media research also presented challenges in moving from proposal to praxis. While I intended to produce digital storytelling, I ended up with footage that deployed complex layers of communication forms spoken into diverse discourse communities. Significant synthesizing work was required to bring the different interviews and their insights together into a story form. The interview footage would have been shoehorned into the simplicity of the digital story tradition if I had stayed with my original plan. So the narrative form I have come up with may have difficulty finding a comfortable home or may have to do the challenging work of making space for itself among new documentaries and educational media resources.

Third, the differences among political time and digital media time and academic time have been challenging to traverse. The serious consequences of different timelines is devastating and clear in the stories of asylum-seekers who set out for Australia in a boat while it was still legal to do so and then were detained in offshore processing facilities on arrival because policy had changed while they were in transit. That reality is a reminder that this is a knowledge mobilization project about a human experience that is currently hypervisible in mainstream media and that is buffeted by seismic national and international shifts in policy and law. I encountered a completely different pace in an unexpectedly long research ethics process due to the combination of digital media methods and the involvement of vulnerable populations, and so early on I had to re-evaluate the number of media outputs I could complete. Academic production is slower than digital media production, and applied media research is even more time-consuming than traditional research. Because praxis unfolds over time, it requires shifting methodology, and this has at times felt unsteady. My approach to steady the research without overturning its ethical integrity has been to hold myself primarily accountable to the local, community relationships on which the research has depended. This has also necessitated holding lightly to all other potential avenues of influence at this stage in the research. Even so, I have struggled with the small, slow nature of a project like this.

Fourth, it is important to acknowledge that despite the significant trust and reciprocity that I had developed with refugee claimant communities prior to embarking on this project, the scope of the project has been necessarily limited by the nature of a two-year postdoctoral fellowship. In addition to my own temporary academic status, which tempered the possibility for establishing formal, long-term partnerships, there was little to no institutional research funding available to postdoctoral researchers. So, in consultation with my community partners, I decided to keep the relationship informal unless a funding opportunity surfaced that would benefit both parties. These limitations have provided me with the opportunity to reflect publicly on the scholarly value of slow, small knowledge mobilization (Glanville 2018c) and informal partnerships (Glanville 2019a) for decolonizing forced migration research methods. My networks have expanded and strengthened *beyond* the scope of my research project, rather than within it. One of the many benefits to this informal relationality has been the way it has allowed me to contribute to constructive public dialogues (Glanville 2019b) and concrete organizational visioning (Glanville 2018b) without compromising the critical nature of my research.

## Conclusion: Ongoing Questions

With each new stage, this project raises interdisciplinary questions about research ethics and the relationship of narratives to the communities they represent. Big picture questions that I continue to grapple with that have particular significance for narrative methodologies in forced migration research include: What concrete support can universities give ethical research that prioritizes relationality, and how can such support account for the slowness that often accompanies that priority? How can narrative research highlight the perspectives of those with refugee experience without increasing the burden of proof on them? If critical theory focuses on the conflictual and oppressive nature of culture, how can this be mobilized in hopeful and communicative narratives without compromising its critiques? What counts as critical knowledge, and what deserves critical attention in this current moment?

In my praxis, questions of form and social change have become inextricably linked: How do we un-pattern humanitarian storytelling without losing the power of familiar story forms for advocacy? How can we use media to diversify perspectives on a cultural narrative in a way that makes the diverse reality feel stronger than the single constructed narrative? What are the politics of a story's ending? Ending a story with a strong statement of opinion and then opening up discussion produces a different effect than leaving the viewer with genuine, open-ended questions, or alternatively creating a tentatively hopeful ending unfinished for imaginative interventions. Is it possible to create media that use cognitive dissonance as a strategy when the medium is digital and intended for cross-cultural contexts? What are the politics of a narrator's voice, including the impact of varying accents and gender on the intended audience's trust? Is the arc of a short digital narrative capacious enough to host multi-voice narration? Do viewers need to recognize themselves in the story to engage with it? And most basically, in the current political moment where asylum discourse is increasingly hyper visible, is it even possible to surprise a viewer with a new narrative pattern?

Further knowledge mobilization questions include: how do we mobilize stories so that they increase knowledge without contributing to hyper visibility? Where is it possible to tell stories that pull us out of our polarized trenches to contribute to a culture of listening? What stories will persist despite the rapid turnover of the media cycle and the public's desire for and consumption of new images, new footage, new stories, and new knowledge? According to whose priorities do we choose which knowledge to mobilize.

NOTES

1 Notice, for instance, the increasing number of academic podcasts (e.g., Migration Conversations Podcast, Global Migration Podcast), collaborative research projects (e.g., The Hostile Environments project), and the work of community-engaged research centres (e.g., the Critical Refugee Studies Collective at the University of California; the work of Stephen High at Concordia's Centre for Oral History and Digital Storytelling).

2 "Digital Storytelling" was supported in part by funding from the Social Sciences and Humanities Research Council. The project's videography was supported by the Dragon Fire Fund, held at the Vancouver Foundation. Dr Kirsten McAllister (Simon Fraser University) served as faculty sponsor throughout.

3 In the second half of this chapter I offer a brief description of how the form was developed. The video is freely available here: https://www.eringoheen glanville.com/listening-1.

4 *Border Story* is currently being embedded in an interactive multi-media

webpage for submission to the *Journal for Artistic Research*. Updates on this resource will be posted at www.eringoheenglanville.com.

5  To further explore critical refugee studies – both theoretical scholarship and applied media projects – readers could engage with the work of the Critical Refugee Studies Collective (2017–20) at the University of California and its online bibliography.

6  Ahmed Danny Ramadan. Interview by author, Vancouver, 6 July 2018.

7  After completing my protocol, I also discovered the document "Ethical Considerations: Research with People in Situations of Forced Migration," a very helpful set of guidelines, including questions for researchers and partner organizations (Clark-Kazak 2017).

8  See Jiwani (2011) for a discussion of "montage" as an anti-colonial media form.

9  See note 2.

**REFERENCES**

Ahmed, S. 2014. "Introduction: Feel Your Way." In *The Cultural Politics of Emotion*, 1–19. Edinburgh: Edinburgh University Press.

Block, K., E. Riggs, and N. Haslam. 2013. *Values and Vulnerabilities: The Ethics of Research with Refugees and Asylum Seekers*. Toowong: Australian Academic Press.

Chouliaraki, L. 2010. "Post-Humanitarianism: Humanitarian Communication beyond a Politics of Pity." *International Journal of Cultural Studies* 13, no. 2: 107–26.

Cisco. 2015. "Cisco Visual Networking Index: Forecast and Methodology, 2014–2019 White Paper." 27 May.

Clark-Kazak, C., with CCR, CARFMS, and CRS. 2017. "Ethical Considerations: Research with People in Situations of Forced Displacement." *Refuge* 33, no. 2: 11–17.

Coleman, D., E.G. Glanville, W. Hasan, and A.K. Hamstra. 2013. "Introduction." In *Countering Displacements: The Creativity and Resilience of Indigenous and Refugee-ed People*, edited by D. Coleman et al., ix–xli. Edmonton: University of Alberta Press.

Eastmond, M. 2007. "Stories as Lived Experience: Narratives in Forced Migration Research." *Journal of Refugee Studies* 20, no. 2: 248–64.

Ellsworth, E. 2008. "Mode of Address: It's a Film Thing." In *Film, Politics, and Ed-*

*ucation: Cinematic Pedagogy across the Disciplines*, edited by K.S. Sealey, 71–89. New York: Peter Lang.

Glanville, E.G. 2013. "Re-routing Diaspora Theory with Canadian Refugee Fiction." In *Rerouting the Postcolonial: New Directions for the New Millennium*, edited by S. Lawson Welsh, C. Sandru, and J. Wilson, 128–38. London: Routledge.

– 2018a. "Refracting Exoticism in Video Representations of the Victim-Refugee: K'Naan, Angelina Jolie, and Research Responsibilities." *Crossings: Journal of Migration and Culture* 9, no. 2: 1–19.

– 2018b. "Storytelling Practices Workshop." Hosted by Kinbrace Community Society, Vancouver.

– 2018c. "Telling a New Story: Digital Storytelling as a Method for Refugee Dialogue." 30 November. School of Communication and Centre for Policy Studies on Culture and Communities, Simon Fraser University, Vancouver.

– 2019a. "Beyond Feedback and Collaboration." Conference paper presented at the Canadian Association for Forced Migration Studies, York University, Toronto.

– 2019b. "Growing Capacity for Refugee Welcome: Stories, Culture, and Discourse." Plenary talk at province-wide consultation, hosted by BC Refugee Hub, Vancouver Immigration Partnership, Mount Pleasant Neighbourhood House, and UBC Migration.

Global Migration Podcast. 2020. Hosted by Doug Ober. UBC Centre for Migration Studies. https://migration.ubc.ca/podcast.

Grabska, K. 2014. *Gender, Identity, and Home: Nuer Repatriation to Southern Sudan*. Oxford: James Currey.

Hartley, J. 2011. "Cultural Studies, Creative Industries, and Cultural Science." In *Digital Futures for Cultural and Media Studies*, 27–58. Hoboken: Wiley-Blackwell.

High, S. 2014. *Oral History at the Crossroads*. Vancouver: UBC Press.

Jackson, M. 2002. *The Politics of Storytelling: Violence, Transgression, and Intersubjectivity*. Copenhagen: Museum Tusculanum Press.

Jiwani, Y. 2011. "Pedagogies of Hope: Counter Narratives and Anti-Disciplinary Tactics." *Review of Education, Pedagogy, and Cultural Studies* 33, no. 4: 333–53.

Levin, B. 2008. "Thinking about Knowledge Mobilization." Discussion paper prepared at the request of the Canadian Council on Learning and the Social Sciences and Humanities Research Council. August. Toronto: Ontario Institute for Studies in Education.

Lewis, P.J. 2014. "Narrative Research." In *Qualitative Methodology: A Practical Guide*, 161–80. Thousand Oaks: SAGE.

Malkki, L.H. 1995. "Refugees and Exiles: From 'Refugee Studies' to the National Order of Things." *Annual Review of Anthropology* 24: 495–523.

Marfleet, P. 2007. "Refugees and History: Why We Must Address the Past." *Refugee Survey Quarterly* 26, no. 3: 136–48.

Migration Conversations Podcast. 2020. Hosted by Jamie Liew. https://migration-conversations.simplecast.com.

Miller, E., H. Little, and S. High. 2017. *Going Public: The Art of Participatory Practice*. Vancouver: UBC Press.

Pinnegar, S., and J. Daynes. 2007. "Locating Narrative Inquiry Historically: Thematics in the Turn to Narrative." In *Handbook of Narrative Inquiry: Mapping a Methodology*, edited by D.J. Clandinin, 3–34. Thousand Oaks: SAGE.

Salverson, J. 1999. "Transgressive Storytelling or an Aesthetic of Injury: Performance, Pedagogy, and Ethics." *Theatre Research in Canada* 20, no. 1: 35–51.

Shome, R. 2009. "Post-Colonial Reflections on the Internationalization of Cultural Studies." *Cultural Studies* 23, nos. 5–6: 694–719.

Siegfried, J. 2001. "Discourse and Knowledge: Theoretical and Methodological Aspects of a Critical Discourse and Dispositive Analysis." In *Methods of Critical Discourse Analysis*, edited by R. Wodak and M. Meyer. Thousand Oaks: SAGE.

Squire, C., M. Andrew, and M. Tamboukou. 2013. "Introduction: What Is Narrative Research?" In *Doing Narrative Research*, edited by C. Squire et al. Thousand Oaks: SAGE.

Trimble, C. 2014. "Why Online Video Is the Future of Content Marketing." *The Guardian*, 14 January.

UN. n.d. "Refugees: Overview of Forced Displacement." Resources for Speakers on Global Issues.

UNHCR (UN High Commissioner for Refugees). 1992. *Handbook on Procedures and Criteria for Determining Refugee Status under the 1951 Convention and the 1967 Protocol relating to the Status of Refugees*. January, Geneva.

Woolley, A. 2014. *Contemporary Asylum Narratives: Representing Refugees in the Twenty-First Century*. London: Palgrave Macmillan.

# Contributors

ADNAN AL MHAMIED is a Syrian PhD candidate at McGill University's School of Social Work. His doctoral research focuses on Syrian refugee fathers in the context of forced migration and their resettlement in Canada. This topic has a strong connection to his personal experience as both a father and an advocate for human rights. He is a researcher associate with the McGill Refugee Research Group and Global Child McGill, and he is affiliated with the SHERPA Centre in Montreal.

RIHAM AL-SAADI is a PhD student in social work. Her dissertation focuses on the acculturation processes of immigrant populations. She is an instructor at the University of Windsor, where she teaches social work courses to undergraduate and graduate students. She has more than ten years of research experience in volunteer, student, and employment roles. She is a current member of the Immigrant Youth Research Group and the Emotional Competence Research Group. She is also a research team member in a longitudinal study on Syrian refugees' resettlement in Windsor-Essex. Riham has worked closely with immigrant populations, primarily immigrant youth, in agencies such as Women Enterprise Skills Training and Ready Set Go. She works in private practice, running Transparency Counselling Services.

NEIL ARYA is a family physician in Kitchener, Ontario, where he is assistant clinical professor in family medicine at McMaster University (part-time), adjunct professor in environment and resource studies at the University of

Waterloo, and scholar in residence at Wilfrid Laurier University. He is a fellow of the International Migration Research Centre (http://imrc.ca) and the Balsillie School of International Affairs, where he is engaged in refugee research. He has run a refugee health clinic for the past eleven years in Kitchener-Waterloo. Prior to that he was the physician for St John's Kitchen's Psychiatric Outreach Project, which caters to the needs of those experiencing homelessness, precarious housing, or street-involvement. He was founding director of the Global Health Office at Western University.

MONA AWWAD holds a bilingual master's degree in public policy and international affairs and is currently working with the Centre for Refugee Studies on the "Syria Long Term Health Outcomes in Canada" project. Her professional background includes political and social research, policy analysis, and specialized support for immigrants and refugees, as well as journalism, translation, and group session facilitation. Mona is fluent in both English and Arabic and has a working knowledge of French.

AZZA AHMED ABDEL AZIZ lives between Khartoum and London. She holds a PhD in social anthropology, with a special focus on medical anthropology from the School of Oriental and African Studies, University of London. Her research focuses on cultural understandings of health and well-being. She has been following the unfolding uprising in Khartoum since December 2018 and has been documenting the everyday protest practices, focusing on artistic expressions. She is also a co-researcher with Kasia Grabska in a project on creative practice, mobilities, and development in Sudan.

SUSAN BANKI is a senior lecturer in the Department of Sociology and Social Policy at the University of Sydney. Her research interests lie in the political, institutional, and legal contexts that explain the roots of and solutions to international human rights violations. In particular, she is interested in the ways that questions of sovereignty, citizenship/membership, and humanitarian principles have shaped our understanding of and reactions to various transnational phenomena, such as the international human rights regime, international migration, and the provision of international aid. Her focus is on the Asia-Pacific region, where she has conducted extensive field research in Thailand, Nepal, Bangladesh, and Japan on refugee/migrant protection, statelessness, and border control. She is currently investigating the local, regional, and international mechanisms (and the interactions between them) that serve as potential levers for change.

MIGUEL ALONSO CAMBRÓN is a social and cultural anthropologist and audio-visual producer based in Spain. His primary line of research is related to sound phenomena from a social point of view, but he is also interested in identity dynamics, intangible heritage issues, sociability in historic neighbourhoods of Southern Europe, historical memory, and audio-visual technologies as applied to social sciences, anthropology and archaeology. He has participated in several projects as editor, cultural activist, sound artist, writer, producer, graphic designer, and audio-visual technician.

EVROPI CHATZIPANAGIOTIDOU is a political anthropologist at Queen's University Belfast. Her research interests lie at the study of migration and diasporas, conflict-induced displacement, and the politics of memory and loss. She has conducted fieldwork in Cyprus, the UK, and Turkey. She has published journal articles and chapters on numerous topics, including the connections between memory and history in the Cypriot conflict, the transnational role of diasporas in peace-building, youth migration and precarity in Southern Europe, and refugees and the politics of representation in Turkey.

CHRISTINA R. CLARK-KAZAK is associate professor in the Graduate School of Public and International Affairs at the University of Ottawa, and past president of the International Association for the Study of Forced Migration. She previously served as editor-in-chief of *Refuge: Canada's Journal on Refugees*, and as president of the Canadian Association for Refugee and Forced Migration Studies. Prior to joining the University of Ottawa, she worked for York University (2009–17), Saint Paul University (2007–8), and the Canadian government (1999–2007). Her research focuses on age discrimination in migration and development policy, young people's political participation, and interdisciplinary methodologies in forced migration contexts.

ILSE DERLUYN obtained her PhD in educational sciences at Ghent University (Belgium) and is currently affiliated as full professor in the Department of Social Work and Social Pedagogy at Ghent University, where she teaches courses in migration and refugee studies. Ilse's main research topics concern the psychosocial well-being of unaccompanied refugee minors, migrant and refugee children, war-affected children, victims of trafficking, and child soldiers. She is also actively involved in supporting refugees and practitioners working with refugees and migrants and in policy research and policy influence. She has published more than one hundred international publications and books. She heads the Centre for the Social Study of Migration and Refugees and is co-director of the Centre for Children in Vulnerable Situations. Besides being the PI of the ERC-SG ChildMove, she coordinates the H2020-project "RefugeesWellSchool."

GIORGIA DONÀ is professor of forced migration and co-director of the Centre for Migration, Refugees, and Belonging at the University of East London. For more than three decades she has worked as a researcher, practitioner, and activist with refugees in Central America, Eastern Africa, and Europe. Her research focuses on conflict and displacement, child and youth migration, psycho-social perspectives in forced migration, refugee voices and representation, and multi-modal narratives.

ERIKA FRYDENLUND, PhD, is research assistant professor at the Virginia Modeling, Analysis and Simulation Center at Old Dominion University. Her research focuses on migration using a modelling and simulation approach. Her current work with Jose Padilla examines the impacts of migration on host communities in Lesbos, Greece; Cucuta, Colombia; and Cape Town, South Africa. Her email is efrydenl@odu.edu.

SHASHINI GAMAGE, PhD, is a researcher, journalist, and filmmaker based in Australia and Sri Lanka. Her research examines the intersections of gender, media, and migration. She is a research associate with the Ageing and New Media group of La Trobe University, Melbourne, where she examines digital media practices of older migrants in Australia (2019–20). Her PhD, supported by an Australia Awards Scholarship, was conducted at La Trobe University (2012–16), where she produced a transnational feminist media ethnography of Sri Lankan women's soap opera cultures in Australia and Sri Lanka, published as *Soap Operas, Gender, and the Sri Lankan Diaspora* (Palgrave Macmillan, 2021). Her work in journalism includes documentaries about women, peace, and security in conflict zones during the civil war in Sri Lanka (2004–10). She founded *Women Talk* (2017), a digital archive of multimedia journalism that documents feminist activism in Sri Lanka, supported by Australia Awards. In a collaboration with the Centre for Migration Research Development, Colombo, and the University of Sussex, she contributed to digitizing narratives of conflict-induced displaced urban migrants for the study *The Unknown City: the (In)visibility of Urban Displacement* (2017–18).

ERIN GOHEEN GLANVILLE (PhD, McMaster) is a lecturer in the Coordinated Arts Program at University of British Columbia, and researches and teaches cultural refugee studies at the University of British Columbia. Formerly she was a postdoctoral fellow in the School of Communication at Simon Fraser University (201719). As part of this research, she has produced educational media on asylum discourse under the title *Worn Words*. She is the co-editor of *Countering Displacements: The Creativity and Agency of Indigenous and Refugee-ed Peoples* (University of Alberta Press, 2012). She has published articles on refugee narratives in *Crossings: Journal of Migration and Culture, Canadian Literature, Global Responsibility to Protect*, and *Intermediality: History of the Arts, Literature, and Technology*, and has contributed to multi-author volumes on pedagogy and globalization. Glanville has used her doctoral work on refugee narratives to facilitate community workshops and organizational storytelling sessions in Australia, Canada, New Zealand, and the United States. www.eringoheenglanville.com.

MARIE GODIN is a British Academy postdoctoral fellow. Her project is titled "Refugees, Social Protection, and Digital Technologies" and aims to explore how the development of tech-social protection initiatives led by, with, or for refugees is contributing to a reshaping of the politics of welfare at the local, national, and transnational levels, with a particular focus on international migration from Sub-Saharan Africa to Europe. She holds an MSC in forced migration from the Refugee Studies Centre, University of Oxford, and a PhD in social sciences from the University of East London. Marie has published extensively on the Congolese diaspora and the politics of "home" and belongings in different contexts. Her broader research interests lie in the area of migration and development, with a focus on diaspora engagement and gender, social protection, and political activism.

KATARZYNA (KASIA) GRABSKA is a social anthropologist whose research focuses on gender, generation, youth, displacement, refuges, return, and identities. She is a senior researcher at the Peace Research Institute in Oslo and a visiting professor at the Institute of Ethnology, University of Neuchâtel, Switzerland. Since 2002, she has been carrying out long-term research among Nuer South Sudanese refugees in Sudan, Egypt, and Kenya, and among returnees in South Sudan. Her book *Gender, Identity, Home: Nuer Repatriation to Southern Sudan* (2014) received the Amory Talbot Award for the best contribution to African studies in 2015. She has also worked on collaborative research about adolescent girls' migration in Bangladesh, Ethiopia, and Sudan, and refugees' involvement in civic change in host countries, including Sudan and Switzerland. Katarzyna works with visual media, feminist methodologies, and creative arts-based and participatory methods in her fieldwork. One of her recent films was made in collaboration with a team of researchers and filmmakers. The long version of the film, *2 Girls*, has been shown at numerous film festivals around the globe.

OULA HAJJAR is a PhD student at the Department of Social Work at McGill University. She is the research coordinator of the Montreal site for the CIHR research project Refugee Integration and Long-Term Health Outcomes in Canada. She was involved in the initial welcoming of Syrian resettled refugees in Montreal and in Germany and remains active in the community.

JILL HANLEY is associate professor at the McGill School of Social Work, where her research focuses on access to social rights (health, housing, labour) for precarious status migrants. She is also co-founder and actively involved with Montreal's Immigrant Workers Centre.

JASON HART is associate professor in the International Development Group at the University of Bath. His research interests coalesce around humanitarian responses to conflict-affected and displaced populations with particular attention to children.

MICHAELA HYNIE, PhD, is a professor in the Department of Psychology and the Centre for Refugee Studies at York University, and past president of the Canadian Association for Refugee and Forced Migration Studies. She conducts mixed-method community-based research on interventions that can strengthen social and institutional relationships to improve health and well-being in situations of social conflict and forced displacement. She has worked in Canada, the Democratic Republic of Congo, India, Liberia, Nepal, Rwanda, Sierra Leone, and South Africa. She currently leads Syrian Refugee Integration and Long-Term Health in Canada (SYRIA.lth), a five-year longitudinal study on integration pathways and health.

NICOLE IVES, associate professor, McGill School of Social Work, has been working with refugee populations in resettlement for nearly thirty years in Canada, Denmark, and United States. Her research focuses on refugee resettlement practice and policy, comparative migration policy, and the role of community-focused, faith-based organizations in resettlement. Current projects include examining long-term health outcomes for Syrian refugees in Canada and recreation as a vehicle to promote integration among refugee children in Montreal. In Montreal, QC, and in Manchester, New Hampshire, Professor Ives is involved with immigrant- and refugee-serving organizations, linking their work with McGill's teaching and research. She is on the board of directors of the Montreal City Mission.

RABIH JAMIL is a PhD candidate in sociology at the Université de Montréal and a member of GIREPS, an interdisciplinary research group on employment, poverty, and social protection. His research interests focus on platform capitalism, digital labour, surveillance, and organization. Rabih has more than ten years of experience in the field of socio-economic professional research with emphasis on informal work and refugees' economic integration. He holds an MSC in development studies from the school of Oriental and African Studies at the University of London.

DANESH JAYATILAKA is a researcher working on forced migration issues. He has a PhD in economics from the University of Colombo (2018) with a split-site scholarship to the School of Global Studies, University of Sussex. His interests include disasters, migration, development, and their intersections, with a special focus on displacement and resettlement in community and urban settings. He co-founded (2012) and chairs the Centre for Migration Research and Development and was co-investigator for *The Unknown City: the (In)visibility of Urban Displacement*. He is presently a co-investigator in two studies: Towards Trajectories of Inclusion: Making Infrastructure Work for the Most marginalised (2020–23); and Holding Aid Accountable: Plural Humanitarianism in Protracted Crisis (2020–23), conducted with the University of Sussex and the Peace Research Institute Oslo.

MAHI KHALAF is the SYRIA.lth project coordinator in BC as well as settlement site manager at ISSofBC. She has worked internationally for fifteen years to support research and building capacity of not-for-profit organizations in the Middle East and southern Africa. In the past five years she has shifted her work to the settlement sector with ISSofBC, where she supported the resettlement of Syrian government-assisted refugees and moved on to manage the settlement program in Vancouver and Richmond, BC. Mahi holds a master's degree in international affairs from Carleton University's Norman Paterson School of International Affairs.

RIM KHYAR, PsyD candidate, UQAM, is interested in refugees' mental health and the relationship between social conditions as job access and mental health.

BEN C.H. KUO is a professor of clinical psychology at the University of Windsor. His research focuses on acculturation, cultural stress and coping, professional help-seeking attitudes and behaviours, and cultural adjustment and mental health issues among immigrants, refugees, and culturally diverse populations. Dr Kuo's clinical experiences extend to clients of diverse backgrounds and issues/concerns; he regularly teaches and supervises clinical psychology graduate students in multicultural counselling and psychotherapy course and practicum.

INE LIETAERT holds a PhD in social work (Ghent University), studying the return and reintegration processes of assisted returnees from Belgium to Georgia and Armenia. Following her PhD, she worked as a post-doc researcher with the ERC Childmove project. She currently works as an assistant professor at the United Nations University–CRIS in Bruges and at the Department of Social Work and Social Pedagogy. Her main research topics relate to return migration, migration governance, reintegration processes, assisted return, unaccompanied refugee minors, migration trajectories, well-being, belonging, and international social work. She is a research member of the Centre for the Social Study of Migration and Refugees and teaches International Social Work at Ghent University. She guides PhD students investigating processes of return and reintegration, unaccompanied refugee minors, and internal migration and displacement. She is currently involved as co-supervisor of the various PhD researches in the ChildMove project.

MAY MASSIJEH is a master's student at York University, where she is studying at the Humanities Department with a concentration on heterotopia and psychogeography between asylum countries and home countries. Her interest in refugee studies began in 2016 when she had the opportunity to pursue a master's in environmental studies at York University. She focused on art-based research, exploring the concept of home and homemaking in the lives of children who experienced forced displacement, using animation and storytelling. She has been working with York University since 2016 as a research assistant as part of syRIA.lth Toronto team along with two other research projects, Client Support Services evaluation and the Nai Children Choir.

RANA MOHAMMAD is a certified interpreter. She works as an international language instructor for adult learning in Kitchener, Ontario. She is also program facilitator at Carizon Family and Community Services in Kitchener, Ontario. She also works as a research assistant at York University.

FIONA MURPHY is an anthropologist based in HAPP, Queen's University Belfast. She specializes in Indigenous politics and movements, refugees, and mobility studies in Australia, Ireland, and Turkey. The key thematics in her work include loss, trauma, memory, and displacement. Her current work focuses on the politics of reparations in the context of the removal and institutionalization of Aboriginal Australian children. She works extensively on the topic of asylum seekers and refugees in Ireland, the UK, and Turkey. She is co-author of *Integration in Ireland: The Everyday Life of African Migrants* (MUP, 2012).

ANNA ODA is a registered nurse with a master's degree in nursing from Ryerson University, Toronto. Currently, she is working at the Centre for Refugee Studies, York University, on coordinating the Refugee Integration and Long-Term Health Outcomes in Canada study. She is also completing her master's in public health, specializing in social and behavioural health sciences, at the Dalla Lana School of Public Health, University of Toronto. Previously, she worked at the Centre for Addiction and Mental Health. She is interested in community mental health, community-based research, newcomer integration and well-being in the post-migration context, healthy public policy, and broader social determinants of health.

JOSE J. PADILLA, PhD, is research associate professor at the Virginia Modeling, Analysis, and Simulation Center at Old Dominion University, Virginia. He works on the study and development of innovative simulation solutions that bridge the human/systems divide by fostering creation through simulation. Padilla's ongoing research focuses on methodological development for M&S of human behaviour using social media data and agents; simulating users, insider threats, and hackers for cybersecurity; and designing and developing platforms for simulation development and data capture.

NICOLE PHILLIPS is an honorary associate at the University of Sydney, where she completed her master's degree in human rights in 2014. Her main research interests include migrant and refugee rights in Southeast Asia, Australia, and the United States. Prior to completing her master's, Nicole studied at Indiana University and the University of Bologna in Italy. She has conducted field research on Bhutanese refugees in Nepal and the United States, and on young Burmese women in Thailand, and has worked in resettlement in the United States.

ANDREA RODRÍGUEZ-SÁNCHEZ is a social worker and musician. Her academic work focuses on peacebuilding through collective musical spaces in Colombia. She holds a PhD from the UNESCO Chair of Philosophy for Peace–Institute for Social Development (Jaume I University of Castellón, Spain) and is currently is a member of the Peace Program at the National University of Colombia. She is also presently the Secretary of the Colombian Association of Music Researchers.

MARINA ROTA is a sociologist with postgraduate studies in criminology in Greece and Belgium. She holds a PhD in sociology from Athens's Panteion University of Social and Political Sciences. She has worked in the field of migration and asylum as a field worker since 1995, mainly with unaccompanied refugee minors and child victims of human trafficking. She has also worked with various organizations, including Doctors of the World, Doctors Without Borders, and the International Organization for Migration and Health. For the past fourteen years she has been training front-line professionals in identifying and supporting people in vulnerable situations as well as victims of trafficking. Since 2017, she has been working at Ghent University as a researcher in the ChildMove project.

KATHY SHERRELL is the associate director, settlement services, at ISSofBC and an affiliate scholar at the York Centre for Refugee Studies. She holds a PhD in geography from the University of British Columbia and a master of arts degree from Simon Fraser University, with an emphasis on refugee resettlement in Canada, including regionalization, legal status, housing, and settlement experiences. Kathy continues to be active in research with refugees. Currently, she is a co-investigator on two pan-Canadian, multi-year refugee research projects, as well as a lead on numerous internal research projects.

NIHAL SOĞANCI is currently continuing her PhD in social anthropology at the Panteion University of Social and Political Sciences in Athens. Her ethnographic research mainly questions how North Cyprus has been collaged and montaged as home in the post–2003 period. At the same time, she is working at the Home for Cooperation, a multicultural community centre in the buffer zone in Nicosia. She is one of the creative directors of the Buffer Fringe

Performing Arts Festival 2020, which questioned the meanings of displacement. She holds an MSc in international public policy with a particular focus on conflict resolution and reconciliation from University College London and a BA in languages and translation, majoring in French, from the University of Surrey, UK.

DINA TAHA is a PhD candidate at the Sociology Department and an affiliate with the Centre for Refugee Studies at York University. Her research interests include critical refugee studies, gender in the Middle East, and decolonizing methodologies. Her dissertation explores Syrian refugee women's survival mechanisms in Egypt, particularly through marriage. She holds a BA in political science from Cairo University and an MA in international human rights law from the American University in Cairo. She has extensive experience with feminist and minority advocacy groups such as Nazra for Feminist Studies and Minority Rights Group International. Dina can be reached at dinataha@yorku.ca.

OCÉANE UZUREAU holds a master's in migration studies from the University of Poitiers. She previously worked as project coordinator at the Observatory of the Migration of Minors (University of Poitiers/MIGRINTER-CNRS) on action research projects with unaccompanied minors newly arrived in France, analyzing access to protective services and local inclusion with local NGOs and institutions. She is currently a PhD candidate in educational sciences at Ghent University (CESSMIR) and a member of the ChildMove team. Her research interests target migrant children's mobilities within Europe, participatory research projects with young people, border-crossing experiences, and social support from NGOs and volunteers available for migrants on the move.

# Index